TIBET: A POLITICAL HISTORY

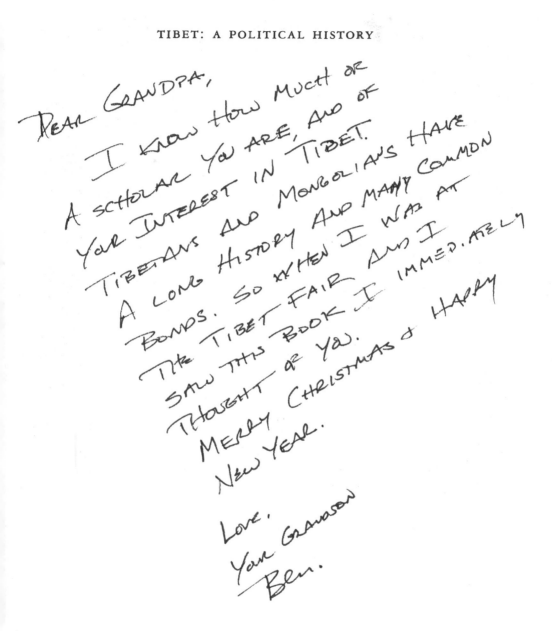

DEAR GRANDPA,

I KNOW HOW MUCH OR A SCHOLAR YOU ARE, AND OF YOUR INTEREST IN TIBET. TIBETANS AND MONGOLIANS HAVE A LONG HISTORY AND MANY COMMON BONDS. SO WHEN I WAS AT THE TIBET FAIR AND I SAW THIS BOOK I IMMEDIATELY THOUGHT OF YOU. MERRY CHRISTMAS & HAPPY NEW YEAR.

LOVE,
YOUR GRANDSON
BEN.

Ruling lamas affixed their seals to official documents to make them valid. The seals had been given to them in turn by the Mongol Khans and the Manchu Emperors. The engraving on this seal of 1909 is in three scripts: (a) the three columns on the left and on the right are in 'Phags-pa script which was devised in the 13th century by 'Phags-pa Lama for Qubilai Khan; (b) the next column on the left consists of the same inscription in *Lantsa,* an ornate Indo-Aryan script used for decorative purposes; and (c) the lines of small characters are proper Tibetan script.

Freely translated, the inscription says:
"Seal of the King of the powerful wish-granting (jewel), who is worshipped by all the gods and men, the Ocean-Lama Vajradhara, the unchangeable all-knowing one who exercises power over all the victorious teaching (of the Buddha), who is the protector of all above earth and of all times, lord of the three worlds and the teachings of the Buddha (which came from) the Glorious Land (i.e. India)."

TIBET

A POLITICAL HISTORY

BY TSEPON W. D. SHAKABPA

POTALA PUBLICATIONS · NEW YORK · 1984

Also by Tsepon W. D. Shakabpa

Bod-kyi Srid-don Rgyal-rabs
    Tibetan History (Vols. I & II in Tibetan)
    Shakabpa House, Kalimpong, India, 1976

Buddha's Relics in Tibet
    Baptist Mission Press, Calcutta, India, 1951

Lha-ldan Raw-sa "Phrul-snang Gtsuq-lag Khang-gyi Dkar-chak"
    A Guide to Jokhang, the Central Cathedral in Lhasa
    Shakabpa House, 1982

ISBN 0-9611474-0-7
Library of Congress Catalogue Card Number 67-13448

First Printing Yale University Press, 1967
Second Printing Yale University Press, 1973
Reissued   Potala Publications, 1984

Contents

Appendix:

Foreword

Tsepon W. D. Shakabpa was born January 7, 1907, in Lhasa. He entered government service at the age of twenty-three and in nine years became Head of the Finance Department, serving concurrently as one of the eight influential spokesmen who presided over the Tibetan National Assembly. In addition to his extensive experience in government, Mr. Shakabpa has traveled abroad. In 1948 he headed the Tibetan Trade Delegation, which traveled around the world.

Following the Communist Chinese occupation of Tibet in 1951, Mr. Shakabpa took up residence in India, where he began work on a study of Tibet's political history. A number of books on Tibet have been published in recent years; most of them are devoted chiefly to religion or to contemporary events. Mr. Shakabpa's study, by contrast, is a balanced presentation of Tibetan political history from earliest times down to the present.

In preparing his book, Mr. Shakabpa has used some fifty-seven original Tibetan sources. Some are rare Tibetan government records; others represent materials not previously cited in English works. It will be noted that when a Tibetan source is cited in a footnote, no page number is given. Although contrary to Western academic methods, this practice is traditional in Tibetan historiography. Beginning with the earliest known Tibetan histories, only the title of a cited work was given—apparently on the assumption that a literate person would be able to locate the page concerned, once he knew which book to read. It was only after working on his history for some time that Mr. Shakabpa came to know the Western method of giving page numbers and publishing data in citations; therefore, his book incorporates the traditional practice for Tibetan sources and the academic method for Western sources. It would have been difficult, if not impossible, for him to rewrite all the citations of Tibetan materials, since some of them were unique government records he copied in Tibet and are no longer available. Moreover, those who read Tibetan will have little difficulty in locating the cited passages; those who do not would find page numbers valueless.

For the convenience of the general reader, Mr. Shakabpa has rendered the Tibetan names phonetically; but aware of their inconsistencies and of the confusion caused by numerous homophones in the Tibetan language, he has wisely included the correct Tibetan orthography for each entry in the Index, as well as in the Bibliography, which will greatly increase the value of his book to the serious student of Tibetan history. The system of orthographic transcription used is that described in T. Wylie, "A Standard System of Tibetan Transcription," *Harvard Journal of Asiatic Studies*, 22 (December 1959), 261–67.

Mr. Shakabpa's book is a unique contribution to our understanding of Tibet, because his work marks the first time that a Tibetan lay official of high rank has written a study of his own country's political history. He sheds new light on certain significant factors in the evolution of that form of religious government unique in Tibet. In addition, he offers new and interesting evidence, which should help clarify the political status of Tibet in modern times.

I first met Tsepon Shakabpa in India in 1960, at which time we discussed at length his work on Tibetan political history. Since then, I have had a continuing interest in his progress, and it is, therefore, with pleasure and a sense of fulfillment that I now have the privilege of writing the foreword to this book, which is the fruition of Mr. Shakabpa's years of work.

TURRELL WYLIE
*Associate Professor of Tibetan
Language and Civilization
University of Washington*

Preface

In 1931 I was summoned to the house of my uncle, Norbu Wangyal Trimon, who was then the senior Minister of Tibet. He spoke to me at length and gave me a thorough briefing on the Chinese war with Tibet and how the Chinese were driven out of the country some years earlier. He further acquainted me with the Simla Convention of 1914, which had been concluded between the British, Tibetan, and Chinese plenipotentiaries, attending under equal powers. My uncle participated in that Convention as the assistant to Lonchen Shatra, then Prime Minister of Tibet and the Tibetan plenipotentiary at the Simla conference. My uncle handed me the drafts and documents of the Convention, together with the traditional ceremonial scarf, and said, "It will help Tibet if you write a political history after studying these documents." As I was quite young at the time, I was not fully aware of the significance of his advice or of the documents.

Early in 1946 my family and I made a pilgrimage to India, where I witnessed extensive movements for independence by the Indian people. While in Bombay, I heard speeches given before large crowds of people by Pandit Jawaharlal Nehru and Sardar Vallabhai Patel. Those speeches moved me to realize the true value of independence. It was then that I really began to prize the documents given to me years before by my uncle. On my return to Lhasa, I pressured responsible officials to safeguard Tibet's independence and to develop diplomatic relations with foreign countries.

Toward the end of 1947, the government of Tibet assigned me to head a Trade Delegation of five men. We were instructed to visit major countries around the world to discuss commercial and political matters. While in India, we had a memorable audience with the late Mahatma Gandhi. Meeting that great man, who led India to independence by means of nonviolence, and hearing his fruitful advice was a truly great inspiration to me. In all the countries we visited, I and the other members of the Trade Delegation endeavored to further knowledge and understanding of Tibet. Owing to the results of this and other missions I have undertaken on behalf of my government and people, I realized that the world stood in need of information on Tibet's historical and political status.

When the Communist Chinese invaded eastern Tibet in 1950, government officials accompanied the Dalai Lama to Yatung, near the Indian-Sikkimese border. When an agreement was signed in the spring of 1951 between Tibet and China in Peking, I crossed over to India, rather than return to Lhasa and be forced to collaborate with the Red Chinese.

In India, I began to work on this book, knowing that there was no comprehensive and accurate political history in Tibetan, much less in English. I was able to secure numerous volumes of ancient manuscripts from Tibet, as well as through the kind assistance of my good friend, T. D. Densapa of Sikkim. I began an extensive study, using my uncle's documents as a background. When His Holiness, the Dalai Lama, visited India in 1956 to participate in the Buddha Jayanti celebration, he encouraged me to complete this book.

After the Tibetan revolt in 1959 and the flight of the Dalai Lama along with thousands of Tibetan refugees, I was appointed the Representative of His Holiness, the Dalai Lama, with the responsibility of looking after the relief and rehabilitation of some 80,000 Tibetans seeking refuge in India, Nepal, Sikkim, and Bhutan. In 1959 Mr. Gyalo Thondup and I appeared before the United Nations General Assembly, when the "Question of Tibet" was presented through the sponsorship of Ireland and Malaya. Being thus occupied, I had no time to work on my manuscript. Finally, on May 15, 1963, I obtained official leave from my duties to complete this book.

First of all, I wish to express my sincere thanks and deepest gratitude to the Asia Foundation, under whose sponsorship I was able to come to the United States, and without whose help the publication of this book would have been indefinitely delayed. I wish to thank the staff of the Yale University Press for its kind assistance and patience, and the staff of the Yale Library, which has an extensive collection of materials on Tibet.

I must equally thank my sons and Ruskin Bond for the help given in the translation of my manuscript into English. I wish to express my appreciation to Professor Turrell Wylie, University of Washington (Seattle), who was kind enough to edit my manuscript and offer valuable suggestions. Finally, I wish to acknowledge the unfailing encouragement given me by my wife, Pema Yudon, who contributed significantly to the completion of this book.

TSEPON W. D. SHAKABPA

List of Abbreviations

All original Tibetan sources cited in this volume have been assigned abbreviated titles, which are listed alphabetically in the BIBLIOGRAPHY, where the full title and author's name are given. Frequently cited Western sources have been assigned abbreviated titles as given below. Complete citations are given in the BIBLIOGRAPHY.

BELL	*Tibet: Past and Present*
BOGLE	Markham, *Narratives of the Mission of George Bogle*
BOUNDARY	*Report of the Officials of the Governments of India*
BUSHELL	"The Early History of Tibet from Chinese Sources"
CHRONICLES	Petech, *A Study of the Chronicles of Ladakh*
DALAI	*My Land and My People*
DOCUMENTS	(See BIBLIOGRAPHY, Tibetan Sources)
HOWORTH	*History of the Mongols from the ςth to the 19th Century*
JASB	*Journal of the Asiatic Society of Bengal*
JRAS	*Journal of the Royal Asiatic Society*
LI	*Tibet: Today and Yesterday*
PELLIOT	*Histoire Ancienne du Tibet*
PETECH	*China and Tibet in the 18th Century*
PHAGDU	"A Short History of the House of Phagdu"
PORTRAIT	Bell, *Portrait of the Dalai Lama*
RICHARDSON	*A Short History of Tibet*
ROCKHILL	*The Dalai Lamas of Lhasa and Their Relations with the Manchu Emperors of China*
SIMLA	(See BIBLIOGRAPHY, Tibetan Sources)
SMITH	*The Early History of India*
TEICHMAN	*Travels of a Consular Officer in Eastern Tibet*
TOMBS	Tucci, "The Tombs of the Tibetan Kings"
TPS	Tucci, *Tibetan Painted Scrolls*
TUN-HUANG	Bacot, Thomas, and Toussaint, *Documents de Touen-houang*
YOUNGHUSBAND	*India and Tibet*

ཞེ་   ༑ང་རང་ལ་ཡོད་ཅི་འདུག་ནག་ཅིག་ལ་དབང་དག་ལ་ཤོག་ཁ་བ།
ནས།   གལ་ཏེ་དགག་ན་གཞི་ལ་ཞིག་ལ་ལ་འདི་ན་ལ་ཉེ་ཡ་ལ།
ཐལ་ལདུ།   ཉལ་ཐ་ལ་པ་ཕུ་གཞི་ལ་ཟིན་ནག་ལ་ལ་འདི་ལ།།བ
༑ང་རང་ནི་ནིལ་ལི་ལ་ཞིན་ཐམ་ལ་ག་ལ་པུ་ལ་ལ་ཁགས།
ད་ལ།   གི་རིལ་ལི་ལི་ལ་ལ་ལི།།ཞེག་ལ་ཐག་ར་ལྔས་ལ།
རང་ལ་ཞིན་གཉིས་ཐུ་ལ་བཐ་ག་ལ་ལ་ཁྲ།   གལ་ཐི་ན་ཐི་ལ་ལཏགས
རག་ལ་ལ་འཊྲི་ལ་ལ་ཐག་ལ་འཆོ་ལྷ་ལ་ཆོ་ལ་ཞེ་ན་ལ་ལུ་ལ།།
ཞི་ཏི་ལ་ཞ་ནཐ་ནག་ཅི་ན་ལ་ཡ་ཐུ་ཞི་ལི་ཆེན་ལ།   པུ་ལ།།
ཞལ།   ༑ཕི་གༀ   ༑ཞི་ཐི་ཅི་ལ་ཞ་ལྔ།།
             ༑

Since Tibet had remained isolated for many centuries there are very few people, who know much about Tibet and its people.   I, therefore, welcome this book, TIBET: A POLITICAL HISTORY by Mr. W.D. Shakabpa.   This is the first of its kind in English written by a Tibetan, and there is no doubt that it will be of immense value in presenting a true picture of Tibet, particularly, today, when there is a great need for it.

THE DALAI LAMA

Swarg Ashram
Upper Dharmsala
Kangra/Punjab
India.

March 12, 1966.

DEDICATED

to my fellow countrymen who are suffering immeasurably under Communist Chinese oppression, and who are waiting earnestly for the day when Tibet will regain her freedom and independence.

I

An Introduction to Tibet

Tibet—The Origin of the Name

According to the writings of early Tibetan scholars, the name "Bod" for Tibet had originated from the name "Pugyal" long before the Bon religion emerged.[1] Others maintain that the name Bod was derived from Bon itself, which is the name of the early religion of the country before the introduction of Buddhism in the seventh century.[2] Yet another group of scholars maintain that the name Bod, orally meaning "fled," was given to the country because the Indian leader Rupati and his followers fled to Tibet after involvement in war with the Pandavas.[3] It is also stated that "Bod" has no specific meaning and is used merely as a form of identification. The Indo-Tibetan border residents refer to Tibetans as Bhotias; a name derived from "Bhota," the Sanskrit name for Tibet.

The modern name of "Tibet," by which the country is known to the world, derives from the Mongolian "Thubet," the Chinese "Tufan," the Thai "Thibet," and the Arabic "Tubbat," which are found in early works. In many poetical writings of Tibet, the country is referred to as "Khawachen" or "Gangjong," meaning "The Abode of Snow," and "Sildanjong," meaning "The Cool Climate Land."

Geographical Position

Tibet has long been known to the world as a forbidden land fortified by snow mountains; but people in general are often uncertain as to its exact location. Suffice it to say that it lies west of China, north of India and Nepal, east of Persia, and south of Russia and Mongolia. It is

1. DEB-SNGON.
2. DEB-DKAR.
3. DGA'-STON.

the highest country in the world. On its border with Nepal stands Mount Everest; and common to the border of Nepal, Sikkim, and Tibet is Kanchenjunga. Between Bhutan and Tibet lies Mount Chomo Lhari, first climbed in 1937 by Spencer Chapman, who became lost on the way down and eventually showed up in Bhutan. Other great mountains such as Kailash, sacred to the Buddhist and Hindu alike, Tsari, Yalha Shambo, Chomo Kharak, Kangkar Shameh, Nyanchen Thanglha, and Machen Pomra (Amne Machen) are studded about Tibet like precious jewels.

At Tachienlu in the east, an iron bridge divides China from ethnic Tibet, and a white stupa known as Chorten Karpo marks the limit of ethnic Tibet's northeastern frontier at Karchu.

The southern border of Tibet is formed by the Himalayas; the western border by the Karakoram range; and the northern by the Altyn Tagh range, which borders on Chinese Turkestan.

Tibet has three main regions, known as the Chol-kha-sum. From Ngari Korsum, in western Tibet, to Sokla Kyao, the region is known as Ü-Tsang; from Sokla Kyao to the upper bend in the Machu (Yellow River) it is known as Dotod (Kham); and from the Machu bend to Chorten Karpo it is called Domed (Amdo). Tibetans say that the best religion comes from Ü-Tsang, the best men from Kham, and the best horses from Amdo. The old divisions of Tibet were known as Trikor Chuksum; ten thousand family units were known as a "Trikor" (myriarchy) and "Chuksum" meant "thirteen." These divisions are no longer used, having been superseded by the division of Chol-kha-sum.

Rivers and Lakes

Four rivers, all having descriptive names, rise near Mount Kailash in the west. The Sengye Khabab (Out of the Lion's Mouth) flows through Kashmir to become the Indus in Pakistan; the Langchen Khabab (Out of the Elephant's Mouth) flows southward to become the Sutlej in western India; the Mapcha Khabab (Out of the Peacock's Mouth) becomes the sacred Ganges (though Gangotri, in India, is the accepted source for Hindus); and the Tachok Khabab (Out of the Horse's Mouth) flows eastward and, joining the Kyichu River south of Lhasa, forms the Brahmaputra, which winds through Assam and Bengal.

A river known as the Ngochu rises in central Tibet and flows through Dotod (Kham) in eastern Tibet and into Burma as the Salween. From northern Tibet, two rivers, the Ngomchu and the Zachu, flow through eastern Tibet, merge, and enter Laos and Thailand as the Mekong. The Drichu River also flows through Kham and into China as the Yangtse. The Machu River, coming from the mountain Machen Pomra in eastern Tibet, passes through Amdo and becomes the Huang Ho (Yellow River) of China.

The largest lakes of Tibet are the Tso Mapham (Manasarowar) in the west, sacred to both Buddhist and Hindu, Namtso Chukmo (Tengri Nor) in the northwest, Yardok Yutso (Yamdok) in central Tibet, and Tso Trishor Gyalmo (Kokonor) in the northeast.

Climate

In northern Tibet, people live up to an altitude of 16,000 feet, and in southern Tibet the lowest areas of habitation are at 4,000 feet, but the majority of the inhabitants live at elevations between 7,000 and 12,000 feet. Lhasa, the capital of Tibet, is situated at a height of 11,000 feet. In the north, the land is not cultivated, but is used for grazing sheep and yak because of the altitude. Areas below 12,000 feet can be cultivated.

The climate of Tibet varies according to the altitude. In general, the air is dry and the sun is strong. In the higher regions, it is colder and there is very little rainfall; but in the lower regions, there is a moderate rainfall and a fairly warm climate. For instance, in Lhasa the maximum temperature is 85 degrees Fahrenheit and the minimum is minus 3 degrees. The maximum rainfall is 18 inches, the minimum, fifteen.

The people of the outside world always imagine the people of Tibet to be living continually among snow and ice. Actually, it does not snow very much in Tibet, but when it does, it takes a long time to melt. The heaviest snowfall on the plateau is about four feet, compared to a frequent ten feet at Simla in northern India. The average snowfall along the southern border of Tibet is seven to eight feet.

Crops and Vegetation

The major products of Tibet are barley, wheat, and black peas. Other products include maize, beans, buckwheat, mustard, and hemp. The willow and poplar, as well as fruit trees like the apricot, peach, pear, apple, and walnut, are quite common. Strawberries, grapes, rhubarb, and mushrooms grow in abundance. Vegetables such as potatoes, cabbages, cauliflower, tomatoes, onions, garlic, celery, radishes, and turnips are common in the lower regions, while in the uplands there is little vegetation except for grass. In the past, the annual grain yield was more than sufficient for the population, and surplus barley and wheat could be stored for 25 to 50 years, because of the favorable climate.

The rose, sunflower, aster, phlox, dahlia, carnation, cornflower, lotus, marigold, pansy, sweet pea, and other flowers accustomed to temperate climates grow well in Tibet. Imported flower seeds from England do extremely well. Wild orchids and other meadow flowers are numerous, and medicinal plants are found throughout the country at lower altitudes.

Wildlife

There is a great variety of wildlife. In different parts of Tibet, one finds the tiger, leopard, Himalayan black bear, red bear, monkey, wolf, fox, marmot, hare, wild dog, wild pig, wild goat, deer, musk deer, antelope, wild yak, wild ass, lynx, rock snake, otter, and porcupine.

The marmot is much sought after as his skin makes a valuable export item. The white marmot, however, is considered sacred by superstitious Tibetans, who believe that to kill one would bring bad luck.

The musk deer always drinks at a particular spot and rubs itself against the bark of a tree. The hunter can usually tell from the deer's tracks whether it is carrying a large amount of musk or not. If it is, a trap is laid near its favorite tree.

The nomadic Tibetans claim that among the wild yaks there is usually one male to about a hundred females. This is not because few males are born. It is believed that the mothers, using their teeth, castrate most male progeny, taking care to leave the healthiest males alone. The uncastrated males remain aloof from the herd and select a female only during the mating season. They are fierce, jealous, and short-tempered, so it is probably just as well for the peace of the herd that there are so few males. The wild ass is said to have a similar custom.

The ardent bird watcher would find the crow, raven, magpie, parrot, owl, eagle, vulture, wild red duck, wild cock, partridge, white grouse, woodpecker, swallow, blackbird, lark, sandpiper, cuckoo,

stork, pigeon, dove, and water-fowl. The cuckoo, swallow, and small
eagle live in the north during the summer, migrating to the south during the winter. It is considered a bad omen in Tibet if any kind of
owl enters one's house at night. The vulture is very common. Cutting
up corpses and feeding the pieces to the vultures is a frequent funeral
practice.

Race

There are two traditions concerning the racial origin of the Tibetan
people. The first may be called the tradition of Indian ancestry. It is
said that a king, or military commander, named Rupati of the
Kaurava army fled to Tibet with his followers following defeat in a
great war with the Pandavas. A large number of learned Tibetans
claim that those people were the ancestors of the Tibetans. This claim
is based on a letter written by an Indian pandit, Shankara Pati (Deje
Dakpo), about one hundred years after the death of the Buddha, in
which he described the migration of Rupati's followers into Tibet.[4]

The second tradition maintains that Tibetans are descended from
monkeys; specifically from a male monkey, an incarnation of the
deity Avalokiteśvara (Chenresi), who produced six progeny through
a mountain ogress. These hybrid monkeys looked like any others, except that they had no tails. Gradually their descendants lost their various simian characteristics. Those who took after the original father became very merciful, intelligent, and sensitive, and did not talk more
than necessary. Those who inherited the characteristics of the mother
ogress were red-faced, fond of sinful pursuits, and very stubborn.

Tradition says this happened near Tsethang in the center of Ü-
Tsang region of Tibet. Behind Tsethang there is a mountain called
Gongpori, where the caves of these monkey ancestors are still to be
seen. The Indian pandit, Atisha, who visited Tibet in the eleventh
century, discovered a document in a pillar of the Jokhang, or central
temple, in Lhasa, that was written according to tradition during the
reign of Songtsen Gampo in the seventh century. This document provides evidence in favor of the second tradition for the origin of the
Tibetan people.[5]

Modern anthropologists claim that Tibetans belong to the Mongol-
oid race. Such a classification seems plausible since Tibetans have had a

4. DEB-SNGON; DGA'-STON; BU-STON.
5. MA-NI; RDZOGS-LDAN; ME-LONG.

close relationship with the Mongols for centuries; but up to now, no comparison of the skulls of the Tibetan and the Mongol have been made. The majority of the people in the Ü-Tsang region of Tibet are short of stature, round-headed, and high-cheek-boned—therefore slightly different from those of the other two regions. The people of Dotod (Kham) and Domed (Amdo) are tall, long-headed, and long-limbed.

Population

No thorough or accurate census has ever been taken in Tibet, and thus only an estimation is possible. When the early religious kings sent troops against China in the seventh century, they were able to recruit as many as 200,000 men.[6] According to Ba Salnang, an early Tibetan chronicler, the fantastic number of 14,000,000 was recruited for another war.[7] Regardless of the validity of these figures, it appears that the population of Tibet has declined over the centuries, because the present estimated population of Chol-kha-sum (the three regions of ethnic Tibet) is about six million. Of this number, approximately 48 per cent are nomads and 32 per cent are traders and agriculturalists. Monks and nuns, drawn from all classes of society, form about 20 per cent (18 per cent monks and 2 per cent nuns).

Towns

The largest town in Tibet is the capital, Lhasa, where the Dalai Lama and the Tibetan government had their headquarters. The population of Lhasa always ranged between 35,000 and 40,000. During the first month of the Tibetan New Year, monks and pilgrims from various parts of Tibet converged on Lhasa for the Monlam festival (Prayer assembly), raising the population to between 70,000 and 80,000.

The second largest town is Shigatse with a population ranging from 13,000 to 20,000. Nearby is the Tashilhunpo monastery, the residence of the Panchen Lama.

The third largest town is Chamdo, in eastern Tibet. There is a

6. PELLIOT, p. 4.

7. The manuscript edition of the *Sba-bzhed* published by R. A. Stein in his *Une Chronique Ancienne de bSam-yas: sBa-bžed* (Paris, 1961) states clearly (line 4, p. 43) that 14,000,000 horsemen came forth (*rta pa bye ba phrag bcu bzhi byung*). Whether this is a hyperbolic number or a scribal error in the original manuscript is impossible to say; but the figure seems impossibly high.

monastery there, and in the past it was the residence of the eastern Governor-general. The town's population was between 9,000 and 12,000.

Gyantse, in central Tibet, is the fourth largest town. The Palkhor Choide monastery is located there. A British Trade Agency was established there in 1904 by the Younghusband Expedition. In 1955, the agency was washed away by a flood, and the Indian Trade Agent, his wife, and the members of staff were lost.

There are many smaller towns scattered throughout Tibet, but there is no need to mention them here.

Transport and Communications

Every Tibetan, be he trader, monk, official, soldier, or pilgrim, traveled by horse or mule, or on foot, while luggage was carried by horse, yak, mule, ox, donkey, or sheep. It was a custom for travelers to garland their mounts with small bells and their pack animals with large bells. This helps to relieve the long silence and strain of a tedious journey. It also helps to frighten away wild animals in jungle regions, and the bells assist the travelers in locating their pack animals during night grazing hours. No single pack-load could exceed eighty pounds, and only two such loads could be carried by one animal, according to a decree of the government.

In western Tibet, sheep were the most common pack animals; each one carrying two ten-pound loads of salt. Each trader had about one hundred sheep, and usually about a dozen traders traveled together. The load was not removed from the sheep's back for several weeks and the animals would try to rest between two small outcroppings so that the load was raised and the pressure eased. It was quite pitiful to see the sheep searching for such a resting place at the end of a day's journey. Sometimes at the end of long journeys, the skin of the sheep came away with the load, when it was removed. The traders sold both the salt and the sheep on their arrival at the Nepalese or Indian border.

In the past when transport was confined exclusively to pack animals, roads were little more than rough tracks, and there were no major bridges. Some rivers were crossed either in small yak-skin boats holding about ten people, or in large wooden ferries carrying about thirty animals and men. In eastern Tibet, there are very strong currents which can be crossed only in canoes hollowed out of the trunks of walnut trees. These hold only two or three people.

Some rivers in eastern Tibet are too swift even for canoes, and in those areas an ingenious sort of ropeway is used. Since the river usually flows between two steep hills, the rope, which is made of strong, thick cane, is inclined at an angle of about sixty degrees, and a small wooden saddle is attached to it. The traveler is strapped into this saddle and then slides, feet first, down to the opposite side. Another rope serves travelers going in the opposite direction. The descent is cushioned by blankets and eased by a sudden upward tilt at the end of the ropeway. Local inhabitants carry their own saddles and are expert at making such crossings. More elaborate arrangements have sometimes had to be made for travelers coming from other parts of the country. Sometimes when large parties or bodies of troops were making these crossings, there were "traffic jams," and people were held up for several days, having to camp on either side of the river. Not only did men, women, and children make the crossings; but pack animals as well. These were lashed upside-down to the ropeway and sent sliding across to the opposite bank.

In the fifteenth century, a traveling mendicant by the name of Thangtong Gyalpo, who begged in order to do good for others, erected 53 chain bridges across rivers in the Ü-Tsang region of Tibet. He constructed the bridges after years of collecting pieces of iron, which he got through soliciting, and then employing the labor of skilled blacksmiths. The bridges proved to be extremely useful to early travelers, and some of them are still in use in remote areas of Ü-Tsang. No animals were permitted to use the bridges.

Until 1956 there was a postal system maintained by runners who carried the post in relays, each man covering four and a half miles before handing over the mail to the next man. This system operated between India and Lhasa, through Sikkim, and between Lhasa and a few other towns within the country. There was also a telegraphic service between Lhasa and India; but, there was no such service for the public in Tibet proper. Military and official correspondence was carried on horseback and relayed from one town to another. Urgent communications, like one advising of the imminent visit of some important official, were attached to arrows to give them greater significance. Any letter attached to an arrow was given priority and forwarded to its destination without any delay.

In 1930 the British Trade Agent made a Jeep road between Phari and Gyantse; but this road lasted only for a few weeks and then had to be put out of service because the local people objected to it on the grounds that it affected their livelihood since they would no longer be able to provide pack animals for transport. An attempt to introduce motor vehicles into Tibet was made by the thirteenth Dalai Lama, who put a few cars on the roads in Lhasa in 1928 on a test basis. As there was no motorable road between Tibet and India, the cars had to be dismantled in India and carried in pieces over the Himalayas by porters.

After 1945, the Tibetan government was able to establish radio stations at such important and strategic places as Chamdo, Nagchukha, and Gartok. Then, after 1951, the Chinese Communists constructed several roads, bridges, and airfields to facilitate military movements in the occupation of Tibet.

Commerce and Economy

There must have been large quantities of gold in Tibet in early times. When the Tibetans were enthusiastically absorbing the Buddhist religion into their country from Nepal and India, they made many gifts of pure gold to the temples and pandits in those countries. They often paid for their purchases in gold as well.

In later times, Tibet's major exports were wool, yak tails (principally imported by the U.S. for use as Santa Claus beards), borax, and salt. Minor exports included the skins of various animals, musk, incense, and a variety of medicinal goods, such as leaves, herbs, bear's bile, and dried deer's blood. Moreover, horses, sheep, donkeys, mules, and goats were exported annually to India, Nepal, and China.

Imports from India included such goods as woolen material, cotton cloth, inferior silk, cotton, wool, kerosene, glass, and miscellaneous machinery. Iron and copper were imported, as well as staples, such as rice, fruits, and medicines. From China, Tibet imported brick tea, silk, porcelain, enamel, and ceremonial scarves (khatag);[8] While Nepal supplied copper articles and rice. It should be noted that before the Communist Chinese occupation of Tibet, starvation was nonexistent, owing to the surplus food storage system. Taxes were generally paid in kind and the excess food stuffs, particularly grain, were stored in gov-

8. The khatag (Kha-btags), or ceremonial scarf of white silk, is a traditional necessity. It has become a custom to use the scarf for many occasions, such as when greeting one or bidding farewell, when paying a visit, and so forth. The exchange of the scarf is quite an elaborate ceremony. They are also used as offerings to sacred images and to venerated lamas.

ernment granaries. It is estimated that the grain reserves were sufficient for three years in case of famine. Except for the importation of
rice, tea, and some fruits and sweets, Tibet was self-sufficient in its
supply of food.

The Tibetan government had no bank of its own; nor did it control
foreign exchange. There was no restriction on imports and exports;
therefore, the exchange rate fluctuated according to the balance of
foregn trade. Markets were controlled by supply and demand. Trade
within Tibet itself was also controlled to a large extent by the
weather. For example, traders from the Kokonor region (Ch'ing-hai
province of China), who sold horses and mules in Lhasa, had to leave
Kokonor in April in order to ensure that fresh grass for their animals
would be available. They would reach Lhasa in August and arrive
back home by February. The yaks they would take back with them
would carry the goods purchased and also provide them with meat
during the winter months. Tibetan travelers found security against
bandits by forming large caravan parties and carrying firearms, the
use of which was not prohibited by law.

Currency

In early times, the barter system prevailed in Tibet, and barley
grain was used to make purchases ranging from horses to clothes. The
barter system has been retained to the present day in remote parts of
Tibet. Even fines were levied in grain. Later on, silver was used for
purposes of trade, but, in the beginning, only according to weight. As
the weights became standardized—ten *karma* to one *sho-gang*, ten *sho-
gang* to one *sang-gang*, and fifty *sang-gang* to one *dotsed*—a form of
currency developed, using these silver pieces as coins.

For a few years after 1750, the coins of Nepal were circulated in
Tibet. One Nepalese silver *tamka* was the equivalent of one *sho-gang*
and five *karma*. In 1792, the Tibetans, using the Nepalese coin as a
model, made their own *tamka* with a Tibetan inscription. Later, copper coins, varying in size according to value, were also minted by the
Tibetan government and embossed with the seal of the lion. Sang-
gang, sho-gang, and karma then became actual coins, not merely units
of weight, and were the equivalent of rupees, annas, and pice. This
currency continued in use until the Communist Chinese occupation.

In 1890 the Tibetan government introduced paper currency. The
first notes were in denominations of five, ten, fifteen, twenty-five, and

fifty *tamka*. Later these notes were called *sang* and issued in denominations of five, ten, twenty-five, and one hundred. Silver coins followed in units of five, ten, fifteen, thirty, and one hundred sho-gang, and one gold coin, which was valued at twenty sang. All notes and coins bore the government seal of the lion and the date of issue. Government-held gold reserves backed up the currency notes. The minting of coins and printing of notes was begun after Tibetan officials had been sent to British India, where they studied the works and methods of the Calcutta mint.

Housing and Living Conditions

There are no significant architectural differences among houses in Tibet, only slight variations in design. It is customary for people to build their houses facing south to make the most of the sunshine. The materials are usually brick and stone. A two-story building usually comes up behind a one-story structure. Windows and doors are outlined in black cement. In early days, firewood was placed on the roof as a protection against thieves; this practice survived as a fashionable custom, and rooftop firewood was arranged in very attractive patterns. Prayer flags flutter above every roof.

Temple architecture has been influenced to a considerable extent by Nepal, India, and China. As for paintings, Tibetan artists work on prescribed models of Buddhist canonical tradition. Three of the most prominent schools of painting are the Karma Gardre of Kham, the Gongkar, Khenri, and the Menthong Ari of Ü. Painting, along with the making of images, was first introduced into Tibet from Nepal and India, and elaborations on these arts were borrowed later from China.

The nomads make very strong, substantial tents of woven yak hair, including the long tail hair. The largest tents are big enough to accommodate one or two hundred persons and are divided into separate rooms. Except for very rich nomads, these people never remain in one place for long. It is essential for them to erect prayer flags over their tents and to burn incense before the entrances. It is always possible to recognize a Tibetan encampment from the number of prayer flags in the vicinity. The nomads keep yak, sheep, goats, horses, and fierce watch-dogs. The agriculturalists keep horses, mules, donkeys, pigs, cattle, poultry, yak, and *dzo*, which is a cross between a *dri* (female yak) and a bull. The dzo is excellent for plowing. The male hybrid is called dzo-pho; the female dzo-mo.

The yak is probably the most useful animal in Tibet. It lives under the most difficult conditions and finds its own food most of the time. It provides transport, milk, and meat. Its skin makes excellent boots, saddlebags, boats, and so forth; while the hair, including the long tail-hair, is good material for making tents and durable clothing. The yak is also used for plowing. The female yak, along with the female dzo-mo, gives good milk, with the dzo-mo producing the greater quantity. Yak butter is used in making a nourishing drink mixed with tea.

Language and Literature

There is no resemblance between the language of Tibet and those of India or China, although the Tibetan script was adapted from an Indian one. The original names for many items brought in from China, India, and Britain were retained and became part of the Tibetan language. Within Chol-kha-sum (ethnic Tibet), there is a wide range of dialects, creating for the Tibetan the same sort of language problems found in other countries. The Ü-Tsang dialect is considered to be the most widely understood. There is, however, only one written language and this gives unity to Tibetan literary culture.

Many scholars assume that the Tibetan script came into being when King Songtsen Gampo (reigned 629–49) sent his minister, Thoa-mi Sam-bhota, and some students to India to study the script of the Guptas. It seems that there may have been some sort of a script in use before that—perhaps one related to the Bon religion—because Songtsen Gampo is said to have written a letter to the King of Nepal asking for his daughter's hand in marriage before the students and minister were sent to India to learn a writing system. According to historical texts, the king did write the letter; [9] however, there is no evidence that there was an earlier Bon script.

The current Tibetan script was derived from the Brahmi and Gupta scripts, which were in use in India as early as A.D. 350. Of the students sent to India, Thon-mi Sam-bhota alone returned to devise a script for the Tibetan language. The amazing similarities of the Tibetan script with those of the Brahmi and Gupta scripts can be seen in Bühler, *Indische Palaeographie*, Plate IV, Cols. I–VII. In my own study of the Gupta script, I am able to read most of the letters, although the meaning of the words is unknown to me.

9. ME-LONG; RDZOGS-LDAN.

Religion and Character

According to early writings, Bon—Tibet's earliest religion—was founded by Shenrab Miwo of Shangshung in western Tibet. The time of Shenrab Miwo's life is a matter of dispute. Some followers of the Bon religion maintain that he was a contemporary of Lord Buddha; while others claim he was an incarnation of the Buddha.[10] Contrary to these is the assertion by still others that Shenrab Miwo was an incarnation of an ardent Buddhist pandit, who later opposed the doctrine of Buddhism.

Buddhism first came into Tibet in the seventh century from Nepal and India; but the actual active propagation began in the eighth century with Padmasambhava. Gradually the Bon religion diminished in influence, but it still exists in various remote areas. Buddhism was not introduced into Tibet all at once, but at different times by different teachers. The principal sects are the Nying-ma-pa, Ka-gyu-pa, Sa-kya-pa, and Ge-lug-pa. Among the minor groups are the Shi-che-pa, Chag-chen-pa, and Ngor-pa; but all are Tibetan Buddhists. There were also adherents to the Muslim and Hindu faiths in Tibet, where there was freedom of religious worship and thought before the Communist occupation.

Tibetans lean strongly on their Buddhist faith and believe in the doctrine of *karma*; which teaches that the rewards and punishments of this life are the result of one's actions in the previous life. This is one of the reasons why Tibetans are very sympathetic, honest, cheerful, and satisfied with their lot. They are loyal, open, gentle, and kind. They enjoy their leisure and, even though their border neighbors of China and India previously relegated women to inferior status, the Tibetans are courteous and treat their women as equals. Such have been the opinions of foreign travelers who have spent some time in Tibet. It is said in Tibet that the people of Ü-Tsang are very religious-minded, the people of Kham are good fighters, and the people of Amdo are worldly and make good businessmen.

Although a feudal system, somewhat similar to that of medieval Europe, prevailed in Tibet before the Communist occupation, there were no restrictions on worship or travel for even the poorest peasants or servants. There was also a special form of social mobility on reli-

10. GRUB-MTHA'.

gious grounds. For example, the present Dalai Lama himself comes from a family of farmers. In fact, incarnate lamas may come from any one of the social classes.

Monastic Life

In view of the fact that religion played such a dominant role in the life of the Tibetans, I shall provide a brief glimpse into monastic life. Thousands of Buddhist monasteries were scattered throughout Tibet: in cities, towns, and villages. Even the tiny hamlet possessed either a monastery or nunnery. The way of life varied slightly from one monastery to another, depending on the sect and the size of the monastery.

Most of the Buddhist sects played important roles in shaping the history of Tibet. In modern times, the Ge-lug-pa, commonly known as the Yellow Hat sect, is predominant with its famous monasteries of Drepung, Sera, Ganden, and Tashilhunpo. Such large monasteries as these are also referred to as *Dansa* (Seat of the Head Lama) or *Chode* (Great Religious Institution). Very small monasteries are sometimes called *Ridro* (Hermitage). The common term for all monasteries is *Gompa*.

Admission to a monastery is open to all classes of the population.[11] When a boy of five or six years of age receives admission to one of the monasteries, he is dressed in monastic robes and the hair is shaved from his head, except for a tiny portion on the crown which is to be offered to the high lama, who will remove it in a ceremonial manner with a blade. The boy receives a new name and is taught to read, write, and memorize the scriptures by heart for a period of two years. Following this elementary education, he takes the vow of a *getsul*, the first stage of monkhood, and he then commences classes in higher studies. He studies intensively and extensively over a long period of time and gradually completes the following subjects: Perfection of Wisdom, Avoidance of Extremes, Canon of Monastic Discipline, Dialectics, Metaphysics, and Logic.

When the boy reaches adult age (18 to 20 years), he may take the vow of a *gelong*, the fully-ordained monk, and is then subject to very strict monastic discipline. The gelong vow may be taken while a monk is still in the process of his higher studies. Additional studies and the successful completion of texts in philosophy and theology enables one to receive the highest of monastic degrees, namely Lharam Geshe,

11. PAD-DKAR.

"Master of Metaphysics." Monks in smaller monasteries are not subject to such rigorous discipline, nor are they eligible to study for the Lharam Geshe degree.

A graduate may remain in the monastery for life or he may enter a hermitage for meditation, following which he will emerge into society and preach to his fellow men. Even higher monastic studies may be undertaken in a separate college of *Ngak* (Tantrism). Graduates of this monastic college are eligible to become Khenpo (abbots), and even possibly the Ganden Tripa (Enthroned-one of Ganden monastery), who is the most learned religious figure in Tibet. By the time a Ge-lug-pa monk becomes a candidate for Ganden Tripa, he is usually well over sixty years of age.

The organization of a monastery in Tibet resembles that of a Western university. Each monastery is subdivided into colleges and dormitories. The government and wealthy patrons support the monasteries by contributions of grain, tea, and butter. The money distributed to the monks as gifts from donors enables the monks to buy clothing and to meet minor expenses. In all of the monasteries, the monks are expected to lead a simple life and to refrain from smoking, drinking, and dancing. Most of the sects impose celibacy on fully-ordained monks.

This survey of monastic life reflects, of course, the way it was in Tibet prior to the Communist Chinese occupation.

The Calendar and Astrology

Throughout this book the reader will find many dates given according to the Tibetan calendar system: for example, the fifth day of the third Tibetan month of the Water-Male-Horse year. Whenever the exact day and month of a given event is known from Western sources, the Western date is given after the Tibetan one. In those cases where there is no available information on the exact Western month and day, only the Western year is given. The reason for this requires an explanation of the Tibetan calendar and the lunar system upon which it is based.

Two factors make it impossible to set up a conversion table between the month and the day of the Tibetan calendar and the Western calendar. The first problem is that the Tibetan lunar year theoretically consists of twelve months of thirty days each, making a total of 360 days. In order to make this coincide with the solar year of 365 1/4 days, an intercalary, or extra, month is added every third year. Unfortunately for the purposes of conversion, the intercalary month is not added consistently at any point, but anywhere among the twelve regular months that is considered lucky for that particular year. Thus the year in which the intercalary month was added can be computed, but its corresponding Western month cannot.

The second problem for conversion results from the need to adjust the theoretical 360-day Tibetan lunar year with the actual lunar year of 354 days. The adjustment is made by omitting certain days. A Tibetan calendar consists of pages marked off in six squares with a number in each square representing the day of the month. The six squares do not correspond to a Tibetan week, but five such pages make a lunar month of thirty days. When a day is omitted from the calendar, the number is omitted from its proper square and the word *chad* (cut off) inserted. That day of the month ceases to exist. The days of the month would then appear thus: 1, 2, *chad*, 4, 5, 6, etc. Moreover, certain days are duplicated. For example, the calendar would appear with a duplicated day thus: 1, 2, 3/3/, 4, 5, 6, etc.

In view of these unpredictable adjustments made in order to keep the Tibetan lunar calendar in agreement with the actual lunar and solar years and to avoid unlucky days, it is impossible to set up a formula for the conversion of Tibetan days and months into their Western equivalents unless one possesses the actual calendar for the year in question. A new Tibetan calendar is prepared towards the end of each year by the official astrologer, who determines which unlucky days are to be omitted and which days are to be duplicated. If it is the third year, he decides where to insert the intercalary month. Only then is the calendar made up for the ensuing year. Thus the Tibetan people do not know precisely what the next year's calendar will be like until it has been prepared by the astrologer.

The new year begins with the rise of the new moon in the Western month of February, except following the year when the intercalary month was added, then it begins in March. Allowing for the difference between the beginning of the new year in the Tibetan and Western systems, the equivalent Western year, at least, can be computed with certainty.

Tibetan months have no distinctive names and are simply numbered consecutively. The seven days of the week are named, as in the Western system, for the sun, moon, and the five visible planets: Mars,

Mercury, Jupiter, Venus, and Saturn. These names are prefixed with the word *Sa* (planet), thus: Sa nyi-ma (Sunday), Sa da-wa (Monday), Sa Mik-mar (Tuesday), Sa Lhak-pa (Wednesday), Sa Phur-bu (Thursday), Sa Pa-sang (Friday), and Sa pen-pa (Saturday).

In ancient times, the Tibetan calendar was based on a twelve-year cycle, each year being named after one of the following animals: mouse, ox, tiger, hare, dragon, serpent, horse, sheep, ape, bird, dog, and hog. This twelve-year cycle was in use until the eleventh century A.D., when the sixty-year cycle was introduced. This system was expounded in the religious text *Du-kyi khor-lo gyu* (Sanskrit: Kālacakra-Tantra) translated into Tibetan in the year A.D. 1027, which became the first year of the first sixty-year cycle. The cycle of sixty years is obtained by combining the names of the twelve animals with those of the five elements: wood, fire, earth, iron, and water. One element name is combined with two successive animal names and to distinguish further between the two successive *element* years, the word *male* is added to the first and *female* to the second. Thus: the wood-male-mouse year is followed by the wood-female-ox year.

Astrology, divination, and the casting of horoscopes play important roles in Tibetan daily life and the lucky and unlucky relationships between the various elements and animals assigned to each year of the sixty-year cycle are carefully observed by the astrologer (Tsi-pa). There is antagonism between certain animals and there are degrees of affinity between the elements. For example, the combination of the tiger and the monkey is an unlucky one, just as iron is hostile to fire, which melts it. Even the months, days, and hours have specific astrological aspects which are unlucky in certain combinations.

As in the case of the preparation of a new calendar at the end of each year, astrology influences Tibetan affairs at various levels. Auspicious days for important occasions ranging from the enthronement of a Dalai Lama down to a departure on a long journey are determined by astrology.

Divination through the use of numbers, rosary beads, dice, and other objects is resorted to by people seeking guidance on sundry matters. Horoscopes are commonly cast for such events as the choosing of a marriage partner and the selection of the proper person to participate in funeral ceremonies, as well as to forecast the events of one's entire life.

Weddings

The wedding ceremony in Tibet varies in different provinces according to family wealth and social position. The preliminaries to a typical Tibetan wedding begin with extensive inquiries made among eligible girls by the parents of the prospective groom. After careful selection of a few girls, the respective parents of the girls are requested to give her in marriage if the horoscopes are in agreement with that of the groom. The names and ages of the groom and the girls selected are presented to a soothsayer and an astrologer to ascertain which one of the girls meets the qualifications. If the girl's parents consent to the proposal after the horoscopes are found to be in agreement, the engagement date will be fixed by the astrologer.

The bridegroom's party will proceed to the house of the bride with ceremonial scarves and gifts. This visit is known as *Long-chang* (Begging-beer). The bride's mother is paid a certain sum of money commonly known as *Nu-rin* (Breast-price). Nu-rin is always paid to the bride's family whether the bride's mother is living or not. After conclusion of this ceremony, an agreement is drawn and sealed by parents before witnesses.

An auspicious day will then be selected for the bride to depart from her home. On the eve of the wedding day, a reception party of horsemen will proceed from the groom's house to the house of the bride. The procession is led by the astrologer, who bears in his hand an arrow-like banner with a scroll of painting hanging from the banner's point. Astrological diagrams, known as *sipaho*, depict the stars and planets. Mystical symbols are also pictured on the painting as a symbol of protection from evil spirits. The party is accompanied by a fully saddled mare, which has already been foaled and which the bride will ride from her home to that of the bridegroom.

Early on the wedding day, the lama of the bride's house will seek the permission of her household deity to give the bride away. The special representative of the bridegroom will then plant an arrow with ribbons of five different colors (da-tar) on the bride's collar after he has explained, in poetical form, the significance of the arrow. He then declares the bride to be married to the bridegroom. The reception party will lead the procession, followed by the bride riding the mare and supported on both sides by attendants. A similar party of horsemen from the bride's house will accompany the procession. Often the bride weeps and faints when departing from her home. She will be accompanied by her best friends to stay with her at her new home for a few days until she overcomes her homesickness.

On the way, the wedding procession will be met by a welcoming party, who will offer them barley beer (chang) while they are still mounted on their horses. Arriving at the gate of the bridegroom's house, the bride dismounts upon a stack of barley grain and brick tea. The bridegroom's mother will receive the bride at the gate with a bucket of milk. The bride dips the third finger of her left hand into the milk and then flicks a few drops of it into the air as an offering to the gods.

The bride is escorted into the family chapel and seated beside the bridegroom, then members of both families will join them, seating in order of seniority. An exchange of scarves and gifts takes place between the two families, after which tea, rice, and wine are served. Following the ceremony, friends of both families come to congratulate the married couple with gifts and scarves. Later, the couple will be taken onto the roof of the house, where prayers will be offered by the household lama to bring the bride under the protection of her husband's family deities. The representative of the bride, while hoisting a prayer flag on the roof of the house, will pronounce her equal in rights as the other members of her husband's family. Lavish parties are given for a few days to celebrate the marriage. The bride is forbidden to visit her parents' home before one month has passed, then she and her husband may call for the first time. After this first visit, the bride may visit her parents any time she wishes. In recent times, the wedding ceremony and customs have become simpler and love-marriages, in contrast to arranged-marriages, are permitted.

Sports

Horses have played a very important part in Tibetan sports. Their speed was tested over distances of four miles, rather than on a fixed, circular course. Some races involved riderless horses; while others took place over short distances, while the rider aimed at a target with a rifle, bow and arrow, or spear. These special events took place only at long intervals, and every lay official had to take part at least once in his life. There were also archery contests with targets and trials for distance. Since prizes were distributed by the government for these contests and public prestige was involved, the officials spent months practicing. The original purpose of the contests was to ensure that the officials were ready to join the military in an emergency; later, the contests became a traditional sport.

Ancient Tibetan custom required a man from each lay-official household to compete in three-mile foot races. Volunteers were not lacking for weight lifting, and even compulsory wrestling was popular. Tibetans enjoy swimming. Racing across rivers, at an angle against the current, was a popular feat of endurance.

The Tibetan equivalent of Western bowls and skittles was a game of throwing round stones considerable distances in an attempt to hit targets of horn or other stones. For broad jumping, a raised earthen ramp was prepared and the competitors formed teams. The impetus gained by running up this ramp and leaping enabled the contestants to reach thirty feet or more. In autumn, kite fever attacks every boy and young man. High winds and clear skies set kites soaring and kite fights filled the skies above Lhasa. The kites were made of colored paper and bamboo, and the strings were coated with glue and powdered glass. Everyone tried to cut the string of his opponent's kite by using his own kite string as a blade. Nowadays, football, tennis, and other games are played, while mah-jongg, dice, and cards are popular indoor games.

Dress

It is said that the early kings of Tibet wore head coverings consisting of a red sash twisted about the cap like a turban, long loose robes, and shoes with toes pointed upwards. This style of garments is believed to have originated with the kings of Persia.[12]

The robes of Tibetan lamas and monks originated with the Indian-style garments of the Lord Buddha, but were later modified to suit the rigorous Tibetan climate. The dress of the lay and monk officials originated partly from Mongolian garments. The rank of a lay official is known by the variations of the color and style of his gown. The man in the street wears a long, coarsely woven, heavy woolen gown, folded back into several wide pleats and held in place by a sash. A sheepskin lining protects against the cold winter air.

As in the West, women in Tibet are fashion conscious. For special occasions, wide-sleeved blouses under long gowns and multicolored, striped aprons delight the hearts of the ladies. Their long black hair is

12. DEB-DKAR.

augmented by plaits of false hair, on which rests the *patruk,* which is a velvet-rolled framework ornamented with pearls, coral, and turquoise. The shape of the patruk varies in different regions of the country. Long gold earrings, studded with turquoise, are looped over the ears, and charm boxes of gold with turquoise and diamonds are worn on necklaces.

The hats worn by men and women in winter are similar in style. They are attractively covered with silk brocade and have two large flaps and two smaller ones edged with fur. In summer, the men prefer Western-style felt hats.

It is interesting to note that the brocade gowns of the abbots and other high clerical officials closely resemble those worn by archbishops in the Roman Catholic Church. Also, the hollow woolen hat worn by all ranks of monks, although varying somewhat in size, reminds one of the helmet of ancient Greece. One might ask whether this style originated in Tibet or perhaps in Persia or India during the campaign of Alexander the Great.

In early times, the soldiers of Tibet wore armor, but in the seventeenth century a strange change took place—cotton clothing, made to resemble armor, was worn instead. After 1916 the military uniform was modeled on British style, but after 1947 there was a gradual change to a pure Tibetan style.

Government

At the apex of the Tibetan governmental structure is the spiritual and temporal ruler of Tibet, the Dalai Lama. In theory, the power of the Dalai Lama is absolute, but in practice he does not exercise his authority without consultation to aid his judgment. During the absence or minority of the Dalai Lama, a Regent (Gyaltsab) is appointed by the National Assembly (Tsongdu) to run the government. The government structure was dualistic in nature with two Prime Ministers (Silon)—one a layman and the other a monk—and the administration was divided into civil and religious branches.

In the operation of the civil administration, the Council (Kashag), which was the chief executive body, attended to all matters of private and national issues. The Council was composed of three lay officials and one monk, each accorded the title of Kalon. The Council was concerned with the studying and expressing of their views on those issues which were forwarded to the Dalai Lama through the Office of the

Prime Minister for final decision. The Council's privilege of forwarding recommendations on the appointment of executive officers, governors, and district officials gave them control over a wide range of governmental activities.

Below the Council, there was an administrative body separated into the following departments: Political, Military, Economic, Judicial, Foreign, Financial, and Educational. Except for the Finance Department (Tsekhang), all other departments were headed by one lay official and one monk official. The Finance Department was composed of four lay officials, each accorded the title of Tsepon. Each of the various departments had the power to make decisions within a certain limit. Beyond that, issues were forwarded, with departmental views, to the Council, which in turn followed a similar procedure.

The administration of religious affairs was attended by the Lord Chamberlain (Chikyap Khenpo) and a Council of four monks known as Trungyik Chemo. On matters of religious issue, this body presented its views to the Dalai Lama through the Office of the Prime Minister. The Lord Chamberlain was also in charge of the Forest Department and the Private Treasury of the Dalai Lama.

A joint session of the four Trungyik Chemo and the four Tsepon was frequently held to discuss matters of political importance and other issues. When the National Assembly met to discuss issues of national importance, the Council of the Trungyik Chemo and the Council of the Tsepon presided over the meeting and acted as spokesmen. The decisions made by the National Assembly were usually not altered and were forwarded to the Dalai Lama through the Council (Kashag) and the Office of the Prime Minister in the usual procedure.

This brief outline reflects the structure of the Tibetan government as it was before the setting up of the Preparatory Committee for the Autonomous Region of Tibet by the Chinese Communists in 1956.

2

The Empire of the Early Kings of Tibet

There is no documentary evidence to enlighten us about the most ancient period of Tibetan history. According to Buddhist tradition, the Tibetan kings traced their ancestry to the son of a noble family of Magadha in Bihar, India, who is said to have been born with long blue eyebrows, a full set of teeth, and webbed fingers. His father, Mak Gyapa, hid the child out of shame, and when he grew up, he wandered into Tibet.[1] The boy arrived at Yalung in Tibet, where the people were adherents of the Bon religion, and there he meet a number of farmers grazing their cattle. The sky was regarded as sacred by the Bon Tibetans. When they asked where he came from, the boy, not understanding their language, gestured skywards and they, thinking he was very holy to come from the sky, decided to make him their leader. Placing him on a wooden sedan-chair, they carried him on their shoulders to their village and there gave him the name Nyatri Tsenpo, meaning "Neck-enthroned King." Until the coming of Nyatri Tsenpo, the Tibetans lived in caves. It is believed that he built the first house, known as Yumbulagang, which is still to be seen in central Tibet. Such, then, is the traditional origin of the first Tibetan king according to the Buddhist historians.

Nyatri Tsenpo and the next six kings are said to have returned to the sky at death by means of a "sky-rope"; and no tombs for them are known. The tomb of the eighth king is said to exist in Kongpo in Ü-Tsang. The Tibetans call that tomb, "The First Tomb of the Kings." This king's name was Drigum Tsenpo and it is from his time that the real history of Tibet begins. Since Drigum Tsenpo was buried in a tomb, it is assumed that he accidently cut the "sky-rope" and could not ascend to heaven at death, as his ancestors had done.

1. RDZOGS-LDAN. On the other hand, BU-STON traces this Tibetan king to the royal family of King Salgyal of Kosala in India.

The son and successor of this king was Chatri Tsenpo, also known as Podekungyal. According to Tibetan accounts, Drigum Tsenpo was killed by a minister named Longam, who usurped the throne. The three sons of Drigum Tsenpo—Chatri Tsenpo, Nyatri Tsenpo, and Shatri Tsenpo—fled into exile. Later on, Chatri Tsenpo was able to re-gain the throne. It is interesting to note that Ssanang Setzen, the Mongolian chronicler and author of *Mongol Khadun Toghudji*, traces the Mongol royal lineage to that of Tibet. Citing Ssanang Setzen, Howorth states that the three sons of the king of Tibet fled when their father was killed by a minister named Longnam, who usurped the throne. The three sons fled in different directions; the youngest, Burtechino, fled to the land of the Bede people, who lived near the Baikal Sea and the mountain Burkhan Khalduna.[2]

According to some accounts, Podekungyal, the ninth king was a contemporary of Wu-ti, Emperor of the Former Han Dynasty, who reigned 140–85 B.C. During Podekungyal's reign, both iron ore and copper ore were discovered. He had canals made to improve agricul-ture and bridges built across streams; these were innovations. A palace, known as Chingwar Taktse, was erected at Chongyas. The ruins of that palace are still be be seen there.

Eighteen generations after Podekungyal, a son of the royal line, named Tho-tho-ri Nyantsen, was born ca. A.D. 173.[3] When he ascended the throne he became the twenty-eighth king according to the Buddhist tradition. It is said that when Tho-tho-ri Nyantsen was sixty years of age, he received a book of Buddhist scripture, while liv-ing in the palace of Yumbulagang. He could not read the book be-cause it was in Sanskrit and there was no one in Tibet at that time who could translate that language. The king called the book *Nyenpo Sangwa* (The Secret) and a secret it remained for many years. Not wanting his ministers to know that the book had come from India, the king told them it had descended from the sky and that he had been shown in a dream that, after four generations, there would be a king able to read and understand the book. Nel-pa Pandita, an early Ti-betan historian, mentions that the book was received through a certain

2. HOWORTH, pp. 32–33.
3. Tibetan histories state that Tho-tho-ri was sixty years old when he received the *Nyenpo Sangwa* (The Secret), which marked the initial introduction of Buddhism into Tibet. This event was of such importance that Tibetan currency notes are dated from the year of that introduction, which is given as A.D. 233. Assuming that date to be correct and if Tho-tho-ri was sixty years old at the time, then he was born ca. A.D. 173.

Pandita Losemtso of India and not from the sky as other learned men maintained.

Four generations later,[4] in A.D. 617, Namri Songtsen, the thirty-second king, had a son named Tride Songtsen, who is better known nowadays as Songtsen Gampo.[5] In Chinese records, he is called Ch'i-tsung-lung-tsan. His birth came just one year before the founding of the T'ang Dynasty, when Kao-tsu became Emperor in 618.

Songtsen Gampo ascended the throne at the age of thirteen. In time, he drew up ten moral principles and sixteen rules of public conduct for his people. A few years later, he sent his minister, Gar Tongtsen with presents and a letter to the Nepalese King, Amshuvarman, to ask for the hand of the Princess Bhrikuti Devi in marriage. Amshuvarman sent his daughter to Songtsen Gampo and she took with her an image of the Akṣobhya Buddha. That image is considered sacred by the Tibetans as it is said to have been blessed by Lord Buddha himself. The Tibetans always refer to the Princess Bhrikuti as *Belsa,* which means "The Nepalese Consort."

A thorough search of Tibetan historical records has failed to reveal the exact date when Songtsen Gampo sent Thon-mi Sam-bhota with sixteen companions to India to learn the Sanskrit language. Thon-mi Sam-bhota went to Kashmir in northwest India, where he had as his tutors Lipi Kara and Devavidyasimha. The Tibetan students who accompanied him to India died there. After Thon-mi Sam-bhota returned to Tibet he used his knowledge of the Brahmi and Gupta scripts to devise a Tibetan script. He then is said to have translated the book, *The Secret,* preserved since the time of Tho-tho-ri Nyentsen, and so its enlightening contents were made known to the people. That book was considered of such importance as the first introduction of the Buddhist religion into Tibet, that modern currency notes are dated in so many years from the arrival of *The Secret,* which is said to have been in A.D. 233.

---

4. There is an unexplainable situation involved in the number of years elapsed between Tho-tho-ri and Songtsen Gampo. My findings indicate that Tho-tho-ri was born ca. A.D. 173 and it is generally accepted that Songtsen Gampo was born in 617—456 years after the birth of Tho-tho-ri; yet, only four kings ruled during the interval. Tibetan accounts say Tho-tho-ri lived to the age of 120 years. Presuming this to be factual, there still remains a period of 324 years before the birth of Songtsen Gampo, which means each of the four intervening kings lived an average of 81 years. Although not impossible, such long lives for successive rulers seems improbable; therefore, this problem requires further research.

5. BU-STON; DEB-DMAR; ME-LONG; LO-TSHIG.

Meanwhile, Songtsen Gampo had been seeking the hand in marriage of the Princess Wen-ch'eng Kung-chu, a daughter of the Chinese Emperor T'ai-tsung. Thokiki, the ruler of the T'u-yü-hun (Eastern Tartars) had also requested an imperial princess, which conflicted with the Tibetan request.[6] Songtsen Gampo then sent his troops against the T'u-yü-hun and defeated them. They also subdued the tribes called Ch'iang, Pai-lan, and Tang-hsiang. Having recruited 200,000 troops in all, the Tibetans then attacked and captured the city of Sungchou.[7] Songtsen Gampo again asked for an imperial princess in marriage as an alternative to war. With his letter of request, he sent the Chinese Emperor a present of a suit of armor finely decorated with gold inlay. The Chinese gave battle but were defeated and so the Emperor finally agreed to give a princess in marriage. Gar Tongtsen, the minister who had served as the envoy to Nepal to escort the Princess Bhrikuti to Lhasa, was sent to the Chinese Court to receive the Princess.

In the year 641, the Chinese Emperor sent his minister, Tao-tsung, Prince of Chiang-hsia, with a company of troops to escort the princess, Wen-ch'eng Kung-chu, as far as the Tibetan border where Songtsen Gampo received her. The princess, referred to by the Tibetans as *Gyasa,* which means "The Chinese Consort," arrived at Lhasa with articles of personal use such as silk, porcelain, and an image of Shakyamuni, the Gautama Buddha. Since this image is also said to have been blessed by the Lord Buddha himself, the Tibetans considered it to be very sacred.

Both Belsa (the Nepalese Princess) and Gyasa (the Chinese Princess) wished to build temples for the images of the Buddha they had brought to Tibet. Gyasa had her temple built and it was called Ramoche Tsukla-khang. Belsa, lacking the necessary astrological guidance, asked the Gyasa for advice on the location for her temple and Gyasa advised her to build it over a small lake. Wondering if Gyasa was misleading her out of jealousy, Belsa spoke to Songtsen Gampo,

6. Desmond Martin, *The Rise of Chingis Khan and His Conquest of North China* (Baltimore, 1950), p. 53, states that since the beginning of the fourth century, the Kokonor area had been ruled by the T'u-ku-hun; but in A.D. 672, they were conquered by the Tibetans and the T'u-ku-hun subsequently fled to China. (The T'u-ku-hun, also known as T'u-yü-hun, are called 'A-zha in Tibetan.)

7. BUSHELL, p. 444; PELLIOT, p. 4. The city of Sungchou here is the modern Sung-p'an in Sze-ch'uan province.

who confirmed, after prayer and meditation, the decision that the correct site was over a small lake. The Tibetans built her temple by filling in the small lake with logs and earth, which had been carried there by a large number of goats. After the temple was completed, an image of a goat was erected beside it in honor of those animals. The temple was called Rasa Trulnang Tsukla-khang,[8] and later became known as the Jokhang. The door of Gyasa's temple faced east towards China and that of Belsa's faced west towards Nepal. During the next generation, the two images were interchanged in the temples for reasons of security when it was rumored that a Chinese army was about to enter Lhasa. The founding of the palace, Tritse Marpo, on the site of the present Potala is also attributed to Belsa.

Meanwhile, the Tibetans had conquered parts of upper Burma[9] and, in 640, occupied Nepal, remaining there for some years.[10] Present day Nepali family names, such as Tsang, Lama, Sherpa, and Tamang, are Tibetan in origin deriving descent from the Tibetans who once occupied Nepal. In that country there is still a pillar called Shila Deva, which was erected by a Newari king, Narendra Deva, on which is inscribed details of the tribute owed to the Tibetan king of the time. In 643, Likme, King of Shangshung became a vassal of the Tibetan ruler.[11]

The Tibetan queen of Songtsen Gampo, Mongsa Tricham of Tölung, gave birth to a son named Gungsong Gungtsen, who, having reached the age of thirteen ascended the throne. He ruled only five years, dying at eighteen, and Songtsen Gampo again took up the ruling powers.[12]

In order to administer the kingdom, Songtsen Gampo appointed six governors (khospon). When these arrived in their respective districts,[13] they made land divisions among the subjects. Class distinctions were made between soldier, attendant, and agriculturalist, and

8. Rasa Trulnang Tsukla-khang literally means: "Goat-earth miraculous-appearance Temple."

9. RICHARDSON, pp. 29–30; BELL, p. 23.

10. DEB-DKAR; DEB-DMAR.

11. TUNG-HUANG, pp. 97–99.

12. DEB-DMAR.

13. DGA'-STON gives the names of only five of these governors: Gar Tsongtsen for Ü-Tsang, Khyungpo Sumsungtse for Shangshung, Hor Jashu Ringpo for Sampa and Kham, Wai Tsangzang Palleg for Chibs in Amdo, and Chogro Gyaltsen Yangong for Thongyab in Drugu. I have been unable to find any record of the name of the sixth governor.

for every thousand families a spokesman was appointed. Each governor had his own military command, distinguished from the others by a distinctive uniform, flag, and color of horse.

In the court at Lhasa, Songtsen Gampo appointed nine ministers of varying rank. In 645, he sent one of these ministers to China to inform the Chinese Emperor that he wished to build a temple in China at a mountain in the province of Shansi. This request was agreed to and in due time the temple was built and it was called the Temple of Wu-ta'i Shan.[14]

In the year 648 the Chinese Emperor sent a goodwill mission to the court of the Indian Emperor, Harsha (606–47). The mission was commanded by Wang Yüan-ts'e, who was accompanied by an escort of thirty cavalrymen. By the time the mission arrived in India, Emperor Harsha was already dead, and because he had had no son and heir he had been succeeded by his minister, Arjuna. Conditions in India at that time were somewhat unsettled and Arjuna himself was intolerant of Buddhism and its followers. Under his order, all members of the goodwill mission were slaughtered, with the exception of Wang Yüan-ts'e and one of his men, who managed to escape to Nepal. From Nepal, which was a dependency of Tibet at the time, Wang appealed to Songtsen Gampo for help and received 12,000 mounted troops from Tibet and 7,000 from Nepal. According to some historians, they marched into India and fought a three-day battle at Hirahati in Bihar, which ended in the capture and deposition of Arjuna,[15] but Indian sources do not corroborate this account.

Arjuna's rival, King Kama Rupa, was delighted at the defeat of Arjuna and, as a token of his approval, sent presents of cattle, horses, and other articles to Songtsen Gampo. The Chinese Emperor was so grateful to Songtsen for his action on behalf of Wang Yüan-ts'e that he stipulated that upon his own death, a statue of the Tibetan King should be erected beside his grave.

In 649, when Songtsen Gampo and his Chinese and Nepalese queens were staying at a place called Phanpo, an epidemic broke out in the region and one of the Nepalese queen's maidservants caught the disease. The disease, not identified by name, is recorded as having been highly contagious and causing a high fever. Songtsen Gampo caught

14. BU-STON states that Songtsen Gampo himself journeyed to China to build this temple.
15. DEB-DKAR; SMITH, p. 304; BUSHELL, p. 446.

the disease and finally succumbed to it.[16] According to later religious historians, Songtsen Gampo and his two queens were absorbed into a statue of Avalokiteśvara in the Jokhang, when the King was eighty-two years old; however, the Tun-huang documents show that Songtsen Gampo died in 649 [17] and the Chinese Princess in 680.[18] The tomb of Songtsen Gampo is located in the Chongyas valley near Yalung.[19]

Songtsen Gampo was succeeded on the throne by his grandson, Mangsong Mangtsen, who was only a child at the time; therefore, Gar Tongtsen, the trusted minister of Songtsen Gampo, acted as regent until the boy came of age.

In 654, at an assembly of ministers and governors, it was decided that the king, the ministers, and the governors should meet once a year to decide future policies and military preparations.[20] In the following year, Tibetan troops were massed along the Chinese frontier in preparation for hostilities against the T'u-yü-hun. The regent, Gar Tongtsen, lived in the Asha (T'u-yü-hun) region for eight years, conducting the military campaigns. The prolonged war finally came to an end when Su-ho-kuei, the T'u-yü-hun chief minister, sought asylum with the Tibetans and revealed to them the defenses of his people, which allowed the Tibetans to defeat the T'u-yü-hun. Mu-yung No-ho-po, the T'u-yü-hun Prince of Ho-yuan, was forced to flee to Liang-chou in China.

In 666 Gar Tongtsen returned to Lhasa from the region of Asha. The following year, he died of a fever; not, as some believe, in battle with the Chinese. Gar Tongtsen had four sons: Gar Tsenya Donbu, Gar Triding Tsendro, Gar Zindoye, and Gar Tsenyen Sungton. Gar Tsenya Donbu became the chief minister, and the other three became military commanders. The Gar family played a key role in the building of the Tibetan empire in the seventh century.

Following the Tibetan defeat of the T'u-yü-hun, refugees began to pour into Liang-chou in such numbers that the Chinese Emperor summoned his ministers to discuss the advisability of going to war with

16. DGA'-STON; DEB-DKAR.
17. TUN-HUANG, p. 30.
18. PELLIOT, p. 10.
19. TOMBS.
20. DEB-DKAR.

the Tibetans, or to relocate the T'u-yü-hun people. The minister, Yen Li-pen, advised against war, at least until the famine, then widespread in China, was over. General Ch'i-pi ho-li expressed his opinion that war against Tibet, because of the great distances involved, would pose problems of transport and supplies. Minister Yen advised the Emperor to wait until the Tibetans mistook his patience for weakness; then when they became arrogant and careless, they could be defeated in one campaign. The minister, Chiang K'o, disagreed and insisted that any delay would allow the Tibetans to become even more powerful and that they should be attacked at once. The discussions led to nothing. War was not declared nor was any decision made regarding the relocation of the T'u-yü-hun.

In 668 a large military fortress was constructed at Dremakhol,[21] and in the following year, the T'u-yü-hun submitted an oath of loyalty to the Tibetan king.

The year 670 was one marked by great military victories for the Tibetans. They marched into the Tarim basin and captured the four garrisons of Anhsi, through which the Chinese had controlled that region. The Emperor appointed Hsüeh Jen-kuei as commander-in-chief of an army of 100,000 men to recapture the four garrisons in Chinese Turkestan. The army was defeated at Ta-fei-ch'uan, and General Hsüeh was degraded for failure. In 671 another Chinese army was ordered against the Tibetans, with Chiang K'o as commander-in-chief; but, he died en route, and the army returned to China.

The Tibetan King, Mangsong Mangtsen, then sent one of his ministers, Jang-jig, who knew both written and spoken Chinese, to China as an envoy. The Chinese Emperor received Jang-jig and asked him various questions about Tibet. Jang-jig informed him that the Tibetan King was so powerful and capable of looking after the affairs of state that he surpassed his brilliant grandfather, Songtsen Gampo. After a few words about the Tibetan way of life, Jang-jig concluded by saying that the Tibetan people are united and all measures are deliberated before carrying them out, and therein lay Tibetan unity and strength. The Emperor then asked Jang-jig why the Tibetans had given asylum to Su-ho-kuei, who had betrayed his own T'u-yü-hun people, and then attacked China; but, Jang-jig only replied that he had been sent to offer presents and had no instructions regarding other matters.[22]

21. TUN-HUANG, p. 14.
22. PELLIOT, p. 7; DEB-DKAR.

In 676 the Tibetans raided Shan-chou and K'uo-chou in the province of Kansu and killed many officers and people before returning to Tibet with their spoils. The Chinese Emperor immediately ordered the Prime Minister, Liu Jen-kuei, to T'ao-ho with soldiers, and another commander, Li Yu, to Liang-chou. Before these armies could advance, the Tibetans raided the towns of T'ieh-chou, Mi-kung, and Tan-ling in Kansu. The Chinese Emperor summoned his commanders and sharply rebuked them for their failure to mobilize their troops in time, thus causing the loss of many towns in the northwest. He demoted them and then appointed his political secretary, Li Ching-yuan, to the rank of general. Reinforcements were ordered up from the provinces of Chiennan and Shannan.

Li Ching-yuan attacked the Tibetans at Longji and defeated them. Bringing up fresh troops, he then attacked in the Kokonor region, where the Tibetan minister, Tsenya Donbu, was staying. Liu Shen-li, a commander with Li Ching-yuan, led his troops too far into the Tibetan lines and, lacking sufficient support, was surrounded and killed. The Chinese army was routed and had to retreat. One of Li's generals, Heich'ih Ch'angchih, led five hundred warriors against the Tibetans in the dark of night and scattered them; but, Li Ching-yuan still returned with his army to Shan-chou, where he too was degraded.

In spite of the strenuous efforts of the most able Chinese generals, no significant gains were made against the Tibetans. The Emperor, Kao-tsung, called a meeting of his ministers to discuss the situation. He lectured them for losing continuously against the Tibetans, whereas in earlier days, they had been able to conquer Korea (Kao-li) easily. When the Emperor asked for their opinions as to what course of action to take, the majority said it would be better to negotiate with the Tibetans; but a few suggested that China should make extensive preparations for a few years and then retaliate. It was finally agreed that the frontier should be garrisoned.[23]

In the same year, 676, the Tibetan ruler, Mangsong Mangtsen, died, but the Tibetans kept his death a secret for three years so the Chinese would not know that the Tibetans were without a leader. At the time of his death, the young queen of Mangsong Mangtsen was pregnant. Although there is some disagreement whether the child was born seven days or one month after his death, it is certain that a son was born shortly after the death of the king. The prince, who was named

23. PELLIOT, p. 9.

Dusong Mangje, was informed of his father's death only when he had reached the age of three years.

In 677 Shangshung revolted, but the revolt was crushed in the following year. During this period, the military might of Tibet was felt sharply in neighboring countries. There were seven outstanding military commanders in Tibet. All were good horsemen and fighters, expert archers and swordsmen, inspiring leaders, and able to race the wild ass and wrestle the wild yak. They were Ngok Dongshor, Ngok Lingkham, Non Gyaltsen, Bas Gosdongchan, Gos Yakchung, Chokro Dongshor, and Non Tridun Yujin.

The chief minister, Gar Tsenya Donbu, died in 685 and was succeeded by his brother, Gar Triding Tsendro. The two younger brothers continued to lead their armies against the Chinese; but, the influence of the Gar family was becoming so great that the brothers' loyalty to the king began to wane. Gar Zindoye was captured in battle in 694 and his brother Tsenyen Sungton was executed in the following year for treason to the Tibetan king. The chief minister himself, Triding Tsendro, was disgraced in 698 for disloyalty; in the following year, he committed suicide, after being defeated by troops of the Tibetan king, Dusong Mangje.

According to Tibetan sources, Dusong Mangje died in the country called Myava in 704.[24] Myava is said to be the kingdom of Nan-chao, which was located in the region of present day Yun-nan province of China. Chinese sources say the Tibetan king was killed while personally leading the army to suppress a revolt in Nepal and northern India.[25]

Tride Tsugtsen, who was only seven years old at the time, succeeded his father on the throne, but his grandmother, Trimalo, served as regent during his minority. Tride Tsugtsen is also known by the nickname Mes-Agtshom (Old Hairy), which was given to him in his old age because of his hirsute appearance. During his reign, three temples called Drakmar Dinzang, Chimpu Namral, and Drakmar Keru were built south of Lhasa.

Some Tibetan sources relate that Mes-Agtshom had a son by the name of Jangtsha, for whom the King had requested a Chinese princess; but the son died before the princess arrived in Lhasa, so Mes-Agtshom himself took her as a wife. This is an interesting story, but

24. TUN-HUANG, p. 40.
25. PELLIOT, p. 12.

one that is contradicted by Tibetan historians themselves. Both Tibetan documents [26] and Chinese [27] give 710 as the year the princess was given in marriage. Mes-Agtshom was only twelve years old at the time and could hardly have had a son, let alone one who was ready for marriage.

The actual account is that a request was made for an imperial princess by Trimalo, the grandmother of the young king, and in 710, a daughter of Shou-li, prince of Yung, was given the title of Princess of Chin-ch'eng. The Emperor himself accompanied her as far as Shih-p'ing hsien. In honor of the princess, he changed the name of that place to Chin-ch'eng hsien. The princess was escorted to Tibet by General Yang Chü. The Emperor had given the princess, Chin-ch'eng Kung-chu, in marriage with the express hope that it would ease the tensions between Tibet and China and bring about an abatement of the border warfare; but his hope was not realized.

According to some Tibetan sources, the Princess Chin-ch'eng was very unhappy after her arrival in Tibet. She was without companions and suffered from the jealous intrigues of the King's other wives. The princess wrote a letter to Kofo Fiwang, a Tibetan vassal in Asha (T'u-yü-hun) country, and requested him to give her refuge as she intended to leave Tibet. Kofo Fiwang was afraid to give her asylum, but he passed her request onto another vassal, She Tahi Ko, who also was reluctant to offer her refuge because it would displease the Tibetan King. He then wrote a letter to the Chinese Emperor informing him that the princess was unhappy and was considering running away from Tibet.

The Emperor then wrote the princess and advised her to remain in Tibet, as any rash action on her part might precipitate a war. He asked her to try and settle down in the Tibetan King's court both for her own sake as well as that of her country. The princess reluctantly agreed to this. Not long afterwards, she began to inquire into the whereabouts of the Buddha image, which had been brought to Tibet by the Chinese princess, Wen-ch'eng Kung-chu, and was later concealed by the Tibetans. After a thorough search, she found the image, where it had been walled up in the Rasa Trulnang temple, and caused it to be placed in the center of the temple.

In A.D. 719, during the reign of the Hsüan-tsung Emperor, there

26. TUN-HUANG, p. 20.
27. PELLIOT, p. 13.

was an increase in Chinese military operations with the view to check
the advances of the Tibetans and the Arabs, who sometimes combined
their forces. Tibet did not escape the attention of early Arabian historians, who knew the country as *Tubbat* and its ruler as *Khakan*.
According to Barthold, the names Tüpüt and Tüpüt-Kaghan are
found as early as the Orkhon inscriptions.[28] Some trade relations were
also established for it is said the Tibetans brought musk to the Muslim
world.

In 730 the Tibetan king requested various classics and histories
from the Chinese Emperor. A minister, Yü Hsiu-lieh, protested that
the books requested contained valuable information on military tactics, defense plans, and deceitful strategems and that it would not be
in the best interest of the empire to send the books to the Tibetans;
but the Emperor disregarded his protest.

In 741 a Tibetan mission was sent to the Chinese Court to carry the
news of the death of the imperial princess, Chin-ch'eng Kung-chu. At
the same time, the mission asked for peace negotiations, but the Emperor refused. Soon after, a Tibetan army of 400,000 men advanced
into China and attacked the town of Ch'eng-feng and then continued
on; but they were stopped at the Ch'ang-ning bridge by General
Sheng Hsi-yeh. The Tibetans later seized the town of Shih-p'u, which
they held until 748, when it was recaptured by the Chinese.[29]

In the year 755 the king, Mes-Agtshom, died. Most Tibetan sources
say he died at Yardok Batsal after being thrown from a frightened
horse; however, the Shol-do-ring pillar, which stands in front of the
Potala in Lhasa and which was erected during Trisong Detsen's reign
(755–97), bears an inscription saying that Mes-Agtshom was assassinated by two ministers, Bal Dongtsap and Langme Zig.

After Mes-Agtshom's death, his son, Trisong Detsen, became king.
Like his father and grandfather, he was a patron of Buddhism and
wanted to encourage the spread of the religion; but he found himself
opposed by many of his ministers, who were devoted to the Bon religion. Mashang Dompa Ke and Takra Lugong were two ministers
strongly opposed to the Buddhist faith. (The latter should not be confused with another minister, Takdra Lukhong, whose name is similar.
Takdra Lukhong, also known as Nganlam Lukhong, was loyal to the
king and his work has been commemorated in an inscription on a

28. W. Barthold, *Encyclopaedia of Islam*, 4 (Leiden, 1913–36), 742.
29. PELLIOT, p. 27.

stone pillar in front of the Potala. A number of Tibetan historians have confused the two names, much to the detriment of Takdra Lu-khong).

There were two junior ministers, Gos Trizang and Shang Nyam-zang, who were willing to help the king patronize the Buddhist religion. They approached various sympathetic ministers, apprising them of their intention to raise a certain issue in the council and asking them for their support. Then they bribed an oracle to predict a great famine and epidemic for the country and a short life for the King unless two loyal subjects offered themselves as a sacrifice for the welfare of the King and the country.

The traditional account is that Gos, the pro-Buddhist minister, and Mashang, the pro-Bon minister, were the two who were to be entombed in accordance with the prophecy. Gos, who instigated the scheme, had made secret arrangements and escaped from the tomb, leaving Mashang to die.[30]

There is another account, which I shall relate here. The prophecy was that two prominent people had to go into exile as ransom. An assembly of ministers was called to discuss the issue and the two junior ministers, Gos and Shang, stood up and declared their long-standing loyalty to the King and volunteered to go into exile. This gesture was received warmly by the assembly and the two ministers were praised for their spirit of self-sacrifice.

The two senior ministers, Mashang and Takra Lugong, seeing that this could result in loss of face for them, voiced a protest and insisted that not only were they the senior ministers, but they were of greater loyalty than anyone else; therefore, they should be given the honor of going into exile. The assembly approved their request, which was just what the junior ministers had expected to happen.

Tibetan accounts say that Mashang and Takra Lugong were sent to a graveyard in Tohlung; but this does not mean that they were killed. The second story says the two ministers were given the privilege of the "living dead," a custom associated with the death of a Tibetan king. Whenever a king died, his most loyal minister would volunteer to be buried with him. In fact, the minister was not really buried but went to live near the king's tomb with a group of "dead men," who were not permitted to see or speak to any other living person. The succeeding king would come annually to his father's tomb to pay homage and

30. SBA-BZHED; DGA'-STON.

to bring him an offering of goods and presents, which were then appropriated by those living as "dead men" near the tomb. The relatives of these men could bring food and clothing for them; but when someone approached the tomb, a horn was blown to warn the "dead men," who had to go promptly into their huts. Only then could the relatives enter the graveyard and leave the offerings. When they had departed, another blow on the horn signaled that the "dead" could then emerge.

If by chance, a horse, cow, or other animal strayed into the graveyard, it was branded by the "dead" and then released. The owner of the animal, finding that it had been branded so, promptly sent it back to the graveyard as a present to the "dead."

Although one tradition says the minister Mashang was buried alive by a trick executed by Gos Trizang, another tradition claims that Mashang and Takra Lugong were exiled to a graveyard, where they became "living dead." [31]

Once Mashang was removed from the political picture, the king, Trisong Detsen, sent one of his ministers, Ba Salnang, to Nepal to invite the Indian pandit, Śāntirakṣita, to come to Tibet and teach the doctrine of Buddhism. Śāntirakṣita accepted the invitation, and when he arrived in the region of Drakmar, he was given a warm welcome by the Tibetan King. It is asserted that after he began to preach, the Bon spirits of the country were so resentful and displeased that they caused storms, lightning, and floods. The people interpreted these omens as a sign that the new religion was not acceptable and Śāntirakṣita, sensing that the time was not yet ripe for the spread of his teachings, returned to Nepal. Before departing, however, he suggested to the king that he should invite the great Indian Tantric Master, Padmasambhava, to visit Tibet.

The minister, Ba Salnang, was again sent to extend an invitation to Padmasambhava, who was in Nepal at the time. Padmasambhava was well versed in the magical arts associated with the tantric form of Buddhism, which was more acceptable to the Tibetan people. With powerful formulas and rituals, Padmasambhava was able to subdue the Bon spirits, which opposed his missionary efforts in Tibet. He vanquished them and caused them to take an oath to defend the new religion; hence, many of these spirits were taken into the Buddhist pantheon.

Padmasambhava was welcomed by the king, Trisong Detsen, and

31. DEB-DKAR.

then Śāntirakṣita was again invited back to Tibet. The king decided to have a monastery built and Śāntirakṣita drew up the plans, using as his model the monastery of Otantapuri, which was laid out in the design of the Buddhist universe.[32] The monastery was built in the region of Drakmar, and when it was completed, after twelve years, it was called Migyur lhungi dubpai Tsukla-khang, meaning "The Temple which is an Unchangeable, Perfect Mass." It is commonly referred to as Samye.[33]

Eager to know if Tibetans were capable of becoming good monks, the king selected seven intelligent men to be used as a trial group. They were Pagor Verotsana, Chim Shakya Tawa, Bas Ratna, Nganlam Gyawa Chogyang, Ma Rinchen Chog, Khon Luiwangpo, and Tsang Legdrub. These neophytes were trained by Śāntirakṣita, and they became the first monks in Tibet. The trial group was so successful that many Tibetans then became monks. A school for the study of Sanskrit was established at Samye and a large number of Buddhist texts from India were translated into the Tibetan language. (Atisha, a celebrated Indian pandit who visited Samye in the eleventh century, wrote that he had never seen such an extensive and thorough system of translation of Buddhist texts, even in India.)

Before he died, Śāntirakṣita predicted that eventually there would come a conflict between the two schools of Buddhism then spreading in Tibet. One was the teaching that enlightenment was an instantaneous realization that could be attained only through complete mental and physical inactivity; this system was being spread by the Chinese monks. The other, which Śāntirakṣita had introduced, maintained that enlightenment was the result of a slow, gradual process, requiring study, analysis, and good deeds. Śāntirakṣita instructed that when the time came, his disciple, Kamalaśila, should be invited from India to defend the Indian system of Buddhism.

The king, Trisong Detsen, called for the debate, and it was held at Samye over a two-year period (792–94). Hoshang, a Chinese monk, defended the "instantaneous system" and Kamalaśila, the "slow

32. See Giuseppe Tucci, "The Symbolism of the Temples of Bsan-yas," *East and West*, VI-4 (Rome, 1956), 279–81. The original monastery of Otantapuri in India was destroyed by Muslims under the command of Ikhtiyar-ud-Din Muhammad, in 1193. See Charles Eliot, *Hinduism and Buddhism*, 2 (London, 1954), 112.

33. According to the findings of Haarh, the monastery of Samye was completed in A.D. 766 and inaugurated in 767. See Erik Haarh, "The Identity of Tsu-chih-chien, the Tibetan 'King' who died in 804 AD," *Acta Orientalia*, 25, 1–2 (1963), 121–70.

system." At the end of the debate, Kamalaśila was declared the winner, and the King issued a proclamation establishing the new religion as the orthodox faith for Tibet. The document was written in gold letters on blue paper and was kept in the court records. The main features of that proclamation were that the Three Jewels (the Buddha, the Dharma, and the Sangha) were never to be abandoned; the various Buddhist temples were to be maintained; the amount of support given to the temples was to be continued; and future generations of the royal family were to uphold the provisions of the proclamation. The document prepared by the King was sworn to by the princes, the chief ministers, the ministers of the interior and the exterior, and the generals. Thirteen copies were made and distributed for preservation.[34]

A great celebration was then held with the King, the royal family, the ministers and officials all in attendance. There were games of archery and horse racing, followed by singing, dancing, and feasting. The celebration marked the proclamation of Buddhism as the religion of the land, the completion of the Samye monastery, and the successful training of the first monks. The following is said to be one of the lyrics sung by the King at the festival:

> Gold, silver, copper, lead, and iron
> are the five metals found in this land of mine;
> Mustard, barley, peas, beans, and wheat
> are the five grains we are accustomed to eat.
> Neither heat nor cold does the climate bring
> to the country of which I am the King.
>
> With great toil have I gathered this treasure
> and I am happy to spend without measure
> in spreading the faith of the Buddha,
> gleaned from the land of India.
>
> It was in Tho-tho-ri Nyantsen's reign
> that *The Secret* first here came;
> translated in Songtsen Gampo's time,
> it has become established in mine.

34. The full inscription of this stele is given in DGA'-STON. The inscription and its translation appears in TOMBS, pp. 94–95 and 43, respectively.

> The temple prayer flags are so fine
> the sun complains it dare not shine,
> the birds object that they cannot fly
> as the flags on the temple are jammed too high.
> This temple, not built by human hand,
> has grown by itself from our sacred land.[35]

It should be noted that the defeat of the Chinese system of Buddhism, which preached "instantaneous enlightenment," may have been influenced by the political events of the time, for there was a constant state of border conflict between China and Tibet throughout the latter half of the eighth century. Repeated battles with the Chinese increased the tension between the two countries to the point where in 763 the king, Trisong Detsen, ordered an army of 200,000 men to proceed from the grounds of the T'u-yü-hun against China under the leadership of four generals: Shangyal Lhanang, Shangchim Gyalzig Shultheng, Takdra Lukhong, and Lhazang Pal. The combined military forces attacked Ching-chou, and its governor, Kao Hui, surrendered to them. Soon after, Feng-t'ien-huen in Pin-chou fell to the Tibetans. The Emperor Tai-tsung (763–804) sent the renowned minister, Kuo Tzu-yi, with a large army to halt the Tibetan advance, but he was compelled to retreat. The Tibetans advanced rapidly toward the Chinese capital of Ch'ang-an, with Kao Hui, the governor of Ching-chou, personally guiding them. The Emperor had fled from the capital, and Kuo Tzu-yi subsequently escaped south into Niu-hsin-ku with his family and a large following.

Once in the capital, the Tibetans set up Ch'eng-hung, Prince of Kuang-wu, as Emperor, who in turn selected Ta-she as the title of his reign. Whenever a new emperor was enthroned in China, it marked the beginning of a new year; therefore, the Tibetans declared that a new year had begun. They obtained a letter from the new Emperor guaranteeing annual tribute and, then, fifteen days later, they withdrew from the Chinese capital.

Reference to the above events is found in an inscription on the south side of the Shol-do-ring stele in Lhasa, dated in the reign of Trisong Detsen. Some of the words have been effaced; but the translation is as follows:

35. BKA'-THANG; SHEL-BRAG.

In the time of King Tride Tsugten (Mes-Agthsom), Nganlam
Lukhong carried out all confidential royal works. King Tride
Tsugten died from injuries done to him by Bal Dongtsap and
Langme Zig, although they were high-ranking ministers.

They attempted to injure the person of the King's son, Trisong
Detsen, and tried to cause internal dissension in the Kingdom of
Tibet. All the facts about Bal and Langme and of their hatred
for the King were brought to the King's notice by Lukhong. The
hostility of Bal and Langme having been proved, they were condemned. Lukhong became an intimate friend of the King.

In the time of Trisong Detsen, Nganlam Lukhong, being in
the King's confidence, was admitted into the great inner councils.
Being experienced in politics, he was appointed Commander of
the campaign in the direction of Khar Tsan (in China).

Since he knew well the art of warfare, he was able to subdue
the Asha, who were subject to China. He took many Chinese territories and imposed taxes there, consequently, the Chinese were
completely demoralized. Yarmo Thang, a part of China . . .
and in the direction of Tsongkha . . . and so forth, from . . .
Ngaphochel by Lukhong . . . enemies who challenged . . .
made the kingdom great . . . gave great counsels . . . being
on intimate terms with the King, he took great trouble for the
benefit of the Kingdom.

King Trisong Detsen, being a profound man, the breadth of
his counsel was extensive, and whatever he did for the kingdom
was completely successful. He conquered and held under his sway
many districts and fortresses of China. The Chinese Emperor,
Hehu Ki Wang, and his ministers were terrified. They offered a
perpetual, yearly tribute of 50,000 rolls of silk and China was
obliged to pay this tribute. When the Chinese Emperor, Hehu Ki
Wang, the father died, the son, Wang Peng Wang, succeeded to
the throne. He was not able to pay tribute to Tibet and the King
of Tibet was offended. Nganlam Lukhong took the lead in counsels for the launching of war by Tibet against China's center, at
the Chinese Emperor's palace Keng-shir. Shangchim Gyalzig
Shultheng and Takdra Lukhong were appointed as the two chief
commanders for the campaign against Keng-shir. They attacked
Keng-shir and a great battle was fought with the Chinese on the

banks of the Chow-chi. The Chinese were put to flight and many were killed.

The Chinese Emperor, Wang Peng Wang, left the fort in Keng-shir and fled to Shem-chow. The Ministers of the Interior, Chewu Keng, Don Kyan, and So Kyan . . . subjects of the (Tibetan) King . . . Tibet . . . Kow-wang, the younger brother of Kim-shing Kung-chu, was made Emperor of China . . . Minister . . . vassals, great and small . . . the (Tibetan) Empire was firmly established and its fame and praise were spread abroad. Lukhong being in the King's confidence took great trouble for the good of the Kingdom.

Some of the words in the inscription have been worn away by time and the elements and others have been effaced by people banging stones against the pillar. This was a custom supposed to bring good luck. The missing words are indicated by ellipses in the above translation.[36] The spelling of Chinese names has been considerably altered in the Tibetan transcription—for example, *Kim-shing* for the Chinese *Chin-ch'eng*—but the account in general agrees with that given in Chinese sources.[37] This inscription appears on the south face of the pillar; other inscriptions, ordered by the King, appear on the east and north faces. These promised special privileges to Nganlam Lukhong and his descendants. They were to be exempt from the death penalty and other severe punishments for whatever they might do, with the exception of treason or disloyalty to the King.

Several years later, in 783, peace negotiations between Tibet and China took place, resulting in the treaty of Ch'ing-shui, which established the boundaries between the two countries. In general, all land in the Kokonor region west of T'ao-chou and the Ta-tu river were ceded to Tibet.[38]

Examples of Tibetan architecture and utensils were discovered under the sands of Chinese Turkestan, where several ancient documents were also found. Two of those documents are letters of protest sent to the administrator of the prefecture of Sha-chou. The first is a letter from two military officers residing at Dankhar palace in Tibet. It is

36. DGA'-STON.
37. PELLIOT, p. 30.
38. PELLIOT, pp. 43–44.

dated in the middle of the winter season in the year of the Dragon, and reads:

> We have received a complaint from the citizens of Sha-chou who were originally from Bal-po that they are being unnecessarily taxed on their small fruit gardens. They are protesting against this, and claim that the palace fruit gardens have more than enough fruit for the civil and military officers. In the future, you are not permitted to tax the fruit gardens of the citizens of Sha-chou.

> > (Signed) Tromsher and Lhazang Salthong
> > (Imprint of the official Dankhar seal).

The second letter was sent by Dunpa Lungchu to the administrator of Sha-chou in the first month of spring in the year of the Pig.

> We have received petitions from two districts informing us that Tibetan civil and military officers are taking Sha-chou girls on the pretext of marrying them; but then work them as servants.

> The people of Sha-chou claim that they have the same rights as other subjects of Tibet. They say that their girls should not be taken away by force into another province. They request to be allowed to marry among their own people in their own province.

> In the future, no girls are to be obtained by force. If, however, a boy and girl like each other, there is no objection to their getting married.[39]

> > (Imprint of seal).

According to the *Debther Karpo,* two well-known battlefields of the early wars with China can still be seen in the Amdo (Kokonor) region, to the north and east of the Machu (Yellow River). They are known today by the Tibetans as Gyatrag Thang (Field of Chinese Blood) and Gyadur Thang (Field of Chinese Graves). Local guides describe the significance of these battlefields to visitors and travelers. Many people living in the Amdo region have family names that are associated with the Ü-Tsang region of central Tibet. The natives of Amdo claim that these people are descendants of soldiers from Ü-Tsang, who fought in the early wars with China and then settled in Amdo territory.

39. DEB-DKAR.

According to the *Yiktsang Khaspa Gache,* during the time of the king, Trisong Detsen, military commanders were given charge of four different zones. Nine daring and athletic commanders were in charge of the north zone. The King is said to have asked them if they had sufficient troops to defend the border or if they needed more reinforcements. The nine commanders replied that they were fully able to defend the frontier on their own and assumed full responsibility for the north zone. Since that time, the area was known as Guthup (The Capable Nine). Later, when the nine commanders asked the King if they should return from the frontier, he asked them to wait until they received his orders. It is said that the orders never came, and so, the nomadic descendants of those nine commanders, who live in the Chone and Zogye regions of Amdo, are now known as the Kamalok (Not to Return Without Orders).[40]

The Tibetans made various military alliances during the time of Trisong Detsen. In A.D. 750, Kolofeng, son of Pilawko, became the King of Siam, and during his reign, an alliance was made with Tibet. In 754 Nan-chao was invaded, and in recognition for his assistance, Kolofeng received the title of "Younger Brother" from King Trisong Detsen.[41] Imohsun, who succeeded Kolofeng as king of Siam, sought assistance from Tibet in 778, and Tibetan and Siamese troops fought side by side against the Chinese in Szech'uan. The Tibetan troops remained with the Siamese for eight years and then returned to Tibet when amicable relations were restored between Siam and China.[42]

According to some Tibetan sources, a religious crusade was launched in the time of Trisong Detsen against the Bedehor, in order to recover an image of Pehar, one of the spiritual defenders of Buddhism in Tibet. The image was then installed in the Samye monastery as a guardian spirit. Also, needing a relic of the Lord Buddha for the great chorten (stupa) of Samye, Trisong Detsen sent men to India to obtain one. Ba Salnang, the minister who had visited India and Nepal in earlier times, wrote that two large bodies of cavalry were sent to India; one through Nepal and the other through Phari in southern Tibet and then into India. It is said that when a maharaja, who then ruled a territory north of the Ganges, saw the Tibetan cavalry bearing

40. GLING-BU; YIG-TSHANG.

41. W. A. R. Wood, *A History of Siam from the Earliest Times to the Year A.D. 1781* (London, 1926), p. 33.

42. Oscar Frankfurter, "Narratives of the Revolutions which took place in Siam in 1688," *Siam Society,* V-4 (Bangkok, 1908), 5–38.

down upon his city, he mistook it for the vanguard of an army. Assuming that it would be followed immediately by foot soldiers and elephants, as was the military practice in India, the maharaja offered to surrender; but it was a religious mission and not sent to make territorial conquests.

The Tibetan troops crossed the sacred Ganges and arrived at Magadha in Bihar. The ruler of Magadha and his followers, knowing the Tibetans would not attack the monastery of Otantapuri, deposited most of their possessions there and then fled eastward; however, the Tibetans continued on to Bodh Gaya. There they made offerings to the sacred Bodh tree, obtained the desired relic, and then turned back towards Tibet. They erected an iron pillar on the banks of the Ganges to mark the site of their crossing.[43]

Tibetan power spread far and wide in the later of Trisong Detsen's reign. In the year 790, the Tibetans recaptured the four garrisons of Anhsi, from which they had been driven in 692 by the Chinese forces of the Empress Wu. The Tibetan army advanced westward to the Pamirs and even reached the Oxus River. As a mark of their distance, a lake in the north of the river Oxus was named Al-Tubbat (Little Tibetan Lake).[44] A few years later, the Arabian Caliph, Harun al-Rashid, aware that the Tibetans were becoming too powerful, allied himself with the Chinese in order to keep the Tibetans in check.[45] Attacked by the allied forces of the Chinese and the Arabs, the Tibetans succeeded in holding their own without substantial loss of territory, in spite of considerable defeats. The expansionistic dreams of the Tibetans were, however, checked; but as Petech has written, "the very fact that nothing less than the coalition of the two most powerful empires of early Middle-Ages was necessary for checking the expansion of the Tibetan state, is a magnificent witness of the political capacities and military valour of those sturdy mountaineers."[46] According to Bretschneider,[47] the Tibetans were continually engaged in launching attacks to the west between the years 785 and 805; consequently their military attention was diverted from China, whose

43. SBA-BZHED; DGA'-STON.

44. Philip K. Hitti, *History of the Arabs* (London, 1956), pp. 208–09.

45. RICHARDSON, p. 29; George N. Roerich, *Trails to Inmost Asia* (New Haven, 1931), p. 100.

46. CHRONICLES, pp. 73–74.

47. E. Bretschneider, *On the Knowledge Possessed by the Ancient Chinese of the Arabs* (London, 1871), p. 10.

frontier provinces suffered less than they had previously. Tibetan sources, on the other hand, make only vague mention of conflict with a country to the west.

The introduction to a catalogue of the articles preserved in the tomb of the fifth Dalai Lama (1617–82) stresses the importance of a certain ritual called *Dasi*. The introduction relates the story of a rumor, which reached the ears of the king, Trisong Detsen. The rumor was that an invasion of Tibet was about to take place and would come from four directions. The pro-Buddhist minister, Gos Trizang, supposedly asked, "Will we kill a hundred or a thousand of the enemy? Or, will we have to flee? Let us have faith in Buddha and consult Padmasambhava, now meditating in the hills of Chimpu near Samye." When consulted, Padmasambhava agreed that the news was serious and advised everyone to perform the ritual called *Dasi*. The invasion never took place.[48]

There is an inscription on a stone pillar near a bridge in Chongyas, which is a testimonial to the power of King Trisong Detsen. It is addressed to the King himself, and reads as follows:

> King Trisong Detsen, because of the efforts of your father and grandfather, our country is powerful and our religion gains in strength.
>
> I have written this inscription to commemorate your great work. You have carried out everything that your father and grandfather desired for the peace and welfare of our country and the improvement of our places of worship.
>
> I have written a detailed report on your valuable work and on the expansion of your Empire. That report is now in your archives.
>
> King Trisong Detsen, you are very different from other neighboring kings. Your great prestige and power is known from Rashi in the west to Longshar in the east, and even in the north and the south.
>
> The extent of your magnificent Empire has brought greatness to Tibet. We are a happy people, peacefully practicing our religion because of your compassionate heart. Not only are you generous and kind to your human subjects, but to all living creatures as well. That is why men have given you the name

48. GSER-SDONG.

Trulgyi Lha Changchub Chenpo (Great Enlightened, Miraculous, Divine Lord).

King Trisong Detsen had four sons: Mutri Tsenpo, Muni Tsenpo, Mutik Tsenpo, and Tride Songtsen. The firstborn son, Mutri Tsenpo, died young, so when Trisong Detsen retired from public life in 797 and went to live at Zungkar, he handed the affairs of state over to his second son, Muni Tsenpo. Some sources say Trisong Detsen died at Zungkar in the following year, and one source, the *Kathang Shetrag*, says that during a horse-racing event in which Trisong Detsen took part, an arrow was shot from amidst the spectators, killing him.

There is much confusion in Tibetan sources concerning the length of Muni Tsenpo's reign and his successor to the throne. Some sources say he reigned about one and one-half years,[49] while others say he ruled for as much as seventeen years;[50] but the latter appears to stem from a misunderstanding of Chinese accounts. There is also disagreement among western scholars; some say Muni Tsenpo reigned from 797 to 804,[51] and some accept the tradition that he reigned about eighteen months (797–99).[52] In view of the deeds attributed to him, such as three social reforms, it would seem that eighteen months was too short a reign period.

It is said in Tibetan accounts that Muni Tsenpo, in an effort to reduce the great disparity between the rich and the poor, introduced land reform and appointed ministers to supervise the equitable distribution of land and property. When the King later asked how the reform was progressing, he found that the rich had become richer and the poor, poorer. Twice, he reorganized his reform plans, but without success. Disillusioned by the failure of his idealistic plan, the King is said to have consulted Padmasambhava, who informed the King that he could not forcibly close the gap between the rich and the poor. "Our condition in this life," Padmasambhava said, "is entirely dependent upon the actions of our previous life and nothing can be done to alter the scheme of things." At least, the account of the unsuccessful plans of the King shows there was an attempt at reform in the early period.

49. DEB-DMAR and DGA'-STON give the length of his reign as one year and nine months, while BU-STON and ME-LONG state one year and six months.

50. DEB-SNGON gives his reign period as seventeen years.

51. CHRONICLES, p. 77.

52. Helmut Hoffmann, *The Religions of Tibet* (New York, 1961), p. 78.

During his reign, Muni Tsenpo based his policies upon the religious records of his father and grandfather. His rule came to an end because of his mother's treachery. Tsephongsa, the mother of Muni Tsenpo, was extremely jealous of her daughter-in-law, Queen Phoyongsa, who had been her co-wife to Trisong Detsen. Phoyongsa was a very young and beautiful girl and before his death, Trisong Detsen had her marry his son, Muni Tsenpo, so she would not suffer at the hands of Tsephongsa. It is said that the mother, Tsephongsa, was so violently jealous of Phoyongsa that she poisoned her son, Muni Tsenpo, in order to get revenge on her rival. It has also been suggested that Muni Tsenpo was poisoned because of the unpopularity of his reform program.

Since Muni Tsenpo had no son and heir, the throne was given to his younger brother. The third brother, Mutik Tsenpo, was next in line of succession, but he was disqualified for the following reason. During the reign of his father, Trisong Detsen, a secret and important meeting was being held relating to the border problem. The King and his ministers were in a room on the first floor of the palace at Samye. The prince, Mutik Tsenpo, unaware that an important conference was in progress, banged on the door of the assembly room in order to gain admittance. The door was opened by Shang Nanam, one of the ministers, who curtly informed the prince that a confidential meeting was in progress. Feeling insulted, the proud and arrogant prince drew his sword and ran the minister through. As punishment, the prince was exiled to Lhodak Kharchu, near the Bhutanese border. When his elder brother, Muni Tsenpo, died, the prince's claim to the throne was passed over in favor of the youngest brother, Tride Songtsen. (In my youth, I visited Lhodak Kharchu to investigate this story. The place, nowadays, is a sparsely inhabited region in a valley surrounded by dense forests. At the time of Mutik Tsenpo's exile, it must have been completely uninhabited. The people of Lhodak Kharchu pointed out to me three caves on the side of a steep mountain, where the exiled prince was said to have lived, repenting his hasty action.)

It is to be noted that Gos Lotsawa, Tsuglag Trengwa, and other Tibetan historians, relying on Chinese records, say that Dzuche Tsenpo was installed as king after the death of Muni Tsenpo. According to Petech, those historians did not realize the true identity of the king mentioned in the Chinese records and therefore produced a new king called Dzuche Tsenpo, a transliteration of the Chinese *Tsu-chih-*

chien.[53] The latest study on this matter is that of Erik Haarh,[54] but it seems that the contradictions and confusions associated with the reigns of Muni Tsenpo and his successor still require further study. For example, Haarh gives the name of the exiled prince as Muruk Tsenpo, and identifies Mutik Tsenpo as Tride Songtsen. There is disagreement also whether Tride Songtsen ascended in 799 or in 804. At least, it may be safely stated that in 804 Tride Songtsen was king. He is commonly referred to as Sadnaleg in Tibetan sources.

Since Sadnaleg was still quite young, he was assisted in his rule by four experienced and capable ministers: Dangka Palgyi Yonden, Nyang Tingzin, Shang Do Trisur, and Nanam Tridragyal. The first two of these ministers were also called *Bande,* because they were Buddhist monks. They carried out the administration in line with the policies of the previous kings.

Indian pandits were invited to Samye to help in the translation of Buddhist texts. Sadnaleg erected the temple of Karchung Lhakhang near Lhasa. As there was opposition to the Buddhist religion at the time, the king called a meeting of his ministers and various vassals from different parts of the kingdom. An extensive document was drawn up pledging support for the propagation of the Buddhist faith and it was signed by the king and all those present. An inscription to this effect was also placed on a pillar in front of the Karchung Lhakhang.[55]

During Sadnaleg's reign, the Tibetan army continued to harass the Arabs in the west. According to *al-Ya'qubi,* the Tibetans even besieged the capital of Transoxania, Samarkand. Al-Ma'mun, the second son of Harun al-Rashid, came to an agreement with the Tibetan governor of Turkestan, who presented al-Ma'mun a statue made of gold and precious stones, which was later sent to the Ka'ba in Mecca.[56]

Sadnaleg had five sons: Tsangma, Darma, Tritsug Detsen (also known as Ralpachen), Lhaje, and Lhundup. The firstborn son became a monk and the last two died in childhood. When Sadnaleg died in 815 at Drak, the ministers bypassed Darma as heir to the throne be-

53. CHRONICLES, p. 77.

54. Haarh, "The Identity of Tsu-chih-chien."

55. For the transcription and translation of the Karchung inscription, see TOMBS, pp. 100–04 and 51–55, respectively.

56. CHRONICLES, p. 78.

cause he was irreligious, harsh, and hot tempered. They gave the royal power to Ralpachen, who was pro-Buddhist. Bande Dangka Palgyi Yonden, the Buddhist monk, served as the chief minister of state. Ralpachen took as his queen a Tibetan girl named Palgye Ngangtsul.

During his reign, King Ralpachen invited three Indian pandits, Śilendrabodhi, Dānaśila, and Jinamitra, to central Tibet and provided them with two prominent translators, Kawa Paltsek and Chogro Lui Gyaltsen. The names of these translators appear at the end of almost all Tibetan books of the period, as they were responsible for the revision of the Buddhist texts, which had been translated earlier. They standarized the terms used for translating Buddhist concepts from Sanskrit. The first dictionary was compiled at that time. Called the *Mahavyupatti,* it was a Sanskrit-Tibetan lexicon and indispensable for those translating Buddhist texts.

After coming to the throne, Ralpachen sent troops under the command of Hrangje Tsen towards the Chinese border. Buddhists in China and in Tibet sought mediation, and finally both countries sent representatives to the border. A meeting was held in 821 and a peace treaty concluded. The text of the treaty was inscribed on three pillars. One was erected outside the Chinese Emperor's palace gate in Ch'ang-an, another on the boundary between the two countries at Gugu Meru, and the third in front of the main gate of the Jokhang at Lhasa. At the time of swearing to uphold the treaty, there were two religious ceremonies performed: the Bon ritual of animal sacrifice and the Buddhist ritual of invoking the sacred trinity of the sun, moon, and stars as witnesses.

The text of this Sino-Tibetan treaty has been translated several times; [57] therefore, it will not be repeated here. Suffice it to say, the treaty reaffirmed the boundaries established by the 783 treaty of Ch'ing-shui and restored the former relationship of mutual respect and friendship. The stone pillar in Lhasa was erected in the year 823. [58] The west face bears an inscription of the treaty in both Tibetan and Chinese. The east side bears an edict by the king summarizing Sino-Tibetan relations. The north side gives the names of the

57. RICHARDSON, pp. 244–45. For a comprehensive study of both the Tibetan and Chinese versions of the treaty, see Li Fang-kuei, "The Inscription of the Sino-Tibetan Treaty of 821–822," *T'oung Pao,* 44, 1–3 (1956), 1–99.

58. This date is given in the inscription as "the 9th year of sKyi rtag." (Li Fang-kuei, p. 4). The use of sKyi rtag as a reign title for Ralpachen is probably due to the influence of the Chinese custom, and it is the only such occurrence in early Tibetan history.

seventeen Tibetan officials who participated in making the treaty, and the south side gives those of the eighteen Chinese officials.

I have seen the Lhasa treaty-pillar, but not the one that was erected in China. The text of the Chinese pillar had been copied out by the then British High Commissioner in China (c. 1913), who then gave it to Kalon Trimon, a Tibetan minister at the Simla Convention of 1913–14. Kalon Trimon, who was my uncle, later gave that copy to me. Comparison shows that it agrees with the inscription on the Lhasa pillar.

The third pillar, which was erected at the border, no longer exists —unless it actually lies in some museum in France, where it is said to have been taken. A well-known resident of the Chinese province of Kansu named Apa Alo told me that his father had seen the fallen pillar at Gugu Meru and that a party of French Tibetologists had been transcribing its inscriptions. Apa Alo himself searched for the pillar, but found no trace of it.

King Ralpachen, in order to build a new temple, sent for expert bricklayers, carpenters, silversmiths, and blacksmiths from China, Nepal, and Chinese Turkestan. This temple, known as Onchang Doi Lhakhang, was situated about thirty miles southwest of Lhasa near the banks of the Kyichu. Ralpachen also introduced from India a new system of weights and measures for silver and grain.

As an encouragement to others to become monks, Ralpachen decreed that for each monk seven households would have to provide for his needs. This appears to be the first case of monastic taxation in Tibet. As a gesture of increased prestige, monks were to be known as "Priests of the King's Head." This title arose from the practice of tying a long piece of string to Ralpachen's hair, to which a cloth was attached. This cloth was then spread out on the floor and monks would sit on it, while they prayed and ate before the king. This practice was only followed when a monk was a guest of the king, who might, on occasion, be in another room.

Although Ralpachen was doing considerable good for the country and its religion, he met great opposition from his elder brother, Darma. Besides the resentment of having been denied the throne, Darma was bitterly opposed to the Buddhist religion. At a meeting with his loyal supporters, Darma considered how to get rid of his brother, Tsangma, who had become a monk, and of Bande Dangka Palgyi Yonden, the king's trusted Buddhist minister. He succeeded in having his brother sent to Paro in Bhutan, where he would be ineffective. Then, Ralpachen was led to believe that the monk minister, Bande, was having a secret love-affair with the Queen, Palgye Ngangtsul.

Bande Dangka was sent to Nyethang, where he devoted himself to religious meditation. Two ministers, Be Gyaltore and Chogro Lhalon, who were loyal to Darma, went to Nyethang to assassinate Bande Dangka. When Bande did not succumb immediately to their knife assault, they suffocated him by stuffing cloth down Bande's throat. There is a preserved head said to be that of Bande Dangka kept at Nyethang.[59]

Only after the assassination of the Buddhist minister did the Queen come to know of the false allegations made against them. She was so distraught by the slur on her honor that she jumped over the palace walls to her death.

One day in 836, Ralpachen was drinking beer and sunning himself in the garden of the Shampa palace,[60] when the ministers Be and Chogro crept up behind him. Grabbing him by the neck, they twisted his head around until his neck was broken.

The pro-Bon ministers then placed Darma on the throne without any opposition. Be Gyaltore was appointed Chief Minister, Be Taknachen became Minister of the Interior, and Nanam Gyatsa Trisum, Minister of the Exterior. They promulgated laws designed to destroy the teaching of Buddhism in Tibet. They had the principal temples—the Ramoche and Tsukla-khang in Lhasa, Trisong Detsen's temple in Samye, and Ralpachen's temple of Onchang Do—sealed up and pictures of monks indulging in strong drink painted on the outer walls.

The Buddhist monks were ordered to choose whether to marry, to carry arms and become huntsmen, or to declare themselves to be followers of the Bon religion by ringing a bell wherever they went. Failure to comply with any of these orders was punishable by death. Two well-known monks, Nyang Tingzin and Ma Rinchenchog, were executed for refusing to abandon their Buddhist faith. The Indian

59. I myself have seen what is said to be the preserved head of Dangka Palyon in a small village called Gyadrong in the Nyethang district. A mausoleum containing the remains of the famous Indian Pandit, Atisha, is located nearby.

60. The Shampa palace, where Ralpachen was assassinated, still stands, enclosed within the walls of the Katsel monastery in the district of Maldro Gungkar, about forty miles east of Lhasa.

pandits and scholars, finding themselves treated with little or no respect, returned to their native land.

Darma was given the name of Lang (Bullock) Darma by the people because they did not like the way he treated them and the religion.
Lang Darma was able to wipe out Buddhism in central Tibet, but not
in other parts of the country where his authority could not be imposed. By 842 religious persecution had become so intense that a
monk, Lhalung Palgye Dorje, who was doing meditation at Yerpa, decided to do something about it.

Lhalung Palgye Dorje set out for Lhasa, wearing a black hat and a
black cloak with a white lining. He smeared charcoal on his white
horse and concealed his bow and arrow in the long, flowing sleeves of
his cloak. When he reached Lhasa, he left his horse tied near a chorten
(stupa) on the banks of the river and walked into the city. He found
King Lang Darma and his courtiers reading the inscription of the
treaty-pillar located in front of the Jokhang temple.

Prostating himself before the King, the monk freed his bow and
arrow without being detected and then, standing up, he fired an arrow
straight at the King's heart. While the King was in his death throes
and the people around thrown into confusion, Lhalung escaped to the
river bank. Mounting his horse, he forced it to swim across the river to
wash the charcoal away and then, reversing his cloak so only the white
lining showed, he returned to Yerpa by a devious route.

A search party set out after him, but no one had seen a man in
black riding a black horse. A fruitless search was made of all the likely
hiding places in the nearby hills and villages. Finally, the searchers arrived at Yerpa, where they were told that a mysterious hermit lived
alone in a cave in the hills. They went up to investigate but finding no
footprints nor signs of human habitation outside the cave, they did
not enter. One man did venture to go inside and he saw a man sitting
at the far end of the cave in the posture of deep meditation. Apparently in a state of trance, the man did not move as the searcher approached him. When he placed his hand over the hermit's heart, he
found the heart to be beating rapidly. The searcher returned to his
home and told his family that he believed the assassin was the hermit
in the cave; but he would not report the matter to the authorities
since he preferred to put the common good above his own self-
interests. A rumor spread that the assassin had been seen and Lhalung

Palgye Dorje hearing this, left his cave and sought refuge in eastern Tibet.[61]

At the time of Lang Darma's death, his junior queen was pregnant. The senior queen pretended that she too was pregnant and finding an abandoned baby, she claimed it as her own son. Several ministers doubted whether the child was hers as it seemed too big for a newborn infant; but some agreed to accept the queen's word and so the child was named Yumtan, which means "Relying on the Mother."

When Lang Darma's son and heir was born to the junior queen, she was afraid he might be kidnapped because of his just claim to the throne, so she took precautions for his safety. She always kept him in the light of the sun by day and of a lamp by night; thus, he acquired the name O-sung, meaning "Protected by the Light."

O-sung succeeded in ascending the throne at Lhasa, and Yumtan went to Yalung and there established a separate lineage of kings. This marked the first schism in the royal line and central authority. Another split in the lineage was caused by O-sung's two grandsons. Tri Tashi Tsekpal, the older grandson, ruled in the province of Tsang. Kyide Nyimagon, the younger grandson, was exiled to Purang in western Tibet, where he established the western lineage of kings.

A number of folk tales have since sprung up about Lang Darma. He was supposed to have had horns on his head and a black tongue. To hide his horns, he arranged his hair in two plaits, tied in a raised knot on each side. No one supposedly knew this at that time, unless it was his hairdresser. It is said that this is the origin of the practice for the Tibetan lay officials to plait their hair in that manner. It is also said that some Tibetans, when they scratch their heads and put out their tongues on meeting high-ranking persons, do so to show that they have neither horns nor black tongues.

The long lineage of royalty which came to an end with the collapse of the Tibetan kingdom, following the assassination of Lang Darma, marked the early period of Tibetan history, which Tibetans regard as the heroic age of the Chosgyal (Religious-Kings).

61. SBA-BZHED; BU-STON.

3

The Struggle for Religious Survival

The assassination of Lang Darma in 842 led to a schism in the royal lineage and the beginning of decentralization of authority. Nothing approaching central authority was restored until 1247, when Sakya Pandita was invested with the right to rule over the Trikor Chuksum (Thirteen Myriarchies) of Tibet by Prince Godan, a grandson of Genghis Khan. The dates 842 and 1247 therefore mark the period of decentralized control in central Tibet, during which time the country consisted of many small hegemonies, which were constantly warring against, or allying with, each other as conditions warranted. These small power enclaves, each with its own fortresses, were ruled by men who gradually became clerics. It would be impossible to reconstruct the history of those various states here, but the more important events of that four hundred year period will be surveyed.

In the year following Lang Darma's proclamation abolishing the Buddhist religion, three hermit monks were living in the hills near Chuwo Ri, south of Lhasa. Their names were Tsang Rabsal, Yo Gyewa Jung, and Mer Shakya Muni. One day, they saw a number of men whom they knew to be monks out hunting with bows and arrows. On making inquiries, they were informed that the practice of Buddhism had been forbidden by law in Tibet and that all monks had to become either husbands, huntsmen, or followers of the Bon religion. The three hermit monks decided to flee central Tibet. According to Tibetan sources, they loaded a number of Buddhist texts on the back of a mule and then passed through Ngari Korsum, the land of the Garlog and the Hor, and arrived finally in Amdo, where nomads living along the Machu (Yellow River) provided them with all their needs in return for religious instruction.

A young man living in the region, who is said to have been a Bon

believer, volunteered to become a Buddhist monk. After his first initiation, he was called Gewa Rabsal; but he was so quick to learn and to
absorb the teachings of the Buddha that the three monks changed his
name to Gongpa Rabsal (All-Wise). Anyone could take the initiatory
Buddhist vow, but to belong to the higher order of monkhood, one
had to take ordination from a monk who had received his teaching in
a direct line from the Buddha. It was customary for a monk to keep a
record of the names of his teachers and a chronological tree of his
teachers' predecessors, back to the Buddha himself. The three monks
from central Tibet were so qualified to give ordination and, in time,
Gongpa Rabsal rose from the junior rank (Getsul) to the senior rank
(Gelong) of monkhood. Gongpa Rabsal took his final ordination
from Tsang Rabsal. For many years after Lang Darma's persecution,
there were no initiations into the order in central Tibet; but Buddhism was kept alive in eastern and western Tibet.

According to tradition, one of the descendants of O-sung, Tsana
Yeshe Gyaltsen, had an estate at Samye in the central Tibetan province of Ü. He studied the historical and religious records of the earlier
kings and learned that Buddhist novices could only take the vows of a
Getsul and a Gelong from fully-ordained monks. As there were no
such monks left in central Tibet, he decided to send some of his people
to Amdo for religious training. He called for volunteers and selected
ten of the most promising young men—five from Ü and five from
Tsang—and sent them to Amdo under his sponsorship, providing
them with presents for their prospective teachers. The names of the
ten were Lumed Tsultrim Sherab, Ding Yeshe Yonten, Rakshi Tsultrim Jungnas, Ba Tsultrim Lodro, Sumpa Yeshe Lodro, Loton Dorje
Wangchuk, Tsongtsun Sherab Sengye, Bodong Upa Dekar, and two
brothers of Ngari Wogyapa.

When the ten young men arrived in Amdo, the teacher, Tsang
Rabsal, was very old, so he assigned the responsibility of training them
to his disciple, Gongpa Rabsal. After they had been ordained as
monks, the ten men returned to Samye in central Tibet, only to find
that their sponsor, Tsana Yeshe Gyaltsen, had died. However, his son,
Ngadak Tripa, offered them patronage. The monks inquired in Samye
if anyone had seen monks before that time, and only one old woman
of seventy-six years claimed to have seen a monk and that was when
she was six years old. This story gives an indication of the length of
time during which Buddhism was suppressed in central Tibet.

Meanwhile, in the region of Ngari in western Tibet, Tsenpo Khore, a grandson of Kyide Nyimagon, had ascended to the throne of the western lineage of kings. He built Toling monastery and then decided to become a monk. Turning over his rule to his younger brother, Songe, Khore then ordained himself a monk and took the name of Lha Lama Yeshe Od. Observing that the practice of Buddhism in western Tibet was degenerating, he decided to send twenty-one lads to Kashmir to learn Sanskrit and to study the Buddhist doctrine. Of those twenty-one, only two survived the heat and rigors of the journey. These two lived to become famous translators; their names were Rinchen Zangpo and Lekpe Sherab. They invited some Indian pandits to accompany them back to western Tibet and on their return, they reported of growing conflict between the Hindus, Buddhists, and Muslims.

The arrival of the pandits in Tibet in 978 was considered to be the beginning of the renaissance of Buddhism, which has been described as "a spark rekindled in the east and spread by a wind blowing from the west." The year 978 became known as the first year of the Restoration of Buddhism, the 746th year of the coming of *The Secret* (Nyenpo Sangwa), and the year 1522 after the death of the Buddha. Although the pandits represented different schools of Buddhism, the Tantric form of the Mahāyāna school was predominant.

Sometime later, Yeshe Od sent an invitation to Atisha Dīpaṅkarajñāna, a great Mahāyāna pandit, then living in the great monastic-university of Vikramaśīla in India. Yeshe Od's representative, Gya Tsonseng, went to India with an escort, carrying the letter of invitation and presents of gold. The invitation read:

> Tibet has been for a long time a land bereft of its religion. If you are the kind of person I think you are—a great teacher and a true champion of Buddhism—you will come to our aid. I am a weary, thirsty person; thirsty for the water of knowledge from your lips. I await your arrival with great impatience.[1]

Atisha declined the presents and the invitation on the grounds that Buddhism was on the wane in India and his presence there was necessary to prevent any further decline. Gya Tsonseng returned to Tibet with Atisha's answer and then went back to India to study under the great teacher. Yeshe Od thought perhaps the gold he had sent to

1. RNAM-THAR.

Atisha was insufficient, so he decided to obtain more. He led a campaign against the Garlog, but was captured and thrown into prison by the Garlog king.[2] He was offered his freedom if he would renounce Buddhism. When he refused, the king demanded gold equal to his weight as ransom.

Yeshe Od had a great-nephew named Changchub Od, who was a monk. When Changchub Od had raised all the gold possible, it was still less than the weight required to ransom Yeshe Od. With a small escort, Changchub Od journeyed to the Garlog prison to visit his great uncle, who told him not to use the gold for his ransom; but to use it to invite Atisha to Tibet. Yeshe Od was very old, and had dwindled to a mere skeleton. He finally died in the prison from old age and the inhuman treatment he had received.

After he returned to Toling, Changchub Od looked for a suitable messenger who could be sent to India with a letter of invitation. He sent a message to a well-known translator named Nagtso, who lived in Gungthang, near the Nepalese border. When Nagtso received the message, he traveled to Toling, where he was warmly welcomed by Changchub Od, who offered him a seat of honor higher than his own. In a very respectful manner, Changchub Od told the story of his own and his great-uncle's tireless efforts to save the Buddhist religion in western Tibet. He also commented on the confusion caused by the doctrinal differences between the Hinayāna and Mahāyāna schools. Changchub Od then said, "You know the way to India. You know the language and are accustomed to the heat. You are the only person who can bring Atisha here. That great pandit is the only one who can clear up the confusion in our country and set us on the right path." Nagtso replied, "It will interfere with my own studies, but I will do it for you. You have done so much for the religion that I cannot refuse your request." [3] Nagtso was then given five assistants, with presents of gold and a letter to Atisha, and was personally seen off by Changchub Od.

Atisha was now an elder at Vikramaśīla monastery in Magadha, the chief seat of Buddhist learning. Nagtso's arrival at the monastery was

2. For a study on the Garlog, see Helmut Hoffmann, "Die Qarlug in der Tibetischen Literatur," *Oriens*, 3 (Leiden, 1950), pp. 190–208. Although the precise locale of the Garlogs is uncertain, they inhabited a region northwest of Ngari Korsum. The Garlog people were Muslims.

3. LAM-YIG. The account given here of Atisha's life in Tibet is based on RNAM-THAR, LAM-YIG, and the Bka'-gdam-pa section of DGA'-STON.

reported by Gya Tsonseng, the Tibetan who had previously become a student there. Atisha suggested that the purpose of the Tibetan's visit be kept confidential as the other pandits would resent any attempts to take him to another country. The Tibetans were invited to become students and they accepted. When Nagtso finally met with Atisha, he told the entire story of the efforts made to bring him to Tibet and stressed the great need for his presence and teachings.

Atisha, realizing the immense trouble to which the Tibetans had gone, was no longer able to refuse the invitation. The decision was a difficult one because of his heavy responsibilities and duties at Vikramaśīla; but during a session of prayer and meditation, he was urged by his tutelary deity, Tara, to go to Tibet, and he then agreed to do so. The abbot of the monastery, Śīlākara, made Nagtso take an oath that he would send Atisha back to India at the end of three years.

A large party now set out for Tibet by way of Nepal. It consisted of Atisha and twenty-four of his disciples; Nagtso and his five attendants; and Gya Tsonseng with two companions. They were well received by the King of Nepal, and then a reception committee from Tibet came to meet them. They passed the year 1041 in Nepal, and the only unfortunate occurrence was the death of Gya Tsonseng.

In 1042, they arrived in western Tibet at the Toling monastery with its Sergye Lhakhang (Golden Temple), built by Lha Lama Yeshe Od. The translator, Rinchen Zangpo, was the abbot of the monastery, which was the first Tibetan monastery built in Ngari. Atisha and his disciples made corrections and revisions of the Tibetan translations of Buddhist texts, clearing up many confusing points. While at Toling, Atisha wrote a Sanskrit work called *Bodhipathapradipa,* which is called *Changchub Lamgye Donme* in Tibetan, meaning "The Lamp that shows the Path to Enlightenment."

As the time approached when Atisha was to return to India, he traveled from Toling to Purang, where he was joined by Drom Tonpa, a layman from central Tibet who had come to become a disciple of Atisha. In the year 1045 they proceeded to Kyirong, near the Nepalese border; for Atisha's three years were up and he was returning to India. At Kyirong, they learned that the road through Nepal to India was cut off because of internal strife. At that point, Drom Tonpa asked Atisha to visit the region of Ü-Tsang in central Tibet, but Nagtso objected that he had given his oath to Śīlākara at Vikramaśīla that Atisha would return in three years. Atisha reassured

Nagtso that, since the return road to India was closed, he would not be held to blame for any delay; moreover, if the community of monks in central Tibet requested him to come, he could not refuse to do so.

Following the collapse of the royal kingdom brought about by conflict between Buddhism and the Bon religion, there emerged in central Tibet many rival principalities, many of which were ruled by lamas, or by laymen closely allied with lamas. Drom Tonpa, therefore, wrote to the prominent priest-chieftains, informing them that he had invited Atisha to visit Ü-Tsang. The various ruling lamas, with all the pomp and splendor they could muster, set out to welcome Atisha. They collected at Palthang, where they awaited his arrival in an impressive array.

When Atisha saw them from a distance, he asked Drom Tonpa who they were, and Drom replied that the priest-chieftains had come to welcome him. Atisha said, "If you have so many priests in central Tibet, you have no need of me here." But, when he moved closer and could see their luxurious trappings, elaborate clothes, horses, and escorts, he realized that his presence was indeed needed, because such a display of affluence was not in keeping with the teachings of the Buddha.

The priest-chieftains tried to outdo each other in their efforts to entertain Atisha. At first, he was the guest of Lhatsun Bodhi Raj, a powerful man at Samye. He stayed there for several months and then was the guest of another religious chief, Khuton Tsondrus Yungdrung, who hosted Atisha at his monastery of Thangpoche. Hosting Atisha had become a matter of prestige, but Khuton Yungdrung, having once received him as his guest, did little to make his stay pleasant and worthwhile. Displeased, Atisha and Drom Tonpa slipped away from Thangpoche and proceeded to the district of On. Bangton, the chief of Nyethang, hearing of this, sent Atisha an escort of two hundred cavalrymen. He hosted Atisha in Lhasa and then at Nyethang, where Atisha lived several years. Finally, in 1054, Atisha died and his remains were preserved in a chorten (stupa) at Nyethang.

Drom Tonpa, who had been appointed his successor by Atisha, built a temple at Nyethang dedicated to Tara, Atisha's deity. Then, he traveled to Rating monastery in 1057, where he enlarged the monastic building. Drom continued to teach to his disciples until his death in 1064.

The teachings of Atisha were subjected to a reformation movement by Drom, and, as a result, a new school of Buddhism came into being in Tibet. To distinguish themselves from the unreformed followers of Padmasambhava, the followers of Atisha and Drom were called Ka-tam-pa (One of the Doctrine); while the unreformed monks were called Nying-ma-pa (One of the Old).

The Sa-kya-pa sect takes its name from that of the Sakya monastery built in 1073 by Khon Konchog Gyalpo. The Kar-ma-pa sect, which is a subsect of the Ka-gyu-pa, arose from the followers of Karmapa Dusum Khenpa, who founded the monastery called Tsurpu in 1155. These, and other monasteries, were to play an important part in Tibetan history in the following years.

It was considered a worthy achievement for any Tibetan prince or local ruler to send scholars to India, or to invite Indian pandits to Tibet. There was considerable rivalry among persons of power, who wanted to acquire reputations as patrons of religious learning. Unfortunately, not all of the Indian pandits reached their destinations safely. There is at least one account of two scholars, who lost their Tibetan interpreters on the way in Tibet and, finding themselves unable to communicate with the local people, they had to make a living as humble shepherds. This is said to have happened at Tanag in central Tibet, and their inscriptions on slates and stones in that area are of great interest to Sanskrit scholars.[4]

4. The names of those two Indian scholars were Trala Ringwa and Meti (RDZOGS-LDAN; DPAG-BSAM).

4

Lamas and Patrons

In the year 1207, the Tibetans learned that Genghis Khan and his Mongol horde were subjugating the Tangut empire, known in Chinese as Hsi-hsia, which was located in the region comprising part of the modern-day Kansu and Ch'ing-hai provinces of China. A council was held in central Tibet and a delegation appointed to proceed to the camp of the Khan and submit to him. Friendly relations were concluded and tribute established; therefore, the armies of the Khan did not invade Tibet.

After the death of Genghis Khan in 1227, the Tibetans ceased to send the prescribed tribute, and relations with the mongols became strained. In 1240 the grandson of Genghis Khan and second son of the new Khan, Ogodai, by the name of Godan, ordered troops against Tibet. Thirty thousand troops, under the command of Leje and Dorta,[1] reached Phanpo, north of Lhasa. They burned down the Rating and Gyal Lhakhang monasteries. The priest-chieftain, Soton, and five hundred monks and civilians were killed, and towns and villages were looted.

Prince Godan then asked his commanders to look for an outstanding Buddhist lama in Tibet, and they informed him about three lamas. The lama of the Drikhung monastery was the wealthiest; the lama of the Taklung monastery was the most sociable; and the lama of the Sakya monastery was the most religious. Godan then sent a letter and presents to the Sakya lama, Kunga Gyaltsen. The letter stated:

> I, the most powerful and prosperous Prince Godan, wish to inform the Sakya Pandita, Kunga Gyaltsen, that we need a lama to

---

1. According to GDUNG-RABS, DPAG-BSAM, and RDZOGS-LDAN, the names of the leaders of the troops sent by Godan were Dorta Nagpo and Gyalmen. Henry Howorth, in citing Sanang Setzen, gives the name as Dorda Darkhan of the Oimaghods (HOWORTH, p. 505).

advise my ignorant people on how to conduct themselves morally and spiritually.

I need someone to pray for the welfare of my deceased parents, to whom I am deeply grateful.

I have been pondering this problem for some time, and after much consideration, have decided that you are the only person suitable for the task. As you are the only lama I have chosen, I will not accept any excuse on account of your age or the rigors of the journey.

The Lord Buddha gave his life for all living beings. Would you not, therefore, be denying your faith if you tried to avoid this duty of yours? It would, of course, be easy for me to send a large body of troops to bring you here; but in so doing, harm and unhappiness might be brought to many innocent living beings. In the interest of the Buddhist faith and the welfare of all living creatures, I suggest that you come to us immediately.

As a favor to you, I shall be very kind to those monks who are now living on the west side of the sun.

I send you presents of five silver shoes [ingots], a silken gown set with six thousand and two hundred pearls, vestments and shoes of silk, and twenty silken rolls of five different colors. They are brought to you by my messengers, Dho Segon and Un Jho Kharma.

[Dated] The 30th day of the eighth month of the Dragon year [1244].[2]

The invitation, which in fact was an ultimatum, was received and accepted by Kunga Gyaltsen (1182–1251), who was also called Sakya Pandita, because of his knowledge of Sanskrit. He departed from Sakya in the year 1244 for the Kokonor region, where the Prince Godan had his camp. Sakya Pandita took with him on the journey two of his nephews, the ten-year-old Phagpa Lodro Gyaltsen and the six-year-old Chakna. The Mongol representative of Godan accompanied the party.

En route, the party passed through Lhasa, where the young Phagpa became a monk, taking his first ordination from Sakya Pandita in front of the Buddha image, brought to Tibet in the seventh century by the Chinese Princess, Wen-ch'eng Kung-chu. Sakya Pandita gave

2. GDUNG-RABS.

many sermons along the way to the Kokonor region and the journey was taking a long time, so he sent his nephews on ahead. By the time he arrived in the camp of Godan in 1247, the two young Tibetans had won the hearts of the Mongols. According to Tibetan accounts, Sakya Pandita met Prince Godan at Lan-chou, the capital of Kansu.[3]

Sakya Pandita instructed Godan in the teachings of the Buddha and even persuaded him to refrain from throwing large numbers of Chinese into the nearby river.[4] This was being done in order to reduce the population; not for economic reasons, but political ones, since a large Chinese population was always a threat to the rule of Prince Godan. This practice was stopped when Sakya Pandita convinced Godan that it was against the Buddhist doctrine.

Sakya Pandita was invested with temporal authority over the thirteen myriarchies of central Tibet. He then wrote a message to the leaders of Tibet telling them that it was useless to resist the Mongols because of their military strength and instructed that tribute was to be paid.[5]

The Tibetans sent a representative to Sakya Pandita asking him to return to central Tibet; but he declined as he felt he was more useful in the Kokonor region, where he was well treated by Godan. He sent to his fellow clerics in Tibet a book he had written. It was titled *Thub-pai Gong-sal*, meaning "The Buddha's Intention." Knowing he did not have long to live, he left his book as a legacy to his country. To the lay patrons and citizens, he sent a long letter of counsel. In essence, it said:

> The Prince has told me that if we Tibetans help the Mongols in matters of religion, they in turn will support us in temporal matters. In this way, we will be able to spread our religion far and wide. The Prince is just beginning to learn to understand our religion. If I stay longer, I am certain I can spread the faith of the Buddha beyond Tibet and, thus, help my country. The Prince has allowed me to preach my religion without fear and has offered me all that I need. He tells me that it is in his hands to do good for Tibet and that it is in mine to do good for him. He has

3. According to HOWORTH, pp. 505–06, the meeting was in a district west of Sining, called Shira Talas, within the limits of Lientsu.

4. GDUNG-RABS.

5. TPS, pp. 10–12.

placed his full confidence in me. Deep in his heart, the Prince wishes, I know, to help all countries.

I have been preaching constantly to his descendants and to his ministers, and now I am getting old and will not live much longer. Have no fear on this account, for I have taught everything I know to my nephew, Phagpa.[6]

A Tibetan representative took this letter back to Tibet, along with gifts for the prominent lamas and their monasteries. Sakya Pandita then gave to Phagpa his conch shell and begging bowl, thus signifying that he had handed over his religious authority to him. In 1251, Sakya Pandita died at Lan-chou, seventy years of age.

Prince Godan died not long after Sakya Pandita and was succeeded in his power by the prince, Kublai, who is known as Se-chen to the Tibetans. In 1253, when Kublai was in command of the Kokonor region, he invited the nineteen-year-old Phagpa to his court and was much impressed with the young monk's learning, and by his intelligent answers to a number of difficult questions. Kublai then asked Phagpa for religious instruction; but the young Sakya lama told him that, before he could receive such teachings, Kublai would have to take an oath that he would prostrate himself before Phagpa, as his religious teacher, whenever they met and to place him before or above, whenever they traveled or sat. Kublai replied that he had no objections to prostrating himself before Phagpa in private during his studies; but that he could not do so in public, as it would involve a loss of prestige and therefore weaken his authority. Kublai further agreed to seek Phagpa's consent before making decisions with regard to Tibet; but insisted that there could be no interference from Phagpa in regard to the internal political affairs of the Chinese and Mongolian territories. Phagpa agreed to these conditions and Prince Kublai received his initiation.[7] According to Howorth, Kublai consented to occupying a lower seat than his lama when taking vows and an equal seat when dealing with matters concerning the government.[8]

According to tradition, Phagpa bestowed consecration on twenty-five of Kublai's ministers on three occasions. The first earned him the spiritual and temporal authority over the thirteen myriarchies

---

6. GDUNG-RABS.
7. Ibid.
8. HOWORTH, p. 507.

(Trikor Chuksum) of central Tibet. After the second, he was given a
relic of the Buddha and invested with authority over the three regions
of Tibet, called the Chol-kha-sum, which comprised Ü-Tsang (central
Tibet), Dotod (Kham) and Domed (Amdo). When Kublai became
Khan in 1260, Phagpa was given the title of Tishri (Chinese: Ti-
shih), meaning "Imperial Preceptor," after the third consecration. He
was also given the "Gyai-me-yur chen-mo," which remains unidenti-
fied. Some scholars say it was a territory of China, while others believe
it was a promise to end the practice of drowning people to control the
population.

Kublai did not wish to tolerate any Buddhist sect other than the Sa-
kya-pa to which Phagpa himself belonged; however, Phagpa insisted
that the other sects be allowed to practice Buddhism in their own way.
This brought Phagpa the support of many of the Tibetan priest-
chieftains; however, the presence of several different sects in Tibet was
to weaken the power of the Sakya ruling family in the years that followed. It is interesting to note that when Kublai was still a prince,
there was another Tibetan lama at his court. That lama was Karmapa
Pakshi, a member of the Kar-ma-pa sect.[9] Future incarnations of the
Karmapa Lama took place after Karmapa Pakshi's death; it is interesting to note that these were the first incarnations recorded in Tibet.

In 1254 Kublai gave a letter of investiture to Phagpa, granting him
supreme authority over Tibet. That letter, which is recorded in a
Sakya text, reads:

> As a true believer in the Great Lord Buddha, the all-merciful
> and invincible ruler of the world, whose presence, like the sun,
> lights up every dark place, I have always shown special favor to
> the monks and monasteries of your country.
>
> Having faith in the Lord Buddha, I studied the teachings of
> your uncle, Sakya Pandita, and in the year of the Water-Ox
> [1253], I received your own teachings.
>
> After studying under you, I have been encouraged to continue
> helping your monks and monasteries, and in return for what I
> have learned from your teachings, I must make you a gift.
>
> This letter, then, is my present. It grants you authority over all
> Tibet, enabling you to protect the religious institutions and faith
> of your people and to propagate Lord Buddha's teachings.

9. DGA'-STON (Kar-ma-pa section); TPS, 2, 627; and HOWORTH, p. 223.

In addition, my respected tutor, I am presenting you with garments, a hat, and a gown, all studded with gold and pearls; a gold chair, umbrella, and cup; a sword with the hilt embedded with precious stones, four bars of silver and a bar of gold; and a camel and two horses, complete with saddles.

In this year of the Tiger, I will also present you with fifty-six bars of silver, two hundred cases of brick tea, and one hundred and fifty rolls of silk, to enable you to build images of the deities.

The monks and people of Tibet should be informed of what I am doing for them. I hope they will not look for any other leader than you.

The person who holds this letter of credentials should, in no way, exploit his people. Monks should refrain from quarreling among themselves and from indulging in violence. They should live peaceably and happily together.

Those who know the teachings of the Lord Buddha should endeavor to spread them; those who do not know his teachings should try to learn all they can. Everyone should read, write, and meditate; to pray to the Lord Buddha, and also to pray for me.

Some people maintain that it is possible to meditate without studying religion; but that is not correct. We must understand first, and then only can we meditate. Senior monks should teach and advise their juniors, and the young monks should follow carefully the teachings of their superiors.

To the monks, I should say that they should realize and be grateful that they have not been taxed; nor has their way of life been altered. We Mongols shall not respect you, if your monks do not conscientiously carry out the teachings of the Buddha.

Do not think the Mongols incapable of learning your religion. We learn it gradually.

I have high esteem for your monks and should appreciate it if they do not embarrass me in public by any undignified behavior.

As I have elected to be your patron, you must make it your duty to carry out the teachings of the Lord Buddha. By this letter, I have taken upon myself the sponsorship of your religion.

[Dated] The ninth day of the middle month of summer of the Wood-Tiger year [1254].[10]

10. GDUNG-RABS.

In 1260, following the death of Mongka Khan, prince Kublai became the new Khan. He requested Phagpa to conduct the ceremony of enthronement. It is said that the lama-patron relationship between the Mongol Khan and the Tibetan lama was like the "sun and the moon in the sky."

In 1265 Phagpa returned to Tibet for the first time since his childhood departure. At Sakya he was received with all honors by the Tibetan chieftains, who came to pay homage to him. He distributed presents and offered them his advice. The actual administration of central Tibet was carried out by an official known as the Ponchen ("Great Master"), who maintained his office at Sakya. Under this official were the thirteen Tripon ("Myriarchs"), who directly ruled in their own myriarchy. The Ponchen appointed by Phagpa was named Shakya Zangpo.

Two years after Phagpa's return to Tibet, a representative of the Khan arrived at Sakya with a letter inviting Phagpa to return to the Mongolian court. Phagpa arranged for an entourage of thirteen officials to accompany him to look after his needs and comfort. The dress of Phagpa and his officials was made to resemble that of the Mongols.

Some of the lamas began to criticize Phagpa for his actions. One of them, Chomden Rigral, a lama of the Narthang monastery, wrote him the following stanzas:

> The sunbeam of the Buddha's faith has been blotted out by
> the clouds of the Ka-gyu-pa sect.
> The people have lost their peace and happiness because of the
> excesses of the officials.
> The lamas of today are dressed like the chiefs of Mongolia.
> He who does not understand these lines is not "exceptional"
> (Phagpa), [11] though he may be called Phagpa.

Phagpa replied to this letter, writing also in poetic meter:

> The Buddha himself admitted that the faith would rise or
> decline according to the times.
> The peace and happiness of the people depends on the Law of
> Karma; it lies not in the hands of officials.
> To win the Mongols to our faith, I must dress like a Mongol.

---

11. The usage of "exceptional" in the English translation serves to illustrate the poetical style of a pun in Tibetan, because Phagpa, the name of the Sakya Lama, means "exceptional."

He who does not understand these lines must be a man deficient in wisdom.[12]

Phagpa set out with his entourage for the Mongolian court. Near
Lhasa, they passed the temple of Ger, and Phagpa expressed his ad-
miration of it, commenting on the good fortune of the lamas, who
possessed such accomplished assistants. Shakya Zangpo, the Ponchen
(a Sakya minister), was accompanying Phagpa up to the border and
overheard his master's remarks. Making a note of the design and di-
mensions of the Ger temple, he resolved to build one similar to it in
Sakya. When Shakya Zangpo returned to Sakya, he began the work of
building the temple; but he died before it was completed. Kunga
Zangpo, who had been an assistant administrator, succeeded Shakya
Zangpo, and brought the temple to completion. The temple, which
was of great size, was known as the Lhakhang Chenmo.

When Phagpa arrived in Mongolia, he was greeted by the wife and
elder son of Kublai Khan. They had come a considerable distance to
welcome him. A colorful function was held to mark the occasion.
When he reached the court in 1268, he presented to Kublai a script he
had devised for the Mongolian language. This script was based upon
Tibetan writing, with the exception that it was written from top to
bottom in columns as is Chinese and not from left to right as in Tibetan and Sanskrit. Kublai was pleased and the new writing system,
which would become known as "Phagpa's Script," was put into official
use. Because of its square form, its use was cumbersome and time-
consuming. The script soon fell into disuse after the death of Kublai
Khan, but there are many important official records written in it.

Phagpa was again honored by Kublai, who bestowed on him the
title of "Prince of Indian Deities, Miraculous Divine Lord Under the
Sky and Above the Earth, Creator of the Script, Messenger of Peace
Throughout the World, Possessor of the Five Higher Sciences, Phagpa,
the Imperial Preceptor." The customary gifts included one thousand
shoes (ingots) of silver and 59,000 rolls of silk.

In his memoirs, Phagpa mentions that in 1271 Kublai Khan was
very friendly with a stranger from a faraway land, who occasionally
came to visit the Khan. The date falls within the time of Marco Polo's
visit to the Mongolian court, and in the account of his travels, Marco

12. GDUNG-RABS. The usage by Phagpa of the phrase "deficient in wisdom" is a pun on the
name of the lama, as Rigral can be rendered "torn knowledge."

Polo mentions meeting the lama of the Khan, but does not give his name.

When Phagpa prepared to return to Tibet in 1274, the Khan decided to accompany him part of the way. Out of fondness for the lama, he remained with him for many months, until they reached the upper bend of the Machu (Yellow River) in the Amdo region. A grand farewell party was given there for Phagpa by the members of the Mongolian court. An equally lavish reception was given by the Tibetan ruling-lamas, who had come to receive the travelers.[13]

After two years on the road, Phagpa arrived back at Sakya in 1276. He died at Sakya in 1280, when he was only forty-six. Some accounts say that he was poisoned by one of his close attendants, who was intriguing against the Ponchen, Kunga Zangpo. The attendant wrote a letter to Kublai Khan in Phagpa's name and accused the Ponchen of disloyalty, and the Khan sent two of his commanders, with a large number of troops, to deal with the matter. Hearing that the Mongols were approaching, the intrigant is said to have poisoned Phagpa and then committed suicide.[14]

The Mongol commanders, assuming that Phagpa had been murdered by the Ponchen, Kunga Zangpo, went to interrogate him. The Ponchen appeared before them in a white robe and a black hat. He denied being disloyal and denied any connection with the death of Phagpa. He declared that if he were executed, the blood from his neck would be white as proof of his innocence. The commanders executed the Ponchen, and it is said that when his neck was severed, the first spurt of blood was indeed white. When Kublai Khan received word of the entire affair, he said that the administrator had worn a white robe as a symbol of his innocence and a black hat as a symbol of the false accusation brought against him. Because the two commanders had failed to make a thorough preliminary investigation, the Khan had them executed. As a result of this story, the Tibetan expression, "If you cut my red neck, white blood will come out" and "You have forced a black hat on my white person" have become common as protestations of innocence.

13. Ibid.

14. Giuseppe Tucci states that some accounts say Phagpa was killed secretly by one of his assistants for fear that Phagpa would discover who had summoned the Mongol army (TPS, 2, 627). The GDUNG-RABS and RDZOGS-LDAN do not mention anything of poisoning; instead they say that Phagpa's bones turned black and had to be mixed with ivory at the time of his embalmment. Perhaps it was because of poison that Phagpa's bones turned black.

In the year of Phagpa's death, 1280, Kublai Khan had finally conquered all of China, and he ascended the throne as the Emperor of China. Before his death, Phapa had sent presents and a letter of congratulations to Kublai on his success.

Chakna, who was the younger nephew of Sakya Pandita, had traveled to the camp of the Mongols with Phagpa. Later, he married a Mongol princess, but died at twenty-nine. His son, Dharmapāla, was appointed Tishri in Peking in 1282. The new Ponchen (administrator) at Sakya in Tibet was Shang Tsun.

Sometime around the year 1286, a yogi named Ugyen Sengge, who traveled habitually between India and Tibet, noted that the advent of the Muslim faith in India was bringing about the extinction of Buddhism. On one of his visits to India, he managed to contact the king of Ceylon and together they contributed to the repair of the great temple at Bodh-gaya. During the reconstruction work, Ugyen Sengge was living with some five hundred other yogis and monks at the northern end of the temple. The gate that was erected there acquired the name of the "Tibetan Gate." [15]

It is said that Kublai Khan was planning to attack India and Nepal (ca. 1286) by sending his armies through Tibet. Shang Tsun, the administrator at Sakya, strongly objected to such a plan. The yogi, Ugyen Sengge, sent Kublai Khan a long religious poem asking him to desist from waging war against India and Nepal.[16] It would seem the Khan was influenced by these protestations; at any rate, the projected war was not undertaken.

Dharmapāla, the Tishri, set out in 1287 for Tibet, but died during the long journey. Later on, during the time of the chief administrator, Ag-len, the myriarchy, Drikhung, which had become very strong, challenged the authority of the Sakya and attacked them. Ag-len, with a large body of troops including Mongol cavalry, defeated them and then, in 1290, marched against Drikhung territory, where they burned the monastery and massacred many monks. Those who escaped fled to places in Kongpo and Dakpo, where they were followed by troops who looted villages on the way. Ag-len's name is still found inscribed on the rock cliffs of Dakpo.

In 1295 the great Kublai Khan died. It can now be seen how the

15. DGA'-STON (Kar-ma-pa section).
16. Ibid.

Mongols acquired military control over Tibet, beginning with the submission by Sakya Pandita to the prince Godan in 1247. Throughout the period, the actual administration of Tibet remained in Tibetan hands. There was a definite change in the relationship between the Mongol ruler and the Tibetan lama during Kublai's reign. A comparison of Godan's letter to Sakya Pandita with that of Kublai to Phagpa will reveal that the first is an example of correspondence from lord to subject; while the second is one of presentation from patron to lama. The latter is an example of the unique central Asian concept of the patron-lama relationship, in which the temporal support of the lay power is given in return for the spiritual support of the religious power. This relationship between the Mongol rulers and the Tibetan lamas cannot be defined in Western political terms. An insight into the attitudes of the Khan is shown by the lengths to which he went to please Phagpa, whom he acknowledged and supported both as his spiritual teacher and as the supreme authority in Tibet. The taking of religious instructions and the making of the long journey into the Amdo region to accompany Phagpa on his return to Tibet are further indications of a relationship based upon mutual cooperation and respect. The patron-lama relationship came into being between Kublai Khan of the Mongols and Phagpa of the Tibetans. It was maintained as the basis of a political-religious relationship between the Tibetans and the Mongols; and, in later times, between the Manchu Emperors and the Dalai Lama. The patron-lama relationship with the Manchus ended in 1911, with the overthrow of the Ch'ing Dynasty.

After the death of Kublai Khan, the power of the Mongols began to decline in China and the strength of the Sakyas began to wane in Tibet. In 1305 Danyi Zangpo Pal (1262–1322) came to the throne of Sakya and reigned eighteen years, assisted by his administrators, Legpa Pal and Sengge Pal. Danyi, the ruling lama, had seven wives. His numerous sons were the cause for the first schism in the singular succession of Sakya power, as four of his sons each established his own palace and continued the family line. The throne of the ruling lama of Sakya was thereafter shared in turns; however, most of the actual power lay in the hands of the Ponchen (administrator) and the various Tripon (Myriarchs).

Kublai Khan had favored the Sa-kya-pa sect, but his successors did not remain devoted solely to it. A Kar-ma-pa lama, Rangjung Dorje,[17] was invited to China to the Mongol court in 1331. Two years later, he acted as a master of ceremony at the coronation of Togon Temür as Emperor of China, and the Emperor bestowed on him the title of "All-knower of Religion, the Buddha Karmapa." Rangjung Dorje died in 1338 in China, during a second visit to the Mongol court.

In 1350, during the administration of Ponchen Gawa Zangpo and the reign of the ruling lama, Sonam Gyaltsen, the province of Ü in central Tibet fell into the hands of the powerful myriarch, Changchub Gyaltsen of Phamo Drupa. This marked the beginning of the end of Sakya power in central Tibet, because Changchub Gyaltsen, a monk, became the founder of the second religious hegemony.[18]

17. Rangjung Dorje, the third Black Hat Kar-ma-pa lama, lived 1284–1338. He is said to have predicted his future rebirth and the fourth Black Hat Kar-ma-pa lama was recognized as the first reincarnation in Tibet (DALAI, p. 16). For a brief study of the successive lamas of the Karma-pa, see Hugh E. Richardson, "The Karma-pa Sect. A Historical Note," *JRAS* (October 1958), 139–64.

18. TPS, *I*, 17-24.

5

The Phamo Drupa, Rinpung, and Tsangpa Hegemonies

The allegation that the Chinese Emperors of the Ming Dynasty
(1368–1644) inherited claim to Tibet from their Mongol predecessors is not valid historically. The Mongols, in building an empire, first
gained control over part of Tibet and then, after many years, finally
conquered China. Tibet gained its independence from the Mongols in
the time of Changchub Gyaltsen (1302–64), and China gained hers
in 1368 under the leadership of Chu Yüan-chang. Moreover, the Tibetan lamas invited to the Ming court were not of the political stature
of those invited earlier to the Mongol court.

The decline of Sakya power in central Tibet led to the rise of
Phamo Drupa to power. The name Phamo Drupa, which means "One
from Sow's Ferry," was given to a monk, Dorje Gyalpo, who came
from Kham in eastern Tibet in 1158 and built a hermitage called
"Sow's Ferry" at a ferry-crossing near Tsethang. He was a very
learned monk and attracted many disciples. In time, a monastery was
built around the hermitage and it became known as the Thel monastery. One of Phamo Drupa's disciples, Chen-nga Rimpoche, later
assumed the seat of monastery. During this time, Dorjepal, a native of
Kham who claimed himself to be a descendant of Lang Lhazig, attracted the attention of Chen-nga Rimpoche. Because of his ability
and accomplishments, Dorjepal was appointed head of the Nedong
estate.[1]

During the reorganization of central Tibet into administrative
myriarchies in the time of Phagpa, Dorjepal was appointed as a
myriarch in charge of the Phamo Dru myriarchy. This governorship

---

1. PHAGDU, p. 202.

remained in the hands of the Lang family, with the seat of the myriarch at Nedong. It was the custom in the Lang family for one son to remain unmarried and to rule the monastery of Thel and the myriarchy. The other sons married in order to perpetuate the family line. Over the years, the family had many ups and downs, and its fortunes were at a low point during the time Changchub Gyaltsen was a boy.

Changchub Gyaltsen was born in 1302, and at the age of twelve, he was sent to Sakya for religious and administrative training.[2] As a lad, he seemed to be a good choice as the future governor of the myriarchy because he was tenacious, diligent, and capable of facing hardship. He entered into training in Shi-tok-pa, one of the four institutions at Sakya, and was the pupil of a famous lama named Nyam-mepa, with whom he and the other trainees remained for seven years. At the end of this period, his teacher asked whether he would like to become a monk or a governor and Changchub replied, "A monk!" His teacher told him he would never make a good monk; but he might make an excellent governor, so he offered Changchub special training in military strategy and in dealing with people from different walks of life.[3]

In order to become familiar with the ways of the common people, he was made to learn cooking, wood-gathering, and looking after horses and cattle. He was also given practice in public speaking and group leadership. Nyam-mepa told him that to become a good leader, one must first learn to serve others, and to direct others in their work, one must be capable of doing it oneself. Changchub took this thorough system of training very seriously. His self-confidence and ambition increased. He got on well with the children of common families, but was always at loggerheads with his fellow students, who came from rich and powerful families.

When Changchub was twenty years old, his uncle, the governor at Nedong, was dismissed from office by the Sakya lama for abusing his authority, and Changchub was appointed as Myriarch. He was given the myriarch's seal, which was made from sandalwood, and he left Sakya, returning to Nedong as governor in 1322. He appointed Shunu Zangpo as his assistant administrator and then set about im-

---

2. Unless otherwise noted, the account given here of Changchub Gyaltsen is based on his autobiography, the BSE-RU.

3. The grand Sakya Lama, Dagnyi Chenpo, is reported to have said that Changchub Gyaltsen was destined to serve the State, not the Church (PHAGDU. p. 204).

proving conditions in his province. He repaired old forts, built a new
fortified palace, planted trees throughout the valley, and constructed
a bridge over the Shamchu River. He also sought to improve the living
conditions of his people and gave them some relief from taxes.

During the governorship of his uncle, the head of the neighboring
myriarchy of Yazang had taken over two hundred and eighty
Nedong families and their landholdings. Soon after taking office as
governor, Changchub attacked Yazang and regained the lost territory. A state of hostility existed between the two provinces for some
time. The dispute over the territory led to a court inquiry being
instituted by the Sakya administrator. The myriarch of Tsalpa was on
friendly terms with the governor of Yazang and managed to bribe the
investigators to lodge a false report on the case. Consequently, the disputed territory was given back to Yazang.

The dispute between Nedong and Yazang continued, and in 1337 a
new Sakya administrator, Odser Sengge, made another inquiry into
the matter; but he too proved susceptible to bribery and the case was
shelved. In 1345 fighting broke out again between the two provinces.
Wangchuk Ralpa, another Sakya administrator, investigated and decided in favor of Changchub; but the Yazang governor would not
accept the findings, and the feud continued.

A personal aide of the Sakya ruling lama appeared on the scene of
intrigue and claimed that he, Sonam Gyaltsen, was a relative of the
former governor of Nedong. At this point, the Sakya lama and his
ministers, who were impatient with Changchub's stubbornness and aggressive nature, ordered Changchub dismissed as governor, and a letter
of investiture as governor of Nedong was given to Sonam Gyaltsen by
the Internal Minister, Wangtson. Sonam set out for Nedong, but
Changchub refused to hand over the governorship of the province to
him. A stalemate developed.

A few months later, the minister, Wangtson, wrote to Changchub
inviting him to come to Drok Lumpa in the region of Ü to receive a
medal of honor to be presented by the ruling Sakya lama. In his autobiography, Changchub admitted that he went to Drok Lumpa suspecting treachery. Before arriving there, he spoke to one of his close
attendants, saying, "If I am arrested, I want you to return to Nedong
as quickly as possible and warn my ministers. They are to prepare
themselves for battle and they must not surrender Nedong, no matter
what they hear about me. Their own survival depends on this. Even if

I am dragged naked through the streets and have my skin torn from my flesh, they must not give up the province."

As he had suspected, he was arrested as soon as he arrived at Drok Lumpa. He was brought before the Sakya minister, Wangtson, who asked why he had not handed over the seal of governorship to Sonam Gyaltsen, who had come with the Sakya lama's letter of authority. Changchub replied:

> It was the first time I had heard that Sonam Gyaltsen was a relative of mine. Where had he been hiding himself all these years? Even if he were my blood-brother, I would still be capable of governing my own province. I have not broken the laws of the Sakya; nor have my subjects complained of my rule. Why should I give up the governorship? Since Sonam has achieved nothing of merit, to give him the governorship would be like asking a leg to do the work of a head.

Changchub remained obstinate, and Wangtson had him imprisoned for ninety-three days, during which he was continually subjected to torture. On the ninety-fourth day, Wangtson sent for him and, after giving him clean clothes and a comfortable seat, spoke to him mildly and persuasively.

"Why don't you give up the governorship?" Wangtson asked. "The Sakya Lama has appointed Sonam Gyaltsen in your place, and it is useless to disobey his orders. If you agree to resign now, I promise you that in two or three years your province will be restored to you."

Changchub replied, "Tie a letter around Sonam Gyaltsen's neck and mine too, then send us to the Sakya Lama to be judged. Otherwise, kill me now and take the governorship."

This placed Wangtson in a difficult position. He did not have the authority to order an execution; moreover, he had arrested and imprisoned Changchub without the Sakya Lama's knowledge; consequently, he had no wish to send him to the Lama for judgment. Wangtson had no other recourse than to release Changchub.

After releasing him, Wangtson wrote to the Sakya ruling lama and reported that Changchub was being defiant and had refused to surrender Nedong to Sonam Gyaltsen. Then, with the support of Wangtson, an alliance was formed between the three provinces of Tsalpa, Yazang, and Thangpoche.

Changchub returned to Nedong, where he received word from one of his friends at the Sakya court that there was rivalry between the minister, Wangtson, and the chief administrator, Wangchuk Ralpa. He advised Changchub to take advantage of this rivalry by forming an alliance with Wangchuk Ralpa against Wangtson. Changchub wrote a letter to Wangchuk and asked him to come to Ü to investigate the true state of affairs in the area. Wangchuk accepted the invitation and, in due course, visited Nedong.

Wangchuk, who had not been a very effective chief administrator, was shown little respect by his subordinates at Sakya; therefore, the grand reception he was given by Changchub and his ministers at Nedong inclined him strongly towards Changchub's cause. He sent a report favorable to Changchub and later, back at Sakya, continued to champion Changchub's cause to the Sakya Lama. The various conflicting reports about Changchub confused the Sakya Lama and, as a result, Changchub was given a few months respite. Unfortunately for Changchub, his new ally, Wangchuk Ralpa, did not last long as chief administrator and was replaced by Gyawa Zangpo.

About that time, the Myriarch of Thangpoche, supported by Wangtson, attacked and defeated the neighboring province of Yardok, whose governor had allied himself with Changchub. The opposing provinces were now prepared for a major conflict. In his autobiography, Changchub records that he became furious when he heard that, during a meeting in Lhasa of the governors of Tsalpa, Yazang, and Thangpoche, the Yazang governor bragged that he would spend his summers in Yardok and his winters in Nedong.

In 1351 fighting broke out between Yazang and Nedong, and Changchub emerged the victor. It was the responsibility of Sakya to decide the issues involved and to confirm either side's loss or gain of territory. The Sakya Lama was slow in making any decision and the governor of Yazang finally appealed to Wangtson for help. Wangtson wrote to the new chief administrator, Gyawa Zangpo, who was then in Ngari in western Tibet, and asked him to return immediately to Sakya.

Returning to Sakya, Gyawa Zangpo held a meeting of the officials, and it was decided to send the teacher, Nyam-mepa, and Nangso Soseng, popular man-about-town, rather than send court officials to negotiate between the two provinces. When Changchub heard that his former teacher was coming to mediate, he sent a message to Nyam-mepa asking him not to come, since the Yazang governor might not accept the judgment of one so friendly to Changchub. Nevertheless, Nyam-mepa came and Changchub then asked him to show favor and consideration to his opponent, so the Yazang governor would not feel slighted. The attempt at conciliation was a failure, for when Nyam-mepa went to Yazang, he could not locate the governor, who had absented himself to avoid the meeting.

With the attempt at mediation ending in failure, it was decided at Sakya to send an army to settle the dispute. If Changchub did not accept Sakya's decision, he was to be executed and the governors of Yazang and Thangpoche dismissed. The three provinces would then be merged into one and governed directly from Sakya. When Changchub heard of this, he reviewed his position carefully. He thought he could successfully resist the Sakya army, because his own troops were well trained, his province was strongly fortified, and he had an alliance with the governor of Yardok province; however, that would amount to open revolt, and he was not yet ready to show his hand.

While Gyawa Zangpo was en route with an army to the troubled area, Changchub sent him a bar each of gold and silver as a present and requested him to deal honestly with the situation, in which case Changchub would be very cooperative. When the chief administrator was within two days journey of Nedong, Changchub went to receive him. When he found Gyawa Zangpo's attendants unusually polite and respectful, he suspected mischief was afoot. He gave them the use of his guesthouse, which was on the other side of the river and about a mile from his fort and palace.

That same evening he went over to pay his respects. He told them that, judging from the way the Sakya officials were conducting the country's affairs, there would never be peace in Tibet. As he was leaving, he turned and said, "Remember, if you kill me, there will be others in the east and in the west, who will come to claim my body and there will be trouble for Sakya. If, however, you are able to satisfy both the Yazang governor and myself in this dispute, your name and the name of Sakya will be perpetuated forever." According to the autobiography, Gyawa Zangpo said nothing in reply, but merely inclined his head in the affirmative, wearing a displeased expression.

The next day, the Yazang governor and his party arrived to participate in the mediation talks. They camped beside the guesthouse.

Changchub instructed his officials to prepare to defend the fort and palace should he be arrested again, and on no account to surrender.

While the mediation meeting was in progress, Changchub and the Yazang governor were surrounded by troops, bound and kept prisoners. The Nedong officers, suspecting something had gone wrong, did not permit Sakya troops to enter the fort. Fearful that his captors might use his governor's seal to send a false order to his officials, Changchub pretended that he had a fever. He asked for a fire and a brew of nutmeg. A charcoal fire was brought to him in a brazier and, leaning over it to inhale the steam of the nutmeg brew, he covered his head and shoulders with his cloak; then, removed his seal and dropped it into the fire.

A guard asked him what was causing that sweet smell and Changchub replied, "My sandalwood seal!"

For three days, Changchub and the Yazang governor faced a court of inquiry. A number of false accusations were brought against Changchub and he was asked to place his seal against these; but he lightheartedly told the court he could not do so as he had burned his seal.

On the third day, he complained of a backache and asked for one of his attendants. He slipped a message to the servant to be taken to his officers in the fort at the first opportunity. The message instructed them to do all that he had already told them and to ignore any orders brought in his name as he had burned his seal.

That same night, he called one of the guards and asked to see Gyawa Zangpo's secretary. Changchub then told him that he had decided to accept the court's decision and that he would surrender his fort and palace. The following morning, Changchub was released from the rack on which he had been intermittently tortured and was taken before Gyawa Zangpo. Feigning fear and repentance, Changchub asked the chief administrator to be merciful to his officials, since they had refused to surrender the fort only because of his orders. He suggested that two of his own attendants be sent with a message asking them to surrender as his officers would not believe any others.

Gyawa Zangpo welcomed Changchub's change of attitude, but insisted that there be witnesses to his proposal, so Changchub then repeated his offer before the court. The two attendants were then sent to the Nedong fort with his message. The officers were suprised at first and almost decided to surrender, but decided against it, when the attendants reminded them of Changchub's earlier message warning them not to accept any orders sent in his name.

Gyawa Zangpo realized he had been tricked and subjected Changchub to severe torture. While he was in agony, Changchub resolved to seize the throne of Sakya, if he ever became free again. Exiled from Nedong, Changchub was placed backwards on a bullock and led along the banks of the river so the townspeople could witness his humiliation. A hat crowned with a yak's tail was set on his head, but he managed to shake it off and it fell into the river. When the Sakya soldiers jeered at him, he said he would soon be riding back to Nedong, because even then he was facing his capital, although the bullock was carrying him away.

Changchub was then taken to a town near Sakya, where he was to be imprisoned. The people came out of their houses to jeer him and they began to throw clods of earth at him. He opened his mouth and caught some of the mud. Laughing, he said, "Yes, now I am eating the mud of Sakya and soon, in the same way, I will be eating Sakya itself!"

Meanwhile, the chief administrator, Gyawa Zangpo, had declared the three provinces of Thangpoche, Yazang, and Nedong to be one province; but since the Nedong officials still refused to surrender, he could not make the merger a reality. His presence was urgently needed back at Sakya, so he left a body of troops across the river from Nedong and then returned.

For some time, there had been growing jealousy between Gyawa Zangpo and the minister, Wangtson, who was in the Sakya Lama's favor and had also been offered a decoration by the Mongol Khan, Togon Temür. Gyawa Zangpo, seeing that his only chance of remaining in power lay in having a strong ally, sent a message to Changchub offering to release him and to restore his rights and titles, provided that Changchub would not rise up against him. Nyam-mepa was a witness to the offer, which Changchub accepted; and thus he was released from prison in 1352, after serving three and one-half months of confinement.

Changchub returned to Nedong, where he received a great welcome from his people. He told his officials that his life had been spared only because they had refused to surrender to Sakya and he praised his assistant, Shunu Zangpo, for keeping them united during his absence. He informed them of the unstable situation in Sakya and suggested that they should attack immediately. Without delay, he marched his army into Yazang and Thangpoche and occupied those provinces. With the assistance of Gawa Zangpo at the Sakya court, practically all of the Ü region was in Changchub's hands. The Mongol Khan in Peking conferred on him the title of Tai Situ, and from then on, he was known as Situ Changchub Gyaltsen.

In 1354 Gyawa Zangpo and Changchub met in the presence of the Sakya Lama, Kunpangpa, and Gyawa Zangpo apologized for the treatment formerly meted out to Changchub. Changchub offered an escort for Gyawa Zangpo on his return to Sakya, but the chief administrator declined it. On his arrival at Sakya, he was arrested by the minister, Wangtson, and thrown into prison, an act which brought Changchub to the rescue. When Changchub was still five days' march from Sakya, Gyawa Zangpo was released from prison, but was dismissed from his official post. In that year all of Tibet with the exception of Sakya itself was in the hands of Changchub.

In the year 1358, the minister, Wangtson murdered the Sakya Lama, who had presided over the reconciliation between Changchub and Gyawa Zangpo. At the same time, a rumor reached Changchub that Gyawa Zangpo had been poisoned in his country residence. He immediately marched to Sakya, imprisoned Wangtson, dethroned the new ruling lama, and replaced four hundred court officials with his own followers.

After Changchub Gyaltsen came into full power, he reorganized the administrative divisions of the State. Instead of the thirteen myriarchies (Trikor), he divided the land into numerous districts (Dzong). He appointed those men among his followers, who were of unquestioned loyalty, to be masters (Dzongpon) of the districts, thus eliminating the potentially dangerous office of the myriarch (Tripon). He posted officials and guards at various places along the border with China and concentrated troops at the important centers in Tibet. The land was divided equally among the agriculturalists, and it was fixed that one-sixth of the crops were to be taken as tax by the administration. New roads and bridges were built where none had existed before. Ferries, consisting of yak-skin boats, were put in service on the larger rivers, and ropeways were laid across those which were too swift, or treacherous, for ferries. For the protection of travelers, military posts were set up on roads passing through bandit-infested areas. This last reform was particularly beneficial since it helped to eliminate the most common hazard of travel in Tibet. Rest houses and provision caches were established on pilgrim routes around the sacred mountains of Tsari and Kailash.

During the reign of the Sakya lamas, suspected criminals had been executed summarily without a hearing, according to the custom of the Mongols. Changchub adopted the practice of the early religious kings of Tibet and devised thirteen kinds of punishment, varying in severity according to the seriousness of the crime.[4] Investigations were carried out before sentence was passed.

Changchub sought to put an end to the system of inherited governorships and tried to raise the standard of living among the common people. He issued a book of instructions on border defense, military strategy, tax collecting, defense of villages against sudden attack, and steps to be taken to avoid epidemics. He instituted several annual competitions between agriculturalists to encourage the growth of better crops and created medals for outstanding service in any occupation. During the New Year celebration, high officials had to wear the costumes of the early kings, a custom which has prevailed up to the present time.

Changchub's palace at Nedong was surrounded by three walls, each having its own gate. No wine or women were allowed to pass through the gate of the innermost wall, because Changchub remained, to the end of his life, a strict Buddhist monk. During his time, the country was so secure that it was said that an old woman carrying a sackful of gold could pass without fear from one end of Tibet to the other; thus, this period of internal security was known as the era of Genmo Serkhor ("Old woman Carrying Gold"). After having been master of Tibet for several years, Changchub Gyaltsen died in 1364 at the age of sixty-three and he was succeeded by Jamyang Shakya Gyaltsen, a nephew who was a monk.

In the year 1368 the Yüan Dynasty came to an end in China when the Mongols were overthrown, and the Ming Dynasty, with its Chinese Emperors, was founded. Then in 1372 Tsongkhapa Lozang Drakpa, the founder of the reformed Ge-lug-pa sect, came to the re-

4. To these thirteen grades of punishment were added another three by the fifth Dalai Lama, who revised and standardized the sixteen grades of punishment.

gion of Ü-Tsang from Amdo.[5] Jamyang Shakya Gyaltsen died the following year and was succeeded by Drakpa Rinchen, who reigned only
eight years before retiring to the Thel monastery. His nephew, Sonam
Drakpa, came to power in 1381 and his four-year reign proved to be a
prosperous time for Tibet. Because the crops were excellent, he became known as the "Fortunate King." He too retired to the Thel
monastery and was succeeded by Drakpa Gyaltsen.

During that period, a minister named Rapten Kunzang Phagpa
acquired considerable popularity by contributing to the construction
of the famous monastery of Palkhor Choide at Gyantse. Another minister, Zingche Drakrin, a relative of the ruling family, was noted for
his stern and harsh nature, which eventually led to his murder by his
colleagues. This was the first sign of an internal rupture in the court
of the Phamo Drupa, which had been refreshingly free from political
murders up to that point. Tsongkhapa, the head lama of the Ge-lug-
pa sect, was troubled by this event as an indication of the instability
of the ruling family and its administration; however, the lama-
chieftain of Taklung used his own wealth to satisfy the discontented
instigators of the trouble.

When the Ming court, following the custom of the earlier Mongol
court, sent to Tibet for a new spiritual teacher, no ruling lama of any
standing would accept the invitation. Deshen Shekpa, the fourth incarnation of the Karmapa Lama, went to China in 1407. The following is a summary of his visit there as recorded by the historian,
Tsuglag Trengwa:

> On the 21st day of the first month of the Fire-Hog year, we
> arrived at the outskirts of Nanking, the capital of the Ming.
> Officials and noblemen on horses welcomed us and placed
> Karmapa on an elephant. At the city gate of Nanking, the Em-
> peror himself received Karmapa. Gifts were exchanged. Karmapa
> presented a gold model of a wheel and a scarf to the Emperor,
> and received, in turn, a conch shell and a scarf. After the
> Emperor had returned to his palace, Karmapa was escorted to the
> guest house.
>
> The next day, we were given the same royal escort and taken
> to the palace for an audience with the Emperor. The Chinese
> monks and officials burned incense, blew on conch shells, and

5. 'JUG-NGOGS.

sprinkled flowers on the road. Some three thousand of the highest officials, wearing exquisite garments and standing in respectful silence, lined the road from the gate to the three palace doors.

The Emperor himself stood at the center door and accompanied Karmapa through it, while the officials entered through the two side doors. Fifty soldiers in armor lined each wall of the audience hall, and another forty stood around the Emperor and Karmapa, who occupied two thrones in the center of the hall. Chinese officials lined the walls, and the attendants of Karmapa were seated on cushions to the right of the guest of honor. Food and drink were served, and dancers performed before the gathering, while the Emperor and Karmapa engaged in conversation through an official interpreter. Afterwards, they left the hall by the main door, and we were escorted back to the guest house.

Other entries, cited by Tsuglag Trengwa, give details of the public sermons delivered by Karmapa and also of the New Year's celebration. Karmapa was showered with gifts and given the title of "Precious Religious King, Great Loving one of the West, Mighty Buddha of Peace."

A number of lamas had been invited to China prior to Deshen Shekpa, and others followed him, but little is known of their visits because their secretaries did not keep detailed diaries as did Karmapa's. It can only be presumed, therefore, that they were equally well received.

The Chinese Emperor, Yung-lo (reigned 1403–24), hearing of the fame of Tsongkhapa, the founder of the Ge-lug-pa sect, invited him to visit China; Tsongkhapa, however, declined the invitation. When a second invitation came, he sent his disciple, Jamchen Choje Shakya Yeshe, to represent him at the Ming court. Jamchen became the Emperor's personal lama and received a title even more impressive than Deshen Shekpa's. It was: "All-knowing, Understanding and Benevolent Peacemaker of the World, Great Loving One, Worshipped by All, Great Prince and Lama from the Happy Steadfast Kingdom of the West, Jamchen Choje, the Great Lama of the Emperor." After receiving numerous gifts, he returned to Tibet.[6]

6. During his visit to Peking, Jamchen Choje founded the monastery of Huang-ssu (Yellow Temple) in China (Sarat Chandra Das, "The Monasteries of Tibet," *JASB*, New Series, 1, April 1905, 112).

The relationship between Tibet and China at that time is clearly indicated by the special treatment and elegant titles bestowed on even
minor lamas, and the refusal of invitations by prominent ruling lamas,
who would send a disciple as a substitute. It seems obvious that the
Ming Emperors viewed Tibet as an independent "Kingdom of the
West."

In 1409, through the patronage of Drakpa Gyaltsen and his minister, Neu Namkha Zangpo, Tsongkhapa was able to institute the first
Monlam ("Prayer") festival in Lhasa. Essentially a religious service,
the Monlam was thereafter held annually, beginning on the first day
of the first month of the Tibetan New Year. For three weeks, the
monks prayed for the peace and prosperity of the world. Eminent
Buddhist philosophers would debate, be examined in public, and be
given honors. Teachers would deliver sermons to the people. It is said
that through all twenty-four hours of each day of the festival, the
voices of teachers could be heard everywhere. In time, the Monlam became the biggest festival in the year. Thousands of pilgrims and more
than 20,000 monks came from different parts of the country for the
festival, which was celebrated outside the Jokhang in Lhasa.

Also in the year 1409, Tsongkhapa founded the first Ge-lug-pa
monastery in central Tibet. Known as the Ganden monastery, it became the third largest in Tibet, housing as many as 3,300 monks. In
1416 Jamyang Choje (1379–1449), a disciple of Tsongkhapa, founded
the Drepung monastery, with the financial assistance of Neu Namkha
Zangpo. In time, Drepung became the largest monastery in Tibet,
housing 7,700 monks. Sera monastery, which became the second
largest, housing 5,500 monks was founded in 1419 by Jamchen Choje,
after his return from China.[7]

On the twenty-fifth day of the tenth month of the Earth-Hog
year (1419), Tsongkhapa died, and his death anniversary is commemorated throughout Tibet by lighting lamps in every house.

During the time of Drakpa Gyaltsen, there was no war or internal
strife in central Tibet.[8] Only twice did he have to send troops into the
region of Tsang; but the disturbances had subsided before their
arrival, and no fighting took place. Grateful for this period of peace
and prosperity, the people called Drakpa, "Gongma Chosgyal Chen-

7. PAD-DKAR; 'JAM-DBYANGS.
8. RDZOGS-LDAN; DPAG-BSAM.

po," meaning "The Great and Superior Religious King." He died at
Nedong in 1432 at the age of fifty-nine.[9] From this time on, the
Phamo Drupa rulers of central Tibet were addressed as Gongma,
meaning "Superior."

During the reign of Gongma Drakpa Gyaltsen, a minister named
Namkha Gyaltsen had been given the administration of the districts
of Rinpung and Sakya. He took the district name of Rinpung as his
family name, in the same way that the Phamo Drupa ruling family
were referred to as Nedong. Sangye Gyaltsen, a younger brother of
Gongma Drakpa, married the daughter of Namkha Gyaltsen of
Rinpung and two sons were born to them, Drakpa Jungne and Kunga
Legpa.

After the death of Gongma Drakpa, a number of his nephews laid
claim to the throne, each with supporters among the ministers. A conference was held to settle the issue, and one of the ministers, Rinpung
Norzang, suggested that they seek the advice of Chen-nga Sonam
Gyaltsen, who was living in retirement in the Thel monastery. The
lama, Chen-nga, was in sympathy with the Rinpung family and made
the observation that most of the claimants were married. He suggested
that the young, unmarried Drakpa Jungne, who was a nephew of
both Rinpung Norzang and the late Gongma Drakpa, be enthroned.

In accordance with the suggestion of Chen-nga, Drakpa Jungne
was appointed Gongma in 1433; but when Chen-nga died in the following year, other claimants began to make themselves heard. They
were banished to Yargyabpa and compensated with gifts of large
estates there. This year, 1434, became known as the one which marked
"The Collapse of the House of Phamo Drupa."

The ensuing one hundred years were marked by a constant struggle
for power between the provinces of Ü and Tsang, whose leaders ad-
hered respectively to the Ge-lug-pa and the Kar-ma-pa sects. The Kar-
ma-pa were subdivided into the Black and Red Hats. One of the
prominent Tibetan historians, Gos Lotsa Shunupal,[10] served at that
time as a private secretary to Gongma Drakpa Jungne, who, unlike his
predecessors, remained at Nedong instead of touring the provinces.

In 1435 the Rinpung family began to make their power and influence felt in the province of Tsang, when Dondup Dorje conquered

9. According to the *Ming Shih*, the year of Drakpa Gyaltsen's death was 1440 (TPS, 2, 694).

10. This is the author of DEB-SNGON. For an English translation of this Tibetan history,
see George N. Roerich, *The Blue Annals* (2 vols., Calcutta, 1949, 1953).

Shigatse and moved his capital from Rinpung to this new town. Viewing this as open opposition to the Phamo Drupa at Nedong, many of the leaders of Tsang began to ally themselves with the Rinpung family at Shigatse.

After a reign of twelve years, Gongma Drakpa Jungne, who had devoted most of his time to religious activities, passed away in the year 1444. His brother, Kunga Legpa, took over his duties, but did not actually come to the throne for three years, when a council of ministers finally decided he was the best choice. Rinpung Norzang and his deputy, Konchok Rinchen, looked after the civil administration.

Kunga Legpa made a tour of Tsang and was well received, except in the Rinpung capital, where he was treated with indifference, even through he was a nephew of Rinpung Norzang himself. This annoyed Gongma Kunga Legpa and he began to favor the deputy minister, Konchok Rinchen. This caused ill feelings between him and his Rinpung relatives.

The minister, Rinpung Norzang, died in 1466 and his youngest brother, Tsokye Dorje, became the next minister with the help of his powerful relatives. He tried to remain neutral in the dispute; but minor disturbances created by the Nedong group, caused him to support the Rinpung faction.

Donyo Dorje, the son of Rinpung Norzang, wanted to build a monastery in Lhasa on behalf of the Kar-ma-pa sect; but the Lhasa administrator, who supported the Ge-lug-pa sect, refused him permission.[11] The monastery was then built outside of Lhasa and Palkhang Chozay put in charge; but monks from the neighboring Ge-lug-pa monasteries descended on it one night and razed it. A Karmapa Lama, Chosdrak Gyatso, narrowly escaped being killed. He took refuge in Lhasa.

Donyo Dorje, who had become the leader of the Rinpung faction at Shigatse, led troops in a retaliation strike against the province of Ü in 1480 and captured several small districts under the jurisdiction of the Lhasa administrator. Then he marched onto Nedong, where he removed from office the deputy minister, Konchok Rinchen, who had been his father's rival.

In the Iron-Ox year (1481) an attack by Donyo Dorje against the Lhasa area itself was unsuccessful. In the same year, all the ministers

11. The accounts given of the Rinpung and Tsangpa hegemonies are based on DGA'-STON, RDZOGS-LDAN, and NYIN-BYED.

converged on Nedong to discuss the dispute that had arisen between the Gongma's supporters and the Rinpung family. As a result of the discussion, Gongma Kunga Legpa was dethroned and compensated with an estate; his more troublesome relatives were not allowed to remain at Nedong. Chen-nga Tsenyepa, a young cousin of the Gongma, was placed on the throne and, in a reversal of prior practice, was allowed to marry.

The most influential ministers were those from Rinpung and, as their power was predominant in both Ü and Tsang, the Phamo Drupa Gongma was a mere figurehead. In 1485, Rinpung forces attacked a district, Gyantse, whose administrators were Nedong ministers; but the latter found an ally in the Lhasa administrator, and the Rinpung were defeated.

Three years later, as a result of internal disputes within the ruling circle of Gyantse district, Rinpung troops again attacked and this time captured Gyantse. Then, in 1491, the young Gongma died and a council of ministers ruled at Nedong for a few months until Tsokye Dorje, Rinpung Norzang's youngest brother took over as regent.

In 1492 Donyo Dorje again invaded Ü, seizing three districts. Years later, in 1498, a prominent citizen of Lhasa, Depa Nangtse, along with his uncle and nephew, were executed on orders from the Lhasa administrator. Using that event as an excuse, Donyo Dorje attacked and captured Lhasa and dismissed the administrator from office. Rinpung forces took over the Lhasa region and remained there until 1517, when they were finally driven out. During that period, the monks of the Drepung and Sera monasteries were not permitted to attend the Monlam festival in Lhasa, because Donyo Dorje was a supporter of the Kar-ma-pa sect.

In the Earth-Sheep year (1499) a conference of Nedong ministers was held to appoint a new Gongma. The selection went to a twelve-year-old descendant, Ngawang Tashi Drakpa. When he had been on the throne five years, a daughter of the Rinpung family was presented to him as a bride. Gongma Tashi Drakpa had two sons, Drowai Gonpo and Drakpa Jungne, by his Rinpung wife. Then, he had several children with a second wife; this resulted in a certain amount of animosity between the two branches of his family. The senior queen and her two sons were sent to the large Gongkar estate; but being relatives of the Rinpung, they were not without their supporters. In time the Gongma resigned and went to his own estates, taking his second wife

and children with him. The throne was left vacant for the sons of his
first wife, and, since the elder son had already died, Drakpa Jungne
became the Gongma.

Officially, the people of the three regions of Tibet still addressed
the Nedong ruler as Gongma, but the Rinpung faction really held the
reins of the government. Most of Ü-Tsang was under their control;
elsewhere, the Gongma was little more than a figurehead. While the
Tibetan overlords were preoccupied with their own intrigues and
squabbles, Mongol tribes seized the opportunity to relocate themselves
in the Kokonor region of northeastern Tibet. Since the Mongols had a
reputation as being invincible fighters, some of the leaders of the Tibetan sects approached them for support.

In 1505 Tseten Dorje, a servant of Rinpung, was appointed Master
of the Stables at Shigatse. He then played a trick on the Rinpung. He
made a request for a permit to collect three hundred sewing needles
from the people of the surrounding areas. It was readily given; however, the written word for *needle* in Tibetan is very similar to that for
armor; so, Tseten Dorje had no difficulty in making a slight alter-
ation on the permit and thus collected three hundred suits of armor.
He gathered men around him and, with the support of the Kar-ma-
pa-sect, Tseten Dorje began to consolidate his own power at Shigatse
and gradually took control of the neighboring areas. He made over-
tures of friendship to Nedong and was appointed a minister. He then
contacted the Mongols living in the Kokonor region of Dranag
Khasum and obtained from the Chogthu tribe a promise of military
support.[12]

In 1512 the ex-Gongma, Tashi Drakpa, called a meeting of all the
ministers to discuss improvements in the maintenance of law and
order in the country. The purpose of the meeting was soon forgotten
in the disputes that arose between rival ministers who had come from
different regions and belonged to different sects. There was more quarreling and vituperation than constructive discussion. The ex-Gongma
could not control the meetings. Meanwhile, the common people were
enjoying an entertaining week, comparing the dress, trappings, and
bodyguards of the numerous ministers. They neither knew nor cared
about the so-called discussions that were taking place; they only knew
that they could benefit them little, for it was a time when the common people suffered much. The religious pressures increased to the

12. MTSHO-SNGON; THUGS-RJE.

point where Ge-lug-pa monks, when going about in small numbers, wore red hats, the Kar-ma-pa color. Once inside their monasteries, they turned their hats inside out and displayed the yellow color again.

In 1516 the Rinpung faction was challenged by the deposed deputy, Konchok Rinchen, who disputed its right to make all judicial decisions. He sent troops into Tsang; but the ex-Gongma intervened, and for three years there was an uneasy truce between Ü and Tsang. In 1517 the Rinpung forces in control of the Lhasa area had to withdraw, and once again the Monlam festival was celebrated by the Ge-lug-pa monks at Lhasa. For a long time, conflict between the religious sects was continued by the ministers, who championed their causes.

When Tseten Dorje died, his son Karma Tensung Wangpo succeeded him as the Depa Tsangpa at Shigatse. Depa Tsangpa was the title given to the ruler of the new power faction established at Shigatse when Tseten Dorje conquered that town in 1565. From an early age, Karma Tensung Wangpo was taught by his father how to use his hands in manual labor, as well as reading, writing, and religious studies. He grew up to be a bold politician and a learned member of the Kar-ma-pa sect, which he supported strongly. Karma Tensung Wangpo strengthened the relations his father had made with the Mongols and, in the next eleven years, took over four large territories in southern Tibet, together with considerable areas in western and northern Tibet.

During this period, the Ming court in China maintained little contact with Tibetan leaders. The Chinese had their hands full dealing with the Mongol tribes, which had penetrated into eastern Turkestan, the Kokonor region in northeastern Tibet, and even southern Russia.

6

The Emergence of the Dalai Lamas

In order to trace the origin of the Dalai Lamas and their emergence to power, it is necessary to go back to the 15th century. The lama, who became known posthumously as the first Dalai Lama, was named Gedun Truppa. He was born in 1391 at Shabtod in Tsang. He took his vows as a Getsul, the first stage of monkhood, before Truppa Sherab at Narthang monastery in 1405. He studied extensively in philosophy and the Buddhist religion. In 1415, he met Tsongkhapa, the founder of the Ge-lug-pa sect and became one of his most important disciples. The great monastery of Tashilhunpo at Shigatse was founded by Gedun Truppa in 1447, with financial help from Dargyas Pon Palzang. The monastery housed about three thousand monks and Gedun Truppa, now famous in Tibet as a Buddhist scholar, became its abbot and was called Panchen Gedun Truppa. He died at Tashilhunpo in 1474 at the age of eighty-four.[1]

In the following year, Gedun Gyatso was born at Tanag Segme in Tsang.[2] He was considered the incarnation of Gedun Truppa and became known posthumously as the second Dalai Lama. He took his first vows in 1486 and studied at Tashilhunpo and Drepung monasteries. His residence at Tashilhunpo was named Gyaltsen Thonpo. This was later to become residence of the Panchen Lama. At Drepung, he built a residence known as Ganden Phodrang. Later, when the fifth Dalai Lama became the temporal ruler of Tibet, the Tibetan Government was referred to as Ganden Phodrang.

In 1509 Gedun Gyatso founded the monastery of Chokhorgyal, which is located about 90 miles southeast of Lhasa. Nearby, there is a

---

1. The DMIGS-BU puts his age at death at eighty-two; but the 'PHRENG-WA and BCU-GNYIS both state that he died at eighty-four.

2. The events of the life of the second Dalai Lama, Dge-'dun rgya-mtsho given here were obtained from his autobiography which is untitled and incomplete.

lake whose reflections were reputed to prophesy future events. It is said that prophecies leading to the discovery of the thirteenth and fourteenth incarnations of the Dalai Lama were seen in the lake's reflections.

Religious conflicts were being fought at this time and, in 1537, while Gedun Gyatso was residing at Chokhorgyal monastery, the forces of the Drikhung monastery attacked those of the Olkha monastery. The latter's defeat led to the loss of eighteen Ge-lug-pa monasteries to Drikhung, which belonged to the Ka-gyu-pa sect.[3] Gedun Gyatso died in 1542 at the age of sixty-five, at the Drepung monastery.

A year later, Sonam Gyatso was born at Tohlung near Lhasa.[4] He was recognized as an incarnation of Gedun Gyatso, the late abbot of Drepung. Sonam Gyatso studied at Drepung monastery and took his final vows from Sonam Drakpa. He proved himself a brilliant scholar and teacher and, in due time, became the abbot of Drepung monastery. A popular person, he helped prevent violence from breaking out between power factions by his personal mediation.

In 1559 the Nedong Gongma invited Sonam Gyatso to visit Nedong. He became the personal teacher of the Gongma, who gave him a special seal used with red ink; a privilege reserved only for a person of great eminence. A year later, fighting broke out in Lhasa between the Ge-lug-pa and Ka-gyu-pa supporters and the efforts by local lamas at mediation were unsuccessful. They then sent for Sonam Gyatso, whose personal services brought the fighting to an end.

In the summer of 1562, the Kyichu river broke its stone dikes and flooded Lhasa, forcing the population to take to boats. Sonam Gyatso and his followers gave extensive relief to those who had suffered from the flood and also helped repair the dikes. He made it a practice that, on the last day of the Monlam festival, the monks would work on the wall which kept the Kyichu river within its banks, and this became a traditional custom.

When the Nedong Gongma, Drakpa Jungne, died in 1564, Sonam Gyatso was asked to say the customary prayers for him. Drakpa Jungne's son was then enthroned. He was followed by two obscure

3. DPAG-BSAM.

4. The account given here is based on the RDZOGS-LDAN and a biography of the third Dalai Lama, titled *Dngos-grub shing-rta,* written by the fifth Dalai Lama.

successors; after that, the power of the Phamo Drupa of Nedong ceased to exist.

Sonam Gyatso went to Tashilhunpo in 1569 to study the layout and administration of the monastery founded by his predecessor, Gedun Truppa. He was requested to remain there as the abbot; but he was already responsible for the monasteries of Sera and Drepung, so he declined the offer; however, he did leave a representative of his at Tashilhunpo.

Altan Kahn of the Tümät Mongols invited Sonam Gyatso to visit Mongolia; but the lama declined. A few years later, Altan Khan sent a large delegation with camels, horses, and provisions to Tibet, again asking Sonam Gyatso to visit him. This time the lama agreed. He left Drepung on the twenty-seventh day of the eleventh month of the Fire-Ox year (1577). He was escorted to the Dam region some ninety miles north of Lhasa by monks of the three great monasteries,[5] representatives of the Nedong Gongma, and various nobles, who gave him a great farewell there.

As the party was about to leave the Dam region, one of the nobles, Sakyong Tashi Rapten, grasped the stirrup of Sonam Gyatso's horse and recited a verse, wishing long life to him. This verse, addressed to the lama as "The Holder of the Faith," became popular and important because of that incident.

Soon after leaving Dam, the party was caught in a blinding snowstorm, which reduced visibility to a few feet. Buffeted by icy winds, they were soon lost on a plateau, which showed no sign of human habitation. Water and grass were scarce and had to be stored on the backs of the camels and used sparingly. Frequently, they were deceived by mirages. All in all, it was one hundred and seventy days before Sonam Gyatso and his party saw civilization again.

In the summer of 1578, the party finally arrived at a Mongolian settlement at the outpost of Chahar. They found the Mongols living in felt tents and keeping cattle, goats, sheep, and horses. These tent-dwellers lived as nomads, eating meat, butter, milk and cheese, and drinking fermented mare's milk (kumiss), the national beverage. A reception party from Altan Khan met Sonam Gyatso at Chahar, and after a few more days of travel, he was welcomed by Altan Khan him-

---

5. These three, known as the Densa-sum, are the monasteries of Sera, Drepung, and Ganden, founded in 1419, 1416, and 1409, respectively.

self, along with a thousand cavalrymen. Together they journeyed on to the Mongol's capital.[6] The Khan, like his subjects, lived in a tent, albeit a very sumptuous one.

Sonam Gyatso began a program of religious instruction for the Khan and his people and on one occasion preached in the open to the entire population. Altan Khan was converted to Buddhism. According to the *Dngos-grub shing-rta,* a biography of Sonam Gyatso, the Khan made the following proclamation sponsoring Buddhism:

> We, Mongols, are powerful because our ancestral race originally descended from the sky, and [Genghis Khan] extended its empire even to China and Tibet.
>
> The Buddhist religion first came to our country in earlier times, when we gave our patronage to Sakya Pandita. Later, we had an Emperor named Temür, during whose reign our people had no religion and our country degenerated; so that it seemed as though an ocean of blood had flooded the land.
>
> Your visit to us has now helped the Buddhist religion to revive. Our relationship of patron and lama can be likened to that of the sun and the moon. The ocean of blood has become an ocean of milk.
>
> The Tibetans, Chinese, and Mongols now living in this country should practice the Ten Principles of the Lord Buddha. Moreover, I am establishing, from this day forth, certain rules of behavior for the people of Mongolia.
>
> Previously, when a Mongol died, his wife, personal servant, horses and livestock were always sacrificed. In the future, this is forbidden! The horses and animals of the deceased may be given by mutual consent to the lamas and monks in the monasteries; and the family, in return, may request the lamas to pray for the deceased. In the future, it is not permitted to sacrifice animals, wives, or servants for the benefit of the deceased. Those responsible for human sacrifices will be executed under the law, or will have their property confiscated. If a horse or any other animal is sacrificed, ten times the number of animals killed will be confiscated.

6. The Tibetan name for the Mongol capital is Khar Ngonpo, meaning "Blue Fort." According to HOWORTH (pp. 423, 429), the chief city of the Tümät Mongols was Koko Khotan, meaning "Blue Town." It was in Khar Ngonpo (=Koko Khotan) that Altan Khan promised the Dalai Lama to raise a golden statue of the Lord Buddha.

Any person who injures a monk or a lama will be severely punished. The practice of blood sacrifice to the onkon [image] of the deceased is forbidden in the future and such statues already in existence must be burned or destroyed. If we hear that such statues are being kept secretly, we will destroy the houses of those who have concealed them.

The people may instead keep the image of Yeshe Gonpo, a Tibetan deity, in their homes and may offer him milk and butter, instead of blood.

Every person should benefit his neighbors and not steal from his fellow men.

In short, those laws already existing in Ü-Tsang [central Tibet] will also be practiced in this country.

In return for his teachings, Sonam Gyatso received a number of presents, together with the title, "Dalai Lama." "Dalai" is Mongolian for "ocean" and connotes that the Lama's learning was as deep and as broad as an ocean. He was also given a seal inscribed with the title: Dorje Chang ("Holder of the Thunderbolt"). Sonam Gyatso then gave Altan Khan the title of "Religious King, Brahma of the Gods" and prophesied that within eighty years the descendants of the Khan would become the rulers of all Mongolia and China.

The open site where the Dalai Lama had preached and where titles and presents were exchanged now acquired a certain sanctity. The Dalai Lama proposed establishing a monastery there, and Altan Khan agreed to finance the project. The monastery was named Thegchen Chonkhor. Many Mongol tribal leaders and even some Chinese notables, hearing of the Dalai Lama's spiritual powers, invited him to their own regions. He visited some of these, including Lan-chou on the Chinese border. The Chinese asked him to use his influence with the Khan to prevent the Chahar tribes from invading Chinese territory and the Dalai Lama succeeded in bringing about a lessening of the conflict.

Tibetan sources relate that the Dalai Lama also accepted an invitation from the governor of the Chinese province of Ning-hsia. There, he began to preach to large numbers of people coming from eastern Turkestan, Mongolia, and neighboring areas in China. At first, it was difficult for the people to follow him, as he spoke in Tibetan only; but the governor solved this problem by providing him with three interpreters. While at Ning-hsia, Sonam Gyatso received an envoy from the Chinese Emperor of the Ming court, who brought presents and an invitation to visit the Chinese capital; but Sonam Gyatso had to decline, as he had already agreed to visit the region of Kham in eastern Tibet.

In order to maintain the close relationship already established between the Dalai Lama and Altan Khan, it was decided to set up a diplomatic office at Tongkhor, also known as Lusar, where representatives of both the Lama and the Khan would remain to channel intercourse. Tongkhor was about halfway between Lhasa and the outpost of Chahar in Mongolia.

The Dalai Lama then left for the region of Kham, where he founded the monastery of Lithang in 1580.[7] Stationing a representative at Lithang, he then moved on to Chamdo, where he was made an honorary abbot of the monastery there. While staying at Chamdo, the Dalai Lama received the news of Altan Khan's death. His son and successor, Dhüring Khan,[8] invited the Dalai Lama to return, and, in 1582, the Lama left Chamdo for Mongolia. On the way, he passed through the Kokonor region, where he built the monastery of Kumbum on the exact site where Tsongkhapa, the founder of the Ge-lug-pa sect, had been born. (The present Dalai Lama was also born in that area.) In the course of his journey, the Lama became the guest of two Mongol tribal chiefs, Dayan Noyon and Junang Khan. In 1585 he finally reached his destination and remained with Dhüring Khan for more than two years. Their relationship resembled that which existed between the late Altan Khan and the Dalai Lama. At the start of his journey back to Tibet in 1588, the Dalai Lama fell ill and died on the way. His body was cremated and the ashes taken to Lhasa, where they were preserved at the Drepung monastery.

A few years later, the Dalai Lama's followers heard reports of a child that had been born in 1589 in Mongolia. The child, a son of a Chokhur tribal chief, was the great-grandson of Altan Khan and was said to be very different from other children. Tibetan monks went to investigate the reports and became convinced that the exceptional child was the reincarnation of Sonam Gyatso, the Dalai Lama. A large number of Nedong officials, representatives of the three great Ge-lug-

7. According to BEE-DUR, the monastery of Lithang founded by the Dalai Lama was named Thupten Jamchengon.

8. Also occurs as Sengye Dugureng Timur (HOWORTH, p. 425).

pa monasteries, and the personal treasurer of the late Dalai Lama then went to Mongolia to confirm the monks' conviction and, if possible, bring the child to Tibet. The parents, however, refused to part with the child until he was older; therefore, the boy was given his religious education and training in Mongolia by Tibetan teachers.

Since this child became the fourth Dalai Lama, named Yonten Gyatso,[9] a close spiritual relationship developed between Mongolia and Tibet, and the Ge-lug-pa sect emerged as the stronger group. The Sa-kya-pa sect, whose influence dated from the time of Sakya Pandita, began to wane.

In 1601, when Yonten Gyatso was twelve years old, the head lamas and monks of the monasteries in Tibet insisted that he should now be brought to Tibet, and they sent a party to escort him. On the way, Yonten Gyatso spent some time at Tongkhor, where the staff of the diplomatic outpost established by the previous Dalai Lama had been strengthened and its duties increased.

When Yonten Gyatso arrived at Lhasa, he was given official recognition at a ceremony arranged by the monastic officials and was enthroned as the fourth Dalai Lama. He was initiated into the monkhood by the ex-Ganden Tripa, Sengye Rinchen. While a student monk at Drepung monastery, he was visited by the humble, but scholarly, lama from Tashilhunpo, Lozang Chosgyan, under whom he continued his studies. Lozang Chosgyan was the first of the Panchen Lamas, having received the title, which means "Great Scholar," because of his learning. Since then, the reincarnations of Lozang Chosgyan have been known as the Panchen Lama.

About that time, the Red Hat subsect of the Kar-ma-pa submitted a poem to the Dalai Lama, which his attendants were unable to translate. Instead of replying in an equally obscure manner, they sent a very strongly worded letter to the Kar-ma-pa Red Hats. This caused some ill feeling, and the Red Hats began to spread a rumor that the attendants of the Dalai Lama were unable to understand poetry— considered a serious defect in educated persons.[10]

A little later, when a lama of the Kar-ma-pa Red Hats visited the Jokhang in Lhasa, he offered to the image of the Lord Buddha a scarf on which, according to custom, he had written his prayers in the form of a poem. When this scarf was shown later to the Dalai Lama's at-

9. NOR-BU; SPYOD-TSHUL.

10. DPAG-BSAM; DGA'-STON.

tendants at Drepung monastery, they misinterpreted the poem as an insult to the Dalai Lama. His Mongolian cavalrymen became angry and conducted a raid on the stables and houses of the Kar-ma-pa Red Hats. As a result, Karma Tensung Wangpo, the Tsang chieftain and Kar-ma-pa supporter, led a large body of troops to Lhasa in 1605 and expelled the Mongols who had escorted the Dalai Lama to Tibet. A struggle for political power ensued. The province of Ü was in the Ge-lug-pa camp, while Tsang province was under the influence of the Kar-ma-pa sect. For some time, Karma Tensung Wangpo maintained the upper hand, capturing several districts in Ü.

In 1606 the Dalai Lama visited the Choskhorgyal monastery and parts of southern Tibet. The Nedong Gongma gave him a fine reception. In the following year, he was invited to Tsang by the Ge-lug-pa monasteries, and the Panchen Lama, Lozang Chosgyan, came a great distance to receive him, while the monks of the Tashilhunpo monastery lined the streets of Shigatse to give him a grand welcome.[11]

Karma Tensung Wangpo, the chief of Tsang, who had his capital at Shigatse, gave no official welcome or offer of assistance to the Dalai Lama; but he did not place obstacles in the way of the Tashilhunpo monastery, which requested the Dalai Lama to become its abbot. Since he was already the abbot of Drepung, the Lama accepted only an honorary abbotship. He then visited other Ge-lug-pa monasteries in Tsang before returning to Gongkar in Ü province.

The head lama of the Kar-ma-pa Red Hats was living near Gongkar, and correspondence was exchanged between the two lamas which might have led to a meeting. Such a meeting might have ended the rivalry between the Ge-lug-pa and Kar-ma-pa sects; but the attendants of both the Dalai Lama and the Kar-ma-pa Lama did not want a truce, and the Dalai Lama's followers hurried him away to the Drepung monastery. People who came to have audiences with the Dalai Lama were searched for messages from the Kar-ma-pa Red Hats. Poems written at the time blame the attendants on both sides for preventing a meeting which might have led to a reconciliation between the leaders of the two sects.[12]

In 1611 Karma Tensung Wangpo died and was succeeded by his son, Karma Phuntsok Namgyal. At his accession, he controlled all of Tsang, Toh (western Tibet), and parts of Ü. The argument arose on the recognition of Kunkhen Pema Karpo's two acclaimed reincarnations:

11. SPYOD-TSHUL.
12. DGA'-STON.

namely, Trulku Pagsam Wangpo, born in Chhogyal, and Trulku Ngawang Namgyal, born in Gardrong. Depa Tsangpa supported Pagsam
Wangpo. Subsequently, Ngawang Namgyal could not stay in Tibet and
thus had to go to Bhutan. Because Ngawang Namgyal went to Bhutan,
Depa Tsangpa twice waged war against that country.[13] Nor is any reason
given for the visit of the Panchen Lama to Bhutan at that time; but it
is possible that he went there to bring an end to the fighting. After a
tour of the southern border, Karma Phuntsok Namgyal visited Lhasa
and sent his private secretary to the Dalai Lama asking for a religious
audience. The Dalai Lama's influential attendant, Sonam Drakpa, objected to such an audience on the grounds that the Depa Tsangpa of
Shigatse was an enemy of the Ge-lug-pa sect; therefore, Phuntsok
Namgyal received a polite note saying that the Dalai Lama was deep
in meditation and could not be disturbed. The Tsang chief was deeply
offended. The sympathies of the general public were with him, for it
was thought that the Depa Tsangpa might have been won over peacefully if he had been given an audience. Phuntsok Namgyal returned
to Shigatse in disappointment.

In 1615 the Shen-tsung Emperor sent an envoy from the Ming
court to invite the Dalai Lama to China for the purpose of blessing the
Buddhist temple in Nanking. Because of his responsibilities at the
Drepung and Sera monasteries, the Dalai Lama had to decline the invitation; however, he agreed to bless the temple from his monastery in
Tibet, which he did by praying with his face towards China and scat-
tering barley grain into the wind.

In 1616 the Dalai Lama was apparently suffering from rheumatism,
for he made visits to some hot springs for medicinal treatments. In
January of 1617 he died at Drepung monastery, aged twenty-eight.
His body was cremated and his ashes shared between the Drepung
monastery, his Mongolian father, and one of his patrons, a Tümät
Teji, in Mongolia.

During this period, there was considerable intercourse between the
Tibetans and the Mongols, and even the exchange of titles between
Altan Khan and the Dalai Lama. Mongolia was an independent country at that time and remained so until the time of the Manchus. On
the other hand, Tibet had little contact with China during the Ming
Dynasty. The Ming Emperors showed little interest in Tibet, except
for those regions that bordered on China.

13. The accounts of the war are mentioned in Ngawang Namgyal's biography.

7

The Fifth Dalai Lama Assumes Power

The insulting treatment that had been accorded Karma Phuntsok Namgyal by the attendants of the fourth Dalai Lama led him to attack Lhasa in 1618. He met with resistance from the monks of Drepung and Sera, who were reinforced by their lay patrons. A number of people in Lhasa were killed, and the hill on which Drepung monastery stood was littered with the bodies of slaughtered monks. The situation became so desperate that the monks of Sera and Drepung had to seek temporary refuge at the Rating and Taklung monasteries in the north.

As a result of that victory of the Tsang forces, a number of small Ge-lug-pa monasteries in Ü were forcibly changed over to the Kar-ma-pa sect. Two Tsang military camps were established outside Lhasa; one cut off the Drepung and Sera monasteries from Lhasa, and the other blocked the main route out of the district. In that way, the two Ge-lug-pa strongholds were effectively blockaded. The Ge-lug-pa monks, who had returned to their monasteries, were severely restricted in their movements.

At the same time, Phuntsok Namgyal built his own Kar-ma-pa monastery at Shigatse at a place overlooking the Tashilhunpo monastery of the Ge-lug-pa. His monastery was known as Tashi Zilnon, meaning "The Suppressor of Tashilhunpo." The stones for this monastery were collected from the hill above Tashilhunpo, and the workers deliberately rolled boulders down on the Ge-lug-pa monks' quarters, killing a number of them. Tashilhunpo monks were harassed whenever they passed the Kar-ma-pa monastery on their way to Shigatse. This persecution continued for some time.[1]

The Mongol soldiers, who had been expelled from Lhasa by Karma Tensung Wangpo in 1605, returned to Tibet in 1619 in the guise of

1. RDZOGS-LDAN; DPAG-BSAM.

pilgrims. This raised the hopes of the Drepung and Sera monks, as the Mongols were supporters of the Ge-lug-pa sect; but the Mongols were not prepared for a major battle, and they merely camped some distance outside Lhasa. Because of their inactivity, the people began to say that the Mongols were "too many for a gang of bandits and too few for the army."

The late Dalai Lama's chief attendant, Sonam Rapten, who was also known as Sonam Chospel, had sent followers to all parts of Tibet in search of the reincarnation of the Dalai Lama. In 1619 he received information on a child that had been born on the twenty-third day of the ninth month of the Fire-Snake year (1617) at Chingwar Taktse of Chongyas. When he learned that the child showed signs of being exceptional, he went to Chongyas, taking certain articles belonging to the late Dalai Lama. It is said the child recognized these as if they were his own property. Wanting further confirmation, Sonom Rapten returned to Lhasa and then sent the Panchen and another lama to see the child. They were fully convinced that the child was the reincarnation of the Dalai Lama.

The fifth Dalai Lama was named Ngawang Lozang Gyatso.[2] Because of the unstable political situation in Tibet, the discovery and whereabouts of the infant Dalai Lama were kept a close secret. He was brought to Nankartse instead of being left at his birthplace or taken to Drepung.

For some time, the commander of the Mongol troops camped outside Lhasa had been in close touch with Mongol monks in the Drepung monastery, who kept him informed of all that went on in the vicinity. In 1620 the Mongol troops made a sudden attack on the two Tsang military camps. Taken by surprise, most of the Tsang soldiers were killed. Another Tsang army prepared to set out to fight the Mongols. Fearing that this would lead to widespread warfare, the Panchen Lama, the Ganden Tripa, and Taklung Shapdrung set out to mediate between the two rival armies. After negotiation, the Mongols agreed to leave; but on two conditions: the Tsang military camps were to be abolished, and the Ge-lug-pa monasteries, which had been forcibly converted to the Kar-ma-pa, were to be restored to their original sectarian status.[3]

2. Information on the life of the fifth Dalai Lama is based on GOS-BZANG, written by Sdesrid Sangs-rgyas rgya-mtsho.

3. SPYOD-TSHUL; MTSHO-SNGON.

After ruling in Tsang for eleven years, Phuntsok Namgyal died in 1621 and was succeeded by his sixteen-year-old son, Karma Tenkyong Wangpo. Two outstanding officials administered Tsang on behalf of the young chief. The death of Phuntsok Namgyal eased the military tension between Tsang and Ü temporarily, so the discovery and identity of the fifth Dalai Lama was revealed in 1622 and he was then brought to Drepung by the representatives of the three great Ge-lug-pa monasteries (Drepung, Sera, and Ganden).

Fearing for the safety of the young Dalai Lama, the Mongol monks and some staunch Ge-lug-pa supporters wanted to take him to Mongolia; but the personal attendants of the Dalai Lama were unwilling to let him go and they quietly took him to the district of E in southern Tibet. They kept him in hiding there for a year. When the situation had improved, he was brought to Drepung. In 1625 he was initiated into the monastic order by the Panchen Lama.

In 1627 two Portuguese Jesuit priests, Estevão Cacella and João Cabral, who had been in Bhutan, arrived at Shigatse, where they were received by Karma Tenkyong.[4] The purpose of their mission was to seek converts to Catholicism, but they met with no success. Although Karma Tenkyong was friendly to them, the Kar-ma-pa monks objected to them on religious grounds. Cacella and Cabral departed for Nepal not long afterwards. Cacella returned to Shigatse in 1630, but he was in poor health, and died one week after his arrival. Karma Tenkyong then sent for Cabral, who was staying in Nepal. Cabral arrived at Shigatse in 1631 but left again in the following year.

When Cabral departed, Karma Tenkyong ordered an escort for him and sent letters and presents for the Nepalese king, requesting him to help the Jesuit priest. Through the assistance of the Nepalese ruler, Cabral was able to pass through Nepal and arrive safely at Patna in India. He is believed to be the first European to have traveled through Nepal. Cacella and Cabral were among the earliest Europeans to set foot in central Tibet. The first missionary to reach Lhasa is said to have been Friar Odoric of Pordenone, who traveled to Lhasa from Cathay in 1328.[5] The Venetian merchant, Marco Polo passed within the frontier of Tibet; but never actually traveled into the country itself.

Meanwhile, the Ge-lug-pa sect was still faced with difficulties in

4. DESIDERI, pp. 19–26.
5. Sir Thomas H. Holdich, *Tibet, the Mysterious* (New York, 1906), p. 70.

central Tibet. Karma Tenkyong, who became known as the Desi Tsangpa ("Regent of Tsang"), did his best to prevent the yellow-hatted Ge-lug-pa from acquiring new converts among the Chogthu Mongols, who had settled around the Kokonor region. At the same time, he encouraged his ally, Donyo Dorje, who was the king of Beri in eastern Tibet and a supporter of the Bon religion, to persecute the monks of the Lithang monastery. Representatives of the three big Ge-lug-pa monasteries and their officials and patrons then decided to hold a meeting to find ways of preventing the extinction of their sect, which they likened to "a lamp flickering in a raging storm." It was decided to approach the Oirat, Dzungar, and Chahar tribes, who were new Mongol converts of the Ge-lug-pa sect.

Three representatives, including Sonam Chospel, were dispatched to Mongolia. They first approached the chieftains of the Oirat and Dzungar tribes, who, because of the close relationship between the Mongols and the Dalai Lama, decided to enter upon a religious war. The actual responsibility for leadership was taken by a twenty-eight-year-old bearded chief of the Qoshot Mongols, Gushri Khan. The plan called for Gushri Khan, with support from Baatur Khungteji of the Dzungars and Urluk of the Torgut Mongols, to march to the assistance of the Dalai Lama.[6] Gushri Khan decided that he would first visit Tibet in the guise of a pilgrim in order to study the situation firsthand. Sonam Chospel then returned to Lhasa with the news of promised support, and other messengers were sent to the west and east. It was arranged that they should all return to Mongolia in one year's time to report on the situation in Tibet.

Since the time of Tseten Dorje, who became the ruler of Tsang in 1565, the Tsangpa ruling family had maintained friendly relations with the Chogthu Mongols. Karma Tenkyong, the Desi Tsangpa, approached them for help, and in 1635 the Chogthu Chief sent his son, Arsalang,[7] with ten thousand troops into Tibet to wipe out the Ge-lug-pa sect. When Gushri Khan heard of this, he collected a small body of troops and intercepted the Chogthu army. A meeting was arranged with Arsalang. There is no record of what happened at that meeting, but as a result of it, Arsalang changed his plans. Having journeyed from Kokonor to the Nam Tso lake (Tengri Nor), a dis-

---

6. MTSHO-SNGON; GOS-BZANG; and HOWORTH, p. 517.

7. MTSHO-SNGON. Giuseppe Tucci gives the name as Arslān, the son of the Sog po of C'og t'u of the Halka (TPS, 1, 60).

tance of some seven hundred miles, Arsalang then stationed his troops near the lake and entered Ü with only his personal bodyguards. Since no one was certain on whose side Arsalang intended to fight, the Kar-ma-pa Lama and his disciples fled at his approach, and Arsalang entered Lhasa without opposition.

He sent a message to the Dalai Lama at Drepung, asking him to come to Lhasa. They met at the Ramoche temple in the New Year of 1635. It was assumed that Arsalang had no intention of showing any special respect to the Dalai Lama and everyone was surprised when he prostrated himself before the Dalai Lama. Arsalang then went to Drepung, where he received religious instruction from the Dalai Lama and gave his word not to do harm to the Ge-lug-pa sect.

Karma Tenkyong, learning that Arsalang had not carried out an attack against the Ge-lug-pa, sent a message to the Chogthu chief to inform him that his son had acted contrary to their plans. Meanwhile, he dispatched troops to Lhasa to expel the Chogthu Mongols. A skirmish took place, but before there could be any serious fighting, the Dalai Lama's representatives, the Ganden Tri Rimpoche and the Ka-gyu-pa Lama, came to mediate. They mentioned in their report that Arsalang was suffering at the time from an epileptic fit. When Arsalang's father received the message from Karma Tenkyong, he sent special emissaries to Tibet, who assassinated Arsalang and two of his followers.

Gushri Khan, shrewdly aware that Arsalang's death made it possible for the Chogthu army to wipe out the Ge-lug-pa faction, decided to attack the Chogthu in their own land immediately. Lacking sufficient troops of his own, he allied himself with the Mongol chieftain, Baatur Khungteji, and they attacked the Chogthu tribal camps in the Kokonor lake region in the spring of 1637. Sporadic fighting took place in the Kokonor gorge, and, after several days, a major battle was fought between two hills. That battle became famous as the Battle of Olango (Bloody-Hill). The Chogthu troops, who survived the fighting at close quarters, scattered and fled. They were pursued by Gushri Khan's younger brother, to whom they surrendered, when their retreat route was blocked by quagmire. The leader of the Chogthu could not be located at first, but after a search lasting several days, he was found hiding in a marmot-hole and was killed on the spot by Gushri Khan's brother.

When the Chogthu Mongols, who were camped near Nam Tso lake

in central Tibet, heard that their tribe had been almost wiped out in
the Kokonor region, they were placed in quandary: whether to march
back to Kokonor or to join forces with the ruler of Tsang. Perhaps
aware that the odds were against them in either case, they remained
where they were and settled down to a nomadic life in Tibet. Their
settlement grew up on the plain of Zamar and their descendants became known as the Sogde (Mongolian Community).

In 1638 Gushri Khan came to Tibet with other Mongolian pilgrims
and received religious instruction from the Dalai Lama. At a ceremony held in front of the image of the Lord Buddha in the Jokhang
temple in Lhasa, Gushri Khan was placed on a throne and given the
title and seal of Tenzin Choskyi Gyalpo (Religious-King and Holder
of the Buddhist Faith). The Dalai Lama also gave titles to Gushri
Khan's officers, and the Mongols in turn gave titles of their own to the
Dalai Lama's subordinates. That was the origin of a number of
Mongolian titles, such as Dzasa, Teji, Ta Lama, and Dayan, which
were used to address high-ranking Tibetan officials up until recent
times.

Gushri Khan then invited the Dalai Lama to visit his country. Unable to leave his duties, the Dalai Lama sent a permanent representative to Mongolia to maintain good relations with the Mongols. After
touring in Ü-Tsang, Gushri Khan left for his newly-acquired territory
in the Kokonor region, where his Qoshot tribe had decided to settle
down.

Meanwhile, Donyo Dorje, the pro-Bon chief of Beri,[8] sent a message to the Desi Tsangpa, Karma Tenkyong, through a traveling
merchant. This message fell into the hands of a Ge-lug-pa representative, who had been sent earlier to that region to study the political
situation. He passed the letter on to Gushri Khan, who found that it
contained the following scheme:

> It is a great disappointment that our allies, the Chogthu tribe,
> have been wiped out. However, next year, I shall raise an army in
> Kham and accompany it to Ü. At the same time, you must bring
> in your army from Tsang. Together we will completely eliminate
> the Ge-lug-pa sect, so that no trace of it will ever be found. The
> image of the Lord Buddha in the Tsukla-khang temple seems to
> have brought about all these wars and it should be thrown in the

8. Beri was also known as Denkhog Chokhorpon in Nangchen (Kham). This is
stated in Tsultrim Rinchen's recorded teachings.

river. We should allow freedom of worship to all religious sects, including the Bon; the only exception being the Ge-lug-pa.[9]

Gushri Khan reacted immediately. By 1639 he was ready to lead his troops into Kham, and he sent a message to the Dalai Lama to inform him of his plan to conquer the Beri chief first and then march against Tsang. The Dalai Lama discussed this matter with his chief attendant, Sonam Chospel, and the Dalai Lama is reported to have said:

> I am supposed to be a lama. My duty is to study religion, go into meditation, and to preach to others. That is the best course for me to follow while I am still young. It seems to me unnecessary to create any more disturbance in the country, as it would only lead to criticism of us by the people. Our relations with the Tsang faction are not as bad as they were last year. They are not persecuting the Ge-lug-pa now, and the harm they caused to Sera and Drepung monasteries was, in fact, the fault of the Ge-lug-pa for refusing to give the Tsang ruler an audience with the fourth Dalai Lama. I see no reason for competing with the Nedong Gongma, or the Ka-gyu-pa and Jo-nang-pa sects. As for us, the Ge-lug-pa, and the Ganden Phodrang, what we have already is more than sufficient. Too many people have suffered in the past and even been killed because of this kind of political activity. I feel that if we are unnecessarily active, we might find ourselves in the same predicament.[10]

Sonam Chospel, the chief attendant, disagreed with the Dalai Lama, insisting that the Ge-lug-pa sect had been unfairly persecuted by the Tsang ruler. In his opinion, the country had to be unified, if there was to be peace throughout Tibet, instead of the country being left in the hands of various chiefs and religious leaders. He maintained that the Ge-lug-pa had always needed a strong backer and since it had one in Gushri Khan, good use should be made of him.

As a result of their discussions, a joint communiqué was sent through a personal courier to Gushri Khan. It read: "It is requested that you destroy the Beri chief, who has been giving much trouble to the Buddhist religion in Kham." No mention was made of the different sects involved; it stated only the threat to Buddhism as a whole and made no reference at all to the ruling Tsangpa. It concluded with

9. MTSHO-SNGON.
10. GOS-BZANG.

the request that Gushri Khan return to his own country after he had accomplished his goal, as it was not the Dalai Lama's desire to have many people killed. The message ended by inviting Gushri Khan's two queens and other pilgrims to visit Ü.

The Dalai Lama later stated in his own writings that he wondered if the "tune of the flute had not been changed to the song of the arrow," because he knew that his chief attendant had engaged in a lengthy discussion with the courier before provisioning and sending him on his way to Gushri Khan.[11]

Gushri Khan took a number of troops from the Parik tribe of Amdo into his army and then marched into Kham. Although the smaller tribes at Beri were soon subdued, the fighting lasted almost one year. Donyo Dorje, the chief of Beri, was finally captured and put to death in the winter of 1640, and by the following year, Gushri Khan had brought all of Kham under his control. Buddhist monks, who had been imprisoned by the pro-Bon Beri chief, were released, and all regions to the west of Tachienlu, including Sa-dam in the south, were restored to Tibetan control.

The news of Gushri Khan's victory over the ruler of Beri reached Lhasa during the Monlam prayer festival of the New Year of 1641. It was assumed at first that Gushri Khan would then return to the Kokonor region; but reports gradually reached Lhasa that the Mongol troops were approaching Ü-Tsang. When the Dalai Lama expressed surprise at this, his chief attendant, Sonam Chospel, told him that he had instructed the courier to tell Gushri Khan that the Dalai Lama would have no objections if the Mongols were to wipe out the Tsangpa opposition after dealing with the opposition at Beri. Sonam Chospel further said that the Tsang ruler was hotheaded and of limited intelligence. Moreover, although the Dalai Lama had only sought to remain neutral, the Ge-lug-pa followers were saying that he had begun to lean towards the Tsangpa.

The Dalai Lama told his chief attendant that he had gone too far in his schemes; but that if they could persuade the Mongols to return to Kokonor instead of invading Tsang, it might yet be possible to avoid bloodshed. The Dalai Lama said, "If, on account of the commitments

11. This refers to a traditional practice in Tibet of giving an oral message to a courier in addition to the written one. The oral instructions usually explain the written message in more detail; but in situations demanding secrecy, the oral message may actually contravene the written one.

you have made, you find it difficult to go to Gushri Khan, then I shall see him myself and try to use my religious influence with him. If we can succeed in persuading him to leave, it will benefit us politically and vindicate our honor." [12]

The attendant refused to agree to the Dalai Lama's plan, saying that it was too late to avoid a showdown with the Tsangpa and that Gushri Khan could not be turned back at that late stage. While they were discussing the matter, a courier arrived from Gushri Khan, with a message informing them he was going to march against Tsang and suggesting that the Panchen Lama be removed from that area for his own safety.

As it would be difficult to escort the Panchen Lama away from Tashilhunpo monastery, which was located in the Tsangpa capital of Shigatse, a letter was sent to him inviting him to come to Lhasa. The letter said that Gushri Khan had returned to the Kokonor region; but two of his queens were on their way to Lhasa and the senior queen wished to see the Panchen Lama. Unfortunately, illness prevented her from traveling beyond Lhasa; therefore the Panchen Lama was asked to come to her.

Shortly after the Panchen Lama left Tashilhunpo, a courier, from the Ka-gyu-pa monastery of Taklung north of Lhasa, arrived at Shigatse with a message for Karma Tenkyong. The Taklung monks reported that Gushri Khan should have turned northward at Taklung, if he intended to return to the Kokonor region; but, in fact, the Khan had continued marching in the direction of Tsang. Alarmed, the Tsang ruler, Karma Tenkyong, sent troops to intercept the Panchen Lama, who was detained at Rinpung but later released.[13]

Sonam Chospel, the Dalai Lama's chief attendant, then assumed full responsibility for what was happening and immediately went north to meet Gushri Khan. A few days later, he dispatched a note to the Dalai Lama saying that he had met the Mongol Khan and had sent a

12. GOS-BZANG.

13. In his autobiography, SPYOD-TSHUL, the Panchen Lama, Lozang Chosgyan, says that as soon as he received the message from the Dalai Lama, he immediately set out for Lhasa. When he arrived at Rinpung, he received a message from Depa Tsangpa, informing him that it was not definite where Gushri Khan was heading; therefore, he should return to Tashilhunpo. Accordingly, the Panchen Lama started his return, when another message from Depa Tsangpa arrived. This one confirmed the fact that Gushri Khan and his forces were advancing on Shigatse, and it requested the Panchen Lama to go to the Khan and halt the advance of the Mongols. The Panchen Lama records that he tried to mediate with the Khan, but without success.

capable, high-ranking official, Tardongnas,[14] to guide him to Tsang. He concluded, saying that he was on his way back to Lhasa, escorting the two queens of Gushri Khan.

The Tsangpa ruler sent out troops from his standing army to guard the borders of his province. Picked troops were kept at Shigatse, where a stockade was erected around the fort and the Kar-ma-pa monastery. Gushri Khan's reputation as an invincible warrior was so great that he met little resistance from the smaller districts and overran thirteen of them with relative ease. He finally reached Shigatse and besieged the Tsangpa ruling faction.

Meanwhile, Sonam Chospel was busy taking over those districts in the province of Ü that paid allegiance to the Tsang province ruler. Where he could not achieve a direct takeover, he created conditions of tension and alert to prevent troops from being sent to the assistance of the besieged capital, Shigatse. Two spies, who had been sent to Tsang by Sonam Chospel, returned and reported that Shigatse was ringed by Mongol cavalry; but the accuracy of the Tsang archers prevented entry into the fort itself. The Mongols controlled the hills around Shigatse and were waiting for the fort to capitulate for lack of food supplies. Its capture could be precipitated only if the Tsang ruler himself should be killed or if there was an internal revolt.

Sonam Chospel, who had not expected the Tsangpa forces to put up such resistance, grew alarmed and admitted to the Dalai Lama that he had made an error in judgment. He suggested that the Dalai Lama should go to Tsang and mediate between the two opposing armies. The Dalai Lama rebuked him, saying,

> I have never spoken a harsh word to you, but today I am so disturbed that I have no alternative but to reproach you. Did I not tell you a number of times that it would be unwise to engage in a war with the Tsang ruler? He is not as insignificant as you think. How can I possibly attempt to mediate when it is already widely known that we sent an official to guide Gushri Khan to Tsang? Even if I did succeed in bringing about an end to the fighting, the Tsangpa forces would take their revenge as soon as Gushri Khan departs for his own country. I made up my mind that we would have to fight the Tsangpa ruler on the very day

14. The syllable *nas* occurring at the end of certain names means literally "from" and implies "the one from such-and-such a place." It is used in the honorific sense and will appear often in names in the following chapters.

Gushri Khan's messengers arrived, advising us to bring the Panchen Lama to safety. We now must go through with this war, which you have so carelessly begun. If Gushri Khan wins, well and good. If he loses, we shall have to leave Lhasa and find some other country to live in.[15]

After receiving this rebuff, Sonam Chospel intensified his own efforts to bring the fighting to a successful conclusion. He prepared to take over the Dongkar fort, a Tsangpa stronghold in Ü, and with the help of monks from Drepung and Sera he captured it in one day. Most of the Tsang-dominated districts in Ü then surrendered without opposition. Some of them even offered to provide troops for the Dalai Lama. However, a few districts in southeastern Ü continued to offer resistance.

Sonam Chospel, who had been keeping up the pretense of neutrality, then openly showed his hand. He marched into Tsang with a large body of troops and joined up with Gushri Khan's camp. He arranged to provide the Mongol army with food supplies, fodder for horses, and fresh weapons, while his own men were set to work constructing giant catapults. On one occasion, they almost succeeded in entering the fort, but were driven back by the rocks and arrows that descended on them from the high walls of the stockade.

The Tsang ruler finally sent word to the Panchen Lama and the Kar-ma-pa Lama, asking them to try to arrange a truce; [16] but, this was no longer possible as Ü had openly entered into the war. On the eighth day of the first month of the Water-Horse year (1642), after fierce fighting, both Shigatse and the Kar-ma-pa monastery, Tashi Zilnon, were finally captured. Karma Tenkyong Wangpo, the Tsang ruler, was taken captive along with his family and retainers. The victory was celebrated in Lhasa by the monks of Sera and Drepung, who hoisted prayer flags on rooftops and burned incense everywhere.

Karma Tenkyong and two of his important officials, Dronyer Bongong and Gangzukpa, were brought to Lhasa and imprisoned at Neu, a nearby fortress. The Dalai Lama was then invited to Tsang by Gushri Khan. He left Drepung on the eleventh day of the third month and when he was two days' journey from Shigatse, he was received with great ceremony by the Khan and Sonam Chospel, accom-

15. GOS-BZANG.
16. SPYOD-TSHUL.

panied by their cavalry. On arrival at Shigatse, they were received by six hundred Mongol cavalrymen and important officials from Toh, Ü, and Tsang, who had come to pay their respects. Monks lined the streets of Shigatse and the people performed folk dances. Passing through the crowd, the Dalai Lama went to Tashilhunpo monastery, where he took up temporary residence.

On the fifth day of the fourth month of the Water-Horse year, corresponding to 2186 years after the death of the Buddha or the Christian year 1642, the Dalai Lama was led in state to Shigatse and placed on a throne in the audience hall of the palace. On two thrones a little lower than his sat Gushri Khan and Sonam Chospel. The Khan then offered the Dalai Lama the *Mendel Tensum,* which is a symbolic offering, consisting of a gold image of the Buddha, a book of scriptures, and a small chorten (stupa) and representing the body, the speech, and the mind of the Buddha, respectively. The Mongol Khan then declared that he conferred on the Dalai Lama supreme authority over all Tibet from Tachienlu in the east up to the Ladakh border in the west. The responsibility for the political administration of Tibet would remain in the hands of Sonam Chospel, who was given the title of Desi. This title, equivalent to that of a prime minister, became the designation of the chief administrators, who served under the fifth and sixth Dalai Lamas. For the first time, the Dalai Lama had become the temporal and spiritual leader of Tibet. All political affairs were handled by the Desi, who referred such matters to the Dalai Lama only when they were of special importance.

On the fifteenth day of the fourth month, the Dalai Lama left Shigatse for Lhasa. He visited various districts on the way and arrived at Drepung a month later. There he made a proclamation declaring that Lhasa would be the capital of Tibet and that the government would be known as Ganden Phodrang, which was the name of his palace at Drepung. He promulgated laws of public conduct, appointed governors to different districts, and chose ministers to form a new government.

A few months later, a Kar-ma-pa supporter named Garpa Yapse planned a revolt against Ganden Phodrang. A general uprising took place. In most of the northwestern districts, it was suppressed by the local officials; but at Gyantse, the officers fled and the Tsangpa supporters took over the district. Troops from Lhasa soon recovered this territory, but in the southeastern region of Kongpo, a major revolt took place, and the monastery of Zingche was burned down by the rebels. Gushri Khan and Sonam Chospel marched to Kongpo and there inflicted tremendous casualities on the rebels, killing over seven thousand Kongpo troops and capturing many more. One of the captives possessed a charm box, which he wore around his neck. In it was found a letter containing all the Kar-ma-pa plans, including the names of those whom they proposed to imprison, execute, or replace. Gushri Khan was so incensed by the contents of that letter he immediately sent orders to the fortress of Neu for the execution of Karma Tenkyong Wangpo and his two officials, Dronyer Bongong and Gangzukpa. With the death of the Tsang ruler, the focal point of the Kar-ma-pa revolt disappeared and the uprising collapsed. This situation might be compared to the execution of Mary, Queen of Scots, which finally brought an end to the many plots against the throne of Queen Elizabeth.

In 1643 Desi Sonam Chospel toured the provinces of Toh (western Tibet) and Tsang, taking a census of the population. In the same year, the rulers of Nepal and Ladakh and various other Indian rulers sent envoys with presents to congratulate the Dalai Lama on his accession to temporal power. Sikkimese records, known as *Bras-ljongs Rgyalrabs*, state that Phuntsok Namgyal, the first ruler of Sikkim, had assistance guaranteed to him if ever it was needed by the fifth Dalai Lama. In the following year, the Ming Dynasty was overthrown, and the Manchus came to the throne of China.

During this period, Monpa monastries were having trouble with the Bhutanese. After Gushri Khan and Sonam Chospel had investigated the situation, they sent seven hundred Mongol and Tibetan troops into Bhutan to assist the Monpa forces. The troops were accustomed to fighting on the high mountains and plateaus of Tibet and had no experience with the dense forests and high temperatures of Bhutan. They marched too far south, lost their bearings, and were surrounded by the Bhutanese. Three prominent officers, Nangso Dondup, Drongtsenas, and Dujungnas, were captured. Their troops scattered and fled, most of them finding their way back to Tibet. This defeat shattered the myth of an invincible Mongol army and, in the future, Mongols were unwilling to fight in the humid southern regions.

In Lhasa, the Dalai Lama decided to build a palace in his newly designated capital city. On a hill stood the ruins of the palace, Tritse Marpo, built ca. A.D. 636 by Songtsen Gampo for his Nepalese queen. The Dalai Lama selected the same site as the location for his palace. The foundations were laid and the work begun on the twenty-fifth day of the third month of the Wood-Bird year (1645). That palace is known today as the Potala.

In 1646 Tibet and Bhutan entered into peaceful negotiations and drew up an agreement which fixed a status quo on the relations that had existed between the Bhutanese and the Monpa people before the fighting broke out. During the rule of the Tsangpa, the Bhutanese had submitted annual offerings of rice. Under the new agreement, the rice offerings were sent to Ganden Phodrang. The peace did not last long; fighting broke out again in the following year. The Tibetan troops came as far as Paro, via Phari, capturing a Bhutanese fort on the way. They camped a few miles out of Paro; but at night, Bhutanese troops took them by suprise and the Tibetans had to leave their tents and supplies behind in their hasty retreat to Phari. The Tibetan commander had to manage with a very common tent; his elaborate and costly one had been captured. That defeat went down as a disgraceful one in Tibetan history.[17]

In 1648 several Ka-gyu-pa monasteries were converted to the Gelug-pa sect and the monks had no choice but to submit to the forcible change.[18] In the same year, the Dalai Lama sent two officials, Lhakhangpa and Badro, to Tachienlu, Chakla, Gyarong, Bah, Lithang, Jun, Gyalthang, Mili, Dan, Gakhok, Lingtsang, Lhathok, and Nangchen, all in eastern Kham, to take a census of the population and to collect taxes from the landholders.[19] A portion of those taxes was used for the support and maintenance of monasteries in Tibet; the remainder was deposited in the treasury of Ganden Phodrang. Fifty-six books on the collection of revenue in these districts were written by the Dalai Lama and sent out from Lhasa.[20]

Between 1649 and 1651, the Shun-chih Emperor of China sent several envoys to the fifth Dalai Lama inviting him to Peking. The Dalai

17. CHOS-KYI-SPRIN. A few years ago, I met the Bhutanese royal family and had the opportunity to speak to them about this early war. I was told by Rani Chuni Dorji that the armor and weapons captured from the Tibetan army were still preserved in the fort near Paro.

18. BEE-DUR.

19. GOS-BZANG.

20. At the time of the Simla conference held in 1913–14, the Tibetan government produced some fifty-six volumes of census and taxation records to refute Chinese claims to these areas of eastern Tibet. The British Plenipotentiary, Henry McMahon, signed each one of the volumes in verification of its contents.

Lama finally accepted on the condition that he would not be asked to remain there long, giving as his reasons the heat and the smallpox epidemic then raging in China.

Before going to China, the Dalai Lama paid the traditional visit to the Chokhorgyal monastery, accompanied by Gushri Khan and the Desi, Sonam Chospel. Then, on the seventeenth day of the third month of the Water-Dragon year (1652), the Dalai Lama left for China, accompanied by thirteen officials representing the different government departments. His retinue and its composition was analogous to that of Phagpa, who had traveled to China nearly four hundred years earlier.

According to Tibetan tradition, the reason why the Manchu Emperor repeatedly extended invitations to the Dali Lama was the prophecy of the third Dalai Lama made in 1578 that the descendants of Altan Khan would become supreme rulers of Mongolia and China in eighty years time. Since Tibetans consider the Manchus to be closely related to the Mongols, the truth of the prophecy seemed to be confirmed.

In the Chinese tradition, however, the reason for the repeated invitations was the good relationship established by the third Dalai Lama with the Mongols. In addition, the fourth Dalai Lama was a Mongol, and this had brought the two peoples even closer together. By inviting the fifth Dalai Lama to China, the Manchu Emperor hoped to persuade him to use his religious influence with the Mongols to deter them from invading Chinese territory.

When the Dalai Lama was ready to depart, the Panchen Lama came from Tsang to the Dam region to see him off. The entire party remained there for six days, and then the Dalai Lama set out for the border. Gushri Khan and the Desi accompanied him for the distance of a day's journey. The Dalai Lama was well received and hospitably treated by Tibetan nomads and Mongol tribes along the way. At Dranag Khasum, near Kokonor lake, he was given a grand reception by the Tibetans. From Sining on, arrangements for his comfort were made by the Manchus.

In the eighth month, the Manchu Emperor recived a letter from the Dalai Lama, asking him to come and meet him at a place just outside the Chinese frontier. The question of whether to go to meet the Dalai Lama as requested in order to show religious respect for him and thereby gain the submission of the troublesome Khalka Mongols to

Manchu rule or not was debated by the Manchu and Chinese officials of the Court. The Manchus wanted the Emperor to go and welcome the Dalai Lama; but the Chinese officials advised the Manchu Emperor to send presents by some prince, without letting the Dalai Lama into China proper. A compromise was reached and it was decided that the Dalai Lama, with a small escort, should proceed into China and he would be met at a proper place by the Manchu Emperor.[21]

Various gifts and a welcome letter were delivered to the Dalai Lama by the Emperor's envoy and then while they were still en route, another envoy arrived with presents on the fifth day of the ninth month. This presentation took place at Ninghsia, where the Dalai Lama left his horse and took to a yellow palanquin sent by the Emperor. On the second day of the eleventh month and still en route, the Dalai Lama was met by a Chinese minister who informed him that the Manchu Emperor would be meeting him shortly. The Dalai Lama was asked to proceed ahead of the others, with only three hundred officials, leaving the rest of the party to proceed the next day. The Emperor's military commander then arrived with three thousand cavalry and informed the Dalai Lama that the Emperor himself would be arriving the following day. He then rehearsed the ceremonies that would take place at the coming meeting.

On the sixteenth day of the twelfth month, the party arrived at the walled city of Khothor. The Dalai Lama entered the city gate and proceeded through two lines of officials. As soon as the palace came in sight, the Dalai Lama's officials had to dismount from their horses, although the Dalai Lama remained in his palanquin. On entering the palace gate, he stepped out of the palanquin on to a carpet of yellow silk. Halfway to the main door, he was met by the Shun-chih Emperor, who just then emerged from his quarters to receive him. The Manchu Emperor clasped the Dalai Lama's hands and they exchanged greetings through an interpreter. They then went into the palace, where presents of Tibetan articles were ceremoniously exhibited before the Emperor by the officials of the Dalai Lama. After a long talk with his host, the Dalai Lama retired to the prepared guest house. Some accounts say that the Emperor was actually out on a hunting trip, when he ran into the Dalai Lama's party; however, the elaborate preparations made by the Emperor's envoys and officials support the Tibetan

21. There is a lengthy account of the Emperor's discussions and arrangements made concerning the reception of the fifth Dalai Lama given in ROCKHILL, pp. 14–16.

account that the Manchu Emperor had deliberately made a journey from Peking for the sole purpose of meeting the Dalai Lama.

On the seventeenth day of the twelfth month, the party arrived in Peking, where the Dalai Lama stayed at the Yellow Palace (in Chinese: Huang Ssu), especially built for him by the Emperor. High Manchu officials came daily to see him, and on the twenty-fifth day, two ministers visited him, bringing him articles necessary for the ceremony at the official Peking meeting with the Emperor. On the first day of the first month of the Water-Snake year (1653), all the officials in Peking came to pay their respects to the Dalai Lama, who gave them a magnificent reception since it was Tibetan New Year's.

On the eleventh day, the day of the ceremonial meeting, the city was gaily decorated. Streets were lined with people, and the scent of flowers and incense filled the air. The Dalai Lama, in his palanquin, was preceded by officials carrying the ceremonial articles. From the palace gates, he walked along on yellow carpeting and between two rows of officials. The Emperor, leading his guest into the audience hall, took his place on a throne in the center of a raised platform, while the Dalai Lama occupied a throne on his right. In front of each throne were tables bearing fifty gold and silver plates, each filled with Chinese sweets and delicacies.

The Manchu Emperor presented the Dalai Lama with a gold plate on which was inscribed the title Dalai Lama Dorje Chang (Superior of the Ocean, Holder of the Thunderbolt) in Manchu, Tibetan, and Chinese. The Dalai Lama, in turn, presented the Emperor with a gold plate and the title Namgyi Lha Jamyang Gongma Dakpo Chenpo (The Great Master, Superior One, God of the Sky, Bodhisattva). The presentations were followed by entertainment, and then the Dalai Lama returned to the Yellow Palace with the same pomp and ceremony that had accompanied his departure.[22]

22. There is considerable contemporary dispute as to the actual happenings and their implications of the Dalai Lama's reception by the Shun-chih Emperor. Referring to ROCK-HILL, Charles Bell states that the ceremony accorded the fifth Dalai Lama could only have been shown an independent sovereign (PORTRAIT, p. 352). Li agrees that Rockhill's statement that "at this period of China's relations with Tibet, the temporal power of the Lama, backed by the arms of Gushri Khan and the devotion of all Mongolia, was not a thing for the Emperor of China to question." However, Li asserts that during the Dalai Lama's audience with the Manchu Emperor he had to kneel before he was given a seat (LI, p. 37). There is no confirmation of this in Tibetan records, which say only that the Manchu Emperor and the Dalai Lama clasped hands. Hugh Richardson pointed out that,

The Manchu Emperor, as well as the Mongol chieftains present, requested the Dalai Lama to give them, in writing, detailed regulations for the proper organization of monasteries. Letters of instruction were issued to all monasteries, to which was affixed the seal of the Dalai Lama.

On the seventeenth day of the second month of the same year, the Manchu Emperor gave the Dalai Lama a farewell banquet, at which he presented his guest with a number of articles made in China. Two days later, the Dalai Lama left Peking with the same splendid ceremony as had been shown him on his arrival. More presents were sent to him, along with the title, "Preceptor of the Lord Buddha's Doctrine, Keeper of Peace in the West, Uniter of the Buddhist Faith beneath the Sky, Superior of the Ocean, Holder of the Thunderbolt."

On arriving at Khar Ngonpo (Koko Khotan) near the Tibetan border, the Dalai Lama sent half of his party ahead to Sining, and ordered them to wait there for him while he toured the monasteries and towns in the Amdo region. Later rejoining his Sining group, he continued his journey. When he was six days away from Lhasa, he was met by Gushri Khan, the Desi, and other important officials of the Tibetan government. The Panchen Lama was now too old to travel, so he sent his representative instead. On the twenty-fourth day of the tenth month of the same year (1653), the Dalai Lama reached Lhasa.

In answer to a request to visit the monastery of Tashilhunpo and the districts of Tsang and Toh, the Dalai Lama began a tour on the sixteenth day of the sixth month of the Wood-Horse year (1654). The Panchen Lama had made preparations to go as far as Rinpung to receive the Dalai Lama; but the latter, realizing that the Panchen, now eighty-three years old, was too old for any travel, wrote suggesting that he send a representative instead. The Panchen Lama agreed; but still made a one-day journey from Tashilhunpo to meet him.

After concluding this tour, the Dalai Lama returned to the Drepung monastery near Lhasa. On the seventh day of the twelfth month of the same year, Gushri Khan died in Lhasa at the age of seventy-

---

as the last British Mission head in Lhasa, he has personal knowledge of unfounded Chinese claims in regard to the ceremony and enthronement of the present Dalai Lama. He goes on to state, "It is probable that his reception of the Dalai Lama was so sincerely effusive that his Chinese court annalists, with an eye to their rigid and artificial conventions, were compelled to add some favourable embroidery to the facts" concerning the Shun-chih Emperor's reception of the fifth Dalai Lama (RICHARDSON, p. 45).

three. After his death in 1655, his two sons, Tashi Batur and Dayan
Khan, ruled jointly; but, in 1660, they divided the realm of Qoshot
power between them, Tashi Batur taking the Kokonor region and
Dayan Khan remaining in central Tibet. The latter's name was Tenzin
Dorje; but after receiving from the Dalai Lama the title of Dayan
Khan, he was known as Tenzin Dayan Khan.

In the year 1656, a Bengali ruler, named Shah Shoojah, sent an envoy to the Dalai Lama with a present of Indian cloth. The Dalai
Lama, in return, sent him a gift of precious stones. In the same year,
Desi Sonam Chospel died; but the news of his death was concealed for
over a year because of the unstable conditions in the country. Until
the new Desi was appointed, the Dalai Lama carried out the duties of
the administrator himself. He had been greatly impressed and moved
by Sonam Chospel's lifework and declared that the Desi had built up a
solid relationship with the Mongols in the same way that "a master
weaver interweaves the threads of a carpet."

In the following year, a Bhutanese chieftan, Chosje Namkha
Rinchen, who had close contacts with Tibet, was killed, along with
twenty members of his family, by his enemies. As a result, Tibetan
troops were once again sent into Bhutan, and although no details are
available, this campaign apparently achieved more success than earlier
ones.

In 1659 the Dalai Lama sent a representative to Mongolia to ask the
various Mongol chiefs to remain united instead of constantly feuding
with each other. As a symbol of their willingness to obey him, Mongol
chiefs in Mongolia and Tibet as well gave him their oaths, marked
with their personal seals: an indication of the extent of the Dalai
Lama's spiritual influence.

On the thirteenth day of the seventh month of the Iron-Mouse year
(1660), Trinley Gyatso was appointed Desi. In the following year,
there was trouble on the Tibetan-Nepalese border, which resulted in
Tibetan troops, under the command of Tashi Tsepa, Gyangdrongpa,
and Mechagpa, being dispatched to drive the Nepalese insurgents
back. This was the first instance of conflict with Nepal, and it was not
to be the last.

In Sikkim, Tensung Namgyal, the son of Phuntsok Namgyal, became the country's ruler and visited Lhasa to pay his respects to the
Dalai Lama and the Desi. Tensung Namgyal asked the Desi's advice
on the introduction in Sikkim of the system of punishments for the

sixteen different offenses, which had been first instituted in Tibet in Changchub Gyaltsen's time.

The Shun-chih Emperor died and was succeeded by his son, the K'ang-hsi Emperor, in the year 1662. In the same year, the Panchen Lama, Lozang Chosgyan, died at the age of ninety-one. Three years later, an urgent request reached the Dalai Lama from the new Manchu Emperor, urging him to send a representative to the Kokonor region to placate the Mongols there, who were constantly harassing Chinese border towns. A representative was dispatched with the Dalai Lama's request, which the Mongols obeyed, and the situation quieted down. An agreement was reached by which the Mongols would cease raiding Chinese territory and, at the same time, trade between China and Mongolia would be resumed.

In 1665 a petition from the Tashilhunpo monastery reached the Dalai Lama, informing him that a three-year-old boy, who seemed to be the reincarnation of the Panchen Lama, had been found at Thopgyal in Tsang. He was requested to recognize the boy as the new Panchen, which he did, and the boy was given the name of Lozang Yeshe. He was designated as the second Panchen Lama and then taken to Tashilhunpo.

The second Desi, Trinley Gyatso, and Tenzin Dayan Khan both died within a month of each other in 1668. Lozang Thuthop was appointed the third Desi, and Tenzin Dayan Khan was succeeded by his younger brother, Konchog Dalai Khan. These two sent troops into Bhutan as a result of a Bhutanese attack on the Achok tribe of the Monpa. Owing to the friendly relations established by the first Panchen Lama during his visit to Bhutan in 1612, a party of Tashilhunpo monks and Kyishod Teji opened negotiations with the Bhutanese, and the former agreement of 1615 was revived. The Dalai Lama was then asked to intervene in a dispute between the related Oirat-Dzungar and the Khalkha tribes in Mongolia. He sent a representative, who was able to settle their dispute.

The young Panchen Lama was now old enough to take his Getsul ordination from the Dalai Lama and he was brought to Lhasa for this purpose. Lengthy discussions took place among the Dalai Lama's officials as to the relative height of the respective thrones. It was finally decided that the Panchen Lama would occupy a throne at the same height as those accorded the Gampo Trulka and the Drukpa Trulku, two prominent lamas.

The Tibetan people were then in the habit of wearing a variety of costumes, some of Mongolian and some of Chinese design. The Dalai Lama decided that there should be a national dress, especially for his officials, who should wear uniforms according to their rank. During the reign of the Nedong and Rinpung hegemons, it had been a custom during the Tibetan New Year for all officials to put on the costumes of the early kings. The custom, referred to as Rinchen Gyancha (Great precious ornamentation), had died out in the time of the Tsangpa rulers; but it was now revived, and the Desi summoned all the oldest officials and monks to help in the selection of these traditional costumes. A system of seating by status and seniority, known as Danyig A-khu Badro, was also devised. The higher the status, the higher the seating, and all of the Mongol chiefs, lamas and monks, noblemen and officials, found themselves alloted fixed places under this system. These regulations were first put into writing and then into practice beginning with the Tibetan New Year of 1672.

At Gyalthang in eastern Kham, the inhabitants had been provoked by the Chinese into disobeying the officials sent from Lhasa; consequently, troops under the Tibetan officers, Kagyad Norbu and Mechakpa, and the Mongol commander, Thula Baaturteji, were sent to Gyalthang to deal with the situation. They succeeded in bringing about law and order. Reporting back to Lhasa, they recommended the execution of twenty ringleaders, but the Dalai Lama decided instead to imprison them for life.

A little later, the Manchu Emperor sent three officials with a message to the Dalai Lama, asking him for the loan of Tibetan and Mongol troops. There was danger of an internal revolt in China, which was being engineered by a dissident minister, and the K'ang-hsi Emperor did not hesitate to approach the Dalai Lama for assistance.[23] The Dalai Lama replied,

> There has always existed a relationship of religious patronage between the Manchu Emperor and the Dalai Lama. Your father, the Shun-chih Emperor, was particularly kind and gracious to me when I visited China, and I have always prayed for the peace and prosperity of your country. However, I do not think

23. The dissident minister is called Pice Chiang Wang in Tibetan records. Rockhill states that Wu San-kuei, Prince of Yunnan, rebelled in 1674 against the K'ang-hsi Emperor and sought friendship with the Tibetans and Mongols (ROCKHILL, p. 19). It appears that Wu San-kuei and Pice Chiang Wang are one and the same.

Tibetan soldiers would be very effective in China as they are not accustomed to fighting in your climate. The Mongols are excellent fighters; but they are difficult to control and you might find them more of a liability than an asset. Both the Mongols and the Tibetans are unaccustomed to the heat and might easily succumb to the smallpox now raging in China. Therefore, I do not think they would be of much assistance to you and feel it would be unwise to send them to China.[24]

The Dalai Lama sent two of his own officials, Khangsar Rapten and Bumthang Sodwang, to China with the returning Peking envoys, for the purpose of gathering firsthand information on actual conditions in China. No sooner had the party left for Peking than three other Chinese officials arrived, this time from the dissident minister. Tibetan officials requested the Dalai Lama not to give an audience or show hospitality to the minister's officials; however, the Dalai Lama told them he would treat all foreigners alike and ordered them to give the new visitors the same reception as that accorded the other foreigners. The Dalai Lama then gave the Chinese minister's representatives the same reply that he had already sent to the Manchu Emperor. He added that he took an impartial view of the affair and would pray for a peaceful solution to the dispute between the minister and the Emperor. Because of the internal strife in China, the Dalai Lama considered it of great importance that the Mongol tribes should remain united. A Mongol, Dalai Khungteji, who had retired to Tibet to devote himself to religion, was now asked by the Dalai Lama to visit Mongolia in order to bring about the reaffirmation of unity. The Dalai Lama sent him with a letter to all the Mongol Chiefs, informing them of the purpose of Dalai Khungteji's visit and asking them to give full cooperation to him as the personal representative of the Dalai Lama.

In 1675 the new Desi, Lozang Thuthop, had to resign. The Ge-lug-pa sect enforces the vow of celibacy on its monks; yet, Lozang Thuthop, who was a monk, had been keeping a mistress for some time. She was a descendant of the Nedong family. When the Dalai Lama learned of this, he instructed the Desi to send his mistress away. The Desi could not bring himself to do so and, therefore, resigned his position. He retired, along with his mistress, to an estate at Zangri.

Sangye Gyatso, a nephew of the second Desi, was asked by the Dalai

24. GOS-BZANG.

Lama to become the Desi; but Sangye Gyatso declined the honor on the grounds that he was too young. Lozang Jinpa was then appointed Desi and served until 1679.

Meanwhile, the time limit of the agreement between the Bhutanese and the Monpa had now been reached and the Monpa spread the rumor that the Bhutanese were planning to attack them. A Tibetan army immediately marched into Bhutan, where the small district headquarters called Tendong Dzong was put to the torch. Negotiations again took place, but no agreement was reached. Trade between Tibet and Bhutan came to a halt and the border between Phari and Tsona was closed. In 1676 the Bhutanese attacked Sikkim and captured three hundred homesteads in the Chumbi valley. Again Tibetan troops marched against Bhutan and the Bhutanese withdrew from Sikkim, giving up the Chumbi valley.

The Dalai Lama, realizing the importance of the towns near the Kham border with China, sent representatives to Gyarong, Golog, Tachienlu, Gyalthang, Chating, and Jun, with instructions to reduce heavy taxation, mediate local feuds, establish new monasteries, and to resettle areas that had been abandoned by the people. Similar steps were taken in central Tibet. Such measures indicate that the Dalai Lama was a great leader both spiritually and politically.

Lozang Jinpa resigned in 1679 and was succeeded as Desi by the twenty-seven-year-old Sangye Gyatso. In the same year, fourteen religious students arrived in Lhasa from Mathura, Varanasi, and Kuru.

The Ladakhi ruler had been harassing Ge-lug-pa monasteries in his region for some time and even sent troops against some western Tibetan districts. Finally, the Dalai Lama appointed Ganden Tsewang, a son of Dalai Khungteji, as a military commander and sent him, together with Mongol and Tibetan troops, against Ladakh. Some fighting took place at Purang, but the Ladakhi troops had entrenched themselves in forts, making it difficult to be captured. Ganden Tsewang decided to bypass the forts and march directly into Ladakh.

Deleg Namgyal, the ruler of Ladakh, took refuge in the fortress of Basgo, then the capital city. The Tibetan-Mongol army laid seige to Basgo. Finally, Deleg Namgyal appealed to the Mogul ruler of Kashmir for aid. Because of the possibility of a long, drawn-out campaign, a meeting to negotiate peace was called. Mipham Namgyal, the great incarnate lama of Bhutan, came to mediate between the Ladakhi ruler and the Tibetan military commander. Deleg Namgyal agreed to give up to Tibet the regions of Guge, Purang, and Rudok and to send trien-nial presents (Lochak) to Lhasa. This treaty of 1684 established the border between Tibet and Ladakh and remained in effect for years to come. One hundred Mongol troops were stationed in the west, and Ganden Tsewang returned to Lhasa to offer the benefits of the treaty as a present to Ganden Phodrang (the Tibetan government).[25]

On the twenty-fifth day of the second month of the Water-Dog year (1682), the fifth Dalai Lama died in the Potala at the age of sixty-eight. From childhood, the fifth Dalai Lama Lozang Gyatso, had been quiet and serious, and, as it became evident later on, a coura-geous and determined person. A man of few words, whatever he said carried conviction. Although a Ge-lug-pa himself, he retained the services of several prominent lamas from other sects, which led to a certain amount of criticism. The Dalai Lama ignored it on the grounds that he preferred to be familiar with the beliefs and teachings of the rival sects than to remain ignorant of their teachings. He was said to be a good Sanskrit scholar, and he wrote many books, includ-ing one on the composition of poetry. He established two academies, one for monk officials and one for lay officials. Mongolian, Sanskrit, astrology, poetry, archery, and horsemanship were taught in addition to the usual religious and administrative subjects.

Politically, the fifth Dalai Lama was very successful in unifying the country. Previously, there had been constant struggle for power be-tween different religious sects, ruling families, and powerful chiefs. The Dalai Lama succeeded in winning the allegiance of the chieftains within Tibet as well as those on the border. Taxation was just and no exemptions were made. Although he was sympathetic in dealing with his subjects, he could be ruthless in stamping out rebellion. In his *Bslab-bya mu-thi-la'i 'phreng-ba,* a book on temporal and spiritual matters, he remarked that no pity should be wasted on a man who had to be executed for his crimes. Through his religious authority, he made his influence felt in the political affairs of Mongolia and other neigh-boring countries, and even among the Buddhist and Tibetan-speaking peoples of China. It is thus understandable why the Tibetan people still refer to him as the Great Fifth.

Some Chinese records state that Gushri Khan was a subordinate of the Chinese, and since he was instrumental in bringing the Dalai Lama

---

25. This account of the Tibet-Ladakh conflict is based on the MI-DBANG and LA-DAGS; also on CHRONICLES, pp. 156–60.

to power in 1642, it would follow that the Dalai Lama was also a subordinate of the Chinese. It has already been shown that the Chahar, Dzungar, Qoshot, and other Mongol tribes were independent of the declining Ming court at that time. There is no question that Gushri Khan helped put the Dalai Lama in power; but he seldom interfered in Tibetan affairs, once he had consolidated the authority of the Dalai Lama. Moreover, religious zeal, supplemented by the respect and faith Gushri had in the Dalai Lama, cannot be ignored as a prime motivation for the Khan's actions. The Khan spent his winters in Lhasa and his summers in the Dam pasturage, sending his Mongol troops to the Dalai Lama or the Desi whenever they were needed. Although he and his successors were known as kings, they occupied a lower position than the Dalai Lama and the Desi in all formal seating arrangements. Gushri Khan, as the independent leader of the Qoshot Mongols, established the temporal rule of the Dalai Lama; but he neither interfered in the administration nor tried to control its policies. All power and authority ultimately lay in the hands of the fifth Dalai Lama, right up to the time of his death.

8

Rival Powers in Tibet

Sangye Gyatso had become Desi just a little over three years before the fifth Dalai Lama's death. As a young boy, he had been trained and educated by his uncle, the Desi, Trinley Gyatso, and when he grew older, he became one of the Dalai Lama's attendants, receiving a thorough grounding in political and religious matters. He became a well-known scholar and, in later years, was the author of works on religious history, medicine, and astrology. The Dalai Lama, who expected great things from Sangye Gyatso, made him the Desi at the early age of twenty-seven, giving him an even higher status than the previous Desi. Sangye Gyatso had the ability to carry out his duties in just the way the Dalai Lama wished.

Some scholars have made the statement that Sangye Gyatso was believed to have been the natural son of the fifth Dalai Lama.[1] It is true that such rumors existed; but there is nothing in Tibetan records to corroborate the story. The fact that the Dalai Lama himself made the previous Desi resign for breaking his vow of celibacy would make it seem unlikely that he himself would have done the same thing. Perhaps the very young age at which Sangye Gyatso was made Desi caused a certain amount of conjecture and it was then said in levity that he was the Dalai Lama's "son."

Although some scholars maintain that the death of the Dalai Lama was known to many people in Tibet,[2] Tibetan sources claim that the death was concealed by Sangye Gyatso for a period of fifteen years,[3]

1. PETECH, p. 9; Hoffmann, *Religions of Tibet*, p. 175.

2. PETECH, p. 9.

3. The second Panchen Lama, Blo-bzang ye-shes, wrote in his autobiography, PAN-CHEN, that on the fourth day of the sixth month of the Fire-Ox year (1697), he received a letter from the Desi, saying, "Up till now, I have concealed the death of the Dalai Lama. His reincarnation has been brought to Nankartse, and I request you to proceed there and per-

a fact stated clearly as well by Sangye Gyatso himself in his book, the *Bai-durya ser-po*. Only the Dalai Lama's personal attendants, a monk of the Namgyal Dratsang monastery, and the Desi knew of the Dalai Lama's death. Officials and subjects alike accepted without question the Desi's announcement that the Dalai Lama had gone into meditation for an indefinite period and could not be disturbed. Anyone wishing to see the Dalai Lama on a matter of extreme urgency could only do so alone and in the privacy of the Dalai Lama's room. Meals were taken into the room as usual and everything was done to make it appear that he was alive and well.

Officials standing outside the room could hear the continuous sound of the hand-drum and bell used in rituals and signifying that the Dalai Lama was deep in meditation. On public occasions, his ceremonial gown was placed on his throne in the audience hall, and those present went through the usual routines as though he were actually present. However, when visiting dignitaries from Mongolia came to Lhasa and asked for an audience, the Desi could not very well turn them away. They were permitted, therefore, to see the "Dalai Lama" in his chambers. On such occasions, the monk from Namgyal Dratsang monastery, who bore a certain resemblance to the fifth Dalai Lama, was dressed in the Dalai's ceremonial robes and made to go through the usual polite ritual with his guests. The visitors, who perhaps had never seen the Dalai Lama at close quarters, were completely taken in by the deception and helped to spread the fiction that he was alive. Titles and presents were given in the audience hall before the Dalai Lama's robes, and his seal was placed on all official orders.

One of the Dalai Lama's attendants recorded in his diary that the Namgyal Dratsang monk soon tired of his forced imprisonment and made an effort to escape from the duties of impersonation.[4] He had to be beaten sometimes and at others, bribed. Indeed, it could not have been pleasant for him to remain within the walls of the Potala under those conditions for fifteen years.

After a few years of the deception, some people did begin to get a

---

form on him the religious rites. In the meantime, I shall dispatch Nyimathang Shabdrung to China to make an official announcement." The Panchen Lama further stated that he was an eyewitness to a declaration made to a large audience at Nyethang by the Desi regarding the reasons for the concealment of the fifth Dalai Lama's death for fifteen years (PANCHEN).

4. RAB-GSAL. The diary referred to here is that of Trulku Ngawang Norbu. Although the existence of this diary is well known in Tibet, I have not had access to it.

little suspicious. A child lama, known as Mindroling Dungsey, of the Nying-ma-pa monastery of Mindroling, sought an audience with the Dalai Lama, with the object of receiving a new religious name. His companions told him to take a close look at the Dalai Lama so that he could later described him to them. The observant young lama described the "Dalai Lama" so accurately that he even mentioned a hat and eye-shade worn by the impostor. The fifth Dalai Lama had been almost bald and possessed large, round eyes, which could not be mistaken; perhaps the hat and eyeshade worn by the impersonator was to hide those striking features.

Sangye Gyatso was then carrying out a multitude of duties, includ-ing those of the Dalai Lama. His administration was faultless. He reg-ularly visited the courts and offices, and there was a seat for him in every government office, in case he should turn up unexpectedly. Often moving about in the guise of a common man, he made it his job to know everything that was going on. Because he frequently visited drinking shops and public places in disguise, the people became careful not to talk too much in public, in case the "flatheaded Desi" was lis-tening. On one occasion, a beer-drinker, on being questioned by the disguised Desi as to his opinion of the government, is said to have re-plied, "My business is drinking beer. All other business is the Desi's."

During the time of Gushri Khan and Dalai Khan, it was the custom for Tibetan and Mongol cavalry and infantry to parade before the Dalai Lama in full armor during the Monlam festival at New Year's time. Then, for two days after the Monlam festival, the troops en-gaged in public contests of skill, after which there was much feasting and awarding of prizes. In time, it became the custom for every offi-cial of high rank to provide cavalrymen or foot soldiers for the Monlam parade and to take the generalship in turn for the annual show. Until recently, this custom was still a part of the Monlam fes-tival. It is said that the Desi, Sangye Gyatso, participated in the public contests held in his time and that no one has ever been able to shoot an arrow as far as he did.

Signs of disunity began to show among the Mongol tribes. Dalai Khungteji was dead, but his son was still living in Mongolia, so the Desi wrote to him in the name of the Dalai Lama asking him to try and unite the Mongols and to recover territory that had fallen into Manchu hands. The Dzungar and Qoshot Mongol tribes then united and began to menace Lanchow in China; but the Chahar and other tribes, because of Manchu intrigues against the other tribes, remained aloof and out of the union.

In 1695 the Potala palace was completed. In the following year, the Desi, Sangye Gyatso, announced that the fifth Dalai Lama had died in 1682 and that his reincarnation was already thirteen years old.[5] In 1697 Nyimathang Shabdrung was sent to the Imperial Court in China to make an official report of the death of the fifth Dalai Lama.[6] The K'ang-hsi Emperor went in person to meet the Tibetan envoy at the second door of the Imperial palace. Nyimathang announced that the Dalai Lama had died years before and that his reincarnation now sat on the throne in the Potala.

The Manchus used this announcement to convince the Chahar, Qoshot, and other Mongol tribes that the Desi had kept the Dalai Lama's death a secret in order to retain power in his own hands. They also accused the Desi of showing disfavor to those Mongols living in Tibet. They then showered money and titles on the Chahar chieftains. All this served to bring about a split between the two tribes on the one side and the Dzungers on the other. The Desi became unpopular with the Qoshot Mongols in the Kokonor region, when they heard the rumor that their fellow tribesmen in Tibet were being ill treated. At the same time, learning that the Dalai Lama was dead, the Qoshots lost interest in trying to recover Tibetan territory lost to the Manchus.

Following the death of the fifth Dalai Lama in 1682, the Desi, Sangye Gyatso, conducted a secret search for his reincarnation and, in 1685, a report reached him that a three-year-old boy of the Monyul area seemed to be the likely candidate. Twice the Desi sent trusted attendants to verify the discovery, and then, in 1688, the boy was taken secretly to Nankartse, where he was educated by teachers appointed by the Desi. Years later, when the Desi finally announced the discovery of the new Dalai Lama, the second Panchen Lama was invited to Nankartse, where he administered the Getsul vows of monkhood and named the boy Tsangyang Gyatso.

In 1697 Tsangyang Gyatso, the sixth Dalai Lama, was enthroned in the Potala.[7] He was a handsome and intelligent youth, who took his religious and political training from the Desi himself. Moreover, the

---

5. GSER-SDONG.

6. ROCKHILL, p. 29. According to HOWORTH (p. 520), the Emperor received Nimatang with great consideration and "went in person to meet him at the door of the second inclosure of his palace, and he accepted his presents."

7. This account of the sixth Dalai Lama is based on LNGA-PA.

Panchen Lama, Lozang Yeshe, visited him several times and gave him religious instructions. About that time, the Panchen Lama was twice invited to China by the K'ang-hsi Emperor. After the matter was discussed with the Desi, the invitations were declined. The reasons given by the Panchen Lama were that his religious studies had not yet been completed and that he feared the smallpox epidemic then prevalent in China. The Manchu Emperor suspected that the Desi intentionally prevented the Panchen Lama from accepting the invitations; but this was not the case. On the contrary, the Panchen Lama wrote to the Desi and expressed the desire to avoid going to China.[8]

As the young Dalai Lama grew up, he became an excellent archer and often went to the park for archery contests. Both the Desi and the Panchen Lama urged the young Dalai Lama not to lead a frivolous life nor waste his precious hours, which should be devoted to religious study. They insisted that the Dalai Lama should take his vows as a Gelong, or fully ordained monk, since he was then twenty years old. The Desi invited the Panchen Lama to visit Lhasa for the purpose of giving the Gelong vows to the Dalai Lama; however, the young Dalai Lama was of a different turn of mind. Instead of taking the vows of a fully ordained monk, the Dalai Lama had decided that the Getsul vows, which he had already taken, did not appeal to him; consequently, he visited the Panchen Lama in Tashilhunpo in 1702 and renounced his Getsul vows to him. The Dalai Lama was there approached by the abbots of the three big monasteries, by Desi Taktse, and by Lhazang Khan, the son of Dalai Khan and grandson of Gushri Khan, all of whom pleaded with the Dalai Lama not to renounce his Getsul vows; but their pleas were of no avail.

Through familiarity, the Dalai Lama gradually lost respect for the Desi and began to wander off on his own, often spending his nights in Lhasa and in Shol, a small village in front of the Potala. Night after night, he roamed through the streets of Lhasa, singing drunken songs with a friend, an official named Thargyanas. He would secretly invite girls into his tent in the park. In short, the sixth Dalai Lama was a man-about-town who enjoyed the company of women. He composed excellent, romantic verses and songs, which became popular.[9]

The Desi, Sangye Gyatso, learned that Thargyanas was acting as go-

8. PAN-CHEN.

9. The collected poems of the sixth Dalai Lama have been published in English translation; see Yu Dawchyuan, "Love Songs of the Sixth Dalai Lama," *Academia Sinica Monograph*, Series A, No. 5 (Peking, 1930)

between for the Dalai Lama in the latter's rendezvous with women and decided to have Thargyanas killed. On the night of the proposed murder, the Dalai Lama, Thargyanas, and his servant had all exchanged clothes with one another, while returning from their nocturnal adventures by way of the Potala's back door. In the dark, they were suddenly attacked by three men. Thargyanas' servant died from a knife wound in the back, perhaps meant for his master. The next day, the Dalai Lama consulted his oracle, who helped him discover the identity of the assassins, who were then legally executed. From then on, the Dalai Lama's relationship with the Desi began to grow cold and distant, since he suspected the Desi to be responsible for the attack.

In his diary, the lama Lelung Jedrung recorded a very complete description of the sixth Dalai Lama, whom he visited about that time.[10] Lelung Jedrung was made to wait a long time, and when the Dalai Lama finally appeared, he was carrying a bow in one hand and wearing the blue silk clothes of a layman. He wore rings on several fingers and had let his hair grow long, instead of the monk's tonsure. The Dalai Lama gave him only a few minutes before hurrying off to the park with his attendants, leaving Lelung Jedrung to conclude his business with the Desi. Lelung Jedrung described the Desi as looking disturbed and depressed, instead of his usual gay self. He too gave the diarist only a brief time, owing to the pressure of official matters.

The courtesans of Lhasa began to sing a song about the sixth Dalai Lama.

> In the Potala, he is Rinchen Tsangyang Gyatso,
> But, in Lhasa and in Shol, he is a gay young blade.

The Dalai Lama himself is credited with many romantic and lyrical verses. The following are two examples of his poetry:

> Last year the crop was young and green
> 'Tis now but withered strands;
> And youth grown old, is dried and bent
> Like bows from southern lands.

> Dear Love, to whom my heart goes out,
> If we could but be wed,

10. SLE-LUNG.

> Then had I gained the choicest gem
> From the ocean's deepest bed.[11]

The houses in Lhasa and in Shol have always been whitewashed, except for a few painted yellow. It is a popular saying that those yellow houses once belonged to the courtesans whom the sixth Dalai Lama favored.

A number of circumstances, including the discontent of the Mongols and the growing estrangement with the Dalai Lama, forced the Desi to resign in 1703; but, before doing so, he had a magnificent golden mausoleum built for the fifth Dalai Lama, whose body had been preserved. The Desi held a prayer meeting which lasted ten days, followed by a procession known as Tsogcho Serbang, which was repeated annually until 1959. Following the resignation of Sangye Gyatso, Ngawang Rinchen was appointed Desi; however, Sangye Gyatso remained behind the scene and continued to have control of the administration.[12]

The chief of the Qoshot Mongols in central Tibet at the time was Lhazang Khan, the grandson of Gushri Khan. Lhazang Khan had assumed leadership of the Qoshot in 1697. During the ensuing years, there developed an increasing animosity between the Khan and Sangye Gyatso. The dispute and disagreement between them arose from conflicting views on the practice of religion, the dispute between Tibetans and Mongols, and particularly on the issue of the Dalai Lama's behavior. The relationship between them grew worse day by day. Finally, a conference was held before the mausoleum of the fifth Dalai Lama in early 1705 for the purpose of mediating the dispute between the ex-Desi and the Qoshot Khan. Present at the meeting were the sixth Dalai Lama, the Lamo Oracle, Taktse Shabdrung, the representatives of the Panchen Lama, and the abbots of the three big monasteries: Drepung, Sera, and Ganden. It was decided that Lhazang Khan should not remain in Lhasa but must return to the Kokonor region and from there continue his amicable relationship with Tibet.

Lhazang Khan, on the pretext of returning to Kokonor, traveled to Nagchukha, where he recruited the Mongols living around that area. Forming a sizable army, the Khan set out for Lhasa in the middle of

---

11. Raghu Vira, *Tibet: A Souvenir* (New Delhi, 1960), pp. 50-51.

12. According to PAN-CHEN, the newly-appointed Desi, Ngawang Rinchen, was the son of Sangye Gyatso.

the year. Hearing of this, the ex-Desi sent troops to check the Mongol advance. Immediately representatives of the Dalai Lama and representatives of the three big monasteries set out to mediate. In the meantime, the Panchen Lama himself was on his way to the front to mediate personally between the two forces. On reaching Shukpola, the Panchen Lama was informed in a letter from the Dalai Lama that successful mediation had taken place and that a cease-fire was in effect.

It was decided that the ex-Desi would not remain in Lhasa, but would move to Gongkar, where he would be compensated for his lost estates. Lhazang Khan was to return to the Kokonor region. Learning of these agreements, the Panchen Lama returned to Tashilhunpo. A few days later, the ex-Desi, Sangye Gyatso, set out for Gongkar and on the way he was captured by Lhazang Khan's men,,who took him to Tohlung Nangtse, where he was executed on the seventeenth day of the seventh month of the Wood-Bird year (1705). Lhazang Khan then came to Lhasa and assumed full political control.

The people and officials of central Tibet are said to have regretted the way in which the ex-Desi met his death, since his only error was to conceal the death of the fifth Dalai Lama for so many years.[13] Following the execution, Sangye Gyatso's supporters were watched carefully. Ngawang Rinchen, who had been appointed Desi by Sangye Gyatso in 1703, disappeared and could not be located, in spite of a thorough search conducted by Lhazang Khan's men.

A number of prominent Tibetans began to support Lhazang Khan. Among them was Pholhanas, a young lay official who was to play an important part in future events. Even though Lhazang Khan had supported the sixth Dalai Lama, once he gained control over central Tibet, he gradually increased his criticism of the Dalai Lama's loose living. Finally, on the first day of the fifth month of the Fire-Dog year (1706), Lhazang Khan summoned the Dalai Lama to his court and went through a recital of the Dalai Lama's numerous failings and vices. The Khan then ordered him to be taken to the Mongol military camp at Lhalu, near Lhasa, and sent attendants to the Potala to collect the Dalai Lama's personal belongings.[14]

---

13. 'DAB-BRGYA gives an account of the looting of Sangye Gyatso's home, near Sera monastery, soon after his execution. The looting was done by some Sera monks acting on the orders of Lhazang Khan.

14. LCANG-SKYA. The attendant, Drakpa-gyatso, records these events in his diary.

The people resented this treatment of the Dalai Lama and showed their displeasure by closing their shops and houses; but, they could do nothing else because of the presence of Mongol troops. The Dalai Lama managed to send a note from Lhalu to one of his lady-friends in Lhasa, in which he said:

> Lend me your wings, white crane;
> I go no farther than Lithang,
> And thence, return again.

No one had any idea what this implied at that time; but later on, when the reincarnation of the Dalai Lama was discovered at Lithang, this message was considered prophetic.

Lhazang Khan had allied himself with the Manchu Emperor, who was taking an increased interest in Tibetan affairs, because of the relationship between the Tibetans and the Dzungar Mongols. It was decided to depose and exile the sixth Dalai Lama. Some Tibetan records state he was to be taken to Mongolia; other sources say that the K'ang-hsi Emperor wanted him brought to Peking.[15] Anyway, on the seventeenth day of the fifth Tibetan month (June 27), the Dalai Lama was declared deposed and was being escorted into exile. When the party passed near Drepung monastery, the monks there swooped down on the caravan and carried the Dalai Lama inside. Monks from Sera and Ganden joined forces with them. Lhazang Khan soon surrounded the Drepung monastery with large numbers of troops. The Dalai Lama was kept in the monastery for three days; but, aware that his presence could only bring destruction to the monastery and its monks, he insisted on being allowed to leave. After telling the Drepung monks he would see them again, he went out of the monastery and returned to his captors.

Again, the escort and the Dalai Lama set out on the road. When they reached the Kokonor region and were near the Kunganor, a small lake south of the Kokonor lake, the Dalai Lama died. The cause of his death remains unknown; Tibetan and Chinese sources merely say it was due to illness.

Once the sixth Dalai Lama was deposed, Lhazang Khan made an announcement declaring that the sixth had not been a true reincarnation of the previous Dalai Lama. He then put forth a young monk,

15. ROCKHILL, P. 34; PETECH, PP. 11–13.

Ngawang Yeshe Gyatso, as the true rebirth and enthroned him in the Potala as the real sixth Dalai Lama.[16] The previous Dalai Lamas had been addressed as *Thamchad Khyenpa* ("The Omniscient One"); but the people referred to the new encumbent as *Kushab* ("Mister"). He was not generally accepted as the true reincarnation of the Dalai Lama by the people.

In 1709 a severe earthquake shook Toh and Tsang, destroying houses and killing many people. The government tried to compensate for the losses, and relief was sent; but lack of help forced many towns to be abandoned.

After a few years, Lhazang Khan heard reports that a reincarnation of the late Dalai Lama had been found in Kham. He dispatched a Tibetan and a Mongol general to investigate the reports. Arriving in Lithang, they were told of a boy named Kelzang Gyatso, who had been born on the nineteenth day of the seventh month of the Earth-Mouse year (1708).[17] When they went to visit the boy, his family claimed that the child was the reincarnation of the late sixth Dalai Lama. The Tibetan general, in order to avoid any harm being done to the child by Lhazang Khan's supporters, said it did not matter whether he was a reincarnation of the late Dalai Lama, because the latter had been declared an imposter. That night, he spoke to the boy's father, admitting that the child did indeed appear to be outstanding. He advised the father to take the boy to a safe place and keep him out of sight; so the family moved to Derge, some distance north of Lithang.

Certain Mongol tribes, who had been in sympathy with the late Dalai Lama, heard of the discovery of his reincarnation and decided to offer the boy recognition and protection. Accordingly, the boy was escorted from Derge to the Kokonor region, where he was warmly received by the Mongols. The Manchus saw this as an opportunity to extend their influence in Tibet. In 1715 a representative was sent to the boy's family to suggest that he enter a monastery and receive religious training. Finally, in 1716, the boy was taken to the Kumbum monastery, where he took up residence.

In central Tibet, Lhazang Khan continued to strengthen his control over the country. His one attempt at military conquest turned out badly, when he and his forces were defeated in a campaign against Bhutan in 1714. In the same year, he received a letter from Tsewang

16. PAN-CHEN.

17. This account of the seventh Dalai Lama is based on LCANG-SKYA.

Rapten, the ruler of the Dzungar Mongols, proposing a marriage alliance between the son of the Khan and Tsewang Rapten's daughter. Tsewang Rapten, who was the son of the late Dalai Khungteji, the strong ally of the late Desi, Sangye Gyatso, had received an appeal from the monks of the three big Ge-lug-pa monasteries at Lhasa to overthrow Lhazang Khan and help install the true Dalai Lama in the Potala.[18] Tsewang Rapten knew his daughter had been in correspondence with Ganden Tenzin, the son of Lhazang Khan, and decided to make political use of this attachment. He wrote to the Khan proposing that their children be married and that Ganden Tenzin be sent to claim his bride.

Lhazang Khan was suspicious of the Dzungar ruler's intentions; but, at the same time, he had hopes of forming a strong alliance with the Dzungar Mongols. He finally decided to consult the Lamo oracle, who went into a trance and uttered certain stanzas, which were interpreted differently by Lhazang Khan and his son. The Khan took the oracle to mean that the visit would be dangerous and should not be undertaken unless the youth was very determined. His son, Ganden Tenzin, insisted that it only meant that there would be trouble if the marriage was postponed. The Khan finally consented, and Ganden Tenzin set out to claim his bride. When he finally arrived in Dzungaria, the homeland of the Dzungar Mongols, he was seized and imprisoned.

In 1717 Tsewang Rapten appointed his brother, Tsering Dondup, as commander of the Dzungar army, which consisted of seven thousand cavalrymen, and ordered the army into Tibet.[19] Once the invasion began, Ganden Tenzin's use as a decoy was at an end, and he was put to death by the Dzungars. Usually, the Mongols, when traveling to Lhasa, entered from the northeast through the Kokonor region; but Tsering Dondup led his troops through Yarkand and entered Tibet in the northwest. To avoid fighting across the country, he let it be known that he was escorting the bride and bridegroom to Lhasa. Lhazang Khan was in the Dam region, when he received a message from an official in Gartok, the government headquarters for western Tibet, informing him that a large troop of Mongol cavalry was en route to Lhasa. Not knowing that his son had been put to death, Lhazang Khan sent a messenger, with an escort of nine soldiers, to

18. ROCKHILL, p. 37.
19. MI-DBANG; HOWORTH, p. 523.

carry a letter to his son. When the messenger saw the Dzungar cavalry
at Nagtsang he left five of the soldiers behind, with instructions to
return and warn the Khan if anything happened to him. He then entered the Mongol camp with the other four soldiers. When they did
not return, the five soldiers rode back to Dam to alert Lhazang Khan
of treachery.

A stockade was hurriedly erected at Dam. Pholhanas was given the
title of Teji and appointed a general. He advised Lhazang Khan to station troops with muskets in the hills guarding the pass between the
Dam region and Lhasa; but the Khan elected to concentrate his
cavalry on the open plateau. By means of spies, the Dzungars had
spread the word that they were coming to Tibet in the name of the
fifth and sixth Dalai Lamas to avenge the execution of the Desi,
Sangye Gyatso, and that they would return all power to the Tibetans
and expel the so-called sixth Dalai Lama, who had been foisted on
them by Lhazang Khan. They advised the Tibetans not to take part in
the fighting that was to come between the Dzungars and the Qoshot
Mongols of Lhazang Khan. When the battle for the Dam region broke
out, the Tibetans, with the exception of Pholhanas, fought only halfheartedly; but the Qoshot Mongols fought spiritedly. In time, the
superior forces of the Dzungars turned the tide of battle on the open
plateau, and Lhazang Khan had to withdraw his forces to Lhasa,
where they made attempts to fortify the city.

The Dzungars approached Lhasa, surrounded it, and began to make
their own preparations for the final assault on the city. The siege continued until the end of November, when the Dzungars were in position and ready for the final attack. They were so well prepared that
they were able to conquer the city itself almost overnight; but
Lhazang Khan held out in the Potala. Realizing that he could not hold
out indefinitely, he sent his son, Surya, out of the Potala with instructions to proceed to the Kokonor region and bring back reinforcements. Surya was captured by the Dzungars. Electing to fight,
Lhazang Khan left the Potala on the first day of the eleventh Tibetan
month of the Fire-Bird year (December 3, 1717) and attacked the
enemy. Engaging in fierce hand-to-hand combat, he killed eleven men
with his own hands, before he himself was struck down and killed.
Thus ended the life of Lhazang Khan, who had ruled Tibet from 1705
until 1717. He had maintained a close relationship with K'ang-hsi, the

Manchu Emperor of China; but, for all purposes, he reigned over central Tibet as an independent military sovereign.

As soon as the Dzungars gained control of Lhasa, they appointed Lhagyal Rapten, previously known as Taktse Shabdrung, to be the figurehead of the Tibetan government.[20] Yeshe Gyatso, the so-called sixth Dalai Lama, was deposed and confined at Chakpori, a medical college established by the late Sangye Gyatso. The Second Panchen Lama says in his autobiography that he pleaded for the life of Yeshe Gyatso, but was not given a clear reply. Although the fate of Yeshe Gyatso is unclear in some sources, it appears that he was sent to China, where he died in 1725.[21] Tibetan lamas and lay officials who had helped Lhazang Khan during his regime were arrested. Four Nying-ma-pa lamas,[22] two relatives of the Panchen Lama, and three highly placed Tibetan officials were executed. Pholhanas was shown leniency because of his friendship with the new Desi, Lhagyal Rapten, and one of the pro-Dzungar lamas; but he was tortured and deprived of his rank. Finally, he was permitted to return to his estate in Tsang.

The Dzungar Mongols had no liking for the Nying-ma-pa sect and ruined two of its finest monasteries. Until then, the Dzungars had been popular with the Tibetan people because they had deposed the false Dalai Lama, killed Lhazang Khan, and restored the post of Desi to a Tibetan; but popular feeling turned against them when they executed the Nying-ma-pa lamas and subsequently attacked their monasteries.

The Dzungars had wanted to bring the seventh Dalai Lama to Lhasa and enthrone him in the Potala; but the young lama was under Manchu protection at the Kumbum monastery in Kokonor. In 1718 the Tibetans petitioned the Dzungars to bring the true Dalai Lama to Lhasa. Tsering Dondup, the Dzungar commander, promised to do so; but he could not prevail upon the Manchus to release the Dalai Lama. This failure increased his unpopularity among the Tibetan people.

The Desi, Taktse Shabdrung, and three Tibetan officials met in secret to write a letter, saying that they recognized the young lama at Kumbum as the reincarnation of the sixth Dalai Lama, and it was sent

20. PAN-CHEN.
21. PETECH, pp. 64, 91.
22. These four lamas were Dodrag Rinzin Chenmo, Meling Lochen, Dongsey Pema Gyumey, and Namling Konchog Chosdrag.

by courier to Kumbum. As soon as the K'ang-hsi Emperor learned that the boy lama had been officially recognized as the seventh Dalai Lama, he sent a delegation to Kumbum to offer his confirmation that Kelzang Gyatso was the reincarnation of the Dalai Lama. The delegation presented a golden seal to the young lama in March of the year 1720. The seal, inscribed in Manchu, Mongol, and Tibetan, read: "Seal of the Sixth Dalai Lama." Thus K'ang-hsi avoided the question of whether the two previous Dalai Lamas were true incarnations or not.

The K'ang-hsi Emperor wrote a letter to the new Dalai Lama and his Kokonor supporters, saying:

> I was made very happy on the day the Dalai Lama was con-firmed. He is a true reincarnation, and everyone must show him due respect. Both I and the descendants of Gushri Khan are his benefactors. For three years, I guarantee to bear all the expenses of the Dalai Lama's attendants and monks, numbering one hun-dred and thirty-four persons.
>
> The Dalai Lama is like a ray of sunshine, which is impossible for any one group of people to obscure. The ray of Buddhist faith will shine on everyone through him. The Mongols in the Kokonor region should remain united and friendly, instead of quarreling among themselves. The Dalai Lama is requested to advise them to remain obedient to the Emperor, although I am sure they do not intend to be disobedient.[23]

Because of the increasing unpopularity of the Dzungar regime, Khangchennas, the Tibetan governor of western Tibet at Gartok, was able to consolidate his own personal power in that region. When he heard that some Tibetan officials were being taken through western Tibet on their way into exile in Dzungaria, he rescued them. He then wrote a letter to Pholhanas in Tsang and upbraided him for sitting idle instead of engaging in rebellion against the country's enemies. Pholhanas, consequently, left his estate in Tsang and set up headquar-ters near the western border. From there, he was able to consolidate control over the five regions of Tsang, leaving the Dzungars in com-mand only of Lhasa and the province of Ü.

Meanwhile, two important Tibetan officials left Lhasa and took refuge in the Kumbum monastery in the northeast. Then, in the mid-dle of 1718, an imperial army of several thousand men, led by a

23. LCANG-SKYA.

Manchu officer, Erentei, advanced through the Tsaidam region to
Nagchukha. There, they were attacked by the Dzungar and Tibetan
troops and defeated. Large numbers of Chinese were massacred; few
returned to China.[24]

Following the Nagchukha massacre, the K'ang-hsi Emperor dispatched a second army under the command of his fourteenth son,
Prince Yün-t'i, to attack the Dzungars and to escort the seventh Dalai
Lama from Kumbum to Lhasa. At the Drichu river, Prince Yün-t'i
left the column and returned to China. The Manchu general, Yansin,
together with three Mongol officers, Tsewang Norbu, Lozang Tenzin
Wang, and Dondup Wang, continued to lead the army, composed of
Mongol and Chinese troops, to Lhasa, escorting the Dalai Lama as they
went.

When Khangchennas and Pholhanas learned that the Dalai Lama
was being escorted to Lhasa by a large army, they collected their
Tibetan troops and advanced on the city. The Dzungars, finding
troops were marching against them from the south and from the
northeast, fled from Lhasa, taking as much loot as possible. Most of
them fled to the northwest and escaped, even though Pholhanas pursued
them for some distance. A few fled to the northeast and managed to
bypass the imperial army near the Dang-la pass without a clash. Another imperial army, led by the Manchu general, Galbi, arrived from
the east, after traveling through Kham from Szechuan.

It is widely believed that the Manchus alone were responsible for
expelling the Dzungars and that they thereby conquered Tibet; but it
must be noted that the Tibetan troops of Khangchennas and Pholhanas had the Dzungars on the run from Lhasa before the Manchu
armies arrived. Moreover, the Manchu Emperor did not send his
armies to "conquer" Tibet; but to avenge the death of his ally,
Lhazang Khan, and to restore the seventh Dalai Lama to his throne.

24. PAN-CHEN; PETECH, pp. 55–56; ROCKHILL, p. 40.

9

The Seventh Dalai Lama and the
Beginning of Manchu Influence in Tibet

On the fifteenth day of the ninth month of the Iron-Mouse year
(1720), the seventh Dalai Lama, Kelzang Gyatso, entered Lhasa and
was enthroned in the Potala.[1] A provisional military government was
then set up in order to restore peaceful operation of the administration. A tribunal was convened to investigate the previous Dzungar
administration and to ferret out Dzungar sympathizers. Since the responsible Dzungars had fled and could not be brought to trial, the
officials found a scapegoat in the elderly Desi, Taktse Shabdrung, and
his two pro-Dzungar ministers. In spite of an eloquent plea by
Pholhanas on behalf of the Desi, the latter was found guilty of having
betrayed the son of Lhazang Khan, named Surya, into the hands of
the Dzungars. All three defendants were convicted and then beheaded.[2] The Tibetan populace resented the execution of the Desi,
who had been a figurehead used by the Dzungars.

The false sixth Dalai Lama was taken from the medical college and
deported to China, where he died some five years later. The Manchus
also built a garrison in Lhasa and stationed troops there to maintain
peace and order. Tsewang Norbu, the Mongol officer under General
Yansin, was given the seal of a Manchu General and appointed commander of the garrison.

1. The accounts given here of the seventh Dalai Lama and Pholhanas are based on LCANG-
SKYA and MI-DBANG.

2. LCANG-SKYA and MI-DBANG state that a temporary council of six members was
formed. The council, consisting of Tibetans, Manchus, and Mongols, saw to the execution
of Desi Taktse, Tashi Tsepa, and A-chos. According to MTSHO-SNGON, the Mongols resented the treatment they had received from the Tibetans. They also thought the Tibetans
had shown better attention to the Manchus; therefore, the Mongols in Lhasa swore, in
front of the tomb of the fifth Dalai Lama, that they would return to the Chinese border
to fight and harass the Manchus. Also see PETECH, pp. 63–64.

A new form of government was also established. The office of Desi was abolished, as it placed too much power in one man's hands. The new government was headed by a council of ministers—two seniors and two juniors—who were to be responsible for the administration. Khangchennas, the governor of western Tibet, was given the title of Dai-ching Batur and appointed chairman of the council. Ngabo, the governor of Kongpo region, was made the other senior minister, and Jaranas and Lumpa became the junior ministers. After 1723 Pholhanas was also a council minister. Jaranas had consistently opposed Dzungar policies, and Ngabo and Lumpa were the two officials who had earlier left the Dzungar regime and took refuge in Kumbum monastery.

In 1722 the K'ang-hsi Emperor died and was succeeded by his son, who became known as the Yung-cheng Emperor. In 1723 the new Manchu ruler began a policy of retrenchment. He withdrew the garrison from Lhasa, leaving the administration of central Tibet entirely in the hands of Tibetan officials, without any military support from the Manchus.

In the first year of the Yung-cheng Emperor's reign, Mongols in the Kokonor region, led by Chingwang Lozang Tenzin, a grandson of the Qoshot Gushri Khan, revolted against the Manchus. The rebellion was suppressed, and in early 1724 the Kokonor region was integrated into the Manchu empire.

Meanwhile, dissension arose within the council of ministers in Lhasa. Chairman Khangchennas and Pholhanas found themselves opposed to the policies of the other three ministers. Ngabo, Lumpa, and Jaranas, who had vested interests in the province of Ü, resented the fact that Khangchennas, who was concurrently the governor of western Tibet, had been made chairman. Pholhanas, whose interests lay in Tsang, advocated alliance with the Manchus, a policy rejected by the three ministers. Subordinate officials, who were responsible for the routine administration of the government, began to drift into one of the two cliques. Preoccupied with their own positions and provincial interests, the council ministers paid little attention to the affairs of the country. Bodyguards accompanied them wherever they went.

The situation continued to degenerate and was reaching a critical point when unexpectedly a mission arrived from the Yung-cheng Emperor in the summer of 1726, bringing instructions that the Nying-ma-pa teachings were to be suppressed. Khangchennas began to carry out a policy of persecution against the Nying-ma-pa, which brought him in conflict with Pholhanas, who was well known for his inclination towards the Nying-ma-pa sect. Pholhanas then found himself at odds with all of the council ministers, so he offered his resignation, which was refused. At that point, Pholhanas learned that his wife was ill and left Lhasa in the spring of 1727 to return to his estate in Tsang. He asked friends to keep him informed of what went on in Lhasa during his absence.

The animosity and hatred directed at Khangchennas for his arrogant and ruthless behavior continued to mount. Then, on the eighteenth day of the sixth Tibetan month of the Fire-Sheep year (August 6, 1727), the council convened in an upper room of the Jokhang temple. A letter was handed to Khangchennas by Ngabo's brother, a subordinate official. As Khangchennas began to read the letter, he was seized from behind by some officials. Ngabo, Lumpa, and Jaranas then drew their knives and stabbed the minister to death. His bodyguards, waiting outside the office, were taken by surprise and also killed. Assassins were sent to Khangchennas' house, where they murdered his two wives, his secretary, and a steward. The two governors of the north, who were friends of both Khangchennas and Pholhanas, were also killed. Men were dispatched to Tsang with instructions to assassinate Pholhanas.

Pholhanas had been warned by friends in Lhasa of the imminent attack on his life. He sent his sick wife into seclusion and left a strong guard to protect her. He then withdrew, with his two sons and sixty men, to western Tibet, where he found Tsang troops stationed along the nearby Nepalese border. These he persuaded to join his cause. He then wrote to the district officials of western Tibet informing them of the assassination of their popular governor and asking them to assist him in avenging the murder. Gashinas, also known as Doring, was a brother of Khangchennas and had become the new governor of Toh (western Tibet). He and other powerful officials sent a large number of troops to join Pholhanas. With his position considerably strengthened, Pholhanas marched back into Tsang.

A contingent of Tibetan troops was stationed at Shigatse under the command of a Tsang general. When the general could not make up his mind over which side to support, Pholhanas had him thrown over the ramparts of the Shigatse fort and took command of the troops himself. His ability to make shrewd decisions and carry them out swiftly earned him the name, Miwang Pholha (Mighty Pholha).

Meanwhile, Ngabo, Lumpa, and Jaranas gathered troops from Ü and Kongpo and marched to Gyantse in Tsang. A battle ensued. The fighting lasted, off and on, for several months without a decisive victory. Finally, the Panchen Lama, the Sakya Lama, and a representative of the Dalai Lama arrived to mediate. A truce was agreed to on the third day of the third month of the Earth-Ape year (April 11, 1728), and the two armies withdrew from battle. The ministers from Ü disbanded their army, but Pholhanas kept his intact.

Shortly thereafter, a man from the province of Ü by the name of Ah-jo Palzang, killed some Tsang people in the district of Nagtsang, to the west of Lhasa. Using the incident as an excuse, Pholhanas broke the truce. He sent his eldest son with nine thousand troops towards Lhasa, while he himself marched north and collected some three thousand nomads and Mongol troops from the Dam region. He then converged on Lhasa from the northeast and entered the city on July 3, meeting only token resistance.[3]

Ngabo, Lumpa, and Jaranas, whose troops had been dispersed after the truce agreement, took refuge in the Potala and begged the Dalai Lama to save their lives. Pholhanas' troops surrounded the Potala. The Ganden Tri Rimpoche and another high lama acted as go-betweens for Pholhanas and the Dalai Lama. Pholhanas asked that the three ministers be handed over to him; and he suggested that in the event his appeal was disregarded the Dalai Lama and his father leave the Potala with an escort for the Drepung monastery. There the Lama would be safe, because Pholhanas intended to force his rivals out of the Potala. The Dalai Lama finally persuaded Pholhanas to allow the three ministers to live in their homes under close guard until a mission en route from the Manchu Emperor should arrive. The three ministers believed the Manchus would support them in their dispute with Pholhanas. Pholhanas, on the other hand, was convinced that the Emperor would support him. Since Lhasa was completely under his control, he agreed to the Dalai Lama's request.

Two months later, a large imperial army under the command of the Manchus, Jalangga, and Mailu, arrived in Lhasa. The expedition had been dispatched by the Yung-cheng Emperor for the purpose of pro-

3. PAN-CHEN; PETECH, pp. 119-20.

tecting the Dalai Lama and putting an end to the civil war. When it arrived in Lhasa, however, Pholhanas had had everything under control since early July. The expedition arrived on September 4th and the Manchu leaders, Jalangga and Mailu, together with the two resident Manchu officials, Senge and Mala, constituted a court of justice to try the ministers and their followers. The trial lasted seven days and ended in the conviction of the three ministers and fourteen of their closest supporters. On the first of November, all seventeen were executed at the foot of the Bamari hill, half a mile west of the Potala. The three ministers were executed by the excruciating process of slicing. The victims were literally sliced into small pieces. This slow, torturous means of execution was carried out in public to cow the Lhasa populace. Two lamas in the group were strangled, and the rest were decapitated. The families of the men were also executed, with the exception of Jaranas' family members, who were deported into slavery in China.

It was also decided that the father of the Dalai Lama, who had been a strong supporter of the three ministers and their policies, was responsible for much of the intrigue in Lhasa; consequently, the Dalai Lama and his father were sent to Garthar, not far from Lithang in Kham. They remained there for seven years, during which time Miwang Pholhanas ruled Tibet. He was an experienced politician and had won the cooperation of the Manchus. His power was strong enough that he was able to ignore the demands of the Lhasa monks and people to recall the Dalai Lama and his father.

The Manchus reestablished the garrison in Lhasa. For the first time, two resident Manchu officials were established in Lhasa. These officials, known as the Ambans, were in charge of the garrison and were the direct representatives of the Manchu Emperor in Tibet. There were two Ambans stationed in Lhasa from then until the fall of the Manchu dynasty in 1911. The position of Amban was always filled by a Manchu.

The council of ministers was reorganized and new members appointed; but the real power and authority remained in the hands of Pholhanas. An efficient administrator, he made certain that his officials carried out their duties and saw to the proper maintenance of the monasteries. He canceled all of the debts owed the government that had accrued over the years and whose interest the taxpayer could not afford.

Miwang Pholhanas decided to provide the money to have a new edition of Tibetan canonical literature made. The wood blocks were carved for the Kagyur first, being completed in 1732. They were blessed by the Panchen Lama and then deposited in the monastery of Narthang, west of Shigatse. The blocks for the Tengyur were completed in 1742 and then blessed by the Dalai Lama. Together, the blocks are referred to as the Narthang edition of the Kagyur and Tengyur.

In 1730 civil strife in Bhutan had developed to the critical point. Two lamas had come forth and claimed to be reincarnations of Shabdrung Ngawang Namgyal, the head lama of Bhutan. Both claimants found supporters among the Bhutanese chiefs, and raids and murders became frequent. The eighth Bhutanese ruler was murdered by his successor for having sent an official to solicit help from Miwang Pholhanas. Tibetan troops invaded Bhutan in 1730 and forced the Bhutanese to recognize one of the claimants as the head lama. They also forced the Bhutanese to give up prisoners and captured territory. The Bhutanese chiefs exchanged letters swearing to uphold the peace. After that, an official representative of Bhutan was required to go to Lhasa and pay his respects and give presents to the Tibetan govenment. This custom, known as Lochak, was continued until 1950. Accommodations and transport were provided free by the Tibetan government to the Bhutanese representative. The settlement of the dispute appears to have been appreciated by the Bhutanese, who sent representatives to Pholhanas and to the Dalai Lama to thank them for their good offices.[4]

In 1733 the Capuchin mission, headed by Francisco Orazio della Penna, left Lhasa and returned to Nepal. The mission had been established in 1707. It was closed in 1711 but reopened again in 1716. The Capuchin fathers had lived through the Dzungarian invasion and occupation of central Tibet; their medical knowledge, much appreciated by the Mongols and the Tibetans, ensured their safety. The Capuchins had been given permission to buy land and build a church on the east side of the Jokhang temple. Even though the Capuchin fathers rendered valuable medical aid to the people, the monastic groups

4. MI-DBANG. 'BRUG-GI gives the same account, with the additional information that the mediation talks were conducted by Karmapa Changchub Dorje and Shamarpa Choskyi Thondup.

pressured for the closure of the Catholic mission. In 1741 the Capuchins returned for another attempt at proselytizing. This met with no success, and the mission was finally abandoned in 1745.[5]

In 1734 the Manchu Emperor sent his younger brother to visit the Dalai Lama at Garthar. He offered to finance the building of a monastery near the border and to provide for its maintenance and the needs of the monks. Later on, the Emperor extended his patronage by paying 5,000 silver *sangs* annually to meet the cost of the brick tea consumed in the monasteries throughout Tibet. In the long run, the Manchus found it cheaper to spend money on monasteries than on troops in order to pacify the border Tibetans. By encouraging more Tibetans to become monks, they were also reducing the number of potential soldiers.

By the year 1735, Pholhanas had everything under control and the government adminstration functioning smoothly; consequently, the Dalai Lama was allowed to return to Lhasa. He arrived there in the month of September, after seven years away. In October of the same year, the Yung-cheng Emperor died and was succeeded by his fourth son, who became known as the Ch'ien-lung Emperor (reigned 1736–95).

In the following year, the tenth ruler of Bhutan, Mipham Wangpo, came to Lhasa to visit the Dalai Lama and Pholhanas. The Dalai Lama wished to wipe out the memory of past conflicts with Bhutan and honored the visitor by sending two private secretaries and twenty officials to receive him outside Lhasa. The Bhutanese ruler, who was shown considerable hospitality, expressed the desire to build a shrine to the deity Avalokiteśvara in Bhutan. A Tibetan lama was sent with him to help design the shrine and to consecrate it.

Lozang Yeshe, the second Panchen Lama, died in 1737 at the age of seventy-four. A year later, his reincarnation was discovered at Tashitse in Shang, and he was given the name of Palden Yeshe by the Dalai Lama.

In 1740 the Bhutanese attacked Sikkim. Because the Sikkimese ruler was still a minor, Tamdin, the ruler's steward, came to Lhasa to request Miwang Pholhanas to send someone to help administer Sikkim until the ruler came of age. A capable man was needed to run the country and deal with the Bhutanese. Rapten Sharpa was appointed as the

5. Graham Sandberg, *The Exploration of Tibet* (Calcutta, 1904), pp. 31–50; Luciano Petech, I CAPPUCCINI MARCHIGIANI.

administrator for Sikkim.[6] In the same year, Pholhanas was given the title of Chün-wang (Prince of the Second Class) by the Ch'ien-lung Emperor.

In the year 1747, Pholhanas contracted a suppurating boil on his neck and in spite of various medical treatments, the "Mighty Pholha" finally succumbed to this affliction. During the nineteen years that he had ruled Tibet, there had been uninterrupted peace and prosperity throughout the countryside. He had allied himself firmly with the Manchu Emperors and was able to exert his influence on the Dalai Lama himself, who described Pholhanas as a brave man given to quick and clear thinking. The Dalai Lama admired Pholhanas' administrative abilities. He described Pholhanas as a man who tolerated no rival and who was never satisfied with his power and position. Although the Dalai Lama was not certain whether his own troubles were instigated by Pholhanas himself or his subordinates, he inclined to accept Pholhanas as a just administrator. Dokhar Shabdrung, a distant relative of Pholhanas and one of his staunch supporters, recorded a poignant account of his meeting with the Dalai Lama.[7] An attendant of the Dalai Lama had been arrested by Miwang Pholhanas, and the Dalai Lama complained bitterly that this had been done not so much to punish the attendant as to hurt the Dalai Lama's feelings. Pholhanas was not even satisfied when the Dalai Lama remained in his chambers and devoted his time only to prayer and meditation. The Dalai Lama is quoted as saying, "Perhaps Pholhanas will only be happy if I retire to Drepung monastery or some hermitage."

It is clear that Miwang Pholhanas did everything in his power to keep the Dalai Lama in harness. Although he was the sole ruler of Tibet, Pholhanas' collaboration with the Manchus provided the grounds for Manchu, and later on Chinese, claims of overlordship in Tibet. This issue, with its never ending ramifications, had its real commencement during the reign of Miwang Pholhanas.

Pholhanas was succeeded by his youngest son, Dalai Batur Gyumey Namgyal, who had been especially groomed for the role by Pholhanas himself. However, Gyumey Namgyal's policies proved to be quite different in spite of his father's training. In addition to being cold towards the Dalai Lama as his father had been, the new ruler was also hostile towards the Manchus. He wrote to the Manchu Emperor and

6. LCANG-SKYA; 'BRAS-LJONGS.
7. LCANG-SKYA; MDO-MKHAR.

the Ambans stating that a Manchu garrison was not required in Lhasa; a Tibetan garrison could maintain law and order just as well. Moreover, it would not exploit the people by stealing their horses and women. He complained that the Manchu Ambans were interfering in Tibetan affairs.

The Ch'ien-lung Emperor agreed to reduce the garrison to a mere one-hundred-man force to serve as a personal escort for the Ambans; but he did not accept the suggestion that a Tibetan garrison should be established.[8] The Emperor directed the Ambans not to interfere in the internal policies of Tibet and to refrain from exploitation, since sufficient money would be sent to meet all of the garrison's requirements.

A rift developed between Gyumey Namgyal and his elder brother, Gyumey Tseten, who had become the governor of western Tibet in 1729. The Dalai Lama tried to mediate between the two brothers; but to no avail; and then, in 1750, Gyumey Tseten mysteriously died.[9] In the same year, Gyumey Namgyal held a meeting with his ministers, following which, he wrote a letter to the Ambans and the Manchu Emperor objecting to the presence in Lhasa of the Ambans and their small escort. He maintained that Tibetan troops were quite capable of guarding the Dalai Lama and the security of the country. The Manchu Emperor had originally reduced the garrison in consideration of the years of peaceful and harmonious relationship between the Manchus and Pholhanas; but, the insistent demands of Gyumey Namgyal aroused doubts as to his loyalty to the Manchu throne.

Gyumey Namgyal secretly made preparations to form an army, with a view to establishing a Tibetan garrison, and to renew contact with the Dzungar Mongols, who were still the antagonists of the Manchus. Some pro-Manchu Tibetans informed the Ambans, who in turn wrote the Emperor accusing Gyumey Namgyal of creating trouble for the empire. The Ambans then decided to take matters into their own hands. On the thirteenth day of the tenth month of the Iron-Horse year (November 11, 1750), they invited Gyumey Namgyal to come and receive some presents, which had arrived for him from the Emperor. Unaware of treachery, Gyumey Namgyal went to the Ambans' residence in Tromzekhang,[10] taking two at-

8. PETECH, p. 187.

9. MDO-MKHAR.

10. This building, situated in the heart of Lhasa city, was formerly the residence of Lhazang Khan.

tendants inside with him. The Ambans, Fucing and Labdon, up-braided Gyumey Namgyal, and then Labdon seized him and impaled him with his sword. His attendants were also killed.[11]

As soon as Gyumey Namgyal's supporters knew what had happened, they gathered reinforcements and besieged the residence of the Ambans. The fighting lasted several hours. The Ambans, Fucing and Labdon, along with over one hundred Chinese soldiers and civilians, were killed and the residence put to the torch. The night was filled with confusion and panic. Some two hundred Chinese—soldiers, merchants, and civilians—took refuge in the Potala and survived the fury of the mob under the protection of the Dalai Lama himself.

The Dalai Lama appealed to his people to refrain from violence and even had posters to this effect put up; but the incensed populace tore them down. They also looted the office of the military paymaster. Lozang Tashi, the attendant of Gyumey Namgyal who had instigated the mob riot, then fled towards Dzungaria, along with some two dozen men. They were pursued, caught, and returned to Lhasa for trial.

During the short three years Gyumey Namgyal was in power, his relationship with the Dalai Lama was no friendlier than had been that of his father. In fact, none of the Tibetan records of the time has anything favorable to say of him or his reign. In spite of his attempts to remove the Manchus and Chinese from Lhasa, their influence prevailed and Tibetan chroniclers could hardly offer open praise for the late ruler. However, his rule did have several positive factors. From the religious point of view, his concern for the Buddhist monasteries in China and Mongolia is evident; therefore, he must have taken a corresponding interest in the well-being of monks and monasteries in Tibet as well. As a politician, he realized that the continued presence of the two Manchu Ambans and the garrison in Tibet would in the long run undermine the independence of the country. He was courageous in his open objection to foreign pressures and steadfast in his secret military preparations. Had Gyumey Namgyal been less hasty and impulsive, he might have lived long enough to see his policies successfully carried out; but, as it was, he lost his life in a struggle for Tibetan independence.

Shortly after the death of Gyumey Namgyal, the Dalai Lama appointed Doring Pandita to look after the administration of the gov-

11. LCANG-SKYA; MDO-MKHAR; PETECH, pp. 198–99.

ernment.[12] He was a learned man, as is implied by his title of Pandita. He was a nephew of the former governor of western Tibet, Khang-chennas.

In January of 1751, Bandi, a Manchu officer arrived in Lhasa and immediately investigated the charges against Lozang Tashi and other members of his mob. Before justice had run its course, Lozang Tashi and six other leaders were executed by the slicing process, six others were beheaded or strangled, and the rest imprisoned. In February, the main military expedition arrived from China under the command of Chao-hui and Namgyal.

On the first day of the second month of the Iron-Sheep year (1751), the Dalai Lama assumed full spiritual and temporal powers over Tibet. He was then directly involved with the actual administration of the government. Under the Dalai Lama was the council of ministers, consisting of Doring Pandita, Tsering Wangyal Dokhar, Sichod Tseten Thonpa, and a monk named Nyima Gyaltsen. The council was known as the Kashag and its ministers were called either Kalon or Sha-pe. They were provided with a special seal, which conferred on them responsibility for the administration of the country. The Dalai Lama urged them to remain united and not repeat the mistakes of the earlier council ministers, which had led to the civil war of 1727–28. The council members took an oath to serve loyally and to carry out the instructions of the Dalai Lama.

The ministers of the Kashag were nominated by the Dalai Lama and seldom represented the same group interests. They were not assigned individual responsibilities or departmental duties. All four ministers had to reach the same decision in matters large and small, including the selection of candidates for district magistrate (Dzongpon), governors (Chikyap), and other offices. The different governmental departments were headed by secretaries, who were responsible to the Kashag for the making of decisions. Since the administration of all departments depended upon the council ministers for final decisions, it sometimes functioned with delay and irresponsibility. This system, which lasted for two hundred years, impeded the progress of the country. Its weakness manifested itself in times of crisis, because there was no one to assume overall responsibility for making decisions. The one point in its favor was that it prevented a dictatorship from developing and reduced dishonesty to a minimum, because each of its mem-

12. MDO-MKHAR; RDO-RING.

bers acted as a check on the other. The Kashag took over the army which had been build up by Gyumey Namgyal and established it as a permanent force. The army consisted of "regulars" for the first time, not part-time soldiers conscripted from the populace during an emergency. Each landowning family was required to provide one member for the army. Two generals were appointed for the province of Ü, with 1,000 troops; and four generals for Tsang, with 2,000 troops.

The Chinese expedition that had come in 1751 had passed through Kham, and complaints began to reach Lhasa of exploitation of the inhabitants along its route. At the same time, the people of Lhasa began to complain that the Chinese were occupying their houses. They asked the Dalai Lama and the Kashag to have the Chinese sent way. Negotiations with the Ambans resulted in the withdrawal of most of the soldiers, leaving the garrison with 1,500 men.

Later, at the request of the Bhutanese ruler, artisans were sent to erect a gold and copper monastery roof at Pungthang and to create a huge multicolored silk scroll to cover the walls of the monastery. Material assistance was sent to the Bhutanese since they were then on very friendly terms with the Tibetans.

In Sikkim, the young Namgyal Phuntsok had come of age. The Tibetan adviser, Rapten Sharpa and the people of Sikkim now asked the Dalai Lama to bless the enthronement of their ruler. Tashilingpa, the district magistrate of Phari was sent to the ceremony with presents from the Dalai Lama.

Two local lords of Jumla and Lo Menthang, living on the border with Nepal, were feuding with each other. Both petitioned the Dalai Lama for assistance and he told them that since they were Tibetan subjects, he could not favor one against the other. He then sent his representatives, Ngor Khenpo and Saga Gopa, to investigate the dispute. It was decided that the lord of Jumla was in the wrong and he was subsequently deposed and replaced by his son. The Dalai Lama gave these vassals instructions for keeping the peace and then presented them with official seals for use on all petitions to him. They expressed their gratitude for the action he had taken in settling the dispute.[13]

The Dalai Lama had been in poor health for some time. He died at the age of fifty on the third day of the second month of the Fire-Ox

13. LCANG-SKYA.

year (March 22, 1757). In the same year, the Battle of Plassey and the consolidation of British power in India took place. The seventh Dalai Lama was a scholarly man. His political life had been marked by difficulties. Only towards the end of his life, did he actually exercise temporal power. Although overshadowed by the political figures of those violent times, the seventh Dalai Lama has been acknowledged superior to the other Dalai Lamas on religious grounds, because of his piety and scholarly achievements.

IO

War with the Gurkhas and the Dogras

Immediately after the death of the seventh Dalai Lama, his attendants, members of the Kashag, and Tibetan government officials met to discuss whether a regent should be appointed to represent the future eighth Dalai Lama or whether the Kashag should assume the duties of the Dalai Lama. It was finally decided to appoint a regent.[1] The unanimous choice fell on a high lama of the Drepung monastery, the Demo Trulku Jampel Delek, who was also personally in charge of the Tengyeling monastery in Lhasa. He was the first of the Tibetan regents, who were to represent the Dalai Lamas during their minority. Early regents were conscientious lamas; but later they acquired the custom of misusing their powers to further their own interests.

The eighth Dalai Lama was discovered at Thopgyal in Tsang and brought to Lhasa by the Regent in 1762, when he was four years old. He received the name of Jampal Gyatso from the third Panchen Lama, Palden Yeshe.[2]

Prior to that time, when an official party was on a long journey, all horses, fodder, and porters had to be provided free by the inhabitants of the region through which the party traveled; but subjects in the monasteries and on large estates had been exempt from this levy. Under a new ruling, the Regent Jampel Delek included those previously exempted, also decreeing that supplies could be collected from the people only on presentation of a letter of authorization from the Kashag.

The Ch'ien-lung Emperor expressed a wish to build two monasteries in Jehol, similar in design to the Potala and Tashilhunpo. The Regent

---

1. The Regent (Rgyal-tshab) is selected by the Kashag and high government officials from among certain prominent and learned lamas.

2. This account of the eighth Dalai Lama is based on YANGS-RGYAN.

readily responded to his request for the services of a Tibetan architect and several lamas and monks. At about that time, the Manchus attacked the Dzungar Mongols and ten thousand Mongol families prepared to flee into Russia. The Regent, mindful of past Tibetan ties with the Mongols—there were still some fifty of their chiefs who held Tibetan titles—interceded on their behalf and brought about an agreement with the Manchus that permitted the refugee families to remain in certain areas of their former territories.

In 1772 the Bhutanese, under the leadership of Desi Shidariva (Depa Raj) invaded Cooch Bihar and took its Raja prisoner.[3]

Since this incursion threatened the peace of Bengal and its neighboring states, Warren Hastings, the Governor-General of Bengal, dispatched an Indian battalion to drive the Bhutanese out of Cooch Bihar. After several skirmishes, the Bhutanese were pushed back as far as Buxa Duar. At that point, the Panchen Lama interceded at the request of the Bhutanese and sent a deputation to Warren Hastings with a letter asking for an end to the hostilities. At the same time, the Panchen Lama sent another deputation to the Bhutanese asking them to release the Raja of Cooch Bihar. Soon after, on April 25, 1774, a treaty of amity and commerce was signed between the British East India Company and Bhutan. Finding it a proper opportunity to open relations between Bengal and Tibet, Warren Hastings sent George Bogle, accompanied by Dr. Alexander Hamilton, a medical officer, through Bhutan to the seat of the Panchen Lama at Tashilhunpo.

Bogle and Hamilton had to remain in Bhutan for three months, during which period the Panchen Lama sought to obtain entry permits for them from the Tibetan government of Lhasa. The Englishmen finally arrived in Shigatse in October 1774. Upon meeting the Panchen Lama at Dechen Rabgya,[4] Bogle and Hamilton presented him with Warren Hastings' letter and presents. A few months after their arrival in Tibet, the government at Lhasa suggested that they return to India. At the time of their departure in 1775, the Panchen Lama forwarded a request to the Governor-General that a site on the banks of the sacred Ganges be set aside for the use of Tibetan pilgrims. Subsequently, Warren Hastings ordered the construction of a house

3. Data on the Bhutanese invasion were obtained from 'OD-ZER, and BOGLE, pp. 1–14, 82–89, 130–71.

4. Dechen Rabgya is the name of a monastery located in the district of Shang about twenty-five miles north of Tashilhunpo.

and a temple on the banks of the Hooghly, opposite Calcutta. According to Bogle, his conversations with the Panchen Lama were conducted in the Hindustani language. Perhaps the Panchen Lama had learned Hindustani from his mother, who was a Ladakhi. In 1783 Captain Samuel Turner and Thomas Saunders arrived in Shigatse to strengthen further the relationship between Bengal and Tibet.

After twenty-one years in office, the Regent, Jampel Delek, died in the year 1777. The Kashag asked the Dalai Lama, who was then about twenty years old, to assume government responsibility; but the Lama declined on the grounds that he had not completed his training. Ngawang Tsultrim of Tsemonling, who was associated with Sera monastery, was appointed the second Regent.

When the Dalai Lama received a letter from the Manchu Emperor inviting the Panchen Lama to China, the invitation was discussed in a meeting of the Regent with the Kashag. Although they considered it unwise for the Panchen Lama to go to smallpox-ridden China where the heat was often unbearable, they finally decided he should make the journey in the interest of the Buddhist religion. On June 17, 1779, the Panchen Lama departed for China by way of Mongolia. When he arrived at Jehol on July 22, 1780, the Ch'ien-lung Emperor was there to welcome him. They then proceeded to Peking, where the Panchen was given a warm welcome. He took up residence in the Yellow Palace (Huang Ssu), which had been built by the Shun-chih Emperor for the Fifth Dalai Lama. The Panchen Lama had great influence at the Imperial Court and used it to prevent Manchu interference in Tibetan affairs and to enhance the authority of the Dalai Lama. That which the Regent and Kashag had feared took place: the Panchen Lama contracted smallpox and died in Peking on November 27, 1780. His body was returned to Tashilhunpo and preserved in a mausoleum.[5]

In the same year, the Regent had to send troops under Kalon Doring Pandita into the Sa-ngan district of Kham, where local leaders had been extending their power to nearby Lithang, Markham, and Gojo, thus, encroaching on the authority of the Tibetan government. Doring Pandita spent two years in the area suppressing those refractory leaders. The culprits were finally executed and their followers exiled.

5. Sarat Chandra Das, "Contributions on the Religion, History, etc., of Tibet," *JASB*, 51–1 (1882), 35; Ernest Ludwig, *Visit of the Teshoo Lama to Peking* (Ch'ien Lung's Inscription), Peking, 1904, pp. 1–19.

The Regent and the Kashag again asked the Dalai Lama to assume office, now that he had completed his training. He agreed to do so, but requested Ngawang Tsultrim to continue as Regent and assist him in his work. On the first day of the sixth month of the Iron-Ox year (July 21, 1781), the eighth Dalai Lama, Jampal Gyatso, assumed power.

It was the custom for the Dalai Lamas to spend a fortnight, every September, at a large park to the west of the Potala, where they would picnic with their officials and bathe in a small spring. Previously, they had stayed in tents on such occasions, but the eighth Dalai Lama decided to build a summer palace there. It was built in 1783 and named the Norbulingka (Jewel Park).

In the same year, the fourth reincarnation of the Panchen Lama was discovered at Panam in Tsang, when he was two years old. He was given the name of Tenpai Nyima by the Dalai Lama.

The Regent, Ngawang Tsultrim, was a straightforward person. He treated the Manchu Ambans with polite courtesy and invited them to all official ceremonies and receptions, but he did not encourage them to take an interest in Tibetan affairs. In order to undermine his influence, the Manchus invited him to China in 1786. They treated him hospitably and kept him there for some time, while the Ambans gained in influence in Lhasa.

Not long after the Regent's departure for Peking, trouble broke out with the Gurkhas of Nepal.[6] The roots of the matter were events that had taken place some years earlier. The Tibetans had been selling wool, sheep, and salt to Nepal and buying, in exchange, rice and silver coins, which were in current use in central Tibet. After a few years, the Nepalese began to add copper to the silver coins, thus debasing their value. In 1751 the seventh Dalai Lama had written to the three Newari kings, who ruled over the principalities of Kathmandu, Patan, and Bhatgaon in Nepal, and asked them to put a stop to this practice. Then, in 1769, Prithvi Narayan, chief of the Gurkhas, overthrew the Newari rulers and consolidated his power over Nepal. In the following year, the Tibetan government sent him presents and a letter explaining the background to the trade previously existing between Tibet and Nepal. They asked him to allow this trade to continue and also apprised him of the problem of the debased silver coins; requesting

6. Data on the war with Nepal are based on RDO-RING, YANGS-RGYAN, and ROCKHILL, pp. 50-53.

that he prevent bad coins from being sent to Tibet. They suggested that pilgrims be allowed to move freely between the two countries. The reply sent by the Gurkha king was courteous but noncommittal.

In 1775 the Bhutanese, through intrigue, persuaded the Gurkhas to attack Sikkim, which lay between Nepal and Bhutan. The Tibetans offered assistance to the Sikkimese, who declined troops but accepted food supplies. At Walung, a treaty was made between Sikkim and Nepal in the presence of two Tibetan representatives, Shalu Khenpo and Dapon Padtsal. Although territorial and commercial issues were settled at this truce, the Gurkhas were annoyed at the Tibetan intervention and were looking for an excuse to attack Tibet. An excuse was found in the controversy over the third Panchen Lama's personal property, which was being claimed by the Panchen's two brothers, Drungpa Trulku and Shamar Trulku; the latter was the ninth Red Hat Kar-ma-pa Lama named Chosdup Gyatso. Shamar Trulku hoped to use Gurkha backing for his claim to the Panchen Lama's property in the Tashilhunpo monastery; while the Gurkhas wanted to use his claim as a pretext for invading Tibet.[7]

While making a routine trip to Nepal to buy medicines and to make offerings at Buddhist shrines, a Tibetan was summoned into the presence of the uncle of the young king of Nepal. He was instructed to return to Tibet with a message saying that since pure silver coins were now being minted, the former impure coins had to be devalued. Also, Tibetan salt being exported to Nepal should not contain any impurities. The Nepalese ruler threatened that unless his demands were met, he would take the Tibetan districts of Nyanang, Rongshar, and Kyirong, which border on Nepal. Moreover, the Shamar Trulku would be held as a hostage until the ruler received a reply from the Tibetan government. At the same time, the Shamar Trulku sent an appeal to the Dalai Lama that he be ransomed on the Nepalese terms. The Kashag, in reply, stated that both the old, impure and the new, pure silver coins were minted and issued in Nepal and that they were Nepal's responsibility. Since the old, impure coins were still widely circulating in Tibet, their sudden devaluation would upset the country's economy. In consideration of improved trade relations, however, the Kashag agreed to a slight reduction in the value of the old coins. As for the quality of the Tibetan salt for export, both Tibet and Nepal had inspectors at the border, whose job was to test the purity of

7. BOGLE, p. lxxvi.

the salt, as well as other commercial products. The responsibility
rested, therefore, with the inspectors to ensure the quality of the exported salt. In addition, the Kashag remarked that the Shamar Trulku
had gone to Nepal of his own accord, and therefore it was no concern
of the Kashag if he was kept a hostage. The Kashag also wrote to the
Shamar Trulku informing him he was welcome to return to Tibet if
he wished; but that he had gone to Nepal of his own volition; therefore, the Kashag did not concern itself with his welfare. The Kashag
letter concluded with an appropriate saying, "Knowing how to shoot,
you bought the bow!"

At the same time, the Kashag issued a warning to all border districts, alerting them to a possible Gurkha attack. When the Tibetan
letter reached Nepal, the Gurkhas immediately prepared to launch an
invasion. Gurkha troops entered Tibet at three places and, guided by a
servant of the Shamar Trulku, they occupied the districts of
Nyanang, Rongshar, and Kyirong. There was resistance from the local
Tibetans; but they were defeated by the large Gurkha army and
suffered heavy losses. By the summer of 1788, they had marched on
Dzongka and Shekar, two towns on different routes that led directly
to Shigatse.[8]

When news reached Lhasa, the Kashag dispatched two generals[9]
with troops from Tsang to halt the Gurkha advance. They were reinforced by an army from Ü. Kalon Yuthok, a minister of the council,
was in charge of the whole operation. The Tibetans entered Shekar
and occupied the fort; but the Gurkhas succeeded in surrounding it.
In a report to the Kashag, Kalon Yuthok said the Gurkhas had four
generals, five thousand troops, and three thousand porters.

The Manchu Amban reported the border conflict to the Ch'ien-
lung Emperor, who immediately dispatched an army commanded by
his aide-de-camp, Pachung, who spoke Tibetan. While this army was
still en route to Tibet, the Tibetans succeeded in driving the Gurkhas
out of Shekar and Saga; but the Nepalese troops still held the four districts first occupied.

An advance unit of the imperial army consisting of two thousand
troops arrived in Lhasa, under the command of Shen T'ai-tu, who in-

8. MDZES-RGYAN states that as soon as news reached Shigatse of the fall of Dzongka to
the Gurkhas on the twenty-eighth day of the seventh month of the Earth-Ape year (1788),
the six-year-old Panchen Lama, escorted by his attendents, fled to Lhasa.

9. These generals were named Dapon Padtsal and Dapon Changlochen.

formed the Kashag that he had been sent to drive the Gurkhas out of Tibet. Not being familiar with the terrain, he asked that Kalon Tenzin Paljor Doring, a young Kashag member and the son of Doring Pandita, be sent along as his guide. Tsepon Dongna Tsade and another official also accompanied them as the army set out for the battle area.

When they reached Shigatse, Shen T'ai-tu was hesitant to advance farther, not knowing what kind of foe he would have to face. Tenzin Paljor Doring made the following entry in his memoirs:

> All arrangements had been made at Shigatse for the speedy advance of the army. Fresh horses and rations were on hand. Still, ShenT'ai-tu spent five days at Shigatse, making a number of petty excuses for delaying the advance. After holding a number of meetings with his officers, Shen told me that if we advanced without waiting for the main body of the imperial army to catch up, we would be inviting defeat and disgrace. If we remain at Shigatse until the main army joined us, our total number would be too great for the resources of the town. He then asked me if I had a solution to the problem. I received the impression that the officer wanted to avoid a fight. I gave my opinion that the Tibetan troops were doing well, and since the Chinese troops looked even more capable, we were certain to defeat the Gurkhas if we advanced. If we attacked and drove the Gurkhas out now, then we would be in a stronger bargaining position when the rest of the imperial troops did arrive. Then, if the Gurkhas did not comply with our demands, we could march into Nepal. Shen T'ai-tu then openly asked me if there was no way in which we could negotiate with the Gurkhas and suggested that I write to the Dalai Lama about it. I told him that I would not pass my responsibilities on to the Dalai Lama. We had been sent to Shigatse to fight, and fight we must! [10]

Finally, the imperial troops advanced halfheartedly on Shekar, causing a lot of trouble to officials on the way. The Tibetans had no intention of making a truce with the Gurkhas; but the father of the new Panchen Lama and the secretary of Sakya, yielding to Chinese persuasion, arrived at Shekar to open negotiations. There had been no recent fighting and winter had set in, which the Chinese used as an excuse to

10. RDO-RING.

remain inactive at Shekar for eight months, where they were later joined by another two thousand troops from the main army.

Meanwhile, the Gurkhas had attacked the winter palace in western Sikkim, forcing the Sikkimese ruler and his family to flee to the capital, Gangtok.[11] Some Tibetan troops, under the command of Dapon Kyibuk, were sent from Shekar to help the Sikkimese. They brought gunpowder and supplies, and with the help of a Sikkimese officer, Drakar, they were able to drive the Gurkhas out of the country in the course of the winter. Much of the countryside had been devastated by the pillaging Gurkhas.

In the spring of 1789, the mediators stationed at Shekar were in correspondence with the Shamar Trulku, who suggested that they come with a representative of the Dalai Lama to Kyirong to negotiate with him and a representative of the Gurkhas. This offer impressed the Chinese as sensible; but the Tibetans were suspicious of the intentions of Shamar Trulku. Four Tibetan generals and Kalon Doring urged the Chinese to make the most of their strong position and bring the war to a definite conclusion, instead of entering into negotiations with the enemy before a single battle had been fought. They pointed out that the imperial troops had come all the way from China to fight a war and the Tibetans so far had ably supported them; but if they asked for a truce now they would be put in the position of pleaders. The Chinese officers turned a deaf ear to these urgings.

The two mediators, accompanied by Kalon Doring and three other officials, left for Kyirong near the Nepalese border, passing through Dzongka, which was still occupied by the Gurkhas. The monasteries and temples at Dzongka had been looted by the Nepalese troops and shrines and images stripped of their gold coating.[12] The Tibetan delegation arrived at Kyirong five days before the Gurkha representative, Bhim Sahib, who came with four officials and the Shamar Trulku. According to the memoirs of Kalon Doring, they were surrounded everywhere by Gurkha troops and made to feel more like pleaders than

11. YANGS-RGYAN; 'BRAS-LJONGS. Markham gives the name of the Nepalese leader as Subah of Murung (BOGLE, p. lxxvi).

12. According to RDO-RING, when the Tibetan delegation neared Dzongka monastery, they were informed by the monks that the golden tombs of early kings had been looted by the Gurkhas and the embalmed corpses were left lying around. The monks claimed to have recognized the corpse of Changchub 'Od, who was responsible for inviting Atisha to Tibet in A.D. 1042. Through the aid of a Ladakhi named Woma Jigpa, who spoke Nepalese, the Tibetan delegation was able to steal the corpse of Changchub 'Od and take it to safety.

negotiators. The Shamar Trulku appeared very proud and pleased with himself.

The negotiations, with proposals and counterproposals, lasted several days. Kalon Doring gave an excellent summary of the talks:

> We agreed to devalue all impure Nepalese coins being used in Tibet. The old coins, which had no impurities, would have the same value as the new coins being minted in Nepal. It was agreed that Tibetan salt would contain no impurities and that the border inspectors would strictly enforce this rule. Rice and salt must be valued at the current market price, to which of course there is no limitation. Any Nepalese rice trader having to stay in Tibet at an inn must be given free accommodation and firewood; but ten per cent of his sales from rice will have to be given the innkeeper. Tibetan merchants are not permitted to enter Nepal for any purpose of trade or exchange. If a Nepalese subject commits any crime in Tibetan territory, he will be tried and punished by the Nepalese representative in that area. Tibetan officials will have no jurisdiction in the case. To recover the four districts captured by the Gurkhas, Tibet must pay Nepal an annual tribute of 300 dotsed. The Nepalese agreed to withdraw their troops immediately on receipt of the first year's tribute.

The final treaty had an addendum, reading: "Three hundred dotsed have to be paid the first year; but if a senior and responsible Tibetan official visits Nepal in the next year and requests a reduction in the amount of tribute, the Nepalese agree to take it under consideration." [13]

Both parties wanted to make the treaty valid, so they invited two Chinese officials to Kyirong from Shekar to act as witnesses. The Chinese expressed gratification that all had gone well and suggested that both the Tibetans and Nepalese send envoys to China to thank the Manchu Emperor for his good offices. The Gurkha leader said that he would let them know his decision in a few days. Apparently having consulted the Nepalese Government, he agreed a few days later to send an emissary to Peking.

The main body of the imperial army returned, while one general with a few troops waited at Shekar to escort the Nepalese envoy to China. A month later, two Gurkhas, Hari Sahib and Bala Bahadur, ar-

13. Ibid.

rived with ten assistants bringing presents for the Emperor. They accompanied the general back to China. The Tibetans also sent an envoy. It is clear from Tibetan sources that the Chinese army was more of a hindrance than a help to Tibet in the war with Nepal. Kalon Doring states in his memoirs that the Chinese were so ashamed of their conduct that they took the original treaty away with them and removed the portion bearing their own seals before showing it to the Manchu Emperor. In a letter he wrote to the father of the Dalai Lama, Kalon Doring said that there was little difference between the Gurkhas and the Chinese. The former looted and killed because they came as enemies; but the Chinese did the same thing and they came as friends. Owing to the misconduct of his subordinate officers and failure in his responsibilities, Pachung, the Manchu aide-de-camp, committed suicide after his return to China.[14]

When they received the first payment of 300 dotsed in tribute, the Gurkha troops withdrew from the four districts. In 1790 the Dalai Lama sent an investigating team to the border districts to report on the condition of these recently occupied areas and the grievances of the inhabitants. Two officials, Tsedron Dondup Phuntsok and Shodrung Dol Pordongpa, were sent to Nepal to request a reduction in the next tribute payment, as provided for in the treaty. The Nepalese government complained that they were of low rank, and they had to return to Tibet without even having had an appointment to discuss the matter.

The Dalai Lama and the Kashag then decided it was time to recall the Regent, Ngawang Tsultrim, from Peking. His administrative experience was sorely needed, and a representative was sent to China to escort him back. The Ch'ien-lung Emperor tried to delay his departure, saying the Regent was needed in Peking; but the Regent promised to send another lama as a replacement. He returned to Tibet and was reinstated as the Regent; while the former Vice-Regent, Tenpai Gonpo Kundeling, went to China in his place.

Once in office, Ngawang Tsultrim criticized and scolded the Kashag for entering into a humiliating treaty with Nepal. The Regent, who was short-tempered and straightforward in his actions, picked up a bowl of barley flour and threw it at the heads of the Kashag, coating them with flour in the best slapstick fashion. He demoted the general

14. ROCKHILL, P. 51.

who surrendered Dzongka to the Gurkhas. Then, discovering that a number of administrative malpractices had been perpetrated by the Dalai Lama's two younger brothers and a finance secretary, the treasurer, the master of the stables, and the caretaker of the Norbulingka, the Regent sent the lot of them into exile. At the same time, he gave credit and promotion to those who had carried out their duties conscientiously.

Two fourth-rank officials, Khenche Thogmed and Tsepon Debugpa, were sent with a letter from the Dalai Lama to Nepal to request the reduction in tribute, which had been refused to their predecessors. Khenche, the monk official, died in Nepal as a result of the heat. The lay official, Tsepon Debugpa, sent a letter to the Kashag saying that he was not recognized by the Nepalese as qualified to enter into negotiations. They wanted a higher Tibetan official, like Kalon Doring, who had the authority to make decisions. It would not be necessary for Kalon Doring to enter Nepal; he had only to come as far as Nyanang on the border, where he would be met by Bhim Sahib and the Shamar Trulku. They would discuss both the question of the tribute and the return of the Shamar Trulku to Tibet under a guarantee that he would not be persecuted.

The Kashag agreed that Kalon Doring should go to Nepal; but their decision had to be sanctioned by the Regent and the Dalai Lama. When the Regent, Ngawang Tsultrim, learned of the Kashag's proposal, he went into another of his rages and accused the Kashag of wanting to join with the Chinese in catering to the Nepalese, who had developed the game of refusing to deal with Tibetan envoys. The Regent said that if the Nepalese wanted their tribute, they could come and get it themselves. The combined armies of central Tibet would be kept in readiness and he, the Regent, in spite of being an old man who had already served a seven-year term as Ganden Tri Rinpoche, would personally command the military operations. He categorically refused to send any more representatives to Nepal to beg for a reduction in tribute and the Kashag had to withdraw its proposal.

Unexpectedly, Regent Ngawang Tsultrim died of a heart attack in the Potala on the twenty-seventh day of the third month of the Iron-Hog year (April 29, 1791). The Vice-Regent, Tenpai Gonpo Kundeling, was halfway to Peking, when he received a message recalling him to Lhasa.

The Kashag, under the pressure of several threatening letters from Nepal, decided to send Doring and Yuthok, both council ministers, together with seven assistants, to Nyanang to negotiate with the Nepalese representative and the Shamar Trulku. On their arrival at Shigatse, the ministers received a letter from the Shamar Trulku, saying he was on his way with two Nepalese and a Tibetan lay official; but that they were held up at Littipakot, where the Tibetan lay feeling ill. He urged the Tibetan delegation to send a physician on ahead and to join them as soon as possible. Traveling all day and night, a physician named Tsarong and his staff reached Nyanang to find the lay Tibetan official already dead. At the same time, the Tibetans received a letter from the Nyanang district officer confirming that the Nepalese party had reached Littipakot, adding that they were busy making warlike preparations and the Tibetans should beware of treachery. The Tibetan delegation forwarded this report to the Kashag before proceeding on its way to Nyanang. A reply from the Kashag caught up with them at Shekar with instructions that they should proceed to Nyanang, but take no troops with them as this might raise the Gurkhas' suspicions and affect negotiations.

At Nyanang, they were met by a few members of the Nepalese delegation, who asked them to send subordinate officials to Dum, a place on the border some fifteen miles south of Nyanang, where the preliminary negotiations would take place. Accordingly, Tengyeling Dzasa and the officials of Nyanang district among others went to Dum to begin negotiations.

Meanwhile, the local Nepalese representatives at Nyanang asked permission to hold their Mahadeva festival celebrations in the courtyard of the Nyanang fort. In the guise of coolies and rice traders, Gurkha soldiers were able to enter the fort and join in the singing, dancing, and drinking of rice wine that continued throughout the night. In the early hours of the morning, they fell upon the Tibetan officials, who had been watching the celebrations. After a fierce fight, the officials were subdued. Kalon Doring, Kalon Yuthok, and a Tibetan general were put in chains and taken over the border into Nepal. Three Tibetan officials and thirty-five attendants were killed in the fighting at Nyanang fort, along with more than one hundred Gurkhas. The preliminary delegation at Dum met a similar fate and were imprisoned in Nepal with Kalon Doring and the others. Doring's memoirs reveal that they suffered many hardships during their confinement. Then,

Gurkha troops were dispatched through Nyanang and Kyirong in the direction of Shekar.[15]

News of these events reached Lhasa at the end of the seventh month of the year 1791. The Panchen Lama had to take refuge in Lhasa because of the threat to Shigatse, which the Gurkhas captured the following month. The Tibetans stationed at Shekar had not been able to halt their advance and the Gurkhas looted wealthy Shigatse homes and the Tashilhunpo monastery. The Tibetan Government gathered troops from Ü-Tsang and Kham provinces for an advance on Shigatse. The Manchu Amban, Pao-t'ai, reported to the Emperor and advised the Dalai Lama and Panchen Lama to move to Chamdo in Kham for their safety. Seeing the Amban's timid attitude, the Lhasa officials began to take it for granted that the city would fall, and they busied themselves removing valuables to places of safekeeping; the general populace itself was thrown into a state of panic. The Dalai Lama was compelled to address a large gathering of people from the balcony of the Jokhang temple, assuring them that the Gurkhas would not come to Lhasa and that he himself had no intention of leaving the city. He told them there was no cause for alarm and he asked all officials to carry on with their routine duties without undue excitement. This succeeded in bringing Lhasa back to a normal state.[16]

The Manchu Amban continued to request the Dalai Lama and Panchen Lama to go to Kham. The more timid of the higher-ranking officers were packing gold, silver, and other portable treasures in readiness for departure. Abbots from the three great monasteries and eminent retired statesmen held a meeting in the Potala, after which they called on the Kashag and upbraided its members for their cowardly behavior. They reminded the Kashag ministers of the Dalai Lama's address given at the Jokhang and complained that some officials were still packing treasures in preparations for flight. Where could they go with those petty treasures, when all the great treasures of the Potala and the Jokhang would have to be left behind? If people of such high rank, possessing extensive estates, could not stay and serve the country at that crucial hour, when would they ever serve it? The abbots of the three great monasteries guaranteed to protect the Dalai Lama and to defend the Jokhang and Potala. They pointed out

15. The number of Gurkha troops that advanced on Shigatse is not given in Tibetan sources; but the figure is set at 18,000 by ROCKHILL (p. 51) and BOGLE (p. lxxvi).

16. YANGS-RGYAN; MDZES-RGYAN.

that there was no point in listening to the Manchus and Chinese, who had proved by their actions in previous years that they could not protect the interests of Tibet. The outspoken attitude of the abbots put an end to all preparations for the Dalai Lama's possible departure and strengthened the morale of the army and its commanders.

The Tibetan army began to attack the Gurkhas at Shigatse and continuously cut off their supplies. An epidemic broke out among the Nepalese troops and this, together with the harassment they received from the Tibetan army, made them retreat to Shekar and Dzongka, taking with them the spoils of Shigatse and Tashilhunpo. In the fourth month of 1792, the Tibetans drove the Gurkhas farther back to Nyanang and Kyirong. At that point, thirteen thousand imperial troops arrived in Tibet under the command of the Manchu general, Fu K'ang-an, who was a relative of the Ch'ien-lung Emperor and also Viceroy of Liang-kuang. Tibetan troops numbered ten thousand, of which seven thousand were from the district of Gyarong near the province of Szechuan and three thousand from Ü-Tsang.[17]

The Tibetan and Chinese commanders, Kalon Horkhang and Fu K'ang-an respectively, sent a joint letter to the Sikkimese ruler, Tenzin Namgyal, informing him that they were advancing into Nepal with a large army and were sending him ammunition through the district officer at Phari so that he could attack Nepal from the Sikkimese side. They agreed that any territory captured by the Sikkimese could be kept by them. The Sikkimese troops did, in fact, capture some territory. They then sent a representative to Shekar to collect more gunpowder and lead.

In the seventh month, fighting took place at Kyirong and Nyanang, and the Tibetan army repulsed the Gurkhas at the fire encounter. When news of the defeat reached Nepal, along with rumors that countless Tibetan and Chinese troops were marching on the country, there was an immediate improvement in the treatment shown to Kalon Doring and the other Tibetan prisoners.

After taking Kyirong and Nyanang, the Tibetans and the Manchu army—well supplied with rations and arms—entered Nepalese territory under the joint command of the Kashag minister, Horkhang, and the Manchu general, Fu K'ang-an. The Gurkhas, after their first de-

17. Some Tibetan sources claim that the combined Tibetan-Chinese forces numbered 40,000; BOGLE (p. lxxvii) says the Chinese force alone consisted of 70,000 troops.

feat, lost confidence and retreated rapidly, offering only token resistance to the advancing forces. They sent an envoy to India to request military aid from the British,[18] and Rana Bahadur Shah ran away on the pretext of going on a hunting expedition. The Shamar Trulku poisoned himself.

A request came to Kalon Doring from the Nepalese king's uncle, who was then acting as ruler for the young monarch, asking that he go to the Tibetan camp and request them to halt their advance. All blame for the hostilities was placed on the deceased Shamar Trulku. Nepalese willingness to negotiate for peace was heavily stressed. Kalon Doring replied that it would be better if either the King himself or his uncle accompanied him on such a mission; but the uncle did not agree with this suggestion. Instead, Kazi Ratna Patte was sent with Kalon Doring in the direction of Kyirong, and Taksa Narayan Sinha with Kalon Yuthok and Tengyeling Dzasa towards Nyanang to plead for peace. Kalon Yuthok and his party met the Tibetan troops coming from Nyanang at Nawakot, only twenty miles from Kathmandu, while Kalon Doring's party met those coming from Kyirong at Theepung, fifty miles from the Nepalese capital.[19]

At Theepung, Kalon Doring met Phajo Lhakhang, the Tibetan general in command of the Ü troops. The next day, he proceeded on ahead one day's journey and met the Manchu general, Fu K'ang-an, from whom he learned that the Tibetan joint commander, Horkhang, had died a few weeks earlier, leaving Fu K'ang-an solely in command. The Nepalese representative with Kalon Doring was held as a hostage, while his attendants were allowed to return to Kathmandu with a message giving the conditions for peace. The conditions were that the Shamar Turlku's wife and followers were to be handed over to the Tibetans and all valuables taken from the Tashilhunpo monastery returned; only then would orders be issued to halt the advance of the army. The Gurkhas were asked to send a responsible man to Theepung to make decisions on behalf of his government. By that time, a replacement for Horkhang, the deceased Tibetan commander, would have arrived for the negotiations.

A few days later, Hor Kunga Paljor Shatra, another Kashag minis-

18. The Nepalese Prime Minister sought British military assistance, but was refused by Lord Cornwallis (BOGLE, p. lxxviii).

19. RDO-RING; RICHARDSON, p. 69; ROCKHILL, p. 52.

ter, arrived as the replacement for Horkhang; and a week later, the
Gurkha negotiators arrived, led by Bhim Sahib and Kula Bahadur. A
treaty was drawn up and even though a Tibetan copy of it is not
available, its essence was recorded by Kalon Doring in his memoirs:

> The Gurkhas agreed to send an envoy to Peking every five
> years to pay his country's respects to the Emperor. Delegations
> would be sent to demarcate the boundaries between Nepal and
> Tibet, and both sides expressed the desire to forget past ill feel-
> ings. The Gurkhas agreed to hand over the followers of Shamar
> Trulku and all Tibetan prisoners taken during the war. The
> Tashilhunpo spoils would also be returned.

Doring's memoirs do not reveal the decisions arrived at concerning
the reduction of tribute, the conditions governing trade between the
two countries, or the devaluation of the old coinage. The Manchus
erected a stone pillar at the foot of the Potala in Lhasa in commemora-
tion of the victory over the Gurkhas. An inscription on the pillar,
dated in 1792, is in Tibetan, Manchu, and Chinese.[20]

During the course of the Gurkha war, the Lhasa populace had put
up posters protesting the exploitation and interference of the Manchu
Ambans in Tibetan affairs and demanding the withdrawal of imperial
troops. Posters and pamphlets circulated at the time of Fu K'ang-an's
stay in Lhasa alleged that the imperial troops had entered Tibet unre-
quested and that their presence had caused a hundred times more
harm to the Tibetans that the Gurkha invasion. It was claimed that
the Tibetans would have been able to drive out the enemy without
any outside help. To placate the Tibetans, the two Manchu Ambans
then serving in Lhasa were removed for misconduct and returned to
China.

Tibetan accounts say that the ashes of the Shamar Trulku were
handed over to the Tibetans, along with the body of one of his followers, who had committed suicide en route to the Tibetan camp. The
lama's wife and twenty of his followers were released. Tibetan prisoners were also released, and over a hundred porters were provided to
carry the Tashilhunpo treasures back to Tibet.

The British governor-general, Lord Cornwallis, had dispatched
Colonel Kirkpatrick to Nepal to enquire into the situation, but, by
the time he arrived, negotiations between Nepal, Tibet, and China had

20. For a translation of the inscription, see BELL, pp. 275–78.

been concluded.[21] The Manchus got the best of the bargain in the treaty, because the Tibetan council minister, Horkhang, had died and his replacement had no real experience at negotiations. The Manchu leaders were taken on a tour of Nepal and were accompanied on their return journey to China by envoys, who were to pay tribute to the Ch'ien-lung Emperor. An elephant sent as a present to the Dalai Lama was also sent with the returning troops.

When everything was settled, the Dalai Lama inquired into the behavior of those conducting the campaign and demoted the two Kashag ministers, Kalon Doring and Kalon Yuthok, as well as Tengyeling Dzasa. The estates of Shamar Trulku and his monastery of Yangpachen were confiscated by the Tibetan government, and a law was enacted that made it a crime for him to reincarnate.

When the Nepalese envoys returned from China, they brought their ruler, Rana Bahadur Shah, the title of Wang and a peacock plume for his hat; both had been presented by the Manchu Emperor and denoted special privileges. Similar honors were bestowed on his uncle, the acting ruler.

Following the war with the Gurkhas, the Ch'ien-lung Emperor promoted the Ambans to the same level as the Governor-General of Szechuan and directed that all petitions, formerly submitted directly to the Emperor, must now be sent to the Ambans first. Imperial forces were stationed at Shigatse and Dingri as outposts to guard against further Nepalese incursions. Prior to 1792, the Ambans were little more than political observers for the Emperor and sometimes not of high ability and resolve. The behavior of such Ambans as the timid Paot'ai caused the Emperor to reorganize the duties of the Ambans in Lhasa and to send more capable men to serve.

The main base for later Chinese claims of sovereignty over Tibet was the sending of military assistance by the Manchu Emperor, Ch'ienlung, to Tibet to drive out the Gurkhas. It is to be noted, however, that the Manchus supplied imperial troops as an ally of long standing and that the imperial troops did not enter Tibet to attack Tibetans or to conquer their country. The "patron-lama" relationship between the Dalai Lama and the Manchu Emperor was predicated on the mutual responsibilities of each. The patron was to provide temporal assistance;

21. BOGLE (p. lxxviii) states that military aid to Nepal was refused because the British had commercial relations with the Chinese and it was necessary for them to maintain good relations with the Emperor.

the lama, spiritual guidance. When the Manchus were strong in China, as they were during the reigns of K'ang-hsi and Ch'ien-lung, the Emperor fulfilled his obligations as imperial patron by sending troops into Tibet against the Dzungars first and then against the Gurkhas. When the Manchus began to decline in power during the ninteenth century, they were no longer able to supply temporal assistance to the Tibetans; consequently, no imperial troops were involved in the Dogra war of 1841–42 or the second Gurkha war of 1855–56. The decline of Manchu power in China led to a degeneration of the control exercised by the Ambans in Lhasa to the point where again they were little more than political observers.

In 1796 a feudal lord, with estates at Lo Menthang near the Nepalese border, had stopped paying his annual tax of gold to the Lhasa government. He claimed that he had been exempted from his tax by the Manchu General, Fu K'ang-an, in gratitude for his services during the Gurkha war. The Kashag informed the lord that the Manchu General had no authority to grant an exemption of tax, as he had come only as an ally to assist in the military campaign. The lord of Lo Menthang was obliged to pay up his tax arrears.[22]

Jampal Gyatso, the eighth Dalai Lama, died on the eighteenth day of the tenth month of the Wood-Mouse year (November 19, 1804) at the age of forty-six. Throughout his reign, he had immersed himself in religious matters and took little interest in politics, leaving the administration in the hands of the Regent.

The Regent, Tenpai Gonpo Kundeling, ruled Tibet for some time after the death of the eighth Dalai Lama. He made arrangements for rehabilitating those people of Toh (western Tibet), who had lost property during the Gurkha war, by exempting them from taxes and giving them supplies of food grains from government granaries. Similar relief was extended to those who had been living along the route taken by the imperial army during its advance against the Gurkhas and its return to China.

Some people, who had earlier protested through pamphlets and posters against the presence of Manchus and Chinese in Tibet, began to complain openly to the Regent and to the Emperor. They accused some Tibetan officials of collaborating with the Chinese, and they also demanded the permanent withdrawal of the Ambans and the gar-

22. YANGS-RGYAN.

rison. Manchu and Chinese officials traveling between Kham and central Tibet began to be harassed by the people.

The Regent asked the people to avoid disturbing the peace and at the same time, wrote to the Manchu Emperor suggesting that the demands be met. The new Manchu Emperor, Chia-ch'ing (reigned 1796–1820), who had succeeded to the throne upon the death of Ch'ien-lung, sent two officials to Lhasa to investigate.[23] Their report on conditions there resulted in the recall of several imperial officers and the reduction of the garrison to about two hundred and fifty men.

As a reciprocal gesture, the Tibetan government arrested and imprisoned the protest movement's ringleaders, Ngawang Solpa, a monk and Tenpa Tsering, a lay official. While the Manchu investigators were in Lhasa, rumors were circulating that the demoted Kalon Tenzing Paljor Doring, who had a summer house close to the residency of the Ambans, was in close contact with them. This, plus the fact that his thirteen-year-old son, Sonam Paljor Doring, had contrived to become a member of the Kashag, angered the Tibetan people. They held demonstrations and accused the ex-minister Doring, his son, and the monk member of the Kashag of collaborating with the Ambans in their own interests rather than those of the country. They were also accused of emptying the government treasury. The people refused to recognize the Emperor of China as their patron, declaring that it would be better to turn to the Gurkhas for future assistance. Regent Kundeling sent Tibetan troops to protect the Ambans and their storehouses. He then placed Tenzin Paljor Doring, his son Kalon Sonam Paljor, and the Kalon Lama Ganden Sharpa under house arrest.

The two Manchu investigators began to disagree, a fact revealed in their reports to the Emperor. Consequently, two new officials[24] were sent to Lhasa to conduct an investigation. They arrived in 1805 and held an inquiry. The Amban Ts'e-pa-k'e was returned to China in chains and the other exiled to Urumchi in Chinese Turkestan. The Manchus were losing influence in Tibetan affairs because of the low quality of officials and ineffective Ambans being posted to Lhasa. Following the investigations, the Regent demoted the two council minis-

23. RDO-RING gives the names of the two officials as Tsewo and an assistant, Shen. Tsewo is the same as Ts'-e-pa-k'e (LI, p. 59).

24. They were Yün and an assistant named Liu (RDO-RING).

ters, Kalon Sonam Paljor Doring and Kalon Lama Ganden Sharpa, and the chief troublemakers among the anti-Manchu demonstrators were exiled from the Lhasa area.

In 1807 a dispute arose over the claims of candidates for the ninth reincarnation of the Dalai Lama. Both were then two years old. One had been born in Kham, the other in Amdo. The Regent sent emissaries to investigate the rival claims, and their report favored the boy from Dan Chokhor in Kham. Both candidates were then brought to the vicinity of Lhasa, where they were examined by the Regent and the Kashag members. Only the Kham candidate was able to distinguish the eighth Dalai Lama's personal effects from mere imitations; therefore he was recognized as the ninth Dalai Lama (1806–1815) and an announcement was made to this effect by the Regent. In the following year, the Panchen Lama gave him the name of Lungtok Gyatso.[25]

After the Gurkha war, the Ch'ien-lung Emperor tried to institute a new system by which the reincarnations of high lamas, such as the Dalai Lama and Panchen Lama, would be determined by lottery. The Emperor sent a golden urn to Tibet in 1793 to be used for the drawing of lots. The names of the candidates were to be written on slips of paper and then one drawn from the urn to determine the reincarnation. Although there were two candidates for the ninth reincarnation of the Dalai Lama, the golden urn system was ignored and the selection made by the Tibetan officials themselves. In the ninth month of the Earth-Snake year (1808), Lungtok Gyatso, the ninth Dalai Lama, was enthroned in the Potala. Representatives from China, Mongolia, Nepal, and Bhutan attended the exotic and impressive ceremony.

For some time, the two chiefs of the Golog tribe in eastern Tibet, Khangan and Khangsar, had been disobeying instructions from the Tibetan Government. Kalon Shatra was sent with troops to deal with them. He spent two years in the district, pacifying the Golog people and ensuring their obedience to Lhasa.[26]

For years, small caravans of Tibetan merchants had traveled to and from Tachienlu and Sining on the Chinese border. Traders to Tachienlu took with them herbal medicines and returned with brick tea; those going to Sining exchanged Tibetan woolen cloth for horses and

25. Data on the ninth Dalai Lama were obtained from YID-'PHROG and MDZES-RGYAN.
26. YID-'PHROG; SA-'BRUG.

mules. Because of the arduous nature of the long journey and the danger of bandits, the traders made the trip only once a year. Group rivalries naturally developed. Prices fluctuated and disputes were common, fostered by the lack of security and control. In an effort to remedy this situation, the Regent appointed trade agents (Garpon) to accompany the caravans to Tachienlu and Sining. The agents administered the trading camps and regulated prices. Using the small troop escorts at their command, they were able to deal with bandits. Trading caravans began to travel together in larger groups and finally in one big party. Security and organization were thus improved. From documents left by the Garpon officials who had traveled to and from Dranag Khasum, Tsoloma, Shangti, and Kormo on Tibet's northeastern border with China, it is clear that the people of those places were then paying taxes to Tibet and that Tibetan law was operative there.[27]

In 1810, while the ninth Dalai Lama was still a minor, the Regent, Tenpai Gonpo Kundeling, died. He was succeeded by Demo Thubten Jigme. Regent Demo was susceptible to occasional mental disorders, but these did not prevent him from administering the country well. In fact, there was no civil strife during his reign, and crops were good. A Tibetan saying arose, "When Demo becomes mad, the country is at peace."

As the political influence of the Manchus began to wane in Tibet, an attempt to exert influence through religious channels was made. Chinese monks in residence in the great Tibetan monasteries persuaded the Tibetan monks that foreign travelers would pose a threat to the Budhist religion.[28] Under pressure from the monks of the three big monasteries of Drepung, Sera, and Ganden, the Government issued instructions to all district officers on the borders to prevent foreign travelers from entering Tibetan territory. This propaganda had such an effect on the minds of the Tibetans that even in later years it was believed that one's faith would be endangered by eating sweets or using soap imported from India. Much later on, even the British en-

27. SA-'BRUG.

28. In 1811 Thomas Manning, traveling in disguise, arrived in Lhasa and met the ninth Dalai Lama. Manning was received by the Tibetans without hostility and he left confirmation of "the bad quality and conduct of the Imperial representatives at Lhasa." (RICHARDSON, p. 72).

couraged a policy of isolation—for different political reasons—by praising the Tibetan way of life and showing it to be preferable to the unsettled conditions prevailing elsewhere.

Because of lack of contact with the outside world, Tibet did not make the kind of progress achieved by other nations. At the same time, the outside world knew almost nothing about Tibet and accepted without question the Chinese or British version of its situation. The Tibetans did not counter these political versions, simply because they did not know about them. It is only since the Tibetans have been forced out of their own country that they have come to realize how isolated they had been from the rest of the world.

During the 1814 Gurkha war with the British in India, the Nepalese King, Girvan-Yuddha Vikrama Shah, appealed to the Tibetan Government for assistance. Although it is not known whether an official reply was sent, there is in existence a letter written by the Regent to the heads of monasteries in Tibet saying that prayers should be offered for Nepal's success in the war, which seems to indicate that Tibetan sympathies were with the Nepalese at that time.[29]

At the age of ten, the ninth Dalai Lama attended the Monlam festival at the Jokhang temple during the New Year's celebration of 1815. He had a severe cold when he left the Potala for the temple and the exposure led to pneumonia. He died on the sixteenth day of the second month of the Wood-Hog year (March 26, 1815).

Two years later, the Regent received the names of five boys, all one year old, who were candidates for the reincarnation of the Dalai Lama. The claims of two boys from Ü-Tsang were dismissed. Of the three Kham candidates, the child born in Lithang seemed the most likely choice. The Manchu Ambans urged that the system of drawing lots from the golden urn be used to avoid a possible dispute. In 1819 all three candidates were brought to Nethang, near Lhasa, where they were visited by the Regent and the Kashag ministers. The Lithang child was by far the most promising; therefore, without making their decision public, the Regent, members of the Kashag, and representatives of the three big monasteries confirmed him to be the tenth Dalai Lama. When the Ambans learned of this, they encouraged the parents of the other two candidates to press their claims. The Ambans were determined to introduce the lottery system decreed by the Emperor, but the Lhasa citizens protested against it.

29. YID-'PHROG.

At that point, the Regent Demo died of smallpox. This was to prove a particularly unfortunate event for Tibet, for the regency was given to Jampel Tsultrim Tsemonling, a less astute and incisive man than his predecessor. In view of the strong public opinion about the Lithang candidate, the parents of the two rival candidates withdrew their claims. For the sake of appearance, the Ambans went to examine all three candidates, before agreeing that the Lithang boy was the proper choice. They instructed the Regent that he was free to make his own decision but cleverly insinuated that he should make it appear that the lottery system of the Manchu Emperor had not been ignored.

In the Water-Horse year (1822), the Regent announced the confirmation of the Lithang candidate as the tenth Dalai Lama, saying that he had been selected by the drawing of lots, even though this was not the case. Subsequent political implications, were to prove the Regent's actions mistaken and short-sighted: the Amban-supervised drawing of lots to select a Dalai Lama has been cited in later times as proof of Chinese so-called "sovereignty" over Tibet. The tenth Dalai Lama, named Tsultrim Gyatso by the Panchen Lama, was enthroned in the Potala with the usual ceremonies.[30]

During the rule of Regent Tsemonling, a detailed study of agricultural conditions was made in the province of Ü. Statistics were collected on food production, family occupations, and population trends. This study, which was without precedence, helped the Regent improve his system of collecting revenues.

In 1832 Mongols, living near Kokonor lake under a leader named Junang Dzasa, attacked and robbed a neighboring tribe of Dranag Khasum. Regent Tsemonling dispatched troops to the trouble spot, under the command of the council minister, Kalon Thonpa and the general, Dapon Sarjung. On the way, they recruited more troops from Derge and Dimchi Nyernga. A number of skirmishes took place with the Mongols, and soon the tribe under Junang Dzasa surrendered. Junang Dzasa, together with his son and some other leaders, was taken to Lhasa to do homage and submit before the Dalai Lama. Two years

---

30. According to CHU-RTA, the majority's choice fell upon the candidate from Lithang, and, owing to the strong public feeling against the lottery system, the Manchu Ambans left the final decision to the Regent. Since the Regent himself confirmed the Lithang candidate as the tenth Dalai Lama, it would seem the lottery system was not used; yet he announced that the choice was by lottery. No doubt strong confusion surrounded the question of the selection of the tenth Dalai Lama. For example, MDZES-RGYAN states that he was chosen by the lottery system.

later, the Regent sent another minister, Kalon Dondup Dorje Shatra with troops to bring to obedience the district of Powo, in southwest Kham. The people of that district, administered by Kanam Depa, refused to pay taxes or to adhere to Tibetan government law. Kanam Depa and the people of the district were brought under control and had to pay their taxes according to the law.[31]

The tenth Dalai Lama, Tsultrim Gyatso, was continually in poor health and did not live much longer than the previous reincarnation. On the first day of the ninth month of the Fire-Bird year (1837), he died, aged twenty-one. He had preferred to mingle with the common people rather than the court officials and was often found sunning himself on his veranda with office clerks. Because of his poor health, the Tibetan government brought him the best physicians and frequently held special prayers for his recovery. One day when the Regent and the Kashag ministers came to see him he said that all the trouble they were taking to make him better was really for their own prestige. He pointed out that the Tibetan people had suffered tremendously during the clashes in Powo and the Kokonor region and that the state of the country was worse than before, in spite of repeated claims by government officers to the contrary. He is reported to have told them, "Whether you are making these improvements, as you claim, or not, the condition of my subjects has deteriorated." Judging from this disillusioned conversation with the Kashag ministers, it would appear that the officials of the time were not carrying out their duties in an efficient manner.

In 1841 two candidates for the eleventh reincarnation of the Dalai Lama were discovered. They were brought to Lhasa and put through the usual tests. The child born in Gathar in Kham in 1838 seemed to be the more likely candidate. In some accounts, it is said that on the twenty-fourth day of the fifth month of the Iron-Ox year (1841), the boy from Gathar was chosen by the drawing of lots. It is possible that this Dalai Lama was selected by lottery; but no details are given and there is no record of a dispute between the Manchus and the Tibetans over his choice. The Panchen Lama gave the eleventh Dalai Lama the name of Khedrup Gyatso at Dechen Sa-nga Khar.[32]

Several years earlier, the Dogra Raja of Jammu had been creating constant trouble on the border with Ladakh and a Ladakhi family, de-

31. DAR-HAN.
32. ROL-MO.

scended from the early kings, was forced to flee into Tibet. Then in 1834, Maharaja Gulab Singh of Kashmir sent Wazir Zorawar Singh and his troops into Ladakh to back up the Dogra forces. After some fighting, Ngodup Tenzin, the minister of Ladakh, surrendered to Zorawar Singh, who in turn deposed the ruler, named Lala, and enthroned the minister Ngodup in his place. Ladakh agreed to pay an annual tribute of five thousand rupees to Kashmir. Apparently he did not live up to the agreement, for six years later Zorawar Singh returned with an army of six thousand troops.[33] Ngodup Tenzin was now deposed and the former ruler reinstated.

Formerly, when Tibetan government traders had returned to Ladakh from central Tibet with brick tea in exchange for cotton cloth and dried fruits, they had been provided with accommodations and transport; but these facilities were ended in 1841. At the same time, Zorawar Singh and Lala, with Sikh and Ladakhi troops, entered Tibet.[34] Lala died at Balti in Tibetan territory and was immediately succeeded by his cousin, who was accompanying the troops. Fighting took place at Ngari Korsum in western Tibet between Zorawar Singh's army and a Tibetan force commanded by the generals, Dapon Shatra and Dapon Surkhang. Zorawar Singh's predominantly Sikh forces defeated the ill-equipped Tibetans and advanced up to Takla-khar in Purang.

Large scale Tibetan reinforcements were sent to western Tibet under the command of the council minister, Kalon Pal-lhun. Fighting lasted several months, and as winter approached, Kalon Pal-lhun intensified his efforts and succeeded in driving Zorawar Singh's troops out of Taklakhar, where the battle lasted five days. Heavy snow began to fall and the half-frozen Sikhs, unaccustomed to such conditions, were unable to prevent the Tibetans from descending upon them. Fierce hand-to-hand combat ensued. While mounting his horse, Zorawar Singh was recognized by Migmar, a platoon commander, who

33. The account given here of the Tibetan-Dogra War is based on LA-DAGS and KHANG-GSAR. (It is to be noted that Kalon Khang-gsar was not involved in this war; but he noted down the events of the war perhaps out of personal interests, because it was one of his subjects, Migmar, who killed Zorawar Singh.) See also the account by Tshe-brtan of Kha-la-rtse, which is included in A. H. Francke, *Antiquities of Indian Tibet*, Tibetan Text 2 (Calcutta, 1926), 245–50.

34. Zorawar Singh's forces were in three divisions. One division advanced towards Tashi-gong, another through Rupshu, and the last marched into Rudok district (Margaret Fisher, Leo Rose, and Robert Huttenback, *Himalayan Battleground*, New York, 1963, p. 50).

hurled a spear at the Sikh leader and brought him to the ground. He then decapitated Zorawar Singh and carried his head back to the Tibetan camp.

Tibetan accounts say that the Sikh army scattered and that over three thousand Sikhs were killed in the course of the foray. Seven hundred Sikhs and two Ladakhi ministers were taken prisoner. The remainder of the defeated army fled towards Ladakh, pursued by the Tibetans almost as far as Leh.[35]

Those Tibetans who pursued the disorganized army finally halted at Dumra, now called Nupra, where they remained for over a year. In 1842 Maharajah Gulab Singh sent eight thousand Sikh reinforcements into Ladakh under the command of Dewan Hari Chand and Wazir Ratun. The subsequent fighting finally ended when the Dogra forces flooded the Tibetan camp. The Tibetan generals, Dapon Shatra and Dapon Surkhang, with approximately sixty troops, were captured and taken to Leh, the capital of Ladakh. Ladakhi records mention a third general, Dapon Ragashag, who was said to have committed suicide on the way,[36] but Tibetan records mention only two generals.

At Leh, the capital of Ladakh, the party was met by Kalon Pal-lhun's representative, who negotiated with Dewan Hari Chand. It was agreed, under a temporary treaty, that the Tibetan troops would be withdrawn from Dumra and that neither party would violate the other's territory. Those prisoners wishing to return to their own country would be allowed to do so. They agreed to draw up a more comprehensive treaty later on. In the meantime, the two Tibetan generals and the captured soldiers were repatriated. One third of the Sikh and Ladakhi prisoners elected to remain in Tibet. The Sikhs were resettled in the warmer regions of southern Tibet by the government and many of them married Tibetan girls. The Sikhs are known to have introduced the cultivation of apricots, apples, grapes, and peaches into the country.

Tibetan records show that Zorawar Singh's army had been well equipped with firearms and cannon, while the Tibetans were armed with swords, spears, bows, and a few primitive muskets brought from Mongolia. The Tibetans admitted that they owed victory to the heavy snowfall. The Tibetan government honored Kalon Pal-lhun. The two Tibetan generals, Shatra and Surkhang, were made members of

35. Fisher, Rose, and Huttenback, pp. 53–54.
36. LA-DAGS.

Yumbulagang, believed to be the oldest existing castle in Tibet, perhaps fourteen or fifteen centuries old. Located in the Yalung Valley.

The Pillar of Shol-do-ring, erected in the ninth century, bearing inscriptions in Tibetan and Chinese of the Sino-Tibetan Treaty of 821.

The Samye Monastery, built by King Trisong Detsen in the eighth century. Located southeast of Lhasa on the north bank of the Tsang-po River.

The Ganden Monastery, near Lhasa, built by Tsongkhapa in 1409.

Costume worn by early Tibetan kings, brought into use by the fifth Dalai Lama. Until recent years this type of costume was worn once every New Year by certain officials of the government.

The thirteenth Dalai Lama and his ministers in Calcutta, 1910. Front row, from left: Lonchen Changkhyim, Lonchen Shatra, His Holiness the Dalai Lama, Lonchen Shalkhang, Kalon Serchung.

Representatives of Tibet, Great Britain, and China at the Simla Convention, 1914. Front row, from left: an assistant to Ivan Chen; Sekyong Trulku, Prince of Sikkim; Ivan Chen, Chinese Plenipotentiary; Sir Henry McMahon, British Plenipotentiary; Lonchen Satra, Tibetan Plenipotentiary; Teji Trimon, assistant; Nedon Khanchung, secretary.

The Tibetan Cabinet with members of the Chinese Condolence Mission of 1934. Seated, from left, Tibetan Ministers: Chikyap Khanpo, Lozang Gelek, Kalon Nangchung, Kalon Trimon, Kalon Lama Changkyim, Kalon Bonshod. Arrow points to Chinese Mission leader, General Huang Mu-sung.

The Rating Regent, in dark glasses, and his party on journey to the famous Lake of Chok-horgyal in search of portents leading to the discovery of the fourteenth Dalai Lama, 1935.

The Tibetan uprising of 1959, showing women demonstrating before the Potala.

His Holiness the Dalai Lama. (Photograph by John Faber.)

Flight of the Dalai Lama into India, 1959. The Dalai Lama is on white horse.

Tsepon Shakabpa with the late Indian Prime Minister Shri Jawaharlal Nehru.

the Kashag and became known by the new title of Kalon (Minister). Migmar, the man who beheaded Zorawar Singh, was given a promotion and rewarded with a small estate.[37]

Kalon Surkhang was asked to join Dapon Peshi, the Tibetan general in western Tibet, and proceed with him to Leh to negotiate the final treaty with Ladakh. After a meeting of the two parties, two letters of agreement were drawn up, one written by the Ladakhis, one by the Tibetans. Each side signed and sealed only its own agreement. (The two letters were later preserved in the Kashag office in Lhasa, where I myself had the opportunity to examine them.) The letters promised everlasting friendship, the recognition of ancient boundaries, and the continuation of trade between Ladakh and Tibet. Tibetan traders in Ladakh were to receive free accommodations and transport as before.

The letters of agreement (translated and reproduced in the Appendix) are quite different from the version quoted in Aitchison's Collection of Treaties.[38] His version includes mention of the Emperor of China among the dignitaries listed in the "agreement"; but, as far as I could determine, the letters of agreement were exchanged only between Ladakh and Tibet, and the Emperor was not mentioned in the letters. Moreover, there were no imperial troops involved in the Dogra war; the so-called Opium War was raging in China against the British and the Emperor could not spare troops to fight in western Tibet. The small garrison in Lhasa was, by that time, composed largely of Sino-Tibetan troops, that is to say, sons of Chinese soldiers and Tibetan mothers, and there had been a deterioration in both the quality and discipline in the garrison. It is generally acknowledged that the defeat of the Dogras was brought about exclusively by Tibetan troops under the command of a Kashag minister.[39]

A recent study of the period states that "the Tibetan signatories had been taken prisoner and it does not appear that any reference was made to Lhasa before the conclusion of the agreement."[40] This does not seem to have been the case. The two generals, Shatra and Surkhang, had been released before the signing of the final agreement and had returned to Lhasa, where each was made Kalon (Minister) in

37. KHANG-GSAR.

38. For Aitchison's version, see RICHARDSON, pp. 246–47. For the Tibetan version, see the Appendix.

39. LI, p. 60.

40. RICHARDSON, p. 247.

the Kashag. Since the agreement cited in the study mentioned refers to Surkhang as a Kalon, it indicates that he had to have returned to Lhasa before the treaty was signed, since he was a Dapon (General) when he first was captured.

On the twentieth day of the ninth month of the Water-Tiger year (1842), the Ladakh ruler sent a letter of agreement to the Kashag through Kalon Surkhang. That letter was stamped with the red seal of the Ladakh ruler and the black seal of the people's representative.

In 1844 the Kashag members held a meeting with representatives of the three big monasteries and other officials in which it was decided to depose Regent Tsemonling and confiscate his estates and documents. No reason for this decision is given in Tibetan accounts. Obviously, however, a Regent who has been in power for twenty-four years is not suddenly removed from office without some reason. A study of documents relating to the period indicates that the Regent was on bad terms with the Panchen Lama, Tenpai Nyima (1781–1854), and that a rebellious attendant of the Panchen Lama had been favored by the Regent and was made an official at Lhasa.[41] It is also believed that there was a dispute between the Regent and the Changkya Hutuktu, a lama of Drepung monastery, over the issue of rights to a certain estate.

Kalon Surkhang and Kalon Chikhang Chagdrongpa, representing the Kashag, went to Tsemonling's house in Lhasa to collect all official documents. The monks of the Sera Mey college at Sera monastery, to which Tsemonling belonged, showed their resentment in a forthright way. They caught the two Kashag ministers at Tsemonling's house and gave them a severe beating. Kalon Surkhang was so critically injured he could not attend to his Kashag duties; he died a few months later.[42]

From September 1844 until May 1845, the Panchen Lama was the appointed administrator for Lhasa, during which period another Regent was being selected. This fact seems to lend credence to the theory that Tsemonling's downfall was connected to his differences with the Panchen Lama. In the spring of 1845, the Panchen Lama resigned, and Yeshe Gyatso Rating was appointed the next Regent. The ministers of the Kashag at that time were Kalon Pal-lhun, Kalon Wangchuk Gyalpo Shatra, and Kalon Chikhang Chagdrongpa. Kalon

41. DOCUMENTS.
42. SHING-'BRUG.

Tashi Khangsar had been appointed to replace the deceased Surkhang. Of the council ministers, Kalon Wangchuck Gyalpo Shatra was to emerge as an important and influential figure.

On the third day of the third month of the Water-Ox year (1853), a trade agreement was drawn up between local border officials of Tibet and Ladakh (see Appendix). The agreement laid down future procedures with the stipulations that the Ladakhis would supply horses to Tibetan trade agencies and that more capable trade agents would be sent to Ladakh in the future and in turn, better envoys to Tibet. Tibetan trade agents were to be provided with kitchen boys and grooms, and exempted from customs duty if they carried proper permits. The Ladakhi traders were to be given a similar exemption. Traders from both countries were to be free to graze their pack-animals in either country.

While this trade agreement was being negotiated, a letter was sent to Dangtse Kharpon, a representative of Thanedar Bisram stationed at Od in Rudok, which read: "The Tibetan and Ladakhi leaders have concluded negotiations regarding our common borders. We have agreed to adhere to the same border demarcations that existed previously. You are requested, therefore, to hand over Od to the Tibetans and to look after your own territory." It was signed by Thanedar Bisram and dated the fourth day of the third month of the Water-Ox year (1853).[43]

The eleventh Dalai Lama, who had been continuing his education, now reached the age of seventeen and was asked by the government to assume power. He was enthroned on the thirteenth day of the first month of the Wood-Hare year (ca. March 1, 1855). Regent Rating resigned and retired to his monastery. Eleven months later, the Dalai Lama died and the Regent, whose experience was valued, was recalled to serve by the Kashag.

Shortly after the death of the Dalai Lama, war again broke out with the Gurkhas, who were then under the power of the minister, Jung Bahadur Rana. The Gurkhas attacked Tibet on the pretext of trade violations and again occupied the districts of Nyanang, Rongshar, Dzongka, and Purang. The Tibetan government sent troops from Lhasa and militia from Kham under the command of Kalon Tashi Khangsar. Fighting ensued and there were casualties on both sides, but the Tibetans were unable to recover their territories. Monks

43. BKA'-SHAG.

from the three big monasteries volunteered to fight and left in large numbers for the battle area, but they did no actual fighting. Before the monks reached the front, the Gurkhas had opened negotiations and requested Tibetan representatives to proceed to Kathmandu.

A ten-point agreement was drawn up on the eighteenth day of the third month of the Fire-Dragon year (March 24, 1856).[44] Under its terms, the Tibetan government agreed to pay annually ten thousand Nepalese rupees to the Gurkha government and to discontinue the collection of duties from Gurkha merchants and traders. Tibet also agreed to give up Sikh and Gurkha prisoners taken in the recent war, together with all captured weapons. The Gurkhas agreed in turn to return to Tibet the districts of Kyirong, Nyanang, Dzongka, Purang, and Rongshar, as well as all arms and yaks belonging to Tibetan subjects. It was arranged that if disputes should arise between Gurkha and Tibetan subjects, representatives of both governments would sit together and jointly adjudicate them. Murderers would be surrendered to their native country's authorities. Those who participated in the war on the side of the enemy were to be respected in regard to their person and property. Thus, Tibet regained its lost districts, but Nepal gained annual tribute and extraterritoriality in Tibet.

44. For a full translation of this agreement, see BELL, pp. 278–80; RICHARDSON, pp. 247–49, which correspond favorably with the original Tibetan text.

II

Desi Shatra and Palden Dondup: Strong Men of the Nineteenth Century

The Regent, Rating, conducted a search for the reincarnation of the twelfth Dalai Lama and found three suitable candidates. The usual tests revealed the superior qualities of a child born of the first day of the twelfth month of the Fire-Dragon year (December 27, 1856) at Olga in southern Tibet. The majority of the Tibetan people tried to persuade the Regent to confirm the child as the Dalai Lama without resorting to the drawing of lots from the golden urn; but Regent Rating maintained that he would have to follow the procedure established in the case of the selection of the eleventh Dalai Lama. A few officials approached him personally and told him that if the lottery was drawn in favor of the child already selected, the people would not object; but, if another child was chosen, they would not be responsible for the consequences.

The three candidates were being kept near Lhasa. With the approach of the Monlam festival and the arrival of monks from the three big monasteries and others, the Regent began to fear trouble and sent troops to guard the children. In the beginning of 1858, Regent Rating risked holding the lottery during the height of the Monlam festival. Fortunately for all concerned, the name of the candidate already selected came up first. The tension created in Lhasa by this matter immediately subsided. The Regent gave the boy the name of Trinley Gyatso and confirmed him as the twelfth Dalai Lama.[1]

Regent Rating was taking advantage of his power position to make liberal use of his seal, dispensing titles and confirming ownership of estates according to his own inclination. Wangchuk Gyalpo Shatra

1. This account of the twelfth Dalai Lama is based on DANGS-SHEL.

held a private discussion with his colleague, Tashi Khangsar, and they agreed that the Regent was using his seal much too frequently. They brought up the issue at an official meeting of the Kashag, and, finding that the other council ministers were of the same opinion, they decided it was harmful to the government for the Regent to have absolute control over the use of his seal. They approached the Regent with the suggestion that a "Keeper of the Seal" be appointed for the Regent, just as there was one for the Dalai Lama, because it would increase the prestige of his position. The Regent agreed, and it was decided in a meeting of the Kashag that Shatra, being the senior council member, should be appointed Keeper of the Seal. A document to this effect was drawn up by the Kashag and submitted to the Regent for his signature.[2] It reached him in the evening, while he was meeting with his adviser, the Lord Chamberlain (Chikyab Khenpo).[3] The Lord Chamberlain warned Regent Rating that the Kashag's plan was a ruse to deprive him of his powers and advised him to find out who was behind the suggestion to institute a Keeper of the Seal. Through Tashi Khangsar, the Regent discovered that Shatra had instigated the affair. Shatra was then summoned to the Regent's office, where he expected to receive the Regent's seal; instead, he found himself falsely accused of a number of malpractices by the Regent, who stripped him of his rank and position. Without being given an opportunity to visit his home, Shatra was exiled from Lhasa to his estates at Nyemo Jako, where it was hoped he would remain quiescent.

Although married, Wangchuk Gyalpo Shatra had been having a love affair with another woman. Full of resentment, his wife was looking for some way to get even with her husband for hurting her pride. While Shatra was a council minister, he had been in frequent communication with Jung Bahadur Rana, the Nepalese minister. In reply to a letter from the Rana minister asking what he was doing at that time, Shatra replied that he had been removed from office and forced to live on his estates. This letter, with a present, was sent to Nepal; but somehow the handwritten copy fell into the hands of Shatra's wife, who forwarded it to a rival in Lhasa. It was promptly handed over to the Regent with the suggestion that Shatra was con-

2. The information given here on Wangchuk Gyalpo Shatra was obtained from BSHAD-SGRA and from records of prominent officials who lived at the time of Shatra.

3. The Lord Chamberlain at that time was Darhan Khentrul Lozang Trinley Namgyal, author of the DAR-HAN and ROL-MO.

spiring with the Gurkhas against Tibet. Regent Rating sent a general, Dapon Thonpa, with a body of troops to Nyemo Jako, with instructions to make sure that Shatra would never return to Lhasa. Being a monk, the Regent could not openly suggest that Shatra be killed; but that is what he implied.

Dapon Thonpa arrested Shatra as soon as he arrived at Nyemo Jako and informed his prisoner of the reason for his action. Realizing that his life was in danger, Shatra began to give Dapon Thonpa a lively and cleverly worded account of his many achievements in Ladakh and Nepal in the service of his country. Dapon Thonpa began to consider it unwise and perhaps ultimately harmful to his own interests to kill so influential and patriotic a person; therefore, he took the Regent's instructions that Shatra was never to return to Lhasa literally. He had Shatra confined to a monastery called Gyalche Gompa and forced him to become a monk. The abbot of the monastery was instructed to keep Shatra a prisoner under close watch.

Shatra deeply resented the treatment meted out to him by the Regent. Using a snuff merchant as an intermediary, he sent a message to Palden Dondup, the treasurer of the Ganden monastery, who had served under Shatra previously and proved himself to be loyal and capable. Shatra asked Palden Dondup to prepare the monks to rebel against the Regent, which the treasurer promptly set about doing. Using the snuff merchant as a messenger, Palden Dondup informed Shatra that he was finally ready for action. Shatra replied that it was too early to move, that it would be better to acquire the cooperation of the Drepung monks, as the Sera monks would be sure to support the Regent. As it happened, in 1862, the Regent had been substituting money for the grain usually provided to the monasteries. The Drepung monks resented this change and by making an issue of it, Palden Dondup was able to arouse feelings of rebellion in the Drepung monastery. The monks of Ganden and Drepung then joined forces and effected the release of Shatra, bringing him to the outskirts of Lhasa.

The Dalai Lama, who was still a minor, and some of his attendants were supporters of Shatra. They sent the Dalai Lama's scarf, with the customary tea and biscuits, to the reception being given to Shatra outside Lhasa by the Drepung and Ganden monks. Since such receptions were only given to high officials, the Dalai Lama's recognition of it gave Shatra considerable prestige in the eyes of the people. It was cus-

tomary to send a scarf to the Dalai Lama in return for his courtesy;
but Shatra waited until he was directly opposite the Potala and then,
in full view of the crowd, got down from his palanquin, prostrated
himself three times before the Potala, and sent in his scarf. This confused the people, who began to think he had been recalled by the
Dalai Lama, and rumors to this effect soon spread through Lhasa.

Escorted by the Ganden and Drepung monks, Shatra proceeded to
his home in Lhasa. He deliberately spread the rumor that he would be
attacking the Regent the next day, and this brought the Sera monks,
as well as government troops, into Lhasa to guard the Regent. Shatra,
with monks from Drepung and Ganden, immediately occupied the
Potala and the Jokhang temple, assuming guardianship of those sacred
places. Shatra appointed himself Desi (Prime Minister) and proclaimed it in the Jokhang. He did not call himself Gyetsab (Regent),
since the Regent remained in power only during the minority of the
Dalai Lama; whereas a Desi could continue even after the assumption
of power by the Dalai Lama. Posters bearing his proclamation were
put up on the walls around Lhasa.

Shatra then sent out a circular to all prominent families and officials
in Lhasa. In it he listed Regent Rating's mistakes: his misuse of his
seal; his holding of an unnecessary lottery to select the twelfth Dalai
Lama to please the Manchus for his own interests; and his paying of
money instead of grain to the Drepung monastery. Declaring that he
was now the Desi, Shatra ended his letter by asking all officials who
wished to stand by Regent Rating to do so now, or else proceed to the
Jokhang temple for a meeting with Shatra. The officials were confused
and in their uncertainty, the majority decided to attend Shatra's meeting. Shatra called his meeting the Gandre Drungche, meaning:
"Assembly of Officials and Monks of Drepung and Ganden." Because
most of the members of the Tibetan government assembled in the
Jokhang with Shatra, the government troops guarding the Regent
abandoned him, leaving only the Sera monks to protect him.

The Ganden and Drepung monks then attacked the Regent's residence and drove him away. He took refuge in the Sera monastery.
From there, he fled to China with the Lord Chamberlain and the
council minister, Tashi Khangsar. The Lord Chamberlain died en
route and his body was found by the pursuers; but the Regent and
Tashi Khangsar escaped across the border. The property and estates of
the Regent, as well as those of Tashi Khangsar, were confiscated by the
Tibetan government and pro-Regent officials were demoted.

Desi Shatra then placed the Dalai Lama in nominal power, even though the Lama was still a minor and had not completed his training. Shatra himself held the reins of government. His loyal friend, Palden Dondup, was taken into government service. In due course, he became a Kalon, or minister in the Kashag, and later on he was to acquire even greater importance.

In China the deposed Regent, Rating, asked the Manchu Emperor to help him return to power; but at that time, China was faced with internal troubles as well as being at war with Britain and France, and the Emperor was in no position to help restore the Regent to his former position in Tibet. All that the Emperor could do was to write a letter to the Desi through the Manchu Ambans in Lhasa, asking him to restore Rating's estates and allow him to return to Tibet unmolested. Shatra referred the letter to the Gandre Drungche, whose members decided that it was a request and not an order; therefore, they would grant the Emperor this favor. Regent Rating died while on his way back to Tibet, but his estates were subsequently restored to his monastic followers.

Meanwhile, Gompo Namgyal, the chief of Nyarong in eastern Tibet, was using his standing army to spread a reign of terror in the areas around Nyarong. Six thousand refugee families poured into Lhasa from Derge, Horkhok, Lithang, Chating, and Dzakhok. They submitted petitions to the Tibetan government for help, and in 1863 the government sent troops to Nyarong under the command of Kalon Phulungwa and Dapon Trimon. The fighting lasted two years. Finally, Gompo Namgyal and his relatives were driven into their fort, which was put to the torch. All perished in the fire. The remainder of the chief's troops surrendered to the government forces and the seventeen districts he had occupied between Tachienlu and Derge were restored to their former chiefs. The Tibetan government stationed a governor in Nyarong who would have overall authority in the area. The local chiefs would be responsible for their own districts but would consult the Nyarong governor about disputes, and they would provide troops whenever the governor asked for them. A document to this effect was signed by all the chiefs of the region. The refugee families then returned to their homes.[4]

As Desi Shatra had no son of his own, he adopted a boy and then appointed him a Kalon at a very young age. His named the lad Kalon Tsering Wangchuk Shatra. Then, after little more than three years of

4. DOCUMENTS.

absolute power, Desi Shatra died about September 25, 1864. Palden Dondup, in order to retain the support of the Drepung monks, appointed a Drepung lama, Khenrab Wangchuk Dedrug, as an assistant to the Dalai Lama. This lama was a very honest and direct man, devoted to his duties, while his subordinates and attendants were strong supporters of Palden Dondup.

In 1868 the Gandre Drungche appointed Palden Dondup as Lord Chamberlain, thus giving him greater control over the Dalai Lama, who was then about twelve years old. Palden Dondup, who was one of the moving spirits of the Gandre Drungche, established an investigatory office to deal with dilatory taxpayers and to accelerate impending departmental decisions.

My grandfather, who was twelve at the time, told me he remembered seeing Palden Dondup and could recollect his features. He was a tall, heavy man, whom little children feared. His officials must have been afraid of him too. He always kept a fresh, bloodied animal skin outside of his office entrance and threatened to sew up in it anyone who disobeyed his orders. He had, in fact, done just that on several occasions, throwing his victims in the river. According to my grandfather, Palden was harsh and mean, and terrorized the people by his decisions; but he was, nevertheless, a courageous man. Because he was only semiliterate and had poor eyesight, his written orders were difficult to decipher. It was customary, when making a new seal, to inscribe on it a word like "prosperity," "peace," or "happiness"; but on the seal for his new office, Palden Dondup inscribed the word "Kyoklo," connoting "crooked work is justified." His spelling was so atrocious that he unconsciously developed his own system of shorthand. When sending for a horse, he wrote a word that looked neither like horse (rta) nor tiger (stag) but could be read for either one. When his servants asked him which animal he was referring to, he grumbled at them for thinking he wanted a tiger, an animal not even found in Tibet. On another occasion, while reading out a judgment in court, an assistant noticed that Palden Dondup was holding his papers upside down. Making a show of dusting Palden's sleeve, the assistant told him about the papers, to which Palden replied, "I am deliberately reading them upside down, because it is an upside-down man we are dealing with here." Palden's harshness served to discipline and improve the working of all governmental departments. His ruthlessness in collecting reserves of money for the government resulted in a surplus that lasted until the Tibetan revolt against the Communist Chinese in 1959.

In 1871 there was talk that Palden Dondup intended to remove the Dalai Lama from office and send him to a hermitage, with a regular salary. The Gandre Drungche called a meeting of the four council ministers at Palden Dondup's residence. When the ministers did not emerge from the house after two or three days, the people began to wonder what had happened to them. Officially it was stated that the meeting was still in progress, but news spread that three of the ministers were actually under arrest and that Kalon Tsogo had been bound in skins and thrown in the river.

Officials who had not been involved in the affair contacted the Dalai Lama's assistant, Khenrab Wangchuk, and asked him to use his influence to put an end to such outrages. Khenrab Wangchuk, knowing that his attendants were supporters of Palden Dondup, sent them to the Drepung monastery to get them out of his way. He then held a meeting with the officials, who were sure that the Sera monks would not support Palden, since they were not represented in the Gandre Drungche. Khenrab Wangchuk wrote to the abbots of Drepung monastery instructing them that on the same day that he would arrest Palden Dondup in Lhasa, they were to arrest and beat his own attendants and any other pro-Palden Dondup monks in Drepung. One of Khenrab Wangchuk's brothers was among those attendants, but he was not spared.

On the day fixed for the coup, Palden Dondup left for his office accompanied by Tsering Wangchuk Shatra. While on their way, they received a warning that they would be arrested as soon as they entered the Potala. Palden Dondup decided to go instead to Drepung for help, but before he reached the monastery he heard that his supporters there had been arrested and whipped. He had no alternative but to take refuge is the Ganden monastery, to which he belonged.

Meanwhile, the Gandre Drungche was dissolved and government troops sent to Ganden. Assisted by monks from Sera, the troops besieged the Ganden monastery and cut off its food supplies, which brought about its surrender. Palden Dondup and his brother left the monastery under cover of night, but while moving along the valley of Gyama, about fifteen miles east of Ganden, they sighted troops pursuing them and then committed suicide. Tsering Wangchuk Shatra and other supporters of Palden were arrested and brought to Lhasa.

On the recommendation of the Ganden Tri Rimpoche, their lives were spared; but they were sent into exile. The Sera monks who had long nursed their grudge, joined the government troops in the attack on Ganden, and several houses were put to the torch.[5]

To replace the Gandre Drungche, a national assembly, called the Tsongdu, was formed. It consisted of the abbots of the three big monasteries of Drepung, Sera, and Ganden and the heads of all governmental departments. The Tibetan government then repaired and restored the houses in the Ganden monastery that had been looted and burned by the government troops.

After assisting and guiding the twelfth Dalai Lama for eight years, Khenrab Wangchuk died in 1872. The Dalai Lama, who was then seventeen, was asked by the Kashag and the Tsongdu to assume his temporal responsibilities, and he took power in early 1873. He reigned for only two years and fifteen days before dying in 1875. During his short reign, the Dalai Lama had two favorites, Rakhamay Chagnang and his Palanquin-Master. These two were able to influence him in granting titles and honors to people they liked. After the Dalai Lama's death, they were accused of having had a hand in his illness and were thrown into prison and tortured. Later, they were sent into exile.

The Manchu garrison at Lhasa then consisted of only a hundred troops, most of whom had been born in Tibet. The Chinese garrison soldiers were rotated back to China every three years, leaving behind them their Tibetan wives and sweethearts, as well as their children. The fatherless boys, on growing up, were taken into the garrison as troops. They wore Chinese uniforms but spoke Tibetan. Because of the crises in China, the Emperor could not spare imperial troops to reinforce the garrison, and the Ambans had to depend on those soldiers of mixed nationality. However, the garrison had no real military duties to perform, because the Ambans' work consisted entirely of attending various ceremonies and reporting to the Manchu Emperor any changes that took place in the Tibetan government. Whenever a new council minister (Kalon) or other official was appointed, presents and unsolicited titles would arrive from the Emperor. When a new temple or monastery was built, the Emperor would send a handsome plaque to be set up in a prominent place as evidence of his patronage. The Manchu garrison was in such poor financial condition that the soldiers, in order to make money, went from house to house performing the

5. DANGS-SHEL; PAD-TSHAL.

Chinese dragon and lion dances during the New Year celebrations or when some important official was promoted. Those troops of mixed nationality were looked down on by both the Tibetans and the Chinese. Moreover, they were usually kept at a distance, because they were said to be suffering from syphilis, which is known in Tibet as "Gyama"—"the Chinese disease."

12

The Thirteenth Dalai Lama and Britain's Border Policy

After the death of the twelfth Dalai Lama in 1875, Choskyi Gyaltsen Kundeling was appointed Regent, and a search was conducted throughout the country for the rebirth of the deceased Dalai Lama. A member of the search party, Gyutod Khensur, reported having seen a reflection of the future Dalai Lama's birthplace in the sacred lake of Lhamoi Latso at Chokhorgyal, some ninety miles southeast of Lhasa. The birthplace was located at Thakpo Langdun in Southeast Tibet, where they subsequently found a boy who had been born on the fifth day of the fifth month of the Fire-Mouse year (May 27, 1876). The boy was only ten months old when discovered and therefore too young to undergo the usual tests.

A year later, Tibetan officials, carrying the twelfth Dalai Lama's personal articles, visited the child, and after giving him the tests, were convinced that he was the true reincarnation. The Regent and the Kashag members decided to confirm the Dalai Lama without the drawing of lots and a document to this effect was drawn up. According to Rockhill, there were three candidates for the thirteenth Dalai Lama and the child from Thakpo was declared the reembodiment of the Dalai Lama after resorting to a lottery in the Jokhang.[1] Li, on the other hand, says that in the case of the thirteenth Dalai Lama, the drawing of lots was suspended because there was but one claimant.[2] Actually there were three claimants for the rebirth of the Dalai Lama; but the choice fell unanimously on the candidate from Thakpo Langdun, after he had been given many religious tests. There was no lottery.

1. ROCKHILL, p. 71.
2. LI, p. 58.

On the first day of the ninth month of the Fire-Ox year (1877), the Regent publicly confirmed the boy as the thirteenth Dalai Lama and had him brought to the vicinity of Lhasa.[3] A year later, the Panchen Lama gave him the name of Thupten Gyatso at the monastery of Gungthang, four miles east of Lhasa. In 1879, on the thirteenth day of the ninth month of the Earth-Hare year, the Dalai Lama was taken in procession through the streets of Lhasa and enthroned in the Potala. Two years later, Tenpai Wangchuk, the fifth Panchen Lama, died and his body was preserved at Tashilhunpo.

Commissioned by the Bengal government to conduct geographical surveys in Tibet in the guise of a student of Buddhism, Sarat Chandra Das, an intelligent and keen observer of life, set out from Bengal and arrived in Tashilhunpo in 1879. He was accompanied by a Sikkimese lama named Ugyen Gyatso. With the assistance of Kyabying Sengchen Lama, Das was able to collect numerous manuscripts and documents. Through the acquaintance and help of the wife of Dapon Phala, who was related to Sengchen Lama, he visited Lhasa and other places in southern Tibet.[4] During his stay from 1881 to 1883, Das was able to gather valuable information and compile reports on important geographical features of Tibet. He constructed new maps of lake Yardok Yutso. Owing to his secret explorations, the Tibetan government suspected Das of working for the Bengal government, and arrangements were made to arrest him, but he escaped. Kyabying Sengchen Lama, the Phala family, and a few others, who had rendered aid to Das, received punishment from the Tibetan government. As a result of this and similar incidents, the Tibetan government became suspicious and cautious in their dealings with British India.

Once a year, the monks of Lhasa led a religious procession through the streets, circumambulating the Jokhang temple. While the procession was making its round in the year 1883, a quarrel broke out between two Tibetan women and a Nepalese shopkeeper over some coral beads, which he accused the Tibetan women of stealing. The incident aroused anti-Nepalese feelings and the monks and lay people soon got out of hand. They made firebrands from rolls of cloth and used these to light their way as they began to loot the Nepalese shops. By morning, every Nepalese shop in Lhasa had been looted, and open conflict

3. This account of the thirteenth Dalai Lama is based on PHUR-LCOG and PAD-TSHAL.
4. Sarat Chandra Das, *Journey to Lhasa and Central Tibet* (London, 1902); Sandberg, *Exploration of Tibet*, pp. 163-72.

with Nepal was imminent. Representatives of the two governments met, and the Tibetan government agreed to compensate the Nepalese businessmen. However, the actual expenses were met by a rich Mongol, Chayan Hutuktu, who was visiting the Dalai Lama at the time.

After twelve years of service as an efficient and popular regent, Choskyi Gyaltsen Kundeling died in 1866. The Dalai Lama was still a minor, so the Tsongdu appointed Demo Trinley Rabgyas as the next regent. In 1888 the sixth Panchen Lama was discovered and the Dalai Lama gave him the name, Choskyi Nyima.

In 1894 the ecclesiastical officials petitioned the Regent regarding the composition of the Kashag, which they claimed was based almost entirely on hereditary principles of succession. Its members had been predominantly lay officials of noble families; while monks and men of learning and achievement were not considered for appointment. The petition was put before a meeting of the Kashag, Tsongdu, and the Regent, and it was decided that henceforth one monk official would serve as a Kashag minister, as had been the custom in the time of the seventh Dalai Lama. It was also agree that heredity would not be a necessary determinant in the selection of Kashag ministers; lesser officials who had a record of achievement and learning would be eligible.

It was the custom for the people to line the streets of Lhasa whenever the Dalai Lama passed by in a procession; but no one was to watch from an upper-story window or balcony, as this would put one above the Dalai Lama's head. On the day of the butter-lamp festival during the Monlam festival of 1895, the streets were decorated with pillars of colored butter and flickering lamps and the people were out in the streets to watch the Dalai Lama go by. Seeing three Chinese officials watching the procession from an upper window, the Tibetan official on duty spoke to the Manchu Ambans about this breach of courtesy. The Ambans said that the officials must have been ignorant of the custom; but when the Chinese owner of the house was interrogated, it turned out that the officials had been aware of the custom but had insisted on watching the procession from above nonetheless. The Tibetans took offense at this and demonstrated in front of the Ambans' residence. To avoid an outbreak of violence, the Ambans made the Chinese officials apologize to the Dalai Lama and to write a letter promising not to commit the same error in the future.[5]

5. DOCUMENTS.

On the eighth day of the eighth month of the Wood-Sheep year
(1895), the thirteenth Dalai Lama assumed power at the age of nineteen, and the Regent resigned from his official duties. The Manchus
exercised very little power in Tibet at that time, and they did not raise
any issues regarding the Dalai Lama's accession to power.

There soon followed what might be called "the case of the en-
chanted shoes." The Nechung Oracle at the Drepung monastery had
twice prophesied that the Dalai Lama's life was in danger. He was
summoned to the Dalai Lama's private chambers, where, after going
into the customary trance, he revealed that a servant of the ex-
Regent, Demo Trinley Rabgyas, had handed a pair of shoes to Lama
Sodgyal. On being questioned, Lama Sodgyal admitted having received a pair of shoes as a present. The pair was at his home and he
agreed to fetch them. At first, nothing was found in the shoes; but
when they were torn apart, a slip of paper, bearing a magical incanta-
tion, was found inside the heel. It contained the Dalai Lama's name
and date of birth and was designed to bring a sudden end to his life.
Sodgyal denied all knowledge of the mystic paper but claimed that
when he tried to wear the shoes his nose would start bleeding. The ex-
Regent and his relatives were arrested and brought before the
Tsongdu, which had made a fair and thorough investigation of the incident. The ex-Regent admitted having dabbled in witchcraft in an
attempt to return to power. While still young and healthy, he had
been suddenly forced to give up his office because the Dalai Lama had
attained his majority. He claimed that other officials had begun to
persecute him as soon as he was out of power and that he had no way
of redress. His two brothers, Norbu Tsering and Lozang Dondan, had
insisted on trying to regain some of his former status. He then revealed other magical formulas, which he had used in an attempt to
bring about his reinstatement. The ex-Regent, Demo, lacked the political maturity of men like Shatra and Palden Dondup, who achieved
their ambitions in a more direct and realistic manner.

The ex-Regent and his two brothers were imprisoned for life at
Lhasa. The estates that he had acquired during his lifetime were confiscated by the government; but those estates which had belonged to
his former incarnations, were turned over to his monastic followers.
While the investigations were in progress, the ex-Regent's followers
had offered bribes to the Manchu Ambans to effect his release. The

Ambans agreed to attend the meeting of the investigating committee, but the Tibetan government refused them admittance, declaring that their interference was not acceptable.[6]

In the year 1900, after completing his religious training, the Dalai Lama made the customary visit to Chokhorgyal and a pilgrimage to southern Tibet. While visiting Samye, he caught smallpox, but recovered within two weeks, and then returned to Lhasa.

The formulation of British policy towards Sikkim, Bhutan, and Tibet had its origin at a time, some fifty years earlier, when the British made Ladakh a dependency of the state of Kashmir. The Tibetans heard that Spiti and Lahul were detached from Ladakh and made administrative units of British India. It was also learned that the British had occupied the former Gurkha territory of Almora and that they were looking for a route to Lhasa, perhaps through Bhutan. These events, combined with Manchu allegations that the British would destroy their religion, made the Tibetans avoid contact with them. At the same time, Britain was aware of China's internal weaknesses and was concerned with the prospect of Russia extending her influence in Tibet. The Tibetans had no intention of being influenced by any outside force; but the British did not know this as the Tibetans refused to make contact with them. The British were concerned with stabilizing the frontiers of India, and when they heard that the Tibetans were in contact with the Russians, it was considered more in the British interest if Tibet were kept under Manchu influence.

Some time earlier, the British had leased Darjeeling from Sikkim.[7] In 1860 they stopped paying the annual rent, later incorporating Darjeeling and six small districts into British territory. Trokhang Dronyer, a Sikkimese official, who had opposed this usurpation of territory, fled to Tibet, where he was given asylum, along with an estate and an official title by the Tibetan government.

A British Colonel and a civilian official, Mr. Ashley Eden, proceeded to the Sikkimese border and demanded a meeting with the ruler. The Sikkimese ruler was then at Chumbi in Tibet, so his eldest son, Sekyong Trulku, represented him. The British officials handed to Sekyong Trulku a twenty-three-point agreement. If the Sikkimese would accept the twenty-three conditions specified in the agreement, then the British would return the six occupied districts and resume

6. Ibid.
7. The account given here relating to Sikkim is based on 'BRAS-LJONGS and DOCUMENTS.

rent payments for Darjeeling. The main features of the agreement were that the Sikkimese ruler was not to remain in Tibet and that Tibet would not be permitted to interfere in Sikkimese affairs. In the following year, because of advanced age, Chagdor Namgyal, the ruler of Sikkim, stepped aside in favor of his eldest son, Sekyong Trulku. As soon as the son assumed power, the British began paying the annual rent for Darjeeling. In 1868 they voluntarily raised the payment by three thousand rupees. In the same year, Sekyong Trulku, after ruling seven years, resigned in favor of his younger brother, Thuthop Namgyal.

Around 1860, a small civil war was in progress in Bhutan. The Bhutanese ruler asked the British for assistance, while his rivals appealed to the Tibetans. The British stepped in first and brought the situation under control. There was talk of making a road through Bhutan and of stationing a British representative in that country. Finally, after five years, four Bhutanese representatives drew up an agreement with the British, who agreed not to interfere in Bhutanese affairs, providing that the Tibetans also did not interfere. The British also agreed to pay Bhutan two hundred thousand rupees for rights to certain forested areas where they were interested in setting up a timber industry. News of this agreement reached Lhasa during the administration of Khenrab Wangchuk (1864–72). A meeting between the members of the Kashag and the Gandre Drungche resulted in the decision that there would be no cause for Tibetan interference in Bhutan as long as the British did not interfere there or try to build a road to Tibet.

In 1875 some British officials were trekking in Sikkim in the region of the Nathu-la pass on the Tibetan border. When the Tibetan government asked the Sikkimese authorities why the officials were near the border, they were informed that the British had asked permission to build rest houses, called Dak Bungalows, for the comfort of officials traveling in the area. The Tibetan government lodged a protest against this, but nothing came of it.

In 1880 reports reached Lhasa from the district officer of Nagchukha in northern Tibet that a party of British travelers was in the region; however, there is no certainty that they were British, because any Caucasian seen in Tibet at that time was taken for a Britisher. The Tibetan government sent officials to ask the travelers to leave and they turned back.

In 1883 the Sikkimese ruler, Thuthop Namgyal, brought his family to Tibet to have an audience with the Dalai Lama. The Tibetan government gave them an unusually fine reception, and before the party returned to Sikkim, everyone from the ruler down to his servants was given presents of clothing. Sixty loads of Chinese brick tea, thirty dotsed, and one thousand khal [8] of barley grain were also presented to the visitors.

Civil disorder again broke out in Bhutan in 1885. Representatives of the rival parties, Alu Dorje and Gongzim Tamdin, were sent to Lhasa to request the Dalai Lama's mediation. The Dalai Lama informed them that Tibet had agreed not to interfere in Bhutanese affairs; but since it was a matter of mediation desired by both parties, who were of the same faith as the Tibetans, he saw no harm in sending his representative, Kalon Rampa, to Paro. Tibetan mediation succeeded in ending the civil dispute and Bhutanese emissaries were sent to Lhasa to express the Bhutanese ruler's appreciation.

Whenever a Tibetan council minister (Kalon) was near the Sikkimese border, it was customary for the Sikkimese ruler to come to Phari to meet the Kalon who represented the Tibetan government. However, when Kalon Rampa approached the border on his way to Bhutan, he was met only by the ruler's brother, Trinley Namgyal, and some representatives. Kalon Rampa was offended and voiced his displeasure. About the same time, it was reported from Tsang that some Britishers had arrived in Shigatse from western Tibet; but permission for them to stay was, as usual, refused.

In 1885, while these various manifestations of increasing British pressure were bothering the Tibetan government, it was learned from the Ambans that the Manchu Emperor had granted the British permission at the Chefoo Convention to conduct an expedition between China and India by way of Tibet. The Tsongdu held an emergency meeting and declared that Tibet was being harassed by the British from all directions and that the Emperor of China had no authority to give anyone permission to pass through Tibet. The Tsongdu members took an oath never to allow the British to enter Tibetan territory and put their seals to it. The Manchus could not force the Tibetans to comply with their order, and to compensate the British, China recognized the British annexation of Burma.

The District Officer at Phari asked the Sikkimese ruler not to allow

8. *Khal* is a unit of measure equivalent to thirty-two pounds in weight.

the British expedition to enter Tibet through Sikkim. The Sikkimese ruler informed the Phari official that he was fully aware of the situation and had already written to Lhasa about the British intention of building a rest house at Kobuk, near the Dzalep-la pass on the Tibetan border, in spite of the fact they had been informed that the Tibetan government might protest it. The Tibetan government was surprised at the Sikkimese report and sent two representatives, Khenche Drugyal and Tsepon Tsarong, to the border to confirm the actual demarcation of the Sikkimese–Tibetan boundary. An old resident of the area recalled that the original boundary was at Renock, which was now in Sikkimese territory. After discussions with the local people, the Tibetan representatives decided to establish a check-post at Lungthur, which was a little deeper in Tibetan territory than Renock. In spite of discouragement from the Sikkimese, who anticipated British displeasure, the fortified check-post was set up in 1887 and manned by an officer with twenty soldiers.

As soon as they learned of the check-post, the British informed the Manchus that the Tibetans were building aggressive fortifications on the border facing India. At the same time, they wrote to the Dalai Lama through the Sikkimese ruler, demanding the removal of the check-post before March 15, 1888; failing which, they would attack the check-post and drive the Tibetans out. The Kashag replied to the Sikkimese ruler that there was no harm in protecting one's own territory and that the Tibetans were prepared to resist a British attack. Two Tibetan generals, Dapon Ngabo and Dapon Surkhang, with nine hundred troops under the overall command of the council minister, Kalon Lhalu, were dispatched to the border.

The Sikkimese ruler worked hard to bridge the gulf between the British and Tibetan governments. He explained to the Tibetans the folly of challenging the might of the British Empire; but the Tibetans had no way of realizing the opposition they would have to face. They had no experience in modern warfare. Changlochen, the officer in charge of the local area, began to move his troops about the border with scant regard for the consequences. His actions brought the British to the border three months before the date given in their ultimatum. Two thousand British troops, with four cannons, arrived at Kalimpong, and Thuthop Namgyal, the Sikkimese ruler, sent a mission there to request them to halt their advance. At the same time, he sent his brother to Kalon Lhalu in the Chumbi Valley to try and per-

suade the Tibetans to withdraw from the check-post. While negotiations went on, the British forces continued to advance, and on the
eleventh day of the second month of the Earth-Mouse year (March
21, 1888), a brief clash took place at the Lungthur check-post.

This was the first time Tibetans had clashed with the army of a
Western power and they were badly defeated by the disciplined and
well-equipped British soldiers. Those who were not killed were pur-
sued by the British as far as Yatung. In the confusion, Dapon
Surkhang and some of his troops found themselves fleeing into
Bhutan.

The Lungthur battle was soon the subject of a Lhasa street song:

> Lhalu has returned,
> But, he's lost the border.
> Lhalu has returned,
> But, he's lost his cannons.
> The fortress we labored a lifetime to build
> Was destroyed in a morning's bombardment.
>
> Ngabo's furious as ever,
> Surkhang to his corner has crept.
> Changlochen, more clever than wolf,
> On his brown horse has flown
> More swift than a bird.

In a country like Tibet where there were no newspapers or other media
to express public opinion, the people put their feelings and criticisms
in songs and poems. This song of the Lungthur defeat is a clever
parody on the names of the officials; for example, Surkhang literally
means "corner house" and Chang of Changlochen is a homonym for
"wolf."

The British army, encouraged by Sikkimese officials who disliked
their ruler, entered Gangtok. The ruler, Thuthop Namgyal, fled to
Tibet and took refuge in the Chumbi valley at his estate; but he was
seized by the British officer, who had occupied Nadong, and asked to
return to Sikkim. Thuthop Namgyal, with his son and officials, turned
back. At Nagthang they were met and interviewed by a British military commander. The ruler's son, his brother, and a lama, were not
detained but allowed to continue on into Tibet.[9] When Thuthop

---

9. The ruler's son and brother were named Tsodrag Namgyal and Trinley Namgyal,
respectively. The lama was named Khachod Lama.

Namgyal arrived back in Gangtok, he found the administration in the hands of a British officer and two of his opponents, the Phothang Lama and Sholdron. His palace had been confiscated and he was given an allowance of five hundred rupees a month for himself and his family. Shortly afterwards, the Sikkimese ruling family was removed to Kalimpong, where they were kept under house arrest for five months before being permitted to return to Sikkim.

Through their intrigues with the British Political Officer, Claude White, Sikkimese officials were making things uncomfortable for their ruler. They exerted pressure on him to recall his son and brother to Sikkim from Tibet, and they expected him to meet the arrears in pay of attendants who had, by custom, served him voluntarily and in rotation and who continued to do so. They also made a number of changes in Sikkimese administration without consulting the Sikkimese ruler and still expected him to put his seal on their orders. Thuthop Namgyal replied that it was the British, and not he, who had forced his son and brother to go to Tibet, where they were now being educated, and he did not want to interrupt their studies at Shigatse. He refused to put his seal on decisions in which he had not deliberated or even been consulted. In addition, he could not pay his attendants out of the small salary he was receiving. They were serving him voluntarily and could be withdrawn if the officials so wished. After speaking of his problems with the Political Officer, the Sikkimese ruler put them in a letter, which he sent to the Governor-General of Bengal. This action obviously did nothing to improve his relationship with the Political Officer.

In the spring of 1892, Thuthop Namgyal, his wife, and ten trusted officials decided to leave for Tibet. This time they did not take the usual route; but went through northern Sikkim in the direction of Tengkye, the district in Tibet where the Sikkimese official, Trokhang Dronyer, had earlier been given asylum and an estate. Thuthop Namgyal was surprised and disappointed to learn that Tibetan district officials had instructed the local people not to assist any Sikkimese. The Sikkimese ruler had no alternative but to make his way to Walung in Nepal. After five days there, while contemplating going onto Kathmandu, the Sikkimese party was arrested by a company of Gurkha soldiers and forcibly taken to the Gurkha camp at Dhanakote, ten days' journey from Walung.

The Gurkha commander explained to Thuthop Namgyal that he

had been arrested on the orders of the Nepalese government, which had been requested to capture and return the ruler to Sikkim. The party was then taken to Shimin, three days' journey from the Indian border, where they were formally handed over to the British Indian police. They were kept at Dotsug, near Darjeeling, for a few months, and then imprisoned at Kurseong in 1893. (The late Maharaja of Sikkim, Tashi Namgyal, was born in the Kurseong prison, during his family's confinement there.) The ruling family was kept at Kurseong for more than two years. During his confinement, Thuthop Namgyal sent a petition to the Governor-General of Bengal, George Nathaniel Curzon. His petition was investigated by British officials, whose suspicions had died down against the ruler when they realized that they had been fostered by the ruler's political rivals. The Commissioner of Darjeeling, P. Nolan, came to Kurseong and informed Thuthop Namgyal that the British government was prepared to forget past differences and reinstate him as the ruler of Sikkim, provided that he would agree to ten conditions. Basically, he was required to set up a governing council and to consult with the British Political Officer before making any decisions; henceforth, he no longer had the same powers as in the past. Thuthop Namgyal accepted the conditions and on the ninth day of the ninth month of the Wood-Sheep year (1895), he returned to Gangtok.

Throughout his life, Thuthop Namgyal had avoided intrigues and did his best to deal straightforwardly with both the Tibetan and British governments; but his opponents had plunged him into difficulties with the British authorities. He was a brave man with strong principles. At the height of his troubles, while in custody at Dotsug, he was told he could be released if he would resign and give up all claims to power in Sikkim; but this he resolutely refused to do. He had caused no harm to the Tibetans or the British in any manner, and he only wanted to secure his hereditary rights.

In 1890 a convention was drawn up in Calcutta by Lord Lansdowne, the Governor-General of India and Sheng-t'ai, the Manchu Amban from Lhasa, without consulting the government of Tibet. The first article of the convention agreement defined the boundary between Tibet and Sikkim, and the second article recognized a British protectorate over Sikkim, which gave them exclusive control over the internal administration and the foreign relations of that country. There was, however, no corresponding acknowledgment on the part of the British of China's authority over Tibet.[10] The remaining six articles related to Tibet, and since she was not represented at the Convention, those articles were not allowed to be put into practice by the Tibetans. The British were aware that China exercised no real power in Tibet at that time; but it suited their interests to deal with the Manchus, because of the advantages they gained from the Convention. It is also possible that, because of the brief clash between the Tibetans and the British at Lungthur, the Manchus were afraid that Tibet and Britain might enter into direct negotiations; they therefore agreed to a Convention to forestall such a possibility.

An addition was made to the Convention, known as the Trade Regulations of 1893, in which the question of increasing trade facilities across the Sikkim–Tibet frontier was discussed.[11] Again, the provisions of that agreement could not be enforced because Tibet had not been a party to the negotiations. It is surprising that the British entered into a second agreement with the Manchus, when they knew from the results of the first agreement that there was no way of putting the agreement into effect. The Manchus had signed on behalf of the Tibetans; yet they were totally unable to persuade or force them to carry out the provisions of the agreement. A Tibetan, Lachag Paljor Dorje Shatra, was sent to Darjeeling to study the situation. He sent valuable reports to Lhasa; but they did not meet with the favor of the government, which still believed that too close a contact with the British would damage the Tibetan way of life and religion.

About that time, a Japanese monk, Ekai Kawaguchi, under the pretext of being a Ladahki monk, was enrolled for studies at the Sera monastery. He was delivering inaccurate information to the British in India through Sarat Chandra Das. Those inaccurate reports led the British to believe that Tibet was receiving military aid in the form of "small firearms, bullets, and other interesting objects" from Russia. Moreover, Kawaguchi estimated that there must have been over two hundred Buriat students in the major monasteries of Tibet.[12] The increasing fear of the establishment of Russian influence in Tibet, which would constitute a grave danger to India, led the British to realize that

10. For the complete text of the Convention, see BELL, pp. 230–81; RICHARDSON, pp. 250–51.

11. The full text of the Regulations is given in BELL, pp. 282–84; RICHARDSON, pp. 251–53.

12. Ekai Kawaguchi, *Three Years in Tibet* (London, 1909), pp. 496, 506; YOUNG-HUSBAND, pp. 313, 319–23.

they could no longer deal with Tibet through China; but that they must attempt to establish direct contact with the Lhasa government. The fact that the Convention of 1890 and the Trade Regulations of 1893 proved in practice to be of not the slightest use was because Tibet never recognized them. Francis Younghusband quotes Claude White, the Political Officer of Sikkim, as saying that the Chinese had "no authority whatever" in Tibet and that "China was suzerain over Tibet only in name." [13]

13. YOUNGHUSBAND, p. 54.

13

The Younghusband Military Expedition and Its Aftermath

Lord Curzon, who was the Viceroy of India from 1899 to 1905, realized the futility of trying to deal with the Tibetans through the Manchu rulers of China; consequently, he sought ways and means to enter into direct negotiations with the Lhasa government. When two Tibetan officials, Dapon Tsarong and Lozang Trinley, the Secretary-General of the Tibetan government, arrived at Nadong with instructions to employ delaying tactics, their indifferent attitude only strengthened British suspicions of Russian involvement in Tibetan affairs. In addition, there was among the Dalai Lama's attendants a Buriat Mongol monk named Dorjieff, who was known to the Tibetans as Tsenyi Khenpo, or as Ngawang Lozang. Dorjieff was an exceptionally learned man, who maintained close religious contact with the Russians. Because of these various factors, Lord Curzon came to the conclusion that an attempt at peaceful negotiation with the Tibetans would end in frustration; therefore, he decided to send a mission to Tibet under the leadership of Colonel Francis Younghusband.

In the sixth Tibetan month of 1903 (July), information reached Lhasa that Colonel Younghusband and his troops were on their way to Khamba Dzong, within Tibetan territory, for the purpose of opening trade negotiations and discussing the question of British relations with Tibet.[1] Lozang Trinley and Tsarong were instructed to hold talks with the British only on the border and not within Tibetan territory. These two Tibetan representatives sent the district officer of Kham-

---

1. Data on the Younghusband expedition were obtained from PHUR-LCOG and DOCU-MENTS, as well as from *Papers relating to Tibet* (Presented to both Houses of Parliament by Command of His Majesty), (London) Cd. 1920 (1904), Cd. 2054 (1904), Cd. 2370 (1905).

ba Dzong and twenty-five soldiers to Giagong, with instructions to prevent the British from entering Tibet and to report back as soon as the British appeared. From Lachen, Sikkim, word came that the British mission, consisting of five officers and seven hundred troops, had already set out on June 19, 1903. Lozang Trinley, the Secretary-General, and General Tsarong left immediately for Giagong.

A few days after reaching Giagong, they were met by a Tibetan-speaking British officer named Captain William O'Conner, accompanied by two hundred soldiers. The district officer asked O'Conner not to proceed farther as Tibetan representatives had arrived at Giagong that very night. O'Conner said he would be proceeding to Khamba Dzong the next day, where his government had agreed to hold the negotiations. He added that he was only the advance party and the leader, with the bulk of the British force, was following behind him.

The next day at sunrise, a bugle sounded and the British troops assembled. Without any delay, they began marching in the direction of Khamba Dzong, headed by O'Conner and a few mounted officers. The two Tibetan representatives immediately ran into the road and attempted to halt them, insisting that the negotiations had to take place at Giagong. O'Conner acted as interpreter for Claude White, the Sikkim Political Officer, who did most of the talking. White said they had the permission of Peking to hold the talks at Khamba Dzong, where a Manchu representative would be present. This statement had no effect on the Tibetans; however, the large number of troops did influence them and they could do nothing but follow the British force.

The British camped a little way beneath Khamba Dzong and encircled their encampment with barbed wire and trenches. At that point, the two Tibetan representatives received an urgent communiqué from the Tsongdu, instructing them that on no account were they to allow a single British soldier or civilian into Tibetan territory. The Tsongdu maintained that the British were enemies of the Buddhist religion and they were only interested in extending their territories. This the Tibetans knew from past experience during their war with the Gurkhas. If the British were sincerely interested in commercial negotiations, they should be content to conduct them at the border. If, however, the British penetrated into Tibetan territory, then Tibetan troops would be sent one after another to stop them.

Although this message from the Tsongdu had been sent much earlier, it had not reached the Tibetan representatives until after the British troops had arrived at Khamba Dzong. Troops from the military centers of Shigatse, Gyantse, and Dingri were being prepared for action. Monks of the three big monasteries, representing the Tsongdu, joined the Tibetan General and Secretary-General at Khamba Dzong. The Manchu Amban's representative at Shigatse, Ho Kuang-hsi, also went to Khamba Dzong to participate in the talks. The British expressed the hope that the Amban himself would come. On the other hand, the Tibetans reiterated their offer to negotiate if the British would return to the border. The Tibetans stated there was no need for any Chinese participation in the talks and Ho Kuang-hsi returned quietly to Shigatse, citing ill health as the reason for his departure.

At that point, Colonel Younghusband arrived at Khamba Dzong, with four hundred troops. He met with the Tibetans and held a number of meetings; but the subject under discussion was always the location for negotiation, and not commercial matters. The Tibetan insistence on a British retreat gave Younghusband the impression that the representatives he was dealing with were not fully accredited officials; therefore, he asked for persons who had full power to make decisions, which would not later be questioned, and he insisted on the presence of the Manchu Ambans.[2] The Tibetan representatives stated that the Ambans had no connection with the commercial affairs of Tibet. They offered to send for a higher official with full powers to negotiate, provided, of course, that the British would agree to hold the talks at the border and not in Tibetan territory. These arguments were repeated for three months; the British army encamped at Khamba Dzong all the while. The British passed their time carrying out impressive military exercises, taking photographs, hiking in the hills, mapping the surrounding country, botanizing, and geologizing.

Khamba Dzong lay in an area under the local jurisdiction of the Tashilhunpo monastery; accordingly, the Panchen Lama's representative and the abbot of Tashilhunpo, at the instruction of the Lhasa government, arrived at Khamba Dzong to try and persuade the British to withdraw; but they too were unsuccessful. No progress whatsoever was made, and finally the British withdrew, probably because of the approach of winter and orders from their government. On the

2. According to YOUNGHUSBAND (p. 124), it was Mr. E. C. Wilton, of the China Consular Service, who suggested that the Tibetan representatives were not responsible officials.

seventeenth day of the ninth month of the Water-Hare year (1903), they returned to Sikkim.

A number of meetings then took place between the Kashag and the Tsongdu. The Kashag stressed the necessity of bringing about a peaceful settlement instead of resorting to military action, for it realized the Tibetans had no adequate reinforcements for such an undertaking. The Tsongdu, on the other hand, was completely ignorant of British military might and it declared that Tibet would fight to the last man. It felt the Kashag had been influenced in its thinking by Paljor Dorje Shatra, the former representative to Darjeeling who now was a council minister (Kalon) at Lhasa. It was rumored about that there was a traitor in the higher councils of the government and the Nechung Oracle was persuaded to go into a trance, during which, he was asked to identify the traitor in the presence of the Dalai Lama and the Kashag. Apparently the Oracle was reluctant to do so, because he did not remain in his trance long enough to pronounce any revelations. Nevertheless, the four Kashag ministers, Shatra, Sholkhang, Horkhang, and the monk-minister, Changkhyim, were arrested and kept in custody in the summer palace of the Dalai Lama. The Tsongdu formed a committee to investigate the Kashag members. Horkhang, who was a timid and inexperienced man appointed to the Kashag as the replacement for the late Lhalu, anticipated harsh treatment from the Tsongdu. Consequently, he committed suicide.

The Tsongdu's investigation cited Shatra's Darjeeling reports, which had been in favor of contacting the British. The Tsongdu claimed it had learned that Shatra had accepted bribes from the British for writing favorable reports. The Kashag ministers were questioned separately about this. Shatra stated the following to the Tsongdu investigators: (1) he had sent his reports to Tibet after personally witnessing and studying the power of the British in India and, because of his loyalty, had submitted only truthful reports; (2) he suggested that the Tsongdu study his reports, especially his advice on future Tibetan policy and the methods to adopt in negotiations with the British; (3) if he had collaborated with the British, they would not have written to the Dalai Lama asking that he be replaced, which caused the Dalai Lama to send Kalon Bumthang to Darjeeling as his senior; (4) he said he possessed a letter from the Nechung Oracle, sent to him while he was at Darjeeling, praising his services to the country, and that letter had been accompanied by the usual greeting scarf; (5)

he asked them not to base their accusations on rumors but to confront him with those persons who had accused him of treachery; (6) he claimed that on his return from Darjeeling, when he was appointed a Kalon, the Nechung Oracle, in front of the other members of the Kashag, had congratulated and commended him on his good work; and (7) he asked for a final decision, either proving him guilty or honoring him for his services to his country: he did not wish to be left at the mercy of rumors.[3]

Kalon Shatra found himself in a difficult position, caught between two accusing forces. The Tsongdu, on the one hand, suspected him of collaborating with the British, since he supported a policy of peaceful settlement. The British, on the other hand, suspected him of collaborating with the Russians through the monk, Dorjieff, since Shatra strongly attacked the Convention of 1890, which the Tibetans never recognized.[4]

Shatra's colleagues, on being questioned, declared that all their decisions had been collective ones, taken for the future good of the country, and they denied any knowledge of Shatra accepting bribes from the British. In spite of their able defense, they were kept in prison for over a year, during which time, four new Kashag ministers were appointed. They were the monk-minister, Chamba Tenzin, Serchung, Yuthok, and the former general, Tsarong. These were the council ministers who were to deal, in time, with Colonel Younghusband.

Towards the end of the year 1903, the Tibetan government received a letter from Claude White, in which he stated that the Younghusband mission was proceeding into Tibet. White requested that a responsible Tibetan official should be sent to Gyantse to await their arrival for negotiations; however, the Tibetan government sent troops instead to Phari, south of Gyantse. In December, the British military expedition arrived at Nadong. It consisted of Colonel Younghusband, Political Officer John Claude White, Captain O'Conner, Brigadier General James Macdonald, and five thousand Sikh and Gurkha troops, armed with rifles, machine guns, and artillery. They

3. DOCUMENTS.

4. Kawaguchi, in *Three Years in Tibet*, claimed that Shatra was the best authority in Tibet on Britain's Indian policy (pp. 502–03). Not only did Kawaguchi mention Shatra's pro-Russian leanings, but Bell stated that "the Dalai Lama's chief assistant in his pro-Russian policy was the Prime Minister Shatra" (BELL, p. 64).

were accompanied by doctors, supply officers, and four thousand porters, as the mission marched to Nadong via the Dzalep-la pass.[5] Local
headmen and the Phari district officers came to Nadong to request the
mission to halt; but they were ignored, and the expedition proceeded
to Phari.

At that point, Tongsa Penlop Ugyen Wangchuk, grandfather of
the present Maharaja of Bhutan, and Kazi Ugyen, grandfather of the
late Prime Minister of Bhutan, Jigme Dorje, arrived at Phari to mediate between the British and the Tibetans. They told the Phari district
officers that talks should be conducted with the British at Gyantse.
They said that they were there to avoid any misunderstanding between the two sides and that they would take the responsibility for
seeing that the British did not destroy any villages or monasteries on
the way. The Phari district officers reported all this to Lhasa.

Meanwhile, the Tibetan troops encamped at Chumik Shonko between Tuna and Guru, where they built a long, loosely piled, stone
wall about five feet high, across the open plain. The Tibetan Secretary-
General and representatives of the three big monasteries were at Guru,
not far behind the army. The commander of the Tibetan troops,
Dapon Lhading, received a letter from the ruler of Sikkim and his
wife, a close relative of Lhading, urging him to hold talks with the
British rather than engage them in a contest of arms. They informed
him of the strong British military reinforcements camping in Sikkim,
making it simple for the British to replenish their army with both
troops and supplies. For the Tibetan army to challenge the British was
like throwing an egg against a rock—the egg could only be smashed![6]

The Tibetan negotiators at Guru wrote to the British at Phari asking them to withdraw; but instead, the British army crossed the Dang-
la pass and entered Tuna. On the twenty-ninth day of the eleventh
month of the Water-Hare year (January 12, 1904), Dapon Lhading
went to Tuna with a small escort and asked to see Younghusband; but
he was refused and had to return to Guru.

During the ensuing month, little happened beyond the exchange of
a few letters and the repeated efforts of the Bhutanese leaders to bring
about a settlement. Then, on the nineteenth day of the first month of
the Wood-Dragon year (March 3, 1904), Younghusband, O'Conner,

5. An account of the strength of the British forces, which crossed the Dzalep-la, is given
in YOUNGHUSBAND, p. 153.
6. 'BRAS-LJONGS.

and a small escort visited the Tibetan camp at Guru. They were welcomed and taken inside the camp, where they were served tea. Younghusband informed the Tibetans that he was proceeding to Gyantse and that Tibetan representatives, who had full powers to negotiate, should meet him there. He mentioned that, in addition to discussing commercial matters, he wanted to discuss the possibility of having the same friendly relations with the Tibetans as the Russians enjoyed. Younghusband assured them that the British troops would not open fire on the way to Gyantse unless they were attacked first. However, the Tibetans made the same objections as before. They agreed to negotiate only if the British returned to Nadong. They denied any political contact with the Russians and claimed that Dorjieff was nothing more than a Buriat Mongol monk in residence at the Drepung monastery. Finally, they insisted that if the British persisted in their stubborn advance, the Tibetans would be forced to oppose them. The meeting broke up after two hours without any settlement having been reached.

A few days later the Tibetan commanders and representatives visited the British camp at Tuna. They were given a military welcome and offered refreshments; but, once again, the discussions ended in a stalemate. On March 30, the Tibetans were handed a letter informing them that the British would begin marching to Gyantse the next day, which would be the fourteenth day of the second Tibetan month. If any attempt was made to halt the advance, the Tibetans would be responsible for the consequences. The Tibetans did not write a reply; but orally informed the messenger that they would have to stop the British if they advanced towards Gyantse. That same evening, the Tibetans discovered that the British had moved up from Tuna and surrounded their camp at Guru.

On the morning of March 31, the Tibetans were waiting behind their low stone wall. As one section of the British force advanced toward the wall, Dapon Lhading and Dapon Namseling, with their escort, came from behind the wall and advanced half a mile to meet the oncoming British. The British officers dismounted and entered into a conversation with the Tibetans. They agreed that their troops would not load their rifles if the Tibetans would put down their arms. While this conversation was in progress, British troops surrounded the wall, setting up guns on high spots. The rest of the British force occupied the hill behind the Tibetan camp. While Younghusband was still talking to the Tibetan commanders in front of the wall, the British troops opened fire, and in a short time the Tibetan force was almost entirely wiped out.

The only Tibetan eyewitness account of the Guru battle was given by a survivor, Tseten Wangchuk, who had commanded twenty-five soldiers. His account follows:

> While we were waiting at the wall during the discussions, a hail of bullets came down on us from the surrounding hills. We had no time in which to draw our swords. I lay down beside a dead body and pretended I had been killed. The sound of firing continued for the length of time it would take six successive cups of hot tea to cool. When the firing ceased, the British troops came into the camp to examine the dead and wounded. They prodded me with a bayonet, but I remained quiet and held my breath. Later, a sore developed where I was pricked by the bayonet. My relative Dondup was wounded in the leg and was taken away with the other wounded by the British troops. Beside me I recognized the dead bodies of Changkyab Drakpala and Singma Khang-chung Akula. Though afraid, I remained in the company of the dead until it grew dark, and then, at night, I ran to Guru. All the Tibetan officials had left, so I proceeded to Dochen, five miles distant, and informed our garrison of what had happened. My wounded relative, Dondup, who had been treated by the British, then returned with fifty others. Dondup informed us that they had been asked if the Tibetans were receiving assistance from China or any other country. He had been informed that the Brit-ish army was such, that if it lost one hundred soldiers today, it could replace them with a thousand tomorrow. Kushab Sahib [Younghusband] possessed glasses through which he could see great distances. The poor peasants were told [by the British] they could return to their homes, as they were not to be blamed for what had happened; but, if they appeared again, they would be killed. They were photographed, and each of them was given five rupees and a package of cigarettes. Those who were seriously injured were given food and medical treatment. A number of Tibetan troops were kept by the British. All this was reported to the commander by Dondup.[7]

7. DOCUMENTS.

Tibetan government records state that over five hundred Tibetans were killed in the fight, including the generals Dapon Lhading and Dapon Namseling, the colonels Rupon Khansar Changma and Rupon Changkhyim, and two monastic representatives. Over three hundred more were wounded, and all Tibetan weapons were captured by the British.

Brigadier General J. R. L. Macdonald sent a telegraphic report of the battle to the Adjutant General in India. In brief, that report, dated March 31, 1904 at Tuna, read:

> Our casualties are—Major Wallace Dunlop slightly wounded; Mr. Candler, 'Daily Mail' correspondent, severely wounded, and seven sepoys wounded. The enemy's loss is nearly 500 killed and wounded, and 200 prisoners, all their camp and baggage, about 60 yaks and 30 mules, with 2 gingalls and a large number of matchlocks and swords, together with a few breechloaders, two of which were of Russian make. Amongst the Tibetans killed was the chief Lhasa Depon and the Lama representative of the Gaden Monastry; also one Shigatse Depon, whilst the Phari Depon was captured, severely wounded.[8]

A few days later, the British force left Tuna, overcame Tibetan opposition at Zamtrang, Soughang, and Neying, and arrived at Gyantse on April 11, 1904. Many Tibetans were killed by the British during their march to Gyantse. The British set up two camps, one at Shodrup and one at Changlo; both were near the river and about half a mile from the Gyantse fort, which was occupied by the Tibetans. The British captured the fort after subjecting it to an artillery bombardment. Dapon Tailing, commander of the fort, managed to escape and then return with reinforcements. For two nights, he attacked the British camp at Changlo, but lost more men than the enemy.

Meanwhile, a representative of the Manchu Amban arrived at Gyantse and informed the British that the Amban was prepared to come personally to Gyantse but was unable to do so because the Tibetan government refused to provide him transport. Younghusband then decided to proceed directly to Lhasa. On the pretext that the Tibetans had opposed him on his way to Gyantse and that no responsible officials had come to negotiate, he declared his intention to deal with the Dalai Lama himself. It is true that none of the officials sent

8. *Papers relating to Tibet*, Cd. 2054 (1904), p. 6.

by the Tibetan government were of high rank or authority; Young-husband was right in this respect.

While the British force was encamped at Gyantse, Captain O'Con-ner proceeded to Shigatse, where he had developed friendly relations with the abbots and officials of the Tashilhunpo monastery. These dig-nitaries even traveled to Gyantse to meet Younghusband. It was sus-pected by some Tibetans that the Sengchen Lama's attendant from Tashilhunpo was living in the British camp and writing letters on their behalf.[9]

The morale of the Tibetan army began to suffer for various reasons. It soon became well known in Ü-Tsang that the British provided med-ical aid to the Tibetan wounded, who were later given cash and presents and then set free. Younghusband was known to be sympa-thetic with the Tibetan soldiers. Moreover, the fact that the British paid well for firewood, grain, and fodder impressed the local inhab-itants.

The Tibetan government continued making preparations to resist the British. They appointed Kalon Lama Chamba Tenzin as commander-in-chief of the Tibetan forces. A defensive wall was built across the valley floor of the Karo-la pass, which lay between Gyantse and Nakartse. Lieutenant Colonel Brander was sent to clear the pass. Instead of marching up the valley route, the British followed some co-operative shepherds along a mountain route, which enabled them to descend upon the Tibetan army from above. Taken by surprise, the Tibetan force was crushed. Over three hundred men were killed and the Tibetan army scattered "like feathers in the wind."[10] The commander-in-chief, Kalon Lama Chamba Tenzin, and his supply officer, Serchung Sey, were at Nakartse, some distance behind the army. When they heard of the defeat at the Karo-la pass, they made a hasty retreat toward Lhasa, but in their panic, they lost their way and found themselves in the Rong district.

After remaining at Gyantse for over three months, Younghusband left on July 14th for Lhasa. Overcoming a token resistance on the Karo-la pass, the British expedition marched on to Nakartse. The ex-pedition stopped over at Nakartse, where the members visited the neighboring monasteries of Samding and Taklung. They relaxed by

---

9. YOUNGHUSBAND (p. 210) mentions a lama who served as a secretary for the British; but no identification was given. Perhaps it was the attendant of Sengchen Lama.

10. KA-BSHAD.

boating on the Yamdrok lake, where they found good fishing and teal shooting.

A council minister, Kalon Yuthok, and several monastic representatives were dispatched to Nakartse to talk with the British; but nothing came from them and the Tibetan people compared their officials to a "reception party." [11] The British force continued its advance and crossed the Gampa-la pass, which lay between Nakartse and the Tsangpo (Brahmaputra) River. On July 29th, the expedition reached the ferry-crossing of the Tsangpo River, where a letter from the Dalai Lama was delivered to Younghusband by the Lord Chamberlain himself. The letter asked that the British negotiate on the spot and not proceed to Lhasa; but Younghusband refused.

The British were only thirty-five miles from Lhasa at that point. The Lord Chamberlain hurried back to Lhasa and informed the Dalai Lama that the British were ferrying arms and supplies across the Tsangpo River in their own boats. The Tsongu and the Kashag held an urgent meeting and decided that, while the Dalai Lama's presence in Lhasa might put an end to the present situation, there was a danger of his being forced to sign an agreement harmful to the long range interests of Tibet. It was concluded that it would be wiser for the Dalai Lama to leave Lhasa.

The Dalai Lama had to interrupt a three-year meditation in which he was engaged. He appointed the Ganden Tri Rimpoche, Lozang Gyaltsen Lamoshar, as Regent during his absence and gave him careful instructions on dealing with the British. The Tri Rimpoche was an honest, forthright person, who could be relied upon in an emergency. The Dalai Lama gave him his seal and told him to release the former Kashag members, who were being kept in confinement, and allow them to return to their estates. At dawn of the fifteenth day of the sixth month of the Wood-Dragon year (July 30, 1904), the Dalai Lama, with a small escort, left Lhasa and went north.

On August 3rd, the British arrived outside of Lhasa, where they set up camp. That same evening, the Manchu Amban, Yu-t'ai, went to visit Younghusband. He repeated his reason for not making the journey to Gyantse as requested by Younghusband and offered to try to bring about a speedy settlement with the Tibetans—a strange offer in view of the fact he had been unable to get the Tibetans to provide transport for the trip to Gyantse. The next day, the Gurkha repre-

11. Ibid.

sentative stationed in Lhasa, Jit Bahadur, and the leader of the Kashmiri Muslims called on Younghusband, who returned their visit on the
following day. The Tsongdu and the Kashag held separate meetings,
one after another; but no one could come to a concrete decision. The
Bhutanese and Nepalese representatives continued trying to bring
about a settlement, serving as go-betweens for the Regent, the Kashag,
and Colonel Younghusband.

Finally, the Regent, without any ceremony, called on Younghusband and opened the door to future negotiations. Younghusband
asked if he and his officers could stay in the summer palace, but the
Regent informed him that the palace was considred sacred and offered
him instead the best house in Lhasa, which belonged to Lhalu, a relative of the twelfth Dalai Lama. Afterwards, the Regent summoned
the Kashag and informed its ministers that his meeting with the British had not impaired his well-being in any way. He said Younghusband was a human being like anyone else and was amenable to reason.
The Kashag now lost its shyness and, according to custom, sent
presents of meat, fruit, and eggs to the British camp. The ministers
then paid a visit to Younghusband.

While discussions were going on, a Tibetan monk managed to get
into the British camp and attacked two officers, captains T. B. Kelly
and A. Cook-Young, of the medical service, severely wounding them.
The monk was caught and questioned; but he refused to disclose the
name of the monastery to which he belonged. Tibetan officials denied
any knowledge of the man, and he was subsequently hanged in public.
During the rest of the time the British remained in Lhasa, a Tibetan
official and a monk delegate from each of the three big monasteries
were kept as hostages in the British camp to prevent a repetition of the
attack on the officers.

Younghusband informed the Kashag of the terms the British demanded to come to an agreement. Discussions took place regarding the
indemnity for the British expedition, the exchange of prisoners of
war, trade between India and Tibet, and common border problems.
The conditions set forth by the British were, on the whole, unfavor-
able to the Tibetans, but the Tsongdu and the Kashag realized there
was nothing they could do about them. The Dalai Lama was away, the
country was weak, and a dispute with Nepal over Kyirong and
Walung had not been settled. Moreover, Chinese troops were harassing
the authorities of the districts of Nyarong, Lithang, Bah, and Chating

in eastern Kham, and the Manchus in Peking were ignoring complaints from the Tibetans. When faced with two enemies, why not make one of them a friend? "Poison sometimes serves as a medicine," said the Tsongdu, accepting the British terms.

A Convention was signed in the audience hall of the Potala on the twenty-seventh day of the seventh month of the Wood-Dragon year (September 7, 1904). Tibet was represented by the Ganden Tri Rimpoche in his capacity as Regent, the four kalon (ministers) of the Kashag, four secretary generals of the Tsongdu, and representatives of the three big monasteries. The British were represented by Colonel Francis Younghusband, the Sikkimese Political Officer, John Claude White, and five other officers. The Convention was witnessed by Yut'ai, the Manchu Amban, Tongsa Penlop, the Bhutanese mediator, and Jit Bahadur, the Nepalese representative. Two hundred British troops lined the walls of the audience hall, and the Potala itself was surrounded by troops and artillery.

Because Tibet had not been represented at the discussions that had resulted in the Anglo-Chinese Convention of 1890, Tibetans had refused to accept it as binding on them. This had created problems for the British government, which finally authorized the military expedition to march to Lhasa and enter into direct negotiations with the Tibetan government. The Convention of 1904 stated that Tibet would uphold the Convention of 1890 and reference was made to the "relations of friendship and good understanding which have existed between the British Government and the Government of Tibet." It is quite clear that the British were dealing with Tibet as a separate and independent state, particularly since the 1904 Convention makes no reference to China or to Chinese authority in Tibet. The Manchu Amban, the Bhutanese representative, and the Nepalese officer merely witnessed the signing of the Convention; but did not sign it themselves.

Article IX of the 1904 Convention is of paramount importance.[12] That article specified that the government of Tibet would guarantee that, without the previous consent of the British government, it would allow: (1) no portion of Tibetan territory to be ceded, sold, leased, mortgaged, or otherwise given for occupation to any foreign power; (2) no foreign power to intervene in Tibetan affairs; (3) no

12. For the complete text of the 1904 Convention, see BELL, pp. 284-87; RICHARDSON, pp. 253-56.

representative of any foreign power to be admitted to Tibet; (4) no concession for railways, roads, telegraphs, mining, or other rights to be granted to any foreign power or the subject of any foreign power; and (5) no Tibetan revenues, whether in kind or in cash, to be pledged or assigned to any foreign power or the subject of any foreign power.

China was regarded as a foreign power under this article as evidenced by Article III of the Anglo-Chinese Convention of 1906 and Article VI of the Simla Convention of 1914. In other words, it is obvious that the provisions of the 1904 Convention between Great Britain and Tibet completely negate any Chinese claim of sovereignty or suzerainty over Tibet.

The 1904 Convention also called for the establishment of trade marts at Gyantse and Gartok, in western Tibet, which with the one already set up at Yatung under the provisions of the Trade Regulations of 1893 gave the British three centers for trade in Tibet. In addition to concluding the Convention with the Lhasa officials, Younghusband obtained two letters from them; one permitting the British trade agent at Gyantse to travel to and from Lhasa on important business; the other giving British officials freedom of movement in setting up the trade mart at Gartok.

An exchange of prisoners took place. The Tibetan government had to pay one thousand rupees as compensation for two Tibetans, who had been in the service of the British but had been captured and beaten by the Tibetans and succumbed to their injuries. The British army had not engaged in looting in the course of the advance and had respected the religion of the country. It had paid generously for the transport and supplies it obtained from the Tibetans and this resulted in a new folksong, which became popular among the people of Lhasa. It ran:

> At first, enemies of our faith they were,
> And then, "Outsiders" we labeled them;
> But, when in the land their rupees did appear,
> They became known as sahibs and gentlemen.

It goes without question that the 1904 Convention was forced upon the Tibetans; moreover, by forbidding Tibet to have any relations with other foreign powers, it served to intensify Tibet's isolation from the rest of the world. At the time Lord Curzon dispatched the British mission to Lhasa, he was under the impression that the Dalai Lama had been in contact with the Czar of Russia, even though the Russian foreign minister, Count Lamsdorff, had assured the British ambassador, Sir Charles Scott, that Russia had no political aspirations in Tibet, only an interest in the Buddhist religion. There is no evidence in Tibetan government records of any political relationship with Russia, except for Dorjieff's diplomatic visits to that country. Kawaguchi, the Japanese monk who visited Lhasa, reported that there were Russian firearms in Tibet, but if that had been the case, the Tibetans would have used such weapons against the British expeditionary troops. Instead, the only arms captured and photographed by the British were old-fashioned matchlocks, spears, axes, swords, and slings; a handful of rifles were the only modern weapons found. Indeed, it was the very lack of modern military equipment that accounted for the massacre of Tibetan troops by the British.

The British Home Government was severely critical of the expedition and of Lord Curzon's aggressive policy, remarking that it was not necessary for a trade mission to travel as an army. The Secretary of State for India criticized the size of the indemnity demanded from Tibet, which had been set at one-half million pounds sterling by the 1904 Convention, and payable in seventy-five annual installments. The indemnity was subsequently reduced to 166,000 pounds sterling (the equivalent of twenty-five lakhs of rupees) to be paid in twenty-five annual installments.[13]

In view of the fact that the 1904 Convention was drawn up directly between the governments of Tibet and Great Britain, without the participation of any third country, it establishes Tibet as an independent country at that time. In fact, Lord Curzon, in a letter dated January 8, 1903 to the Secretary of State for India, stated thus: "We regard Chinese suzerainty over Tibet as a constitutional fiction—a political affectation which has only been maintained because of its convenience to both parties."[14] The Manchu Amban had wanted the 1904 Convention signed in his own residence, but the Ganden Tri Rimpoche and Younghusband insisted on its being signed in the audience hall of the Potala, in order to make it as legal as possible. In fact, Younghusband asked the Amban how he managed to pass the time of day in Lhasa without any work to do.

13. YOUNGHUSBAND, pp. 337–39; LI, pp. 97–99.
14. Papers relating to Tibet, Cd. 1920 (1904), p. 154.

It is also clear that the ministers of the new Kashag were incompetent people in the field of foreign diplomacy; but they had seen their predecessors fall in disgrace and were naturally hesitant to commit themselves to any bold plan of action. The Nechung Oracle was greatly relied upon for his prophecies as a way of delegating responsibility for decisions.

Winter was approaching as the Younghusband expedition began its return journey, departing from Lhasa on September 23, 1904. When it reached Gyantse, Captain O'Conner was stationed there as the Trade Agent, with a small staff to assist him. Accompanied by Vernon Magniac, O'Conner traveled to Shigatse, where he met the Panchen Lama and established relations with him, much like George Bogle had done in 1774. A month later, the Panchen Lama journeyed to Calcutta, taking with him lavish presents. He was received by the Prince of Wales and Lord Minto, which marked the beginning of friction beween Tashilhunpo and the Lhasa government.

In 1906 Great Britain signed an agreement with China that ratified the Lhasa Convention of 1904. This was done without the knowledge of the Tibetan government. This agreement, known as the Adhesion Agreement of Peking, was amended in 1908 in an agreement called the Tibet Trade Regulations, 1908, in the presence of a Tibetan representative, Kalon Tsarong. Kalon Tsarong was later assassinated. It was claimed in Tibet that Kalon Tsarong had signed the 1908 Regulations without first consulting the Tibetan government of the Dalai Lama. In addition, the Tibetan government knew nothing about another Convention signed by Great Britain with Russia in August 1907, which related to Persia, Afghanistan, and Tibet.[15]

It will be remembered that shortly before Younghusband arrived at Lhasa, the Dalai Lama had gone northward to the monasteries of Taklung and Rating in the company of a small escort. While at Rating monastery, he decided to go on to Mongolia, and he sent a message to the Regent, the Ganden Tri Rimpoche, in Lhasa to this effect. After three months of arduous travel, the Dalai Lama reached Outer Mongolia. At that time, Outer Mongolia was divided into four provinces and was ruled by the Jetsun Dampa Lama, who was known to

---

15. PHUR-LCOG. For the full text of the 1906 Convention, see BELL, pp. 287–89; RICHARDSON, pp. 256–58. The text of the 1908 Regulations appears in BELL, pp. 291–97; RICHARDSON, pp. 260–65. For the text of the 1907 Convention with Russia, see BELL, pp. 289–91; RICHARDSON, pp. 258–60.

the Mongolians as Bogdo Gegen. His capital was at Urga, also known as Ulan Bator Khoto. When he heard that the Dalai Lama had entered his country, he sent his brother and two ministers with a palanquin to meet him. It took the Dalai Lama's party twenty-eight days to reach Urga, where he was received by the Jetsun Dampa Lama. The Dalai Lama stayed at Urga for over a year, occasionally touring the countryside. The reverence he received from the Mongolians made Jetsun Dampa somewhat envious, and for some time relations between the two lamas cooled. Finally, the Mongolian ministers brought about a reconciliation between them.

In 1906 the Dalai Lama returned to the Kokonor region and visited the Kumbum monastery, where the founder of the Ge-lug-pa sect had been born. Two invitations reached him, while he was there. One was from the Tibetan government urging him to return to Lhasa; the other was from the Manchu court asking him to visit Peking. He was informed by Kham officials that the Chinese were constantly causing trouble on the border, so the Dalai Lama decided that a short visit to China might be beneficial.

Towards the end of 1907, the Dalai Lama reached Sian-fu, which had been the Chinese capital known as Ch'ang-an during the T'ang Dynasty. There he received another letter from the Tibetan government urging his return; but he replied that the former Kalon, Paljor Dorje Shatra, should be appointed Lonchen (Prime Minister) to look after the administration, together with the Regent. Shatra declined the offer unless his two former colleagues, Sholkhang and Changkhyim, should also be reinstated. Finally, all three of them were made Lonchen, with authority over the Kashag. Although they took over the actual responsibilities of the government, they acknowledged the seniority of the Regent and gave the Kashag ministers precedence in ceremonial matters.

In 1908 the Dalai Lama left Sian-fu for Peking, visiting various Buddhist monasteries en route. At Wu-ta'i-shan in Shansi province, he was visited by William W. Rockhill, the American Minister to China. This was probably the first contact between Tibet and the United States. He was also visited by the Japanese Buddhist priest, Sonya Otani, with whom the Dalai Lama exchanged a Buddhist text. They discussed the possibility of a monastic student exchange between their two countries. As a result of his meeting with Otani, the Dalai Lama later met the Japanese ambassador, Gonsuke Hayashe, in Peking. The

Japanese military attaché, Masanoni Fufushima, also met the Dalai
Lama there and gave him an explanation of the Japanese military
training system. Those first contacts between the Dalai Lama and the
Japanese led eventually to the training of Tibetan troops in 1913 by a
Japanese military expert. While in Peking, the Dalai Lama was also
visited by Sir John Jordan, the British Ambassador to China.

On the third day of the eighth Tibetan month of the Earth-
Monkey year (September 27, 1908), the Dalai Lama was received in
Peking with great ceremony. He stayed in the Yellow Palace (Huang
Ssu), originally built for the fifth Dalai Lama, and recently renno-
vated. He was received at the railway station by the Mayor of Peking
and the internal and external ministers.

When the Dalai Lama learned that he would be required to perform
kowtow in an audience with the Emperor, he refused to go to the
court.[16] However, arrangements were made and the Dalai Lama met
The Empress Dowager, Tz'u-hsi, and later, the young Emperor, Kuang-
hsü. Tibetan records show that the Emperor appeared to have no authority and to be under the influence of drugs. He spoke very little
and seemed a lifeless individual. The Empress Dowager gave all orders
and was obviously the real power behind the throne. The Dalai Lama
had talks with her and with the Foreign Office (Wai-wu-pu), lodging
complaints that Chinese officials were interfering in Kham and collecting taxes from the Tibetan inhabitants of the region. He said that
China's relationship with Tibet had always been one of religious
patronage and mutual help; therefore, he called for the withdrawal of
Chinese troops and officials from the Kham region. The Empress
assured the Dalai Lama that their previous relationship would not be
altered; however, the Foreign Office officials appeared displeased with
the Dalai Lama's insistence on a purely religious relationship. They did
agree, finally, to curb the excesses of the Chinese troops and officials in
the Kham region. The representatives of the Foreign Office referred to
the 1906 Agreement between China and Great Britain and requested
the Dalai Lama to see that the terms of that agreement were carried
out. No document of agreement was drawn up after those discussions,
because there was obviously a difference of opinion between the Dalai
Lama and the Foreign Office, even though it was not permitted to
come into the open. The Dalai Lama was well aware that the Empress
Dowager's rule was secretly disliked and opposed not only by her ministers, but by the Chinese populace as well. The high degree of corrup-

16. ROCKHILL, P. 78; YOUNGHUSBAND, P. 380.

tion among the officials of the Manchu court, as witnessed by the Dalai Lama, was ample evidence of the decline of Manchu power.

During the round of entertainment in Peking, the Tibetans noticed that the Emperor could not feed himself, but had to be helped by one of his several wives. He died childless in November of that year, and almost immediately after his death, the Empress Dowager followed him to the grave. According to rumor, the Empress had made a drug addict of the young Emperor in order to rule the country herself, and had taken poison after his death. On the ninth day of the tenth month of the Earth-Ape year (1908), a young cousin of the late Emperor was enthroned under the reign title of Hsüan-t'ung. The Dalai Lama was present at the enthronement of what proved to be the last of the Manchu emperors of China.

Three weeks later, the Dalai Lama began his return journey to Tibet. He remained a few months at the monastery of Kumbum, where he made a number of reforms in the administration and rituals of the monastery. On his arrival at Nagchukha on the second day of the eighth month of the Earth-Bird year (1909), he was received by the Panchen Lama and representatives of the Ganden Tri Rimpoche and the Manchu ambans. At Phurbu Chok, he was met by the three Lonchen, whom he personally confirmed as Prime Ministers and who now accepted all the privileges due them.

On the ninth day of the eleventh month, the Dalai Lama entered Lhasa with great formality and ceremony. After two days in Lhasa itself, he reentered the Potala. He was presented with a new seal by the Tibetan people, on which was inscribed "By the prophecy of the Lord Buddha, Gyatso (=Dalai) Lama is the holder of the Buddhist faith on the face of the Earth." Much importance was attached to this seal as it was a symbol of Tibetan independence and a mark of defiance against Manchu or Chinese interference. This defiance was further exemplified by the fact that the seal was presented by the people of Tibet at a time when a strong Chinese army was advancing toward Lhasa.

After the trouble over Nepalese coinage in the year 1792, silver coins had been minted in Tibet, each embossed with a lion's head and the date of its minting. From 1910 on, the name of the Tibetan government, Ganden Phodrang, was put on all new silver coins, which the Dalai Lama issued and put into circulation on his return from China. He also established a Foreign Bureau in Lhasa, which was headed by Teji Phunkhang and Khenchung Gyaltsen Phuntsok. Both of these officials became council ministers (Kalon) later on.

14

The 1910 Chinese Invasion of Lhasa and Tibet's Struggle to Maintain Her Independence

In 1896 some of the territories of the Nyarong governor were taken from him by the Chakla chieftain in eastern Tibet. The governor demanded the return of the territories, but the Chakla chieftain was backed by the Chinese from Szechuan, who sent him troops under an officer named T'ang-li. The Chinese captured a considerable amount of Tibetan territory in eastern Tibet, and the chieftain of Derge and his entire family were taken prisoner and sent to Szechuan. The Derge chieftain's father and mother died in prison; but intervention by the Tibetan government resulted in the release of two of his sons. Authority over Derge was conferred on the eldest son by the Tibetans, and after negotiations with the Chinese had been concluded, T'ang-li's troops were withdrawn.[1]

Similar local clashes occurred during the next few years. In 1903 the Chinese began to establish themselves with troops in the territories of Garthar (where the seventh Dalai Lama had lived for several years), Jun Dondupling, and other places.[2] Meanwhile, the new deputy Amban, Feng-chien, on his way to Lhasa, stopped over at Bah. He commented on the large number of monks in the local monastery and suggested that some of them would be more useful if they returned to agricultural pursuits. The monks took offense at the

---

1. DOCUMENTS.

2. The account given here of Chao Erh-feng and the 1910 Chinese invasion of Tibet is based on SIMLA and on information acquired from officials and citizens associated with the events.

Amban's remarks and murdered him and his escort.[3] Chinese troops were dispatched from Szechuan, under General Ma Ti-t'ai,[4] to deal with the Bah monks, who, having no nearby Tibetan troops to support them, were outnumbered and forced to surrender. The Chinese general arrested 322 monks whom he suspected of having had a hand in the Amban's murder. The monks were executed, their property confiscated, and some of the monastery buildings put to the torch. Ma Ti-t'ai then returned to Szechuan.

On the pretext of continuing investigations into the affair, Chinese troops again come to Bah in 1905 under the command of Chao Erh-feng. Four monks were killed and the monastery heavily fined.[5] The monks of the neighboring Lithang monastery protested against the unfair treatment of the Bah monks, who had already been punished. Chao Erh-feng summoned the two Tibetan government representatives from Lithang and asked them if it was true that the Lithang monks were objecting to his methods. When the two Tibetans confirmed the report, Chao had them executed on the spot. This quelled the aggressiveness of the Lithang monks, but the people of nearby Chating began making preparations to assist Bah. When he learned of this, Chao sent his troops to Chating and 1,210 monks and laymen were killed.

In June of 1906, Chao Erh-feng's troops descended on the Gongkar Namling monastery.[6] Four monks went out to offer the monastery's surrender, but they were executed on the spot. The others fled into the forest, leaving behind two aged monks and three kitchen attendants, all of whom were slaughtered. Similar attacks were perpetrated on the Yangteng monastery, where forty-eight monks were killed; the rest escaped into the forests. Both monasteries were looted of their gold shrines, silver ornaments, and stocks of grain. The Buddhist scriptures were burned. Most of the loot was sent to Szechuan, where the brass and copper objects were melted down to make coins. A deputy commander of Chao's raided the Lagang monastery, where twenty-five

---

3. In addition to Feng-chien's remark and his measures for reform, his followers had been guilty of pillaging the Tibetans (YOUNGHUSBAND, pp. 369–70).

4. Ma Ti-t'ai is the spelling of this general's name in Tibetan records; but TEICHMAN gives it as Ma Wei-ch'i.

5. TEICHMAN, pp. 21–22.

6. According to YOUNGHUSBAND (p. 371), Chao Erh-feng led some 2,000 foreign-drilled troops, equipped with rifles of German make and four field-guns, when he attacked the monasteries.

monks were killed in the fighting and nine of their leaders later executed. The Chinese general soon became known among the Tibetans as
"Chao the Butcher."

It was proposed by Chao Erh-feng that the area from Tachienlu
westward to Kongpo Gyamda be made into a new province of China.
Kongpo Gyamda is a village about 120 miles east of Lhasa. Although
never subjugated and integrated into the Chinese provincial system,
the area proposed by Chao appears on twentieth-century Chinese
maps as the province of Hsi-k'ang.[7] In 1907 Chao sent troops to Tsa
Menkhung in southern Kham, where thousands of loads of grain were
taken from the inhabitants without payment being made. In 1908
Chao, reinforced with troops from Szechuan, declared that since the
Tibetans were in contact with the British, he would establish a local
government at Chamdo and then march to Lhasa.[8]

In Lhasa, a letter written by the Regent and the Kashag to the
Manchu Emperor protesting Chao Erh-feng's depredations was
handed over to the Amban, Lien-yü, who refused to forward it to
Peking. Because the Amban persisted in refusing to forward the letter,
the Regent, Ganden Tri Rimpoche, assumed that the Amban and
Chao Erh-feng were acting in agreement, probably without the Emperor's knowledge; therefore, the Kashag sent a representative to Calcutta to telegraph the Chinese Foreign Office and Military Department (Chün-chi-pu) at Peking, asking them to order Chao to
withdraw from Kham. An appeal was also made to the British to use
their good offices on this matter with China.[9]

There was no reply from Peking. Meanwhile, the Chinese garrison
at Lhasa was reinforced with six thousand troops and the Amban
wrote to the Kashag, informing it that all troops in Tibet were now to
be under the command of Chung-yin, a Manchu who had been appointed commander-in-chief. The Kashag refused to acknowledge the
Amban's order. Tibetan troops outnumbered the Amban's garrison
in Lhasa; but because the Dalai Lama was still in Chinese territory, the

7. TEICHMAN (p. 33) says that Fu Sung-mu, the chief assistant of Chao Erh-feng, proposed that the area be made a Chinese province to be called Hsikang.

8. Although some sources state that Chao Erh-feng himself marched to Lhasa with his
troops—cf. E. T. Williams, *Tibet and Her Neighbors* (Berkeley, 1937), p. 121, and Zahiruddin Ahmed, *China and Tibet, 1708–1959* (Oxford, 1960), p. 18—it is clear that
Chao Erh-feng never traveled beyond Chamdo, where he set up his headquarters.

9. See TEICHMAN, p. 27, for the telegraphic appeals made by the Tibetan government to
the foreign powers of Europe and America.

Tibetan government had to tolerate numerous acts of aggression in Kham out of concern for the Dalai Lama's personal safety. The Manchu Emperor was weak and could no longer control his provinces, whose governors began making their own decisions and policies.

In 1909 the Tibetan government learned that a large Chinese force was being sent to Tibet to police the trade marts, as provided under the Trade Regulations signed at Calcutta in April 1908. The Tibetans objected to the Chinese policing of the trade marts and offered to provide troops themselves, if any were needed. The Kashag made several protests to the Amban, demanding the withdrawal of Chinese troops from Tibetan territory; the Amban's reply was to bring in the troops sooner than planned.

Anxious that the Dalai Lama should arrive in Lhasa before the Chinese troops, the Tibetans sent a representative, Khenchung Chamba Choszang, to Kham with orders to halt the Chinese troops, until Peking should reply to the telegram sent from Calcutta. The Chinese troops had advanced four days' march from Chamdo. Khenchung met them at Tar Dzong and delivered his instructions for them to halt; but the Chinese ignored his orders and placed him under arrest. The Chinese were well equipped with modern arms; however, they carried no food supplies, preferring to halt every fifteen miles or so and help themselves to whatever the local inhabitants could be forced to provide. When they arrived at Kongpo Gyamda, Khenchung Chamba Choszang and eight of his escort were executed on the orders of the Amban.

The Dalai Lama arrived back in Lhasa in December of 1909. Representatives of the Tsongdu were asked to meet the Chinese army and attempt to detain it. Fearing execution, they took with them a deputy of the Nepalese representative in Lhasa and a leader of the Kashmiri Muslims. The deputy Amban, accompanied by the Nepalese representative, went to the Dalai Lama and assured him that the Chinese army was intended merely to police the trade marts. It would be dispersed as soon as it reached Lhasa and would not interfere in the internal affairs of Tibet. As security, he offered to give the Dalai Lama a letter to this effect. The letter arrived the next day. It contained the general assurances already given by the Amban; but reference to the "internal affairs of Tibet" was omitted and instead, it guaranteed that there would be no interference in the "religious affairs of the Dalai Lama."

On the third day of the first Tibetan month of the Iron-Dog year (1910), the Chinese army, under the command of Chung-yin, reached the banks of the Kyichu river, where it was met by the Amban's bodyguard. At three o'clock in the afternoon, the Chinese marched through Lhasa, firing on members of the Lhasa police, killing or wounding a number of them. They also fired on the Jokhang temple, and then, passing through the streets, attacked Teji Phunkhang, the head of the Foreign Bureau and organizer of the Monlam festival, who was on his way to the temple with his colleagues. Phunkhang's horse was killed under him. He himself was arrested, beaten, stripped of his ornaments, and taken to the Amban's residence. His colleague, Tsedron Jamyang Gyaltsen, and Phunkhang's personal servant were killed.

The Chinese then made their presence further known by firing at the Potala. The Dalai Lama immediately appointed a new Regent, Tri Rimpoche Ngawang Lozang Tsemonling, and provided him with an assistant named Khenche Khenrab Phuntsok Neushag. He told them he would have to leave for Yatung, near the Sikkimese border and instructed them to take over his responsibilities. As soon as it grew dark, the Dalai Lama, accompanied by his three Prime Ministers, the council minister, Kalon Serchung, two deputy ministers, Kalon Tenzin Wangpo and Kalon Samdrup Phodrang, and the Medical Adviser, Chamba Thubwang Ngoshi, crossed the Ramagang river and journeyed westward in the direction of Chaksam. (When the present Dalai Lama fled during the Tibetan revolt in 1959, he crossed the same river but then traveled southward.)

The next day, the Amban learned of the Dalai Lama's flight and asked his troops for volunteers to bring back the head of the Dalai Lama. Wu, a Chinese officer,[10] and a Chinese-Tibetan named Gyalgodong, volunteered. They were given three hundred cavalrymen, with whom they pursued the Dalai Lama's party.

On the evening of his arrival at Chaksam, the Dalai Lama received a message that his pursuers were only ten miles away. He immediately left for the monastery Yardok Samding, the seat of the abbess Dorje Phagmo, who is one of the few Tibetan Buddhist nuns considered to be an incarnation. (Reincarnations of Dorje Phagmo are selected in much the same manner as those of incarnate lamas.) A few Tibetan

10. This officer, called Wu Kon-tai in Tibetan sources, was later captured in eastern Tibet and sentenced to life imprisonment at Sengye Dzong.

troops remained behind with the attendant, Dazang Dadul, to delay the Chinese. At sunrise of the next day, the Chinese cavalry arrived at Chaksam, where they were attacked by Dazang Dadul's small force. The Chinese were held up for two days and suffered a number of casualties. Dadul was rewarded in later years for his heroism at Chaksam.

From the Samding monastery, the Dalai Lama sent a message to Basil Gould, then British Trade Agent at Gyantse, asking for asylum in India if necessary. The Dalai Lama then journeyed on to Phari, where he was visited by the commander of a small contingent of twenty-five Chinese troops stationed at Yatung, one day's journey south of Phari. The commander asked the Dalai Lama not to cross over into India and offered to write a full report to the Manchu Emperor and the Amban at Lhasa. The Dalai Lama said that he would consider the request when he arrived in Yatung.

The Dalai Lama was receiving daily reports that the Chinese were still in pursuit from the north. As he continued his trip, almost the entire population of Dromo (Chumbi Valley) and Phari turned out to accompany him to Yatung as bodyguards. The Chinese were warned not to appear on the streets of Yatung on the day the Dalai Lama passed through. Meanwhile, a military officer and the British Trade Agent arrived at Phari from Gyantse to accompany the huge party to Yatung. The party traveled without further interference from the Chinese troops. After passing through the gates, the Dalai Lama was welcomed by David Macdonald, the British Trade Agent at Yatung, and spent the night at his residence. Macdonald had been to Lhasa with the Younghusband Mission in 1904. He spoke and wrote Tibetan very well, and gained the friendship and goodwill of many Tibetans.[11]

The Dalai Lama's original plan had been to remain at Yatung and from there conduct negotiations with Peking, but when he heard that Chinese troops had arrived at Phari, only one day away, he finally decided to cross over into India. Before leaving Yatung, the Dalai Lama left a letter with Macdonald to be forwarded to the British officials in India. In view of the fact that the British had invaded Lhasa a few short years earlier, causing the Dalai Lama to flee to Mongolia, the

11. Macdonald served as the Trade Agent at Yatung for about twenty years (1905–25). He authored books on Tibet, including *The Land of the Lama* (London, 1929) and *Twenty Years in Tibet* (London, 1932).

contents of the letter he now sent the British are interesting enough
to warrant reproducing it in full. It read:

> The Chinese have been greatly oppressing the Tibetan people
> at Lhasa. Mounted infantry arrived there. They fired on the in-
> habitants, killing and wounding them. I was obliged, together
> with my six ministers, to make good my escape. My intention
> now is to go to India for the purpose of consulting the British
> government. Since my departure from Lhasa I have been greatly
> harassed on the road by Chinese troops. A force of two hundred
> Chinese Mongol infantry were behind me at Chak-sam, and I left
> a party of my soldiers to hold them back. A small fight took
> place there, in the course of which two Tibetans and seventy
> Chinese were killed. I have left the Regent and acting ministers
> at Lhasa, but I and the ministers who accompany me have
> brought our seals with us. I have been receiving every courtesy
> from the British government, for which I am grateful. I now
> look to you for protection, and I trust that the relations between
> the British government and Tibet will be that of a father to his
> children. Wishing to be guided by you, I hope to give full infor-
> mation on my arrival in India.[12]

Traveling via the Dzalep-la pass, the Dalai Lama arrived in Kalimpong, where he was the guest of Raja Kazi Ugyen of Bhutan. The
house in which the Dalai Lama lived is known today as Bhutan House,
and to the Tibetans, it is still called Migyur Ngonga Phodrang, meaning "Palace of Unchanging Delight," because of its association with
the thirteenth Dalai Lama.

After a week at Kalimpong, the Dalai Lama went to Darjeeling,
where he stayed in a house called Padabuk. There he was visited by
Charles Bell, the Political Officer of Sikkim, who acted as his liaison
with the government of India. The Deputy Commissioner of Darjeeling looked after all aspects of the Dalai Lama's security.

Several telegrams were sent to Peking to request the withdrawal of
Chinese troops from Tibet; but these were studiously ignored. Moreover, reports appeared in Indian newspapers that the Manchus had
deposed the Dalai Lama and were choosing his successor by a lottery.
The Manchu Amban circulated similar reports in Lhasa. The Dalai

12. BELL, p. 109.

Lama then decided never to have direct negotiations with the Manchus or the Chinese; instead, he invoked one of the articles of the 1904 Lhasa Convention and appealed to the British to intercede on his behalf. The Dalai Lama, on his arrival in Calcutta, received a seventeen-gun salute in his honor and was escorted in a regal carriage to Hastings House.

The Dalai Lama met the Viceroy, Lord Minto, on March 14, 1910, and gave him an account of Chinese deceit and aggrandizement in Tibet. The following are extracts from the private interview as recorded by Butler, who began his account thus: "His Excellency, the Viceroy, received the Dalai Lama in private audience at Government House, Calcutta, this afternoon at five p.m. There were also present Mr. Bell, Political Officer, Sikkim, who acted as interpreter, and myself." The account went on to say that after compliments, in the course of which the Dalai Lama expressed his cordial thanks for the hospitality extended to him and the kindness of his reception, His Holiness said that he had had a trying time in his journey from Lhasa and was in danger from the Chinese soldiers who pursued him. At the time that he left Lhasa, there were 500 of the old Chinese troops and 40 newly-arrived ones, who were the advance guard of a force of 2,000 men then only two days' march from Lhasa. In all, some 2,700 troops had come into Lhasa and its neighborhood lately, according to the information he had received. That total number of Chinese troops in Tibet was not required for Tibet alone. The Chinese had designs on Nepal, Sikkim, and Bhutan, which they intended to subdue, and that would destroy the last vestiges of the Lamaist religion. The Chinese had more than once interposed to prevent amicable direct relations between the Tibetan and British governments. The Sikkim dispute of 1888 and the Younghusband mission of 1904 were due entirely to the actions of the Chinese. While in Peking, His Holiness had asked the British Minister to eliminate the harmful intervention of the Chinese.

The Dalai Lama went on to tell the Viceroy that under the Trade Regulations of 1908, direct relations between the British and Tibetan governments had been assured, and he was appealing that the rights of the Tibetans in this regard should be observed. He asked that he might be restored to the position of the fifth Dalai Lama, who had negotiated with the Emperor of China as the ruler of a friendly state, and he asked that the Chinese troops be withdrawn.

When questioned by the Viceroy as to whether he knew the terms of the treaties, in which the British government had entered with China and Russia, His Holiness replied that he was studying them.

The Tibetan government claimed the right of direct dealing with the British government, and it did not recognize the 1890 and 1906 Conventions, in which it had played no part. Moreover, the Dalai Lama said he had had no communications from the Chinese at Lhasa since he had left Phari. He would not return to Lhasa under the present political conditions there, as the promises made to him had been disregarded. He would not trust the written word of the Peking government as it had violated the promises given him by the late Empress Dowager.

When questioned by the Viceroy as to what he intended to do if he did not return to Lhasa, the Dalai Lama replied that he could not say at the moment, but that unless the matter was satisfactorily settled, he would not return to Lhasa. He denied that he had intrigued against China. He had only been two months in Lhasa before he fled. The Amban was altogether hostile. The Dalai Lama had come away with his ministers and the seals of office. With the Regent, whom he had appointed, he had left the seal that was used in the signing of the 1904 Convention, but his own seal he had with him. Moreover, he had had no contact with the Regent since he left. The Chinese intercepted all official letters and he had no official communication with Tibet. Some private letters had come through, but any communication had to be secret.

During the interview, the Dalai Lama sought to clarify the issue of Dorjieff, the Buriat Mongol, who had visited the Czar of Russia. His Holiness stated that Dorjieff was now in his own country. He had been one of seven assistants to his chief spiritual adviser and had never had anything to say except about spiritual matters.

At the end of the interview, the Dalai Lama said that he had made his appeal and asked what would be the answer. His Excellency, the Viceroy, said that he was very glad to have the opportunity of entertaining His Holiness and of meeting him. He had given instructions that every consideration should be shown to him, but he said that political questions of importance required due consideration and that he could not say more than that he would communicate His Holiness' remarks to His Majesty's government. The Dalai Lama then repeated his expressions of gratitude to the Viceroy and took his leave.

The Viceroy suggested that in the meantime the Dalai Lama enjoy the sights of Calcutta. While showing the Dalai Lama every consideration, the Viceroy was careful not to commit himself to any promises of help, perhaps because he was not very clear as to Britain's own treaty obligations with China and Russia. After spending a few days in Calcutta, the Dalai Lama returned to Darjeeling.

Only two of the original council ministers, Kalon Lozang Trinley and Kalon Tsarong, were still in Lhasa. The Dalai Lama, at the time of his departure, had instructed the Regent Tri Rimpoche to appoint Dekyi Lingpa and Khenchung Gyaltsen Phuntsok as deputy Kalon. The Chinese deposed Lozang Trinley and disqualified Dekyi Lingpa and Gyaltsen Phuntsok, forbidding them to enter the Kashag. Tsarong was the only one kept in office. His new colleagues, appointed by the Chinese, were Tenzin Chosdrak, Rampa, and Lanthongpa. The Regent's assistant, Khenrab Phuntsok Neushag, was arrested by the Chinese and condemned to death; but on the appeal of the Regent, his life was spared and he was dispatched in chains to Tachienlu.

In Lhasa, Tibetan police were replaced by Chinese. The Dalai Lama's personal effects, which were still on their way back from China, were confiscated at Nagchukha. His property in the Potala and Norbulingka (the summer palace), as well as the vast treasury of the Tibetan government, were removed by the Chinese. The Lhasa armory and magazines were emptied, the mint and ammunition factory seized, and the houses of those ministers who had fled with the Dalai Lama systematically pillaged. The property of the ex-Regent Demo, who had been found guilty of plotting against the Dalai Lama in 1899, was restored to his family.

Many districts that had formerly sent their revenue direct to Lhasa began to send it to the Dalai Lama at Darjeeling through merchants and travelers. To put a stop to this, the Chinese set up check-posts along the border and searched all travelers to India. Before long, Tibetans in Lhasa began defacing and removing posters put up by the Chinese. Monastic representatives and Tibetan officials protested to the Manchu Amban against the deposition of the Dalai Lama. Neither the Tibetan people nor their government would cooperate with the Chinese dictatorship at Lhasa. In eastern and southern Tibet, Chinese nationals were frequently attacked.

The Chinese, now realizing that they had made a mistake in declaring the Dalai Lama deposed, instructed the Amban to send Lo Ti-t'ai to Darjeeling to offer the Dalai Lama the restoration of his titles and to request him to return to Tibet. The Chinese official arrived in India in September 1910.

In reply to Lo Ti-t'ai, the Dalai Lama wrote the following letter:

> To Lo Ti-t'ai from the Dalai Lama: On the tenth day of the ninth month of the Iron-Dog year [1910], I received through you an urgent message from the Peking political and military departments asking me to return to Lhasa. In reply, I have the following to say: The Manchu Emperors have always shown great care for the welfare of the successive Dalai Lamas, and the Dalai Lamas have reciprocated these feelings of friendship. We have always had each other's best interests at heart. The Tibetan people have never had any evil designs on the Chinese.
>
> In the Wood-Dragon year [1904], when the British expedition arrived in Tibet, I did not consider taking any assistance except from Peking. When at Peking, I met the Emperor and his aunt, and they showed me great sympathy. The Emperor committed himself to taking care of the welfare of Tibet. On the strength of the Emperor's word, I returned to Tibet, only to find that on our eastern borders, large bodies of Chinese troops had massed and many of our subjects had been killed. Monasteries were destroyed and the people's rights suppressed. I am sure that you are fully aware of this.
>
> Furthermore, the Amban at Lhasa, Lien-yü, had been reinforcing his troops with the object of occupying Lhasa. On several occasions, I objected to this; but he turned a deaf ear to my appeals. When the troops were on their way to Lhasa, I sent my representative, Khenchung, to meet them and explain my position; but the military officers executed Khenchung and seized his possessions.
>
> While on their march, Chinese troops had exploited the people and the monasteries to such an extent that my subjects and the monastery monks requested permission to retaliate. Had they done so, it would not have been impossible for us to defeat your army, owing to our knowledge of the terrain. However, a fight by my subjects against your troops might have been construed as against the Manchu Emperor. I, therefore, asked my ministers to negotiate with your officers and to protect your representatives

in Lhasa. I also wrote to the Emperor asking him to withdraw these troops. All this is clear in the records held by both the Chinese and the Tibetans. I have several times explained this by wire to the Peking Political Department; but I have received no reply.

At Nagchukha, on my way from China to Lhasa, I wrote several notes to the Amban, informing him that China and Tibet must continue their long-standing friendship; but, instead of listening to my appeal, he insisted on bringing more troops to Lhasa. The advance of the Chinese troops coincided with the Monlam festival being held at Lhasa, at which thousands of monks from different monasteries had come together. In order to avoid a clash, the Nepalese representative at Lhasa called on the Manchu Amban to prevent any trouble from arising. The Amban refused to do anything about it; instead, he sent his bodyguard out to meet the advancing troops. On the way, they fired on the Lhasa police, killing some of them. They also fired on the Jokhang temple and the Potala palace.

The eleventh Dalai Lama's nephew, Teji Phunkhang, and Tsedron Jamyang Gyaltsen, were Tibetan government officials assigned to administer the Monlam festival. On their way to the Jokhang temple, they were met by the troops, who fired on them. Tsedron Jamyang and Teji Phunkhang's servant and horse were killed. Teji Phunkhang was then beaten and taken away to the military camp. The people of Lhasa were so outraged that they wanted to take revenge; but I restrained them from doing so. I still hoped we could negotiate with China and avoid unnecessary bloodshed. Not knowing what would happen if I were captured, I appointed a representative in Lhasa to continue negotiations and I then came to the border of Tibet and India in order to personally conduct negotiations with China.

My ministers had appealed to me to remain in Lhasa; but had I done so, a situation similar to the Muslim invasion of India might well have taken place, which resulted in many religious institutions being destroyed. As I did not want this to happen in Tibet, I came here especially to negotiate for my country, not caring what hardships I might have to endure. When I arrived at Phari, I was asked by the Chinese official of Yatung to remain at the Phari monastery and negotiate with Peking and with the Manchu Amban in Lhasa by wire. I thought this arrangement would be ideal; but when troops arrived to take me alive or dead, I had no choice but to cross the Indian border.

At Kalimpong, I came to know that the Manchu Emperor had already issued orders that I had been deposed from office. This was published in Indian newspapers, and even in Lhasa, posters were put up announcing that I was now an ordinary person and that a new Dalai Lama would soon be chosen. Since the Emperor has done everything on the recommendation of the Manchu Amban in Lhasa, without considering the independence of Tibet and the religious relationship between our two countries, I feel there is no further use in my negotiating directly with China. I have lost confidence in China and in finding any solution in consultation with the Chinese.

I have contacted the British, because the 1904 Convention permits us to deal directly with them. The Chinese are responsible for this action of mine.

During my stay in India, Amban Lien-yü has moved Chinese troops all over Tibet and has exploited Tibetan subjects to extremes. They have stopped my supplies and censored my letters from Tibet. They have sealed the treasury in Lhasa, emptied our armory, and seized our mint factories. Khenche Khenrab Phuntsok, assistant to my representative at Lhasa, aged seventy years, who was completely innocent, was imprisoned without cause and sent to Tachienlu. Judicial cases that had already been decided were reopened. Tibetan government property and the property of Tibetan officials and monasteries have been illegally seized.

You are fully aware of this inexcusable illegal action taken by your troops; yet, you inform me and my ministers that the situation in Tibet is peaceful and that status quo is being maintained. I know that this has been said to persuade me to return and I also know that it is false.

Because of the above, it is not possible for China and Tibet to have the same relationship as before. In order for us to negotiate, a third party is necessary; therefore, we should both request the British government to act as an intermediary. Our future policy will be based on the outcome of discussions between ourselves, the Chinese, and the British. Are you able to agree to the participation of the British in these discussions? If so, please let me know.

In case you are not agreeable to this, I am handing you a letter containing the above facts, written in both the Manchu and Tibetan languages, which I would like you to forward to the Emperor. Please explain carefully to the Emperor the contents of my letter. (Dated) Thirteenth day of the ninth month of the Iron-Dog year [1910].

(SEAL OF THE DALAI LAMA) [13]

That winter, the Dalai Lama made a tour of the Buddhist pilgrimage places. He visited Lumbini, Bodh Gaya, Sarnath, and Kushinagara, where the Lord Buddha was born, became enlightened, delivered his first sermon, and died.

Meanwhile, the officials of the Panchen Lama in Tibet, hoping to use the Panchen for their own purposes, invited him to Lhasa in January 1911. He stayed first in the Jokhang temple and then moved to the Norbulingka (summer palace of the Dalai Lama). This annoyed the Tibetan people, who became even more outraged when the Panchen Lama began to fraternize with the Manchu Amban in public, accompanying him to parties and the theatre.

During the Butter-lamp festival, the Panchen Lama and the Amban placed themselves in sedan chairs and were taken in procession around Lhasa in the same manner in which the Dalai Lama was normally escorted. The Lhasa populace participated in the ceremony, but only to the extent of dropping mud and old socks on to the heads of the Panchen and the Amban as they passed. It was also the occasion for a new Lhasa street-song:

> The slovenly attired monk
> On the roof of the Jokhang,
> Would have been a thief
> If it were not for the arrival of the dawn.

"Dawn" in the song refers to the Tibetan resistance movement, which prevented the Panchen Lama from accepting the Dalai Lama's administrative duties, which the people suspected the Chinese were preparing to offer him. From the private correspondence that passed between the Dalai Lama and the Panchen Lama, it is evident that the Panchen held the Dalai Lama in high regard; he was involved in this unpleasantness only because of the collaboration of his officials with the

13. DOCUMENTS.

Chinese. Since that time, ill feeling has continued to exist between the Lhasa officials and the Panchen's Tashilhunpo officials.

Among the Chinese troops in Lhasa, there were many who had been enlisted in Szechuan. Some were ordinary soldiers, while others belonged to the Ko-lao-hui, a secret society of revolutionists. Because of rivalry among the soldiers and the insufficiency of their pay in Tibet, clashes took place within the Chinese army. The Amban had the local leader of the Ko-lao-hui executed; but this only led to recriminations and murder among the Chinese officers. Political dissensions and personal feuds resulted in the defection of a Chinese colonel, Hsieh Kuo-liang, and three other officers to the Tibetan side. They joined the Sera monastery as monks.

In October 1911, the revolution led by Sun Yat-sen overthrew the Manchus in China. When this news reached Lhasa, the members of the Ko-lao-hui mutinied. They attacked the Amban's residence and looted his house. The Amban fled from Lhasa and took refuge near the Drepung monastery; but the mutineers caught up with him and carried him off to Shigatse as a hostage. Chung-yin, the Manchu commander-in-chief, intervened on behalf of the Amban and secured his release. Afterwards, the mutineers called for the other army units stationed at outlying points to join them for the march back to China and home. This brought additional Chinese troops to Lhasa "whose plunder on the way and in the capital aroused widespread ill-feeling among the Tibetans." [14]

Chao Erh-feng had maintained his headquarters at Chamdo; but, on receiving news of the revolution in China, he returned to his capital in Szechuan, leaving his deputy in command of the troops in Kham.[15] In the following year, Chao was executed.[16]

News spread throughout Tibet that the Dalai Lama was about to return from exile. This caused the Chinese troops and civilians in Ü-Tsang to be constantly harassed. Kanam Depa of Poyul in southeastern Tibet openly revolted against the Chinese. Imperial troops, under Lo Chang-chi, were sent from Lhasa towards Poyul; but, because of the

14. LI, p. 67.

15. According to Tibetan records, the name of Chao's deputy was Din Kon-tai. TEICHMAN (p. 33) states that Chao's place on the frontier was assumed by General Fu Sung-mu, his chief assistant.

16. After leaving Chamdo, Chao Erh-feng became the governor of Sze-chuan. In 1912 he was executed by Yin Ch'ang-heng, a revolutionary leader (TEICHMAN, p. 41). Also see Williams, *Tibet and Her Neighbors*, p. 122.

steep, rocky roads leading to that remote area, the Chinese lost many
men on the way and had to return without being able to suppress the
uprising.

A number of the Dalai Lama's junior officials in Darjeeling volunteered to return to Tibet and fight. They arrived in Tsang and organized uprisings. They attacked the Chinese at Shigatse and Gyantse;
but they suffered severe losses and had to return in disgrace to Darjeeling, where for a time they were ridiculed by the senior Tibetan officials. They were summoned into the presence of the Prime Minister,
Lonchen Shatra, expecting to be reprimanded; but the shrewd
Lonchen praised their efforts. He declared them to be heroes, saying
that he was sure they would be more successful in their next venture.
Inspired by his confidence in them, the young officials returned again
to Tibet, where they did an excellent job of organizing guerrilla resistance. Eventually, they succeeded in driving the Chinese out of
Shigatse and Gyantse. Later on, these young officials were all made
generals.

The Dalai Lama then moved from Darjeeling to Kalimpong, where
he again stayed at Bhutan House. From there he sent his sealed orders
to Lhasa, addressed to Tsepon Norbu Wangyal Trimon and the
Secretary-General, Chamba Tendar, who was later to become a Kalon
and governor of eastern Tibet. Tsepon Trimon was later to become an
assistant to Lonchen Shatra at the Simla Convention, with the rank of
commander-in-chief. (Eventually he rose to the position of a Kalon
and succeeded Chamba Tendar as governor in eastern Tibet.)

The Dalai Lama instructed these two officials to organize in secret a
War Department and to prepare for military action. They were told
that if they wished to consult him, they should get into direct contact
with him at Kalimpong. This statement implied that the Kashag was
to be kept ignorant of their plans; nevertheless, Chamba Tendar and
Trimon did at least contact prominent monks in the Sera monastery.
By that time, the Chinese military dictatorship in Lhasa was weak and
inefficient. Chinese soldiers were selling their guns and ammunition to
Tibetan merchants. Chamba Tendar and Trimon sponsored their own
merchants to buy Chinese firearms, while they secretly organized the
recruitment of Tibetan soldiers.

The proud and patriotic Sera monks, aware of the preparations that
were being made, became bold enough to provoke the Chinese openly.
This roused the suspicions of the Chinese leaders, who held a meeting

in Lhasa to discuss the situation. They complained that they were getting no help from Peking and that it was becoming increasingly difficult to live off the Tibetans and their land. Loans were no longer forthcoming from the Tibetan government. The Chinese assumed that if they put pressure on the government, it might provoke an attack by the Sera monks; therefore, they decided to risk an attack on Sera itself, even though they were uncertain as to the extent of opposition they would have to cope with in so doing.

When Trimon and Chamba Tendar learned of the Chinese decision to attack Sera, they contacted the Banagshol tribe of the Kham region, and deployed them to defend Sera. On November 2, 1911, the Chinese attacked the monastery. They captured and burned the surrounding hermitages and laid siege to the monastery itself. The three Chinese officers who had earlier defected to become monks now made themselves very useful to the Tibetan defenders. One of them, Hsieh Kuo-liang, emerged from the monastery at night and penetrated the Chinese lines. He spread the fiction that the monks were approaching from behind and thus diverted the attention of the Chinese so that the Sera monks were able to take the offensive. The Kham tribesmen fought so fiercely that the Chinese were unable to make any headway, even though the fighting lasted ninety-six hours.

Meanwhile, in Lhasa, Trimon and Chamba Tendar had openly declared war, and when this news reached Sera, the Chinese troops abruptly stopped fighting and immediately marched on Lhasa. Lhasa itself was then divided into two zones; the northern being occupied by Tibetans, the southern by Chinese. The front doors and windows of every house in town were blocked with sandbags. Communicating passages were made from one house to another by breaking through the walls. A stockaded street separated the two zones.

Both the Tibetans and the Chinese dug underground tunnels into each other's zone and laid fuses to explode kegs of powder placed under important outposts and houses. These tunnels were made in zig-zag fashion to lessen the shock waves from the explosion. To draw the Chinese to the site of a planned explosion, the Tibetans would launch a brief attack on that area. Because the Tibetans repeatedly used the same tactic, the Chinese finally ignored this ruse and the explosion would take place in an area already evacuated. In order to detect underground digging, earthen jars were buried at floor-level and their rims smeared with mud. The slightest vibration would cause the mud to trickle into the jars.

There were very few large scale engagements. Insults were hurled from windows, and, because random sniping took place in streets dividing the two zones, it was dangerous to stand near an open window. By the end of almost a year's fighting, one third of Lhasa had been subjected to devastation and ruin. Tsepon Trimon himself was wounded in the arm; but he concealed his injury and continued to perform his duties. The Sera monks and the Banagshol Khampa joined in the fighting at Lhasa and made frequent raids on the Chinese cantonment at Drapchi, just outside the city. Many men were lost in their attacks on that well-fortified garrison.

Chinese outposts in Tsang and near the Indian border were being consistently attacked and captured by the Tibetans, who had returned from Darjeeling. The roads to Kham and the Indian border were blocked and the fleeing Chinese headed for Lhasa, where they felt there would be safety in numbers.

In Kalimpong, Dazang Dadul, the hero of the Chaksam battle, was made a commander-in-chief of the Tibetan forces and in January 1912 was sent to Lhasa to work in close cooperation with the War Department set up by Trimon and Chamba Tendar. The Chinese troops were facing a grave food shortage. They might have capitulated sooner; but they were able to hold out longer by moving into the friendly Tengyeling monastery in Lhasa, which belonged to the followers of the late Regent Demo. There they found supplies sufficient for another six months. This resulted in another Lhasa street-song, which described the prolongation of the war even after the arrival of the new commander-in-chief.

Dazang Dadul, Tsepon Trimon, and Chamba Tendar called a secret meeting of the Tsongdu, at which it was decided to arrest all pro-Chinese Tibetan officials, before there were any more defections like that of the Tengyeling monastery. As a result of this decision, the members of the Kashag were all arrested. Kalon Tsarong, his son, and Kadrung Tsashagpa, the secretary of the Kashag, were shot for having close relations with the Chinese. The other three Kalons, who had been appointed by the Chinese, namely, Tensing Chosdrak, Rampa, and Langthongpa, were imprisoned. Phunrabpa, a secretary-general, Mondrong, a treasurer, and Lozang Dorje, a monk official, were executed for being on friendly terms with the monks from the Tengyeling monastery. At the outbreak of the fighting in Lhasa, this monastery had declined the offer of government troops for its protection and the three executed officials had guaranteed its defense. There was no longer a Kashag and all important matters were now deliberated by the War Department and the Tsongdu, sometimes in consultation with the Dalai Lama in India.

During his stay in India, the Dalai Lama was very well treated by the British and relations between India and Tibet consequently improved considerably. Since preparations were being made for his return to Tibet, the Dalai Lama wrote to the Viceroy, through Charles Bell, thanking him for the hospitality shown by the British government during his two-year stay in India. He made known his intention to return to Lhasa. He likened the situation in Tibet to a reservoir which requires constant replenishing if it is not to dry up. Due to the revolution in China, the Chinese troops in Tibet were not being reinforced and the level of the Chinese reservoir was falling fast. As the Tibetans were fighting with very high morale, the Dalai Lama hoped that they would soon drive out the Chinese. Even more important to him at that point was the future of Tibet itself. He reminded the Viceroy of his request for British participation in settling future problems between China and Tibet. Charles Bell, who was given the letter, was also apprised of its contents.

While at Kalimpong, the Dalai Lama had been shown great consideration by Raja Kazi Ugyen, whose house he had occupied. The Dalai Lama expressed his appreciation for the Raja's hospitality by conferring on him and all his descendants the Tibetan rank of Rimshi (Fourth Rank).

On the tenth day of the fifth Tibetan month of the Water-Mouse year (1912), the Dalai Lama left Kalimpong for Tibet, via the Dzalep-la pass. At Yatung, he remained a week at the residence of the British Trade Agent, David Macdonald. From there, he wrote to various monasteries and chieftains in eastern Tibet, encouraging them in their opposition to the Chinese and promising them early liberation. He also wrote to the Banagshol Khampa tribesmen, complimenting them on their brave action at Sera and Lhasa.

Shekar Lingpa, who had been a secretary in the Dalai Lama's service at Darjeeling, was appointed a Kalon to fill the place of the late Tsarong minister. Shekar Lingpa was a straightforward, elderly man, known as an accomplished poet. While in Darjeeling, he had written a number of moving poems in remembrance of Lhasa. Not long after returning to Tibet, Shekar Lingpa died.

Two hundred monks from the monasteries of Sera, Ganden, and

Drepung volunteered to escort the Dalai Lama back to Lhasa. They were led by Ragashar. At the same time, two well-known Khampas, Nyima Gyalpo Pandatshang of Markham and Chopatshang of Gojo, voluntarily brought an armed escort of Khampas to join the Dalai Lama. They were to protect him day and night until Lhasa was reached.

The Panchen Lama, who seemingly regretted his fraternization with the Chinese, journeyed with his officials from Tashilhunpo to welcome the Dalai Lama at Ralung. Continuing on his journey, the Dalai Lama spent some time at the Samding monastery near lake Yardok Yutso.

In Peking, Sir John Jordan, the British Minister, met with the new Chinese President Yüan Shih-kai, and protested the Chinese military action in Tibet and their attempt to make Tibet a province of China.[17] In time, the President sent a letter, via India, to the Amban Lien-yü, ordering him to return to China. The letter instructed him to appoint the Manchu commander, Chung-yin, to continue the usual duties with the help of a council of Chinese officers. The Chinese would have been glad to return to China, but all roads out of the country were in the hands of the Tibetans.

Lacking reinforcements and supplies, the Chinese could not hold out for long in Lhasa. They contacted the Tibetan War Department through the Nepalese representative and offered to surrender. Both Lien-yü and Chung-yin wrote to the Dalai Lama at the Yardok Samding monastery requesting that a representative of the Dalai Lama be present at the time of surrender. The Dalai Lama sent Lonchen Changkhyim, Sera Mey Tsawa Tritrul, and Tsedron Tenzing Gyaltsen to Lhasa to accept the surrender and to conduct negotiations.

The talks began in the presence of the Nepalese representative. The Chinese agreed to hand over all their arms and ammunition, and they requested permission to return to China, via Kham. They asked the Tibetan government to supply them with transport and supplies for the return trip to China. They also appealed for compensation for properties that would have to be left behind. Because there were Chinese troops still in Kham, the request to return via Kham was refused, but the other requests were granted. The Chinese troops would be allowed to return to China via India. Lien-yü and Chung-yin were permitted to retain thirty rifles for their own protection. Those Chi-

17. LI, p. 131; PORTRAIT, p. 354; Williams, p. 123.

nese who had married Tibetan women would be permitted to take their wives and children with them, if their families were willing to go. Those who wanted to remain in Tibet could do so if they agreed to become Tibetan subjects.

The following is a copy of a telegram received from the Viceroy of India relating to the surrender agreement.

> From the Viceroy, 3 September, 1912. (Repeated to Peking). Foreign Secret. Tibet. My telegram of 28th August last. Trade Agent at Gyantse telegraphs 31st August: Lamen Kempo, Dalai Lama's confidential adviser, informs me that Agreement dated 12th August runs as follows:
> Article I. All Chinese arms and ammunition to be stored under the charge of representatives of both parties and the Nepalese.
> Article II. As soon as provisions of Article I have been fulfilled, Chinese officials and soldiers to return to China via India; Tibetan people providing food, etc., on the way to India.
> Article III. Traders and others claiming to be Chinese to be protected by Tibetans provided that they behave and observe laws of Tibet.
> Paragraph 2. Chinese, however, according to Lamen Kempo, have been slow too fulfill the conditions laid down. First before parting with arms they demanded that Wang Kong Thal, one of the officers who had surrendered to Tibetans, should be handed over. Tibetan Government finally agreed when the Nepalese representative had undertaken responsibility for the safety of the man. Then on 23rd August, Chinese deposited 840 magazine rifles, 4 Maxim guns, 160 pronged guns, 90 jingals, and 90 sealed boxes, most of them said to contain ammunition; however, they would not permit Tibetan authorities to examine contents of boxes and refused to hand over pistols and bolts of rifles. Moreover, Lien and Chung demanded retention of thirty rifles each for their guards. This was agreed to, but it is suspected that both retained many more weapons than the stipulated number. Then, on 21st and 22nd August, when the date of departure was discussed, Chinese demanded that Tibetans should raze all recently constructed fortifications and also move 800 maunds of grain from the Trapchi Barracks to the southern part of the city where Lien is living.

Paragraph 3. By their dilatory and obstructive tactics, Chinese cause irritation and some alarm to Tibetan Government.[18]

The agreement was signed on the thirteenth day of the sixth month of the Water-Mouse year (August 12, 1912). It stipulated that the Chinese would leave Lhasa within fifteen days; but they prolonged their stay by seven months. The Dalai Lama remained at Yardok Samding monastery and at Chokhor Yangtse until they had departed. While staying at Chokhor Yangtse, the Dalai Lama was informed that the Chinese President, Yüan Shih-kai, had restored his titles to him. Charles Bell who had been closely associated with the Dalai Lama in India, wrote:

> Yüan Shih-kai, the President of the Chinese Republic, tele-graphed to him [Dalai Lama], apologizing for the excesses of the Chinese troops, and restoring the Dalai Lama to his former rank. The Dalai Lama replied that he was not asking the Chinese Government for any rank, as he intended to exercise both temporal and ecclesiastical rule in Tibet. Thus the god-king made clear his declaration of Tibetan independence.[19]

The Chinese were to leave in three groups. The first group departed; but the other two began fighting again from their base at the Tengyeling monastery. The Tibetans were severe with them, cutting off their food supplies and reducing them to a state of starvation. Finally, they were forced to surrender. On January 6, 1913, Chung-yin and the last of the Chinese troops were forcibly set upon the road to India. Some monks of the Tengyeling monastery, fearing punishment, disguised themselves as Chinese soldiers and accompanied the party to India.

The Tibetan government sent a representative to escort the Chinese up to the Dzalep-la pass. Those who were unable or unwilling to make their way back to China settled down in India in Kalimpong, Darjeeling, and Calcutta, and some stayed in Sikkim. Their descendants are still living in those places today.

On the sixteenth day of the twelfth month of the Water-Mouse year (in January 1913), the Dalai Lama finally returned to Lhasa amid great pomp and celebration.

18. DOCUMENTS.
19. PORTRAIT, P. 135; RICHARDSON, P. 105.

15

Further Evidence of Tibetan
Independence

As a result of the Dalai Lama's constant efforts from Darjeeling and
the persistent struggle of the Tibetans themselves, every single hostile
Chinese was driven out of central Tibet. A number remained in
Kham, but the Tibetans were in the process of driving these out as
well when the Dalai Lama returned to his capital.

Shortly after his return to Lhasa, the Dalai Lama issued a proclamation to all his officials and subjects throughout Tibet. This proclamation, as well as the earlier refusal of Yüan Shih-kai's offer of rank,
are regarded in Tibet as formal declarations of independence. This
proclamation is dated the eighth day of the first month of the Water-
Ox year (1913):

> I, the Dalai Lama, most omniscient possessor of the Buddhist
> faith, whose title was conferred by the Lord Buddha's command
> from the glorious land of India, speaks to you as follows:
>
> I am speaking to all classes of Tibetan people. Lord Buddha,
> from the glorious country of India, prophesied that the reincar-
> nations of Avalokiteśvara, through successive rulers from the
> early religious kings to the present day, would look after the wel-
> fare of Tibet.
>
> During the time of Genghis Khan and Altan Khan of the
> Mongols, the Ming dynasty of the Chinese, and the Ch'ing
> dynasty of the Manchus, Tibet and China co-operated on the
> basis of benefactor and priest relationship. A few years ago, the
> Chinese authorities in Szechuan and Yunnan endeavored to
> colonize our territory. They brought large numbers of troops
> into central Tibet on the pretext of policing the trade marts. I,

therefore, left Lhasa with my ministers for the Indo-Tibetan border, hoping to clarify to the Manchu Emperor by wire that the existing relationship between Tibet and China had been that of patron and priest and had not been based on the subordination of one to the other. There was no other choice for me but to cross the border, because Chinese troops were following with the intention of taking me alive or dead.

On my arrival in India, I dispatched several telegrams to the Emperor; but his reply to my demands was delayed by corrupt officials at Peking. Meanwhile, the Manchu Empire collapsed. The Tibetans were encouraged to expel the Chinese from central Tibet. I, too, returned safely to my rightful and sacred country, and I am now in the course of driving out the remnants of Chinese troops from Do Kham in eastern Tibet. Now, the Chinese intention of colonizing Tibet under the patron-priest relationship has faded like a rainbow in the sky. Having once again achieved for ourselves a period of happiness and peace, I have now allotted to all of you the following duties to be carried out without negligence:

(1) Peace and happiness in this world can only be maintained by preserving the faith of Buddhism. It is, therefore, essential to preserve all Buddhist institutions in Tibet, such as the Jokhang temple and Ramoche in Lhasa, Samye, and Traduk in southern Tibet, and the three great monasteries, etc.

(2) The various Buddhist sects in Tibet should be kept in a distinct and pure form. Buddhism should be taught, learned, and meditated upon properly. Except for special persons, the administrators of monasteries are forbidden to trade, loan money, deal in any kind of livestock, and/or subjugate another's subjects.

(3) The Tibetan government's civil and military officials, when collecting taxes or dealing with their subject citizens, should carry out their duties with fair and honest judgment so as to benefit the government without hurting the interests of the subject citizens. Some of the central government officials posted at Ngari Korsum in western Tibet, and Do Kham in eastern Tibet, are coercing their subject citizens to purchase commercial goods at high prices and have imposed transportation rights exceeding the limit permitted by the government. Houses, properties, and lands belonging to subject citizens have been confiscated

on the pretext of minor breaches of the law. Furthermore, the amputation of citizens' limbs has been carried out as a form of punishment. Henceforth, such severe punishments are forbidden.

(4) Tibet is a country with rich natural resources; but it is not scientifically advanced like other lands. We are a small, religious, and independent nation. To keep up with the rest of the world, we must defend our country. In view of past invasions by foreigners, our people may have to face certain difficulties, which they must disregard. To safeguard and maintain the independence of our country, one and all should voluntarily work hard. Our subject citizens residing near the borders should be alert and keep the government informed by special messenger of any suspicious developments. Our subjects must not create major clashes between two nations because of minor incidents.

(5) Tibet, although thinly populated, is an extensive country. Some local officials and landholders are jealously obstructing other people from developing vacant lands, even though they are not doing so themselves. People with such intentions are enemies of the State and our progress. From now on, no one is allowed to obstruct anyone else from cultivating whatever vacant lands are available. Land taxes will not be collected until three years have passed; after that the land cultivator will have to pay taxes to the government and to the landlord every year, proportionate to the rent. The land will belong to the cultivator.

Your duties to the government and to the people will have been achieved when you have executed all that I have said here. This letter must be posted and proclaimed in every district of Tibet, and a copy kept in the records of the offices in every district.

From the Potala Palace. (Seal of the Dalai Lama) [1]

About one month before the Dalai Lama's proclamation of independence in Tibet, a treaty was entered into by Tibet and Mongolia on the fourth day of the twelfth month of the Water-Mouse year (January 1913), which was signed at Urga. In that treaty, both countries declared themselves free from Manchu rule and separate from China. As sovereign states, they agreed to strengthen the ties of friendship and religion already existing between them. The Dalai

1. DOCUMENTS.

Lama, as Sovereign of Tibet, approved of the formation of an independent Mongolian state, while the Jetsun Dampa Hutuktu acknowledged Tibet as an independent and sovereign state.[2]

After the Dalai Lama's arrival in Lhasa, Regent Tsemonling resigned, having been rewarded with the title Sha-cin-til-gig-che for his competent work during the Dalai Lama's exile. Chamba Tendar was made a Kalon and Trimon was appointed deputy commander-in-chief, with the title of Teji. Dazang Dadul was made senior commander-in-chief with the title of Dzasa. He married the daughters of the late Kalon Tsarong and took the latter's family name, thus coming into possession of Tsarong's estates, family rights, and retainers. Eight nomadic estates in Dam were given to the Sera monastery in reward for its loyal services, while the Ganden monastery acquired half the district of Tsona. In a similar way, all those who had worked for the return of the Dalai Lama were rewarded with titles and estates.

The Tengyeling monastery was disendowed. Its guilty monks were exiled and the rest dispersed to other monasteries. Punishments were inflicted on all those who had cooperated with the Chinese. On the other hand, those Chinese who had lived in Tibet for generations and had offered no resistance to the Tibetans were permitted to remain in Tibet.

The thirteenth Dalai Lama was the first to introduce paper currency into Tibet. Notes were issued in denominations of five, ten, fifteen, twenty-five and fifty *tamka*. The paper used was hand-made and the design traditional. After a few years, two students were sent to Calcutta to make a study of the printing of Indian currency, and on their return to Tibet, they increased the highest denomination to one hundred *sang*. Postage stamps were introduced at that time, and a little later, gold and silver coins were minted.

The close relationship that had developed between the Dalai Lama and the British government resulted in the latter sponsoring the education of four Tibetan students, who were sent to England for a Western education. Khenrab Kunzang Mondrong majored in mining engineering, but on his return to Tibet he did not have the opportunity to put his specialty into practice. Instead, he became the Dalai Lama's personal interpreter and also served as superintendent of the Lhasa police. The second boy, Sonam Gompo Gokharwa, studied military

2. For the text of the 1913 treaty with Mongolia, see BELL, pp. 304–05; RICHARDSON, pp. 265–67.

science; but he died shortly after his return to Tibet. The third boy, Rigzin Dorje Ringang, became an electrician. When he returned, he introduced electrification into the city of Lhasa and the Dalai Lama's summer palace. He was also employed as a translator to the Dalai Lama and the Tibetan government. The fourth boy, Wangdu Norbu Kyibuk, was trained in survey work and telegraphy. He developed further the telegraph network in Tibet and also became a magistrate in Lhasa, working for some time in the Foreign Bureau. The boys had been accompanied to England by Tsepa Lungshar, a brillant but volatile, ambitious man who learned a great deal in England. On his return to Tibet, he became a Finance Secretary and Head of the Military Department. After the death of the thirteenth Dalai Lama in 1933, he attempted to bring about a revolution in Tibet, but failed in the attempt.

In 1913 a retired Japanese military expert, Yasujiro Yajima, visited Lhasa and was given charge of one section of the Tibetan army, which he trained in Japanese methods of warfare. During his six years in Tibet, Yajima adopted Tibetan manners and customs; but the headquarters he built for the Dalai Lama's bodyguards were created in Japanese traditional style. Another Japanese, Togan Tada, who knew the Tibetan language, came to Tibet in 1913 and lived as a monk in the Sera monastery for eleven years. He was well versed in Buddhist philosophy. (In 1961 he was instrumental in bringing some Tibetans to Japan for Buddhist studies. He now lives in Tokyo.) A third Japanese, Bunkyo Aoki,[3] came to Tibet in 1912 to stay first for a year in the Drepung monastery and then one and one half years with Phunkhang in Lhasa.

The Dalai Lama was determined to clear the hostile Chinese out of Kham. He speeded up army recruitment and imported equipment from aboard that could not be made in Tibet. Food stocks were increased. For the first time, a council minister (Kalon) was sent to Kham as the governor, with overall civil and military authority. Kalon Chamba Tendar was the minister appointed to the governorship. He took with him eight generals,[4] a large civil and military

3. Bunkyo Aoki authored a book, titled *Study on Early Tibetan Chronicles* (Tokyo, 1955), which presents his attempt to rectify the discrepancies in the dates found in early Tibetan history.

4. The eight were Dapon Phulungwa, Dapon Jingpa, Dapon Tethong, Dapon Khyungram, Dapon Tailing, Dapon Tsogo, Dapon Marlampa, and Dapon Takna.

staff, and carried full authority to appoint members of his staff as administrators in the districts over which he exercised control.

While exerting military pressure on the Chinese, the Dalai Lama continued to press the British into arranging a tripartite conference.[5] The Chinese did not like the idea of British mediation in their affairs with the Tibetans, but they could find no alternative. They had watched Mongolia pass under Russian control and were apprehensive of Tibet coming under the influence of the British. The Chinese wanted the conference to be held either in Peking or London and they did not agree to the Tibetan representatives being accorded equal status with the Chinese and British representatives. By making such objections, they hoped to delay the conference for some time, but the presence of the Tibetan troops under Chamba Tendar in Kham made them reconsider their position.

The British chargé d'affaires informed the Chinese that the representatives were to attend the conference on equal footing. By sending its plenipotentiary, Ivan Chen, to the tripartite conference, the Chinese government in effect had accorded equal status to the Tibetan representative and recognized the treaty-making powers of Tibet.[6]

In the credentials of the Tibetan plenipotentiary, issued by the Dalai Lama, is stated: "I hereby authorize Sridzin Shatra Paljor Dorje to decide all matters that may be beneficial to Tibet, and I authorize him to seal all such documents."

The plenipotentiary, Lonchen Paljor Dorje Shatra, with Teji Norbu Wangyal Trimon as his assistant, as well as monastic representatives, arrived at Darjeeling, where they received a telegram from Sir Henry McMahon, the Secretary in the Indian Foreign Department and the British plenipotentiary to the conference, asking them to proceed immediately to Simla. A liaison officer escorted them. When they arrived at Simla, they were met at the little railway station by Charles Bell and the Viceroy's secretary. Lonchen Shatra called on the Viceroy and Sir Henry McMahon soon after his arrival. His visit was returned by McMahon and the Viceroy's secretary. The Viceroy entertained the Tibetan and Chinese representatives at a banquet, where he made a

5. The information given here on the Simla conference was obtained from SIMLA.

6. A recent Indian government report states: "the fact that the Chinese side themselves had referred to these negotiations of the Tibetan Government regarding the boundary showed that the Chinese Government recognised Tibet's right in the past to have foreign relations on her own and deal with matters concerning her boundaries." (BOUNDARY, p. 15.)

speech expressing his hope that the conference would result in a settlement agreeable to all parties concerned.

At a preliminary meeting, the British were represented by Sir Henry McMahon, assisted by Charles Bell and Archibald Rose; the Chinese by Ivan Chen and an assistant. The Tibetans were represented by Lonchen Paljor Dorje Shatra, assisted by Teji Trimon. Credentials were exchanged between the plenipotentiaries, and the Tibetans were asked to produce their proposals on the following day.

Lonchen Shatra told Charles Bell that the Dalai Lama wanted the following terms included in the agreement: that (1) Tibet was to manage her own internal affairs and (2) external affairs, with reference to the British on important issues; that (3) no Chinese Amban, officials, or soldiers would be stationed in Tibet, only traders; and that (4) Tibetan territory would include the eastern region up to Tachienlu, some of which had passed under Chinese control.[7]

The Tibetans produced evidence to show that Tibet had been an independent state from earlier times up to the present and that the relationship between the fifth Dalai Lama and the Manchu Emperor had been of a purely religious nature, even though the Chinese interpreted it as a political union. The Tibetan official showed that, as a result of Chao Erh-feng sending Chinese troops into Tibet on the pretext of policing the trade marts, war had broken out and the Chinese expelled. The Tibetans were seeking confirmation of their independence and the acknowledgement of the Dalai Lama as the spiritual and temporal sovereign of Tibet. They demanded that the Conventions of 1906 and 1908, signed at Peking and Calcutta respectively, be declared invalid. They pressed for a frontier with China that would include all Tibetan peoples and territories up to the Kokonor in the northeast, and to Tachienlu in the east. They wanted a continuation of their religious relationship with the Buddhist monasteries in Inner Mongolia and China. Finally, they demanded idemnity from the Chinese for the destruction and loss of property caused in Lhasa and the Kham region by Chao Erh-feng's troops.

The Chinese based their claim to Tibet on its conquest by Genghis Khan. The fifth Dalai Lama, they said, was given a title by the Manchu Emperor. At the time of the invasion of Tibet by the Dzungar Mongols, and later by the Gurkhas, they said the Chinese army had come to the assistance of Tibet. They alleged that in the time of the

7. BELL, p. 152.

K'ang-hsi Emperor, the Tibetans had asked for the presence of a Manchu Amban in Lhasa to advise the Tibetan government and for Chinese troops to protect the country. They claimed that Chao Erh-feng had come to eastern Tibet to investigate the murder of the Amban, Feng-chien, at Bah, and that troops were sent to Lhasa to police the trade marts in accordance with the terms of the 1908 Trade Agreement. They said that, because the Dalai Lama had not taken the advice of the Amban, Yü-Kang, but listened instead, to Dorjieff, the British had come to Lhasa in 1904. As a result of that expedition, China had paid an indemnity of twenty-five lakhs of rupees (166,000 pounds sterling) on behalf of the Tibetan government; consequently, it felt entitled to claim Tibet as an integral part of China. The Chinese insisted on the right to station an Amban in Tibet, with 2,600 troops, to control the foreign and military affairs of the country. One thousand of those troops would remain with the Amban and the remainder would be stationed wherever he decided. Their avowed aim was to restore the political status of Tibet to that described in the Anglo–Chinese Convention of 1906. Finally, they insisted that the boundary between China and Tibet should be placed at Gyamda, not far to the east of Lhasa.

The Chinese claims were verbal and there was no historical foundation for many of their statements. They could produce no records to prove Chinese administration of the territories in eastern Tibet. The Tibetans, on the other hand, went to the Simla conference well prepared. They produced extensive documentary evidence to support their claims. They offered in evidence fifty-six volumes of government documents, consisting of revenue records, lists of houses, officials, and headmen in the disputed areas, bonds of allegiance, and others. Sir Henry McMahon signed them in verification of their contents.[8]

The Tibetans refuted the various Chinese claims. Referring to Genghis Khan's conquest of Tibet, the Tibetan representative pointed out that the Khan was a Mongol, not a Chinese. It was further pointed out that at that time, Mongolia was separate from China; moreover the Khan never took over the actual administration of Tibet. As for the title given the fifth Dalai Lama by the Manchu Emperor, it was in exchange for a title given the Emperor by the Dalai Lama. Regarding the Dzungar Mongols, they were driven out of Tibet by Tibetan forces. In the war with the Gurkhas, the Manchu Emperor had sent

8. SIMLA.

imperial troops to help; but he did so as an ally of the Dalai Lama and not as the sovereign of Tibet. There was no evidence offered that the Tibetans had asked for troops and an Amban in the time of the K'ang-hsi Emperor.[9] As for the indemnity China paid for the 1904 British expedition, it was a fact that the British government had reduced the indemnity and then the Chinese quickly paid it, without being asked to do so by the Tibetans. To further refute this last claim, Lonchen Shatra recalled that a Mongolian nobleman had paid compensation to the Nepalese on behalf of the Tibetans, when Nepalese shops were looted in Lhasa; but that did not give Mongolia any claims on Tibet.

In an attempt to resolve the irreconcilable stands taken by the Chinese and Tibetan representatives, Sir Henry McMahon, on February 17, 1914, proposed a division of the disputed area into Inner and Outer Tibet, with Chinese suzerainty over Tibet. The Tibetans were unwilling to accept any form of Chinese overlordship in Tibet, and the Chinese were unwilling to accept the proposed boundaries; but for the sake of settling the dispute, the Tibetans reluctantly agreed to McMahon's proposal.

Under the terms of the proposed convention, Britain and China would recognize that Tibet was under the suzerainty of China. China would recognize the autonomy of Outer Tibet and would agree to abstain from interfering in the administration of that area, as well as in the selection and installation of the Dalai Lama. China was not to convert Tibet into a Chinese province, and Britain was to make no annexations. The Chinese would not send troops into Outer Tibet or attempt to station officials or establish colonies there. All Chinese troops and officials still in Tibet had to be withdrawn within three months of the signing of the Convention. The Chinese would be permitted to send a high official, with an escort not to exceed three hundred men, to reside in Lhasa. The governments of Great Britain and China agreed not to enter into any negotiations regarding Tibet, either between themselves or with any foreign power. But the Treaty of September 7, 1904 between Tibet and Great Britian specifically states that Tibet and Great Britain may make treaties directly.

Article nine of the Convention described the Sino–Tibetan bound-

---

9. The Imperial troops, which came to Lhasa in 1720, had been requested by Lhazang Khan, who had taken over in central Tibet (PETECH, p. 55). The first Ambans were stationed in Lhasa in 1728, during the reign of the Yung-cheng Emperor, who was the son of K'ang-hsi (PETECH, p. 269).

ary and the other borders in the following way: "For the purpose of the present Convention the borders of Tibet, and the boundary between Inner and Outer Tibet, shall be as shown in red and blue respectively on the map attached thereto." [10]

In the notes of exchange, which were to follow the main body of the convention, Tibet is mentioned as being "a part of Chinese territory", a concession determinedly resisted by the Tibetans and which was not stated in the main text. Other stipulations made in the notes included one saying that Outer Tibet would not be represented in the Chinese Parliament, and another limiting the British Trade Agencies' escorts to seventy-five per cent of that of the Chinese high official.

Although Ivan Chen initialed the draft of the Simla Convention, the government of China ordered him not to sign the final document. The continuous counter-proposals and delays began to annoy the British. Finally, the following communication was sent to the Chinese government on June 25, 1914: "As it is, the patience of His Majesty's Government is exhausted and they have no alternative but to inform the Chinese Government that, unless the Convention is signed before the end of the month, His Majesty's Government will hold themselves free to sign separately with Tibet." [11] Nevertheless, the Chinese government still refused.

Sir Henry McMahon and Lonchen Shatra then proceeded to sign the final document, with the following included:

> The plenipotentiaries of Great Britain and Tibet accept the following treaty. The Government of Great Britain and the Government of Tibet will recognize and abide by the Convention already concluded. The powers granted to China under the Convention shall not be recognized by Great Britain and Tibet until and unless the Government of China ratifies the Convention. This treaty, in two copies each of the English and Tibetan versions respectively, has been sealed and signed on the tenth day of the fifth month of the Wood-Tiger year, corresponding to July 3, 1914. [12]

The governments of Great Britain and Tibet subsequently ratified the Convention; but the government of China refused to do so. The

10. BOUNDARY, p. 110.

11. BOUNDARY, p. 113.

12. For additional details on the Simla conference, see BELL, pp. 148–59. For the complete text of the Simla Convention, see RICHARDSON, pp. 268–72.

ratification of the Convention by Great Britain and Tibet in effect eliminated Chinese claims of suzerainty over Tibet and reaffirmed Tibetan independence and treaty-making powers. Subsequently, the British and Tibetan plenipotentiaries signed a new trade regulation consisting of eleven articles to replace those regulations made in 1893 and 1908, which were canceled under Article VII of the Simla Convention.[13]

The boundary demarcation between Tibet and India to the east of Bhutan, commonly referred to as the McMahon Line, was also agreed upon at the Simla Convention. Earlier, in March of 1914, Sir Henry McMahon and Lonchen Shatra had negotiated the common border and a boundary line drawn on a map. This was given to Lonchen Shatra for confirmation by the Tibetan government. Following are notes that were exchanged between the two plenipotentiaries.

> To: Lonchen Shatra, Tibetan Plenipotentiary. In February last, you accepted the India–Tibet frontier from the Isu Razi Pass to the Bhutan frontier as given in the map (two sheets), of which two copies are herewith attached, subject to the confirmation of your Government and the following conditions: (a) the Tibetan ownership of private estates on the British side of the frontier will not be disturbed, and (b) if the sacred places of Tso Karpo and Tsari Sarpa fall within a day's march of the British side of the frontier, they will be included in Tibetan territory and the frontier modified accordingly. I understand that your Government have now agreed to this frontier subject to the above two conditions. I shall be glad to learn definitely from you that this is the case.
>
> You wished to know whether certain dues now collected by the Tibetan Government at Tsona Jong and in Kongbu and Kham from the Monpas and the Lopas for articles sold may still be collected. Mr. Bell has informed you that such details will be settled in a friendly spirit, when you have furnished him the further information, which you have promised.
>
> The final settlement of this India–Tibet frontier will help to prevent causes of future dispute and thus cannot fail to be of great advantage to both Governments. A. H. McMahon, British Plenipotentiary. Delhi, March 24th, 1914.[14]

13. The full text of the 1914 Regulations are given in RICHARDSON, pp. 272–75.
14. SIMLA; RICHARDSON, p. 267.

Lonchen Shatra sent McMahon a letter accepting the boundary as delineated.

> To: Sir Henry McMahon, British Plenipotentiary to the China–Tibet Conference. As it was feared that there might be friction in the future unless the boundary between India and Tibet is clearly defined, I submitted the map, which you sent me in February last, to the Tibetan Government at Lhasa for orders. I have now received orders from Lhasa, and I accordingly agree to the boundary as marked in red on the two copies of the maps signed by you, subject to the conditions mentioned in your letter, dated March 24th, sent to me through Mr. Bell. I have signed and sealed the two copies of the maps. I have kept one copy here and return herewith the other. Sent on the twenty-ninth day of the first month of the Wood-Tiger year (March 24, 1914), by Lonchen Shatra, the Tibetan Plenipotentiary. Seal of Lonchen Shatra.[15]

On August 4, only a month after the conclusion of the Simla Convention, Great Britain entered into World War I. Lonchen Sholkhang, the joint Prime Minister, was instructed by the Dalai Lama to send a communication to the Political Officer of Sikkim and offer support to Britain in the war against Germany.[16] The following is a translation of Lonchen Sholkhang's letter to Basil Gould, the Political Officer of Sikkim at that time.

> Dear Mr. Gould: We understand from the recent newspapers and from Lonchen Shatra's letter that the situation in Europe is unstable, owing to the declaration of war by Germany against Britain and France. His Holiness, the Dalai Lama, has directed me to write and tell you that, although the Chinese are waging a rigorous war against us in different parts of Kham (eastern Tibet), Tibet is willing to send one thousand Tibetan troops to India, to the support of your Empire, because we realize that the existence of Tibet depends on the continuance of Great Britain's Empire. Kindly reply to my letter at your earliest convenience, after putting our proposals before your Government. With my greeting scarf, Lonchen Sholkhang. Third day of the seventh month of the Wood-Tiger year.[17]

15. SIMLA; RICHARDSON, p. 268.
16. H. H. Dodwell, ed., *The Cambridge History of India*, 6 (Cambridge, 1932), p. 77.
17. SIMLA.

As the letter was transmitted through Lonchen Shatra, he must have had an English translation made for Basil Gould and kept the original Tibetan letter himself.

The reply from Basil Gould in Sikkim was addressed to Lonchen Shatra, who had transmitted the letter for Lonchen Sholkhang. It read:

> Dear Lonchen Shatra: Thank you for your letter dated the fifteenth day of the seventh month. Immediately after I received your letter, I conveyed its substance to our Government in India, and I have received a reply from them saying that the British Government was deeply touched and grateful to His Holiness, the Dalai Lama, for his offer to send one thousand Tibetan troops to support the British Government. Please inform His Holiness that the British Government will seek the support of Tibet whenever the need arises. With greeting scarves from B. J. Gould, Political Officer of Sikkim. Twenty-seventh day of the seventh month.[18]

The Dalai Lama took the Political Officer's letter at face value and, in spite of his preoccupation with the troubled areas of Kham, kept one thousand of his best troops in readiness for helping Britain "Whenever the need arises." Those troops were kept available until the end of World War I.

On the seventeenth day of the ninth month of the Wood-Tiger year (1914), Lonchen Shatra and his delegation returned to Lhasa. After making a full report to the Dalai Lama and the Tibetan government, he commended his assistant, Trimon, for his earlier service in the War Department at Lhasa and for his excellent work at the Simla Convention, particularly for his documentation of the proceedings. As a result of this, Trimon was made a Kalon. Dazang Dadul, known as Tsarong since his marriage, was also made a Kalon, while continuing to act as a commander-in-chief of the Tibetan army.

There was a homeopathic medical college in Tibet at Chakpori; but there was no public school devoted to astrology. The Dalai Lama then founded a public school for both medicine and astrology on the site of the abandoned Tengyeling monastery. The government bore the financial expenditures of all the trainees, who, after completing their

18. Ibid.

studies, were sent to different districts. Free medicine was provided to the poor.

British troops were stationed at Gyantse to protect the trade marts as stipulated in the trade regulations. The Dalai Lama sent Dzasa Dumpa and Teji Doring with some troops to Gyantse to study the British military system. Modern army drill, hitherto unknown to the Tibetans, was now adopted as part of Tibetan military training. Two years later, the military system of the combined Chinese and Mongol army was incorporated into the training of one Tibetan regiment. A Mongol officer, Tenpai Gyaltsen, who had been trained in Russia, was given the command of another regiment, which he disciplined and drilled according to the Russian system. The Japanese officer, Yasujiro Yajima, took over the training of a fourth regiment.

These four regiments, which had been trained in foreign systems, were finally brought to Lhasa, where for four days they were made to parade, maneuver, and engage in competitive exercises before the Dalai Lama, officials of the government, and the public. After this display, it was decided that the Tibetan army would be modeled along British lines thereafter. It was provided with a national flag, which was carried by each regiment, with a regiment number to distinguish one from the other.

The Tibetan government sent Sandrup Phodrang, Dingja Kyibuk, Norgay Nangpa, and a few selected soldiers to Quetta and Shillong to be trained in artillery and machine-gun warfare. The Tibetan army had for some time been increasing in its superiority over the Chinese, and the officers and soldiers were eager to undergo special training and to serve afterwards in Tibet.

16

Clashes Between Tibetans and Chinese in Kham

When Kalon Chamba Tendar was dispatched with troops to Kham in 1917, he made his temporary headquarters at Lhodzong, in the proximity of Chinese-occupied areas, from which troops, under the command of two generals each, were sent out in three different directions to drive out the Chinese. After many months of fierce battles, Tibetan troops recaptured Rongpo Gyarapthang, Khyungpo Sertsa, Khyungpo Tengchen, Riwoche, Chaksam Kha, Thok Drugugon, Tsawa Pakshod, Lagon Nyenda, and Lamda.

The Chinese stronghold was at Chamdo, the capital of Kham province, where most of their troops were stationed. The Tibetans, having recovered most of the surrounding areas, then converged on Chamdo. It was a well-fortified place, and the fighting lasted several months. With the cooperation of the local inhabitants, who had suffered a great deal under the Chinese, the Tibetans were able gradually to cut off all supplies to Chamdo. The Chinese were eventually forced to surrender.

Instead of sending the Chinese prisoners eastward across the Kham border, where they might prove to be troublesome again, the Tibetans escorted them all the way to the Indian border and left them there to make their way home. General P'eng Jih-sheng, the Chinese commander who had held Chamdo for some time, felt humiliated by his surrender and refused to return to China. He was given an allowance and permitted to settle at Dowa Dzong in southern Tibet. This was done even though General P'eng was notorious for his intolerant attitude towards the Tibetans, who in turn had held him responsible for the destruction of the great monasteries of Chamdo, Draya, and

Yemdo in previous campaigns. P'eng was regarded as the archenemy of the Tibetans after the end of Chao Erh-feng.[1]

Gara Lama, a Tibetan fifth columnist, was arrested along with the captured Chinese. He was sent as a prisoner to Jayul; but he managed to escape from there a few years later and fled to China, where he died during a civil war. Among the Chinese captured at Thok Drugugon, the Tibetans recognized Wu, the officer who had volunteered to pursue the Dalai Lama after his flight from Lhasa to India. Wu was imprisoned for life at Sengye Dzong. Gyalgodong, the Chinese-Tibetan, who had helped Wu, was killed in the fighting at Tenchen. His body was identified because of his eleven fingers. His head and hands were sent to Lhasa in a parcel.

(As a boy in Lhasa, I witnessed the arrival of captured Chinese prisoners, all of them in a terribly emaciated condition. When decapitated heads and severed hands were carried through the streets, people held their hands to their noses.)

The Tibetans lost many men in the fighting. Three of their best generals—Dapon Phulungwa, Dapon Jingpa, and Dapon Tailing—died in battle. Kalon Chamba Tendar made Chamdo the permanent headquarters of the Tibetan governor-general of Kham. Tibetans still living in Chinese-occupied areas began to fight before the main Tibetan army could move up, and being ill-equipped and poorly organized, they suffered severe losses. Exhausted from continuous fighting, Kalon Chamba Tendar had to give his troops a rest before going to the aid of the Tibetans in Chinese-held regions. During the rest interval, he made promotions, awarded rewards and punishments, and appointed district officers to administer the territories he had recaptured.

Finally, he sent troops to assist the Tibetans fighting in Markham, Draya, Sangyen, Gojo, and Derge, and those areas were liberated. In the southeast, troops penetrated as far as the Chinese province of Yunnan. The troops, which had recaptured Derge, were approaching Tachienlu and the local people became so excited that the Chinese appealed to Britain to mediate and bring about a cease-fire.[2]

Eric Teichman of His Britannic Majesty's Consular Service, acting on behalf of the British government, was sent to negotiate a truce. The Chinese General, Liu Tsan-ting, proceeded from Bah to Chamdo

1. An interesting account of the recapture of Chamdo by the Tibetans was written by one of General P'eng's officers. It is given in TEICHMAN, pp. 54–56.

2. DOCUMENTS; TEICHMAN, p. 58.

to meet with Kalon Chamba Tendar. On August 19, 1918, a tripartite agreement was signed by the three representatives, Teichman, Liu Tsan-ting, and Chamba Tendar. The territories under dispute were divided between Tibet and China. The boundary corresponded roughly with the course of the upper Yangtze, with China retaining the regions to the east of it, excepting the areas of Derge and Beyul. The Tibetans, however, retained control of all the monasteries in the areas that passed to the Chinese.[3]

A supplementary agreement was drawn up on October 10, 1918, which called for the withdrawal of troops and the cessation of hostilities between the Chinese and the Tibetans, all to be done by October 31st. This agreement, witnessed by Eric Teichman, was signed by Han Kuang-chun and the Chakla Gyalpo for the Chinese, and Khenchung Lozang Dondup, Dapon Khyungram, and Dapon Tethong for Tibet.[4]

It is clear from the wording of those agreements, and the events which led up to them, that Tibet was a power not to be ignored. References to the governments of China, Tibet, and Great Britain in the agreements and the fact that China had to appeal to the British to mediate should be evidence enough of Tibet's independence.

When the Tengyeling monastery in Lhasa was confiscated for its pro-Chinese activities, evidence was found among the seized documents of the complicity of three leading monks from the Loseling college in Drepung monastery. These three monks were defrocked and imprisoned at Lhasa. Over three thousand monks from the Loseling college then demonstrated in front of the Dalai Lama's summer palace, demanding the release and reinstatement of the three monks. The Dalai Lama refused to release them on the grounds that they had indulged in traitorous activities. Moreover, the Loseling monks had not made their appeal through the proper channels. The organizers of the demonstration were arrested and punished.

A few years after the death of the Prime Minister, Lonchen Changkhyim, Tibet lost another of the three prime ministers, who had been appointed earlier by the Dalai Lama. Lonchen Shatra, the Prime Minister who had served Tibet so well at Simla, died in 1923. Lonchen Shatra's achievements as a minister for the Tibetan government will long be remembered. Sir Charles Bell, who had worked with him at

3. DOCUMENTS; LI, p. 144.
4. DOCUMENTS; RICHARDSON, pp. 119–20.

Simla, wrote, "he showed a knowledge of men and a grasp of political affairs that came as a surprise to many at the Conference. His simple dignity and his charm of manner endeared him to all who met him in Simla or Delhi." [5] The only surviving Prime Minister was the aging Lonchen Sholkhang. During his remaining years, he was asked to train Langdun, a young nephew of the Dalai Lama, who was being groomed for the Prime Minister position.

Formerly, prominent monasteries and families possessing large estates paid very little revenue to the government. However, the government had to incur considerable expenses in order to maintain a standing army, and it was decided to create an office to revise the system of taxation and to implement the collection of revenue. Revenues were then fixed in proportion to the size of estates. The Tashilhunpo monastery of the Panchen Lama, which owned large estates, had thus to pay a considerable amount in taxes. This caused dismay among the Panchen's officials. Personal relations between the Dalai Lama and the Panchen Lama were amiable, but the Panchen's officials, conscious of their own cooperation with the Chinese, felt that the new taxes were being imposed on them as a form of punishment. Fearing other reprisals, they and the forty-year-old Panchen Lama, Choskyi Nyima, fled to China via Namru and Sining on the fifteenth day of the eleventh month of the Water-Hog year (1923).

The governor of Shigatse, on learning of the Panchen Lama's sudden departure, immediately set out for the British Trade Agency at Gyantse, where he telegraphed the news to Lhasa. The Tibetan government sent a delegation to intercept the Panchen Lama. It went as far as Namru, but was unable to catch up with the Panchen's party, which had planned its flight in advance. A Lhasa representative was sent to Tashilhunpo to carry on the administration of the monastery in the absence of the Panchen Lama.

When the Panchen Lama arrived at Peking in February of 1925, he was given a warm reception. The Kuomintang Nationalist Chinese party was rising to power in China and officials of the Panchen Lama used him to influence the Kuomintang government against the regime in Lhasa. The question of the Panchen Lama's official status arose; however, because of the unstable situation in China at that time, as well as the thirteenth Dalai Lama's prestige and abilities, the Kuomintang government could do nothing to help the Panchen Lama

5. BELL, p. 158.

in his dispute with the Lhasa government. The Panchen Lama remained in China.

In Tibet, the Dalai Lama realized the importance of an English education for his people. He approached the British government for help, and a school was started at Gyantse, under the supervision of Frank Ludlow. In 1926, only three years later, the school was closed because of objections from the monastic groups, who felt that it would prove harmful to the religion.

Following the Chinese occupation of Lhasa, the police system had declined and become ineffective. The Dalai Lama invited the Superintendent of Police in Darjeeling, Sonam Laden La, to establish a police department in Lhasa. Laden La, who was of Tibetan extraction, trained several hundred policemen and was appointed Superintendent of Police in Lhasa, with the title of Dzasa. He was assisted by Mondrong Khenrab Kunzag, the Rugby-educated mining engineer.

By the 1920s, the Tibetan army had become very strong. The older generals, who had served the country well and loyally in the past, were still campaigning in Kham. The new generals in Lhasa were young men, some of whom had been trained in Gyantse and India; they were inclined to show off a little. A rumor gained ground in Lhasa that there were differences of opinion between the civilian and military officials. The rumor became reality during a meeting of the Tsongdu, where the taxation of estates belonging to the Kashag ministers and the generals was being discussed. The young generals, led by Kalon Tsarong, interrupted the meeting and demanded military representation in the Tsongdu (National Assembly). This was something unheard of, and Lungshar, one of the heads of the Tsongdu, who was jealous of Tsarong's growing power, encouraged the monks to make a big issue of it. The Norbulingka and the Potala were heavily guarded by monks in anticipation of a military takeover; but the generals, who had not expected this reaction, hurriedly handed over their weapons to their troops.

The Dalai Lama intervened directly in the dispute. As a result of his inquiry, the military was accused of unlawfully interrupting a meeting of the Tsongdu. Two generals, Dapon Shasur and Dapon Tsogo, and one minister, Kalon Khemey (also known as Kunzangtse), were dismissed. Tsarong was then sent to Yatung to inspect the mint called Norbu Tsokyil; after which, he visited India and Nepal. While he was one day's journey from Lhasa on his return trip, he received orders that he had been relieved as commander-in-chief of the armies. He remained a Kalon, or council minister, for some time after that.

Dzasa Dumpa was appointed commander-in-chief to replace Tsarong. Dzasa Dumpa was a lazy, impractical man. These qualities well suited the political ambitions of Lungshar, who took advantage of them to get appointed Defense Secretary. In 1922, Kalon Chamba Tendar, who was serving as the governor of Kham at Chamdo, died, and Kalon Trimon was sent as his successor.

A Tibetan subject named Gyalpo had married a Sherpa girl of Nepalese nationality and then opened a shop in Lhasa, which he called Sherpa Gyalpo. In 1922 he began to sell liquor and tobacco without a permit and the Lhasa magistrate decided to arrest him. News of his imminent arrest reached Gyalpo, and he took refuge in the house of the Nepalese Resident officer. The Nepalese officer was under the impression that Gyalpo was a Gurkha and refused to hand him over to the Tibetan authorities. The Lhasa police then forced their way into the Nepalese Residence and arrested Gyalpo. Because of the extraterritoriality rights of the Nepalese granted in the treaty of 1856, this incident almost led to war between Nepal and Tibet, and the British had to intervene to clear up the misunderstanding. Lungshar was largely to blame for the whole affair, because he had insisted on the arrest of Gyalpo after he had taken asylum in the Nepalese Residence.

At about that time, the British government requested permission to build a motor road from Yatung to Gyantse to facilitate transport to and from their trade agencies. A temporary road was built and gas stations erected near rest houses. Three cars were put into use on the road and made the trip twice; however, the local people, who had made their livelihood by providing animals for transport, objected to the use of motorcars and the road project had to be abandoned.

The ruler of the district of Poyul, who had earlier been a payer of small revenue to the Tibetan government, had successfully resisted Chinese attempts to collect larger taxes and had even repulsed a Chinese invasion. Encouraged by his success, he later became unwilling to pay any taxes whatsoever to the Tibetan government and prevented Tibetan officials from entering his territory. Kalon Trimon, serving as governor of Kham, at first tried a peaceful approach with Kanam Depa, the ruler of Poyul, by appointing Rutsa Khenchung as his representative. Because of Rutsa Khenchung's exploitation, Poyul subjects disobeyed his orders and subsequently killed a servant and fifteen Tibetan government troops.

In 1926 Kalon Trimon completed his three-year term of governorship at Chamdo and was succeeded by Kalon Menkhab Todpa. The new governor sent a regiment, under Dapon Takna, to Poyul. The general penetrated deep into the region; but was ambushed in a different part of the country and was killed, along with many of his troops. Later on, more troops were again sent against Poyul, which finally fell to the combined assault. Kanam Depa and some of his followers took refuge in Assam, where he died five years later. Finally, in 1931, two district officers, with a small garrison, were stationed in Poyul.

It had always been the custom to allow Mongolian monks and pilgrims to enter Tibet without restriction. In 1927 some Buriat Mongolian monks, led by a man named Zangpo, came to Lhasa via Nagchukha, with the object of promoting friendly relations with the Tibetan government and spreading Soviet propaganda. As they were already in Lhasa, the Dalai Lama gave them an audience; however, he based himself on the terms of the Simla Convention with the British, which forbade negotiations with foreign powers, and the pro-Soviet Buriats had to return without gaining any concessions. A year later, another Soviet–Mongol mission arrived in Lhasa led by a Soviet military officer from Mongolia. After remaining several months in Lhasa, they too returned after receiving nothing more than an audience with the Dalai Lama.

The Chinese government had made a number of attempts to send a representative to Tibet; but permits were refused to all Chinese wishing to enter the country. In 1927, when the Tibetan abbot, Kunchok Jungnas of the Yungon monastery in Peking, was returning to Tibet, President Chiang Kai-shek gave him a letter for the Dalai Lama. In it, the President offered the Dalai Lama full support if he agreed to Tibet becoming part of China. He also offered to return the Panchen Lama to Tibet without making any conditions for the return. As this was the first time Chiang Kai-shek had written to him, the Dalai Lama welcomed the letter and the messenger. The Dalai Lama gave his reply to the abbot, in which he welcomed the possibility of friendly relations, but declined the suggestion that Tibet become part of China.

In 1930 Miss Liu Man-ch'ing, whose father was Chinese and mother Tibetan, was permitted to enter Lhasa on an unofficial visit. She carried a letter from President Chiang Kai-shek, and also made several informal approaches suggesting closer ties with China; but she was given no encouragement by the Tibetan government.

By that time, Kalon Tsarong, Tsepon Lungshar, and Kuchar Kunphela, all favorites of the Dalai Lama, had become very powerful in Tibet. They were, however, extremely jealous of each other. Tsepon Lungshar, on assuming command of the army, discovered that a considerable quantity of ammunition was missing, and his predecessor, Tsarong, could not account for it. In 1925 Tsarong was stripped of Kashag membership, but allowed to retain the title of Dzasa in consideration of his past services. Up to then, separate departments had been responsible for the mint, paper currency factory, and ammunition factory. The Dalai Lama then combined them under one department and called it the Drapche Lekhung. Tsarong and Kunphela were placed at its head. The new department improved the quality of paper currency, imported ammunition, and established electrification in Lhasa, using the services of Ringang, who had been educated at Rugby in England.

The real strong man was Kunphela, with whom even the Kashag ministers were careful. He was the only man, apart from the Dalai Lama, who had his own private car. It was an Austin A-40, and when Kunphela drove about Lhasa, he created quite a sensation. Towards the end of the thirteenth Dalai Lama's reign (died 1933), Kunphela had created a new regiment called Drong Drak Makhar, consisting of over one thousand sons of prominent families. This regiment received special clothing, food, accommodations, and other facilities. Its headquarters were near Kunphela's offices, and it was his intention that this regiment should help him to remain in power.

When Charles Bell visited Lhasa in 1920–21, he was given the honorary title of Lonchen. Later, Major F. Bailey, Colonel James Weir, and Frederick Williamson, the succeeding Political Officers in Sikkim, were each automatically referred to as Dreche Lonchen (Prime Minister of Sikkim), when they visited Lhasa once every two years. Those visits were made both to improve British relations with Tibet and to mediate in disputes with China, which were still taking place in Kham.

The first American to visit Lhasa was Suydam Cutting, who made three trips to Tibet: in 1930, 1935, and 1937. On one of his visits, he was accompanied by his wife, who was the first Caucasian woman to be officially invited to Tibet by the government. The Cuttings developed a strong friendship and constant correspondence with the thirteenth Dalai Lama, who presented them with a pair of Apsos, a special Tibetan breed of dog. Suydam Cutting was responsible for obtaining an autographed photograph of President Hoover, which the Dalai Lama accepted with a sentiment of good will toward America. The following is from a letter of the Dalai Lama, which touches on it:

> It is sincerely hoped that, this country being a purely ecclesiastical kingdom, you will solicit the state department to render international assistance as far as it is in their power to do so, in order that the Buddhist religion may flourish uninterrupted and that we may enjoy exercising our true right of sovereignty and above all to enhance the prosperity of the people.[6]

In 1931 the Beri and the Dargyas monasteries, east of the Yangtse river, began fighting with each other. The Chinese governor of Szechuan, Liu Wen-hui, supported the Beri monastery and sent troops to its assistance. The Tibetan regiment stationed at Derge assisted the Dargyas monastery and drove the Chinese out of Beri, penetrating almost as far as the Kanze district. The Chinese government sent representatives, T'ang Ko-san and Liu Tsan-ting, to arrange a cease-fire. If the Tibetans had agreed to one at that point, they might have acquired a considerable amount of territory; however, they felt confident of capturing Tachienlu and refused to negotiate with the Chinese.

The Dalai Lama was trying to obtain a settlement with the Kuomintang government at Nanking; but this proved useless as Nanking had no control over the province of Szechuan. Liu Wen-hui, after making extensive preparations, counterattacked later in the year and thrust the Tibetans back. The Dalai Lama intensified his efforts to obtain a settlement through the British; but this too led to nothing.[7]

Kalon Menkhab Todpa had completed his term of governorship in Kham and was succeeded by Kalon Ngabo. Reinforcements and arms had been sent from Lhasa, but in 1932 the Tibetans, who had been pushed back across the Drichu (Yangtze River), were ready to negotiate. A temporary cease-fire was entered into at Kamthok Drukha, between the Tibetan generals in the field and Liu Wen-hui's officers. The

---

6. Suydam Cutting, *The Fire Ox and Other Years* (New York, 1940), p. 177.
7. For details on the last years of the thirteenth Dalai Lama, see RICHARDSON, pp. 134–37.

governments of Tibet, Britain, and China were unaware of this cease-fire. The generals responsible were later demoted by the Dalai Lama.

At about that time, in Sining, General Ma Pu-fang, a Muslim war-lord acting independently of the Chinese government, had aided and abetted one monastery in a dispute with another. Tibetan troops were dispatched to intervene, but when they had advanced as far as Jyekundo, they were repulsed by Chinese reinforcements and suffered a serious defeat at Dan Chokhorgon. During the battle, two outstanding Tibetan colonels, Drashi Rupon Nangrak and Mekyok Rupon Sangda Lasampa, were captured, and large numbers of men, arms, and ammunition were lost. The demoralized Tibetan troops retreated to Chamdo, Riwoche, and Tengchen. Once again, negotiations were attempted through Colonel Weir, the British representative then in Lhasa; but the Chinese government disclaimed any influence over Ma Pu-fang.

At Chamdo, Kalon Ngabo was in a difficult position. My maternal uncle, Secretary-General Ngoshi Thupden, was sent from Lhasa to govern northern Kham, while Kalon Ngabo looked after the eastern sector. Troop reinforcements and new weapons were sent with Ngoshi. Officially, I also accompanied him as a private secretary; but in reality, I had been instructed by the Dalai Lama to take photographs of the Chinese and their weapons. When Ngoshi arrived at Tengchen, he found that the Tibetan troops had retreated from Ch'ing-hai, even though Ma Pu-fang's forces had not pursued them; consequently, a large expanse of unoccupied territory lay between Tengchen and Nangchen. Ngoshi ordered the Tibetans back to their former positions in the unoccupied areas.

Kalon Ngabo died soon afterwards, and until his replacement arrived, Ngoshi had to assume governorship of both northern and eastern Kham. Katsap Tethong arrived after a few months to take over the control of eastern Kham. The two governors met at Lagon Nyenda to discuss future plans before returning to their respective posts.

Using a lama as their liaison officer, the Chinese opened negotiations with Ngoshi, whose reputation as a brave and dignified leader had impressed them. A treaty was signed in the second month of the Water-Bird year (June 15, 1933) at Nangchen Tetsagon in Chinese territory. Dapon Surkhang Surpa and Tsedrung Dorje Yugyal signed the treaty on behalf of the Secretary-General Ngoshi. I myself accom-

panied them as "Keeper of the Seal" and took a number of photographs of the Chinese camp, as well as of the signing of the treaty and
other functions. General Ma Pu-fang was represented by Ma Shun-chi
and Li Tsen-mo. Under the terms of the treaty, it was agreed that the
boundaries between China and Tibet that has existed before the fighting would be restored and respected. This represented a gain for the
Tibetans. Prisoners of war were to be exchanged. If the Tibetans violated the treaty, Riwoche, Chamdo, and Tsawa Pakshod were to be
handed over to Sining. If the Chinese violated it, they would have to
surrender the twenty-five districts of Dimchi. The treaty was carried
out without any violations from either side. Ngoshi was then asked by
the Dalai Lama to return to Lhasa to resume his former duties.

In 1932, a year before his death, the thirteenth Dalai Lama gave his
officials an outline of his policies, which they were asked to follow. The
following is a summary of that testament.

After recalling his early works for the country, the Dalai Lama said
he had done so not for his own credit but for the information of his
officials and his own satisfaction. He expressed a wish to retire but
knew it was not possible to cease serving his country. Realizing that he
was now fifty-eight, he said that he knew it would not be long before
his days would come to an end. He had taken great care to keep Tibet
independent between the great countries of India and China, and at
the same time, troops had been sent by him to the borders of Kham to
challenge those who had invaded Tibetan territory. Remarking on the
advent of Communism in Outer Mongolia, he described how monasteries were being destroyed and the Jetsun Dampa's reincarnation had
been disallowed. Monks were being forced into the army. The Dalai
Lama predicted that Communism would come to Tibet sooner or
later, either from outside or within. Its arrival could be averted only if
precautions were taken from that time on; otherwise, the whole country could become slaves to the system and it would be difficult for the
people "to live through the day and night." There was still time and
opportunity for making preparations and building up the country's
strength. Everyone should cooperate in this, so that the country would
not have any regrets in the future.[8]

A few months before the Dalai Lama's death, the Lonchens and the
Kashag ministers assured him that all officials would carry out their
duties efficiently and that the monasteries were praying for his long

8. PHUR-LCOG.

life. In his written reply, the Dalai Lama expressed his appreciation of the monasterial prayers and he said that if the officials carried out their duties with sincerity, there would definitely be success. But, if they continued as they were doing at present, like brass masquerading as gold, putting off today's duties until tomorrow, then they would regret it. He told his officials that the welfare of the country depended entirely on them.[9]

This was the last recorded statement of the thirteenth Dalai Lama. In November, he caught a cold, which continued to worsen until, in the evening of the thirteenth day of the tenth month of the Water-Bird year (December 17, 1933), he died.

Ever since assuming power, the thirteenth Dalai Lama had improved the discipline of the monasteries. In spite of his many duties, he found time to test monks annually in the Norbulingka and to adjudicate their dialectical debates. During the Monlam festival, he made further examinations and carefully graded the monks. Those who passed the examinations with the first grade had a chance of becoming a candidate for the position of Ganden Tri Rimpoche.

Charles Bell, who was a very close friend of the Dalai Lama, remarked that "he was determined to free Tibet as far as possible from the Chinese rule. The majority of the Tibetan race were with him in this and saw in him the leader of the National Party and the only means of attaining their goal."[10] Bell mentioned further that the Dalai Lama once informed him, "The Chinese way . . . is to say or do something mild at first, then to wait a bit, and, if it passes without objection, to say or do something stronger. If this is objected to, they reply that what they said or did has been misinterpreted and really meant nothing."[11]

In the field of politics, this strategic approach of the Chinese is well known today. Politically, the Dalai Lama was successful in keeping the Chinese out of Tibet. By creating a balance of power between China and India, he was able to maintain Tibet's independence. Those officials and subjects who had done good work were rewarded; those who had failed were punished accordingly. His agents kept him informed of any bribery and corruption among his officials. Capital punishment and amputation, widely practiced in some districts, were

9. Ibid.
10. BELL, p. 140.
11. Ibid., p. 130.

abolished, except in the case of those who had plotted against the government. The Dalai Lama prohibited the dismissal of old servants, and children were not allowed to send their aged parents away. He made a law preventing free transport from being demanded by almost every official and fixed the rates that could be charged by those providing transport. A limit was placed on the interest charged by money lenders. If a landlord did not cultivate his land, another cultivator had the right to work it. In such cases, the land was to be free of tax for the first three years. After that, ten per cent was to be paid to the government and five per cent to the landlord for as long as the cultivator worked the land. Physicians were sent to different districts. Women in childbirth and sick animals were treated free.

Every official had to wear traditional Tibetan clothes. Tobacco, opium, and liquor were prohibited from entering the country. Gambling was made an offense. The Dalai Lama said these vices were weakening the country's manhood and resulted in much waste of time and money. He discouraged women from buying jewelry and expensive clothes in competition with each other, because the wives of poor officials were getting into debt. It had become impossible to enter high society without possessing costly ornaments. These reforms were unpopular with the rich and the privileged; but the majority of the people acclaimed the thirteenth Dalai Lama as the best that Tibet had ever known.

W. W. Rockhill, the American Minister to China, who met the Dalai Lama several times during the latter's visit to Peking in 1908, described the Dalai Lama in the following way.

> He is a man of undoubted intelligence and ability, of quick understanding and of force of character. He is broad-minded, possibly as a result of his varied experiences during the last few years, and of great natural dignity. He seemed deeply impressed with the great responsibilities of his office as supreme Pontiff of his faith, more so, perhaps, than by those resulting from his temporal duties. He is quick tempered and impulsive, but cheerful and kindly. At all times, I found him a most thoughtful host, an agreeable talker and extremely courteous. He speaks rapidly and smoothly, but in a very low voice. He is short in stature, probably about five foot six or seven inches, and of slight build. His complexion is rather darker than that of the Chinese, and of

a ruddier brown; his face, which is not very broad, is pitted with small pox, but not deeply. It lights up most pleasantly when he smiles and shows his teeth, which are sound and white. In repose his face is impassive, and rather haughty and forbidding. His nose is small and slightly aquiline, his ears large, but well set on his head. His eyes are dark brown and rather large with considerable obliquity, and his eyebrows heavy and rising markedly towards the temple, giving him a very worldly expression, which is further emphasized by his moustache and the small mouche under his lower lip. His hands are small and well shaped; on his left wrist, he usually carries a rosary of "red sandalwood" beads with silver counters. When walking, he moves quickly, but he does not hold himself erect, a result of passing most of his life seated cross-legged on cushions. His usual dress is the same dark red one worn by all lamas, with a waistcoat of gold brocade and a square of the same material covering his ch'ablu, and hanging down below his waist in front.[12]

After the death of the thirteenth Dalai Lama, there was no war until 1950; however, the struggle for power in the Tibetan officialdom depreciated the strength of the government's policies.

12. ROCKHILL, pp. 91–92.

17

The Whirlwind of Political Strife

The Dalai Lama was the head of the Tibetan government and its backbone consisted of the Silon (Prime Minister), the Kashag (Council of Ministers), the Yigtsang (Council of Monks, whose members were called Secretary-Generals), the Tsekhang (Council of Lay Officials, whose members were called the Finance Secretaries), and the Tsongdu (National Assembly). The young Prime Minister, Silon Langdun, who was appointed to office in 1926, was a little too soft for politics, but, being the Dalai Lama's nephew, he was shown considerable respect. Kunphela, Lungshar, and Tsarong, the three favorites of the Dalai Lama, assumed important roles in the Tibetan government as a result of their rivalry for power and prominence.

Kunphela headed the Mint Department and had the rank of Khenche. He also controlled the importation and distribution of arms and ammunition. To keep himself in power, he had established the new regiment called the Drong Drak Makhar, which was composed of sons from well-to-do families. Kunphela impressed the people as the "strong man of Tibet," during the latter part of the thirteenth Dalai Lama's reign.

Lungshar, who assumed the rank of Tsepon and took over the military, had been a close adviser to the Dalai Lama. Although an intelligent politician, he had been dismissed from military command for having arrested Sherpa Gyalpo in the residence of the Nepalese representative in Lhasa without the approval of the Dalai Lama. Lungshar strongly suspected Kunphela of having had a hand in his dismissal. In spite of his downfall from such a prominent position, Lungshar continued to dominate the Tsongdu in his capacity as a Tsepon.

Tsarong, the third favorite, was a capable man with foresight. He was clever and progressive; but his political aspirations had been damaged by his removal from the post of commander-in-chief of the army and his subsequent demotion from the Kashag. Tsarong continued to work with Kunphela in the Mint Department, but he remained in the background and avoided deep involvement in politics.

The sudden death of the thirteenth Dalai Lama in 1933 left Tibet in a state of political instability. Tsepon Lungshar realized that in order to strip Kunphela of his power, he would have to bring about the disbandment of the Drong Drak Makhar regiment. He secretly instigated the troops into tendering their resignations on the grounds that army life was hard on them, especially since they were the sons of well-to-do families. Being used to a comfortable homelife, the troops were not unwilling to offer their resignations.

On the third day after the death of the Dalai Lama, the entire Drong Drak Makhar regiment demonstrated before the Norbulingka, while the Kashag and Tsongdu were in session. The regiment demanded its own disbandment. The Kashag ordered the troops to return to their post, offering to meet their demands in due course. However, the regiment abandoned its military post, which protected the nearby Government Mint, and returned to Lhasa.

Influenced by Lungshar, representatives of the three big monasteries proposed to the Tsongdu that monks be sent to replace the deserters at the Mint's military post. The council minister, Kalon Trimon, suggested that it was unwise and unnecessary for monks to do the work of soldiers and he proposed that half of the Dalai Lama's bodyguard be sent to the Mint post as replacements. He then ordered the post to be taken over by troops from the bodyguard and issued instructions that they were to shoot anyone who tried to hinder them from occupying the post.

On the fourth day after the Dalai Lama's death, the Tsongdu, at the suggestion of Lungshar, met to discuss the suddenness of the death of the Dalai Lama. Subsequently, Kunphela and two personal attendants of the Dalai Lama were arrested for failing to provide adequate information on his illness. They were found guilty of keeping the government in ignorance and of failing to give the Dalai Lama adequate medical attention. Kunphela and the two attendants were subsequently exiled to Kongpo.

Shortly afterwards, the Tsongdu held a lottery to select a Regent from the two candidates, Rating Rimpoche and Tri Rimpoche. Rating Timpoche, whose personal name was Jampal Yeshe, was selected and on the eighth day of the first month of the Wood-Dog year (in January, 1934), he became the Regent of Tibet. He was assisted by Silon Langdun, the young Prime Minister.

After causing the downfall of his opponent Kunphela, Lungshar might have been able to assume control of the government had he been successful in replacing the Drong Drak Makhar regiment with monks loyal to him. This plan was thwarted by the actions of Kalon Trimon. Lungshar had gathered support from among the young officials and established an organization known as the Kechog Kuntun, meaning "Happy Union." Within this organization there was an inner circle which discussed the implementation of highly confidential matters. The public policy of those political bandits, headed by Lungshar, was to bring about a change in the government civil services; but the private policy and main political objectives of the organization were known only to the inner circle.

An important member of the organization, a sagacious man named Rimshi Kapshopa, informed Kalon Trimon that Lungshar planned to assassinate him. Trimon informed the Regent Rating of Lungshar's plot and then sought temporary asylum in the Drepung monastery. Meanwhile, the Kashag, having learned from the Regent of the plot, arrested Lungshar and Kapshopa; the latter's arrest was a cover-up to protect him. An investigative committee found certain documents in Lungshar's possession, which confirmed the existence of the plot. His aim had been to overthrow the government, in addition to the planned assassination of Trimon. The committee, after making a thorough study of the evidence, passed a sentence on Lungshar depriving him of his eyesight and sending him to prison for life. This rare penalty was reserved for acts of high treason.

After the expulsion of Chinese civil and military officials from Tibet in 1912, no Chinese had been permitted to enter the country in an official capacity until 1934, when the Chinese government requested permission to send a special mission, under General Huang Mu-sung, to offer religious tribute and condolences for the late Dalai Lama. The Chinese had taken advantage of the times to enter Tibet, because it would have been difficult for the Tibetan government to refuse permission to a mission of religious nature. General Huang Mu-sung and his party arrived in Lhasa in April 1934, via eastern Tibet. At the same time, a similar mission sent by the Indian government, arrived under the leadership of Rai Bahadur Norbu Thondup, a member of the staff of the Political Officer of Sikkim.

After offering condolences at the Potala, the Chinese General visited the Regent and other high officials and gave them lavish presents. Informal discussions followed and finally, with great diplomacy, Huang presented three proposals for settling the remaining differences between Tibet and China: that (1) Tibet must agree to become part of China, that (2) Tibet's national defense must be assumed by troops of the Central Government of China, and that (3) a Chinese commissioner should be stationed in Lhasa.

In reply, the Tibetan government referred to the terms of the Simla Convention of 1914 and agreed to accept the Chinese suzerainty it stipulated if the Chinese government would ratify that Convention. It was also stressed that the British government should be a party to any agreement reached between Tibet and China. The Tibetan government further demanded the return of certain territories east of the Drichu (Yangtze river), such as Derge, Nyarong, and Horkhog. They also agreed to allow the Panchen Lama to return to Tibet, but only on the condition that he and his followers came without a Chinese escort.[1]

The Tibetans remained adamant in their demands and no settlement was forthcoming. Finally, General Huang departed for China, leaving two liaison officers behind to continue talks between the two governments. These officers were in possession of a wireless transmitter, which they promised to hand over to the Tibetan government once a settlement was reached.

By the end of 1934, news of the Dalai Lama's death and the arrest of Kunphela reached Topgyal Pangdatshang, a supporter of Kunphela and a leader of the militia at Markham in eastern Tibet. Topgyal gathered his forces and attacked the government troops of General Dapon Nornang, which were stationed there to protect the border. Dapon Nornang was away from the area when this attack took place. The government troops were badly beaten and Markham was captured by Topgyal's militia.

Topgyal Pangdatshang planned on organizing the province of Kham into an independent state, and he distributed pamphlets to this effect. Two or three months later, government forces under the Gov-

1. DOCUMENTS.

ernor-General of Chamdo defeated Topgyal's militia and drove his troops into Chinese-occupied Bah, east of Markham. The Tibetan government negotiated with the Chinese government for the return of Topgyal; but the Chinese would neither assist Topgyal nor agree to return him to the Tibetans. They permitted him to remain in Bah, hoping that he might prove useful in their future political aspirations.

Rabga Pangdatsang, an elder brother of Topgyal, was also involved in the affair; but Yarphel Pangdatsang, the eldest brother, who was living in Lhasa, knew nothing of the Markham incident. When the Tibetan government learned of Topgyal's activities in the east, it had Yarphel's house in Lhasa surrounded. Yarphel, a shrewd and wealthy man, apologized on his brother's behalf and settled the matter by compensating the government for the damage done through his younger brother's rashness.

In 1934, because of the struggle in China between the Communists and the Nationalists, over one hundred thousand poorly-equipped Communist troops, driven by Nationalist force, began the "Long March" to the northwest. They moved into the Tibetan territories of Horkhog, Bah, Lithang, Nyarong, and Derge. The Tibetan government dispatched troops to check the infiltration, and the Chinese fugitives were eventually forced to continue on to northwest China. This was the first time that Chinese Communists had set foot on Tibetan soil.

Following the death of the thirteenth Dalai Lama, the search for his reincarnation was begun in accordance with the established traditions. In the spring of 1935, Regent Rating and Kalon Trimon journeyed to the Chokhorgyal monastery to view the vision in the sacred lake of Lhamoi Latso. Among the staff selected by the Kashag to accompany Trimon, I was appointed Kadrung Letsap (Acting Secretary to the Kashag).

Chokhorgyal is a small monastery founded by Gedun Gyatso, the second Dalai Lama. The climate in the area is rather uncertain, with frequent snowfall, intermittent rain, sunshine, and strong winds. Ten miles east of the Chokhorgyal monastery lies the sacred lake, protected by towering snow-peaks. It is somewhat circular in shape and a mile in circumference.

When we arrived, we scattered and remained in solemn silence. The Regent and officials were in deep meditation, for it was believed that each person would see a different vision. I confess that I did not see any vision; but the Regent was said to have seen the three Tibetan syllables *A*, *Ka*, and *Ma*, and then some village scenery. Many people have told me that they have seen visions of their future in the sacred lake; others, like myself, have seen nothing at all, even with the greatest effort.

From Chokhorgyal, the Regent journeyed to his birthplace at Rame in Dakpo Gyatsa, a remote little village about two days journey by horse. The villagers had built a small temple on the spot where Regent Rating had been born. A wooden peg driven deep into a large rock was to be seen in front of the temple. We were told that when the Regent was a child of three, he had hammered the wooden peg into the solid rock. When asked why he had done this, the child is said to have replied that he was expecting a rich caravan of guests from afar to take him home and that the peg would be needed to tether their horses. Astonishingly enough, the search party, which was looking for the reincarnation of the Rating Rimpoche, had arrived in the village that very evening and later had taken the child and his family away to the Rating monastery.

The Regent spent ten days visiting his birthplace and meeting with his relatives. I was surprised to find that such a capable man had been born among economically deprived and physically unattractive relatives and among villagers who had never before seen such luxurious trappings as those that belonged to the Regent's party. The whole party camped in tents. For three nights, each time lasting into early dawn, the Regent and Kalon Trimon discussed something of a serious nature. On the fourth morning, to my utter disbelief, Kalon Trimon asked me confidentally to draw up his resignation papers. I expressed my surprise and asked Trimon the reason for his sudden decision to resign at the peak of his career. He told me that both he and the Regent had agreed to submit their resignations. As I could not comprehend the reason, I requested Trimon not to rush into any decision; but he returned to Lhasa and subsequently resigned from office. The Regent toured southern Tibet for a while and then returned to Lhasa, where he presented to the Tsongdu a detailed report of his mission to the sacred lake. Having received his report on the signs relevant to the location of the rebirth of the Dalai Lama, the government organized three search parties. Their leaders were Phurchok Rimpoche, assigned to search Dakpo and Kongpo in southeastern Tibet; Khangser Rim-

poche, assigned to Kham and Jang in eastern Tibet; and Keutsang
Rimpcche, assigned to Amdo and Arig in the far northeast.

Meanwhile, the sixth Panchen Lama continued to live in exile in
China. He made several attempts to return to Tibet. In 1932 his representative, Ngachen Ta Lama, conveyed the Panchen Lama's wishes to
the Tibetan government. At that time, the thirteenth Dalai Lama
agreed to allow the return of the Panchen Lama and his followers and
to restore to him his former rights, powers, and estates, subject to the
following basic conditions: (1) in addition to the usual taxes, the
Panchen Lama should pay the new tax imposed by the Tibetan government to support the national defense program, and (2) the Panchen Lama should enter Tibet accompanied only by his Tibetan attendants.[2]

In the following year, when the Dalai Lama died unexpectedly, the
Regent and the Kashag felt that it would be unwise for the Panchen
Lama to remain in China for a greater length of time. A cablegram
was sent to the Panchen Lama through the Tibetan representatives at
Nanking, requesting his speedy return, subject to the conditions laid
down by the late Dalai Lama. In addition, the Tibetan government
agreed to provide all transportation and facilities to welcome the Panchen Lama into Tibet and to escort him to his estate at Tashilhunpo.
Apparently no clear-cut reply was given to the Tibetan representatives when they visited the Panchen Lama to deliver the cablegram.
One of the representatives, Chosphel Thubten, told me personally that
it would have been a good thing if the Panchen Lama had accepted
the conditions laid down by the Tibetan government; but he treated
them with disdain.

The main delay in the return of the Panchen Lama to Tibet was
caused by the announcement made in 1935 by the Nationalist government of China that the Panchen Lama would establish his headquarters at Sining, and then enter Tibet with a Chinese representative and
an escort of five hundred Chinese soldiers. The Panchen Lama was
given a title by the Nationalist government that declared him to be a
"Special Cultural Commissioner for Western Regions." The Tibetan
representatives informed the Chinese government in Nanking that the
Tibetan government would not recognize the title conferred on the
Panchen Lama. Moreover, it objected to the proposed escort of five
hundred Chinese soldiers. The Tibetans approached the British gov-

2. Ibid.

ernment in India, which in turn raised this objection to the Chinese Foreign Office in Nanking through its ambassador, Sir Alexander Cadogan.

In the past it had been the usual procedure for the British Political Officer in Sikkim to visit Lhasa whenever there arose an important question to be discussed between the British and Tibetan governments. When the Chinese mission under General Huang Mu-sung received permission from the Tibetan government to visit Lhasa to offer condolence for the late Dalai Lama, the Assistant Political Officer in Sikkim, Rai Bahadur Norbu Thon-dup, also came to Lhasa—officially for the same reason, but in reality to watch the proceedings of Huang Mu-sung.

Now that China planned to send armed troops to escort the Panchen Lama into Tibet, F. W. Williamson, the Political Officer in Sikkim, visited Lhasa at the request of the Tibetan government to help look for a solution. Shortly after his arrival, Williamson fell ill and his condition went from bad to worse. The British government in India sought permission to land an airplane in Lhasa to take Williamson to India for medical treatment; but the request was turned down by the Tibetan government. No airplane had ever been allowed to land in Tibet before and the granting of this concession to the British could well have placed the Tibetan government in a difficult position regarding similar requests from other nations. Unfortunately, the Tibetan government's attitude was of no help to Williamson, who died a few days later.

Basil Gould succeeded Williamson and arrived in Lhasa accompanied by Brigadier General P. Neame of the Indian Eastern Command. Through Basil Gould, the Tibetan government requested the British government to fulfill its treaty obligation by making the Chinese government understand the Tibetan government's objections to the sending of an armed escort with the Panchen Lama. Basil Gould said that he would inform His Majesty's government in London and put a strong recommendation to it that it use its influence in the matter. He further stated that the Chinese mission under Huang Mu-sung had left two liaison officers with a wireless transmitting set at Lhasa. Gould requested similar rights for the British to establish a mission with a wireless under Hugh E. Richardson, the trade agent stationed at Gyantse.

When the Tibetan government heard the news that the Panchen

Lama was returning to Tibet via Jyekundo, with an armed Chinese escort, it dispatched Doring Teji to meet him. Instructions were issued to the Governor of eastern Tibet to provide all necessary accommodations to the Panchen Lama; but the Chinese escort was not to be allowed to enter Tibet. About the same time that the Governor learned of the Panchen's arrival with his escort at Jyekundo in March 1937, he also heard of the arrival in Tachienlu of a large number of the Panchen's followers bearing his treasures. The Governor sent an official to instruct the Panchen Lama to proceed without the armed Chinese escort; however, a representative of the Panchen Lama arrived in Chamdo and informed the Governor that the Chinese escort intended to accompany the Panchen Lama.

Several months passed without the counterdemands being settled. Meanwhile, the secretary of the Panchen Lama sent an urgent communication to Tashilhunpo containing the news that the Panchen was due to arrive with twenty Chinese officials and five hundred armed Chinese soldiers capable of opposing any Tibetans, who objected to their entry into Tibet. The communication, with an arrow attached to it signifying great urgency, also showed the route that the Panchen Lama's party would take on the way to Tashilhunpo.

When this urgent communication was intercepted at Lhasa, the Kashag passed it on to the Tsongdu. Its contents displeased the Tsongdu, which decided that the Panchen Lama could not enter Tibet with a Chinese escort. If the Panchen should insist, then he would have to submit a written statement to the effect that the escort, after a rest period of one month, would return to China via India. Also, no member of the Chinese escort party would be allowed to interfere in the affairs of Tibet. The written guarantee must be witnessed by a representative of a third nation. If the Panchen Lama did not agree to the provisions set forth by the Tsongdu, Tibetan troops would be ordered to halt his entry into Tibet.[3]

The Chinese government at Nanking was informed by Tibetan representatives of the Tsongdu's decision. In the meantime, the Panchen Lama had left Jyekundo and arrived at Rakshi Lungon. To make certain that the Panchen Lama was informed of the Tsongdu's decision, the Governor sent a copy of the decision to Dapon Namselingpa and Horche Khenchung, whose duties were to guard the Tibetan border at Chaksamkha and its neighborhood. At that point, the Chinese escort

3. Ibid.

received orders from the Nationalist government to withdraw from Rakshi Lungon. The Panchen Lama then returned to Jyekundo to await developments. He fell ill, and died in Jyekundo on December 1, 1937.

Without the Panchen Lama, his followers would find it difficult to enter Tibet. On the other hand, the prospect of returning to China was not a happy one, as China was now at war with Japan. Consequently, his followers took the Panchen Lama's body and proceeded to Horkhog in eastern Tibet. When they were in Tachienlu, they plotted against the Tibetan government with some of the discontented local Khamba tribes; but they were forced to leave that area and go to Derge as a result of skirmishes developing between themselves and Liu Wen-hui, the Chinese Governor of Tachienlu.

When the Tibetan Governor at Chamdo heard of this, he immediately dispatched a mission to ask the Panchen Lama's followers to return to Tibet with their master's body, assuring them that they would not be subjected to punishment. The followers then separated into two parties. One party returned to Sining in Ch'ing-hai province and the other returned to Tibet with the Panchen Lama's body. The Tibetan government sent Datsap Chokpe to receive the latter party, which arrived at Tashilhunpo in 1938.

In the same year, the young Regent Rating often spoke of resigning from the regentship. The Kashag and the Tsongdu made repeated attempts to prevent this. The Regent was a young man in good health and no reason was seen for him to resign. When pressed for the reason for his dissatisfaction, the Regent replied that his position was such that whenever something came up, he had to consult the Prime Minister, who held joint power with him. This prevented him from making any decisions on his own and consequently delayed matters that needed quick, decisive action.

The Kashag and the Tsongdu, after careful consideration of the Regent's problem, decided it would be best for the Prime Minister to resign in order to facilitate the functions and decision-making power of the Regent. Accordingly, the Prime Minister, Silon Langdun, was asked to withdraw from political activity; but he would retain a nominal prime ministership. Much to the surprise of the Kashag and the Tsongdu, Silon Langdun gladly accepted the proposal of a nominal role. He resigned from political activity on the thirtieth day of the second month of the Earth-Tiger year (1938). At the time of his resignation, his supporters doubted his willingness to resign and an atmosphere of fear and tension enveloped Lhasa; however, the crisis passed, because Silon Langdun, a man of good heart and understanding, stepped down without a sign of regret or resentment.

Soon after that, the Tibetan government received reports from each of the three search parties about candidates most likely to be the reincarnation of the Dalai Lama. Instructions were issued to bring the three candidates to Lhasa for religious tests. Keutsang Rimpoche's search party encountered some difficulty in bringing its candidate to Lhasa from Taktser in the Kokonor region, which formerly was a Tibetan territory and now under Chinese administration. The representatives of the Kumbum monastery and the Muslim Governor of Ch'inghai, Ma Pu-fang, demanded proof that the Taktser candidate was the reincarnation of the Dalai Lama. The Tibetan government replied that confirmation could not be made until all three candidates from different areas of Tibet came to Lhasa and sat for the religious tests. In the meantime, the Taktser candidate was initiated into monkhood at the Kumbum monastery in the Kokonor region. Eventually, the search party was allowed to take the boy to Lhasa after paying a ransom of four hundred thousand Chinese dollars (equivalent to about $92,000 in U.S. currency) to the Governor of Ch'ing-hai.[4]

In July 1939, the larger assembly of the Tsongdu held a special meeting in one of the Dalai Lama's rooms, Dedan Khil, in the Potala. One of the four secretary-generals (Trungyik Chemo) read the reports of the three search parties. One report commented on the successful tests fulfilled by the Taktser candidate, which were given by Keutsang Rimpoche. He pointed out that the vision as seen in the sacred lake by the Regent coincided with the description of the candidate's village as reported by Keutsang's party. He also informed the Tsongdu that the Nechung Oracle and various Lamas also confirmed the Taktser candidate to be the reincarnation. The Secretary-General went on to add that the government had not yet confirmed any of the candidates, owing to the problems encountered in bringing the child from the Kokonor region. Now that the Taktser child was well into Tibetan territory, the Secretary-General informed the Tsongdu that the Tibetan government accepted the Taktser candidate as the fourteenth Dalai Lama. The Tsongdu unanimously confirmed this accept-

4. DALAI, pp. 25–28.

ance and declarations were subsequently issued throughout Tibet to that effect.

The Tibetan government's preparations for the entry of the Dalai Lama into the capital had to be rushed through, since the whole affair was kept under a cloak of secrecy until the last moment. Kalon Bonsho led a party of officials to Nagchukha to receive the Dalai Lama on behalf of the government. I was selected by the Kashag as one of the officials to accompany Kalon Bonsho. We had to travel night and day on horseback to reach Nagchukha before the Dalai Lama. From Nagchukha we traveled another three miles to Gashi Nakha, where we received the four-year-old Dalai Lama, who was borne in a palanquin known in Tibet as a *treljam*. The Dalai Lama's party also included his family members. Kalon Bonsho offered a greeting scarf at the first meeting with the Dalai Lama; later, a welcoming ceremony was performed at dawn in his tent. It was then that the child was officially proclaimed the fourteenth Dalai Lama with the offering to him of the *Mendel Tensum*. The Regent joined the party at Dam Uma Thang and together they journeyed for a few days stay at the Rating monastery.

It was customary for most of the Dalai Lamas to visit Rekya, a small hermitage. After two days at Rekya, the Dalai Lama's party was received at Dogu Thang by the rest of the government officials, the abbots of various monasteries, and the representatives of Britain, China, Nepal, and Bhutan.

The whole procession marched gloriously through the streets of Lhasa on the twenty-fifth day of the eighth month of the Earth-Hare year (October 8, 1939). A visit was made to the Jokhang temple and then the procession moved on to the Norbulingka, the summer palace of the Dalai Lama.

On the thirteenth day of the tenth month of the Earth-Hare year (1939), Regent Rating shaved the fourteenth Dalai Lama's head before the image of the Lord Buddha in the Jokhang temple and named the boy Tenzin Gyatso. The date of his enthronement was fixed for the fourteenth day of the first month of the Iron-Dragon year, corresponding to February 22, 1940. The Kashag cabled the government of China, the British government of India, the King of Nepal, and the Maharajas of Bhutan and Sikkim, informing them of the date of the enthronement. The British government of India was represented by

Basil Gould, the Political Officer in Sikkim. The representatives of Nepal and Bhutan were already in Lhasa. The Chinese government sent as its representative Wu Chung-hsin. The Chinese claim that Wu chung-hsin was sent to Tibet to officiate at the installation of the Dalai Lama,[5] but in reality, Wu Chung-hsin's presence at the ceremony was of no greater significance than the presence of the representatives from the other countries.

Later on, the state astrologer and the soothsayer predicted that Regent Rating's life would be short if he did not devote himself to prayer and meditation. Rating resigned from his post and recommended Taktra Rimpoche Ngawang Sungrab, the senior tutor of the Dalai Lama, as his successor. At the request of the Kashag and the Tsongdu, Taktra Rimpoche accepted the regentship in the first month of the Iron-Snake year (1941).

Early in 1942, during World War II, the supply route between India and China via Burma was cut off by the Japanese. The governments of India and China wished to build a military supply route through the southeastern Tibetan district of Zayul. Kung Ching-tsung, the Chinese liaison officer in Lhasa, and Rai Bahadur Norbu Thondup, leader of the British Mission, approached the Bureau of Foreign Affairs in Lhasa to request the government of Tibet for permission to open a military supply route through Zayul. This request was forwarded by the Kashag to the Regent Taktra, who referred the matter to the Tsongdu. The Tsongdu refused to allow military supplies to pass through Tibet. The Chinese government threatened to wage war if the Tibetan government did not give its consent, and even instigated the provincial governors along the border to initiate hostilities. Tibetan troops were ready to face any aggression. Finally, the Chinese road surveyors were recalled to China and the crisis eased.

Rai Bahadur Norbu Thondup strongly requested the Tibetan government to agree to the supply route proposal and even warned that a continued refusal might result in the loss of British support. The Tibetan government explained to the British Mission that Tibet desired to remain in a neutral position; yet, they did not wish to embarrass the British government in India, therefore they would permit goods that were not of a military nature to pass through Tibet to China.

In the same year, the Tsongdu asked Kung Ching-tsung, the Chinese liaison officer, to leave Tibet for having violated a Tibetan law.

5. LI, pp. 180–85.

He had detained a Lhasa policeman who had entered his house to arrest a Nepalese and a Tibetan who had quarreled on the street and then ran into the Chinese residence. In 1943 the Chinese government requested the Tibetan government to permit the entrance of their liaison officer, Shen Tsung-lien, and a small staff, via India to replace Kung Ching-tsung. The Indian government asked the Tibetan Foreign Bureau if it would permit Shen Tsung-lien and his staff to proceed to Tibet via India. The Tibetan Foreign Bureau gave its consent, following which the Chinese party left India for Tibet. This was the procedure followed whenever a Chinese wished to enter Tibet. Shen Tsung-lien, through his fine diplomacy, was successful in improving the strained relations between China and Tibet.

In late 1942, Lhasa received its first official visit from the Americans. Captain Ilia Tolstoy, accompanied by Lieutenant Brooke Dolan, was assigned by the Office of Strategic Services in Washington to discover routes to convey supplies to China through Tibet. The American visitors were warmly received by the Tibetan government. They had an audience with the Dalai Lama, to whom they presented a letter and a picture from President Roosevelt. Other presents were also given. After remaining in Lhasa for about a month, Ilia Tolstoy and his party were accompanied to the Chinese border by Tibetan escorts and entered China by way of Sining.

The following is the letter sent to the Dalai Lama by President Franklin D. Roosevelt:

THE WHITE HOUSE
WASHINGTON   July 3, 1942

Your Holiness:

Two of my fellow countrymen, Ilia Tolstoy and Brooke Dolan, hope to visit your Pontificate and the historic and widely famed city of Lhasa. There are in the United States of America many persons, among them myself, who, long and greatly interested in your land and people, would highly value such an opportunity.

As you know, the people of the United States, in association with those of twenty-seven other countries, are now engaged in a war which has been thrust upon the world by nations bent on conquest, who are intent upon destroying freedom of thought, of religion, and of action everywhere. The United Nations are fighting today in defense of and for preservation of freedom, confident that we shall be victorious because our cause is just, our capacity is adequate, and our determination is unshakable.

I am asking Ilia Tolstoy and Brooke Dolan to convey to you a little gift in token of my friendly sentiment toward you.

With cordial greetings, I am

Very sincerely yours,
(Signed) Franklin D. Roosevelt

His Holiness
> The Dalai Lama
>> Supreme Pontiff of the Lama Church,
>>> Lhasa

The following is a translation of the Dalai Lama's reply to President Roosevelt:

The Honorable Franklin D. Roosevelt
President of the United States of America
The White House
Washington, D.C., U.S.A.

Dear Mr. President:

We received with the greatest gratification your letter and the tokens of goodwill (your autographed photo and an exquisite gold watch showing phases of the moon and the days of the week) through Envoys, Capt. I. Tolstoy and Lt. Brooke Dolan, who arrived here safely for the purpose of visiting the Pontificate and the city of Lhasa.

We are happy to learn that you and the people of the United States of America take great interest in our country and it is of special significance that the people of the United States of America, in association with twenty-seven other countries, are now engaged in a war for the preservation of freedom, which has been thrust upon them by nations bent on conquest and who are intent upon destroying freedom of thought, of religion, and of action everywhere.

Tibet also values her freedom and independence enjoyed from time immemorial and, being the great seat of the Buddhist Religion, I am endeavoring, in spite of my tender age, to uphold and propagate our religious precepts and thereby emulate the pious work of my predecessors. I earnestly hope and pray for a speedy termination of hostilities so that the nations of the world may enjoy a lasting and righteous peace, based on the principles of freedom and goodwill.

As a token of my regard, I am sending herewith a scarf of honor, three Tibetan coins of the first precious metal [gold], my photo, and three handsewn *thangka* [religious scrolls], depicting the sextet blessed with long existence, the four dutiful brothers, and the eight lucky signs, all framed in blue brocade silk, etc.

Yours sincerely,
Dalai Lama of Tibet
(Seal of the Dalai Lama of Tibet)

Dated the nineteenth day of the first Tibetan month of the Water-Sheep year; corresponding to February 24, 1943.

In 1944 a U.S. military aircraft, piloted by Lieutenant R. E. Crozier, crash-landed in Tibet at a place called Doh near the famous monastery of Samye. The four-motor cargo plane was on a supply run from China to India, when it lost its way and ran out of fuel. The Tibetan government extended every assistance and hospitality to the American crew members, who were escorted to the Indian border. The United States diplomatic mission in India gave its assurance that in the future no U.S. aircraft would fly over Tibetan territory. The Tibetan government was thanked for the help it had extended to the American fliers.

The government of Tibet realized that English-speaking Tibetans were most essential for the conducting of government affairs, but there were only a handful of Tibetans who had some knowledge of the English language. After approaching Basil Gould of the British Mission in Lhasa on this matter, the Tibetan government was able to obtain a Mr. Richard Parker from England to teach English in Lhasa. A school was established in the spring of 1945. A few students were selected by the government to attend the school. After a few months, a strong protest was made by the monasteries on the grounds that the school would affect the religious beliefs of the country. This protest led to the closing of the newly-opened English school. (This event was not without precedent. A similar incident had occurred in 1926, when an English school established in Gyantse in 1923 was closed for the same reason.) The Tibetan government subsequently sent a number of students to study in India under government scholarships. Several more students, sent by private families, joined the government-sponsored group in India.

The Chinese government had always tried to influence the monasteries of Tibet, and at this time they found a weapon in the person of Geshe Sherab Gyatso, a learned Buddhist scholar, formerly at the Drepung monastery, but now working in China for the so-called Commission for Mongolian and Tibetan Affairs. Sherab Gyatso attempted to return to Tibet and had come as far as Nagchukha; but the Tibetan government refused him entry, because it learned that he intended to spread Chinese propaganda in the monasteries. When China fell under the Communist regime some years later, Sherab Gyatso became a Communist tool.

In 1945 two German prisoners of war, Heinrich Harrer and Peter Aufschnaiter, escaped from the British internment camp at Dehra Dun in India. They entered Tibet, where they received asylum since Tibet maintained a position of neutrality throughout World War II. During their seven-year stay in Tibet, Harrer and Aufschnaiter lived in harmony with the Tibetan people. They helped construct a canal for irrigation purposes, plant trees, and build a river bank. As a result of his experiences, Harrer wrote a book, titled *Seven Years in Tibet*.

At the end of World War II, the Regent, Taktra Rimpoche, dispatched a mission to congratulate the Allies on their victory. The mission was headed by Dzasa Thubten Samphel and Dzasa Khemey. Hugh Richardson, then head of the British Mission in Lhasa, warned the Bureau of Foreign Affairs that if the mission should attend the National Assembly in China, the government of Tibet would be violating the Simla Convention of 1914. The Kashag explained to Richardson that the mission did not intend to attend the National Assembly in China; its only objective was to convey congratulations on the Allied victory.

To the British government in India, the mission delivered presents and a congratulatory message through the Viceroy, Lord Wavell. Complimentary presents and a message were also conveyed to the United States government through its representative in New Delhi. The mission then left for China. While there, the mission, without the permission or orders of the Tibetan government, attended the Chinese National Assembly on May 5, 1946. The members of the mission claim that they had gone only to watch the proceedings, because the Chinese had installed their own so-called representatives to represent Tibet in the Chinese National Assembly. The mission further stated that it neither recognized nor signed the new constitutional law passed by the Assembly.

In the following year, the government of Tibet, in response to an invitation from the Indian government, sent a delegation, led by Teji Samdup Photrang and Khenchung Lozang Wangyal, to the Inter-Asian Conference held in Delhi on March 23, 1947. The Tibetan national flag was hoisted and a speech delivered to the Conference. The following speech was given by the Tibetan delegation:

> Our Tibetan Government received an invitation to join in the Asian Relations Conference. We are a country which administers its subjects on the basis of religious aspirations. India, being the motherland of Buddhism, has had friendly relations from ancient times with Buddhists, especially we Tibetans. Therefore, our government has sent us here to attend this great Conference to maintain our peaceful relations based on religion. In a similar way, we are very glad to meet representatives from all the Asian countries in this Conference and we wish to express our sincere gratitude to the great Indian leaders, Mahatma Gandhi, Pandit Jawaharlal Nehru, and Mrs. Sarojini Naidu, and to all the distinguished representatives, who have gathered in this Conference. As for the future, all the Asian countries should feel as brothers towards each other, a feeling based on spiritual relationships, so that in this way we might hope that there will be everlasting peace and unity in Asia.

For years, grain had been lent to Tibetan subjects on interest by the government, by landholding monasteries, and by wealthy individuals. Though the interest rate was low, there had been instances where the subjects failed to pay on schedule and, in time, these unpaid interests increased considerably. The poor debtors suffered a great deal. The government at Lhasa issued orders in 1944 which freed the heavily-pressed subjects from paying the interest arrears that had piled up over the years. The subjects of the district of Lhundup Dzong in Phanpo, hearing of the government's order prohibiting the collection of interest arrears from hard-pressed subjects, determinedly refused to pay interest due to the landholdings of the Sera Che and Ngagpa col-

leges of the Sera monastery, which had lent grain to the subjects of
Lhundup Dzong. The subjects were supported by the District Officer
(Dzongpon) in their refusal to pay the interest arrears. A quarrel ensued between the District Officer and the interest-collectors of the
Sera Che and Ngagpa colleges, which resulted in the District Officer
being severely beaten by the collectors. The officer subsequently died
as a result of the injuries sustained in the beating. The government appointed an investigative committee to look into the dispute. The
members of the committee demanded that the Sera Che and Ngagpa
colleges hand over the guilty persons to the government. The colleges
defiantly refused to hand over the culprits. The monks of the colleges
staged a protest by not attending the first two days of the Monlam
festival in 1945.

The situation went from bad to worse. The government representatives finally forced their way into the Sera Che and Ngagpa colleges
and arrested those who had been responsible for the death of the District Officer. The abbots of the colleges were demoted and new ones
installed.

In the same year, the Sera Che college, to which the ex-Regent, Rating, belonged, invited him to preside over the opening ceremonies of
an old temple that had been repaired. About this time, a rumor circulated in the city of Lhasa that the Regent Taktra was going to resign
and that the ex-Regent would resume the regency. This rumor caused
some excitement and speculation among the people of Lhasa. It appeared that there had been an earlier understanding between Rating
and Taktra to share the regency in alternation; the latter was to resign
on grounds of old age and the former to resume the office for a second
time. The understanding led, however, to a strained relationship between the two and the reigning Regent refused to bow out from the
powerful office. The Sera Che and Ngagpa colleges affair and now the
struggle for the regency cast a dark shadow of mystery, fear, and intrigue over the land.

A year later, in November 1946, Tsepon Lhalu, the son of Lungshar, was ambushed at night, while returning to his home from Lhasa.
Several shots were fired, but none hit any of the men. Only one horse
was killed. Once more the government set out to investigate the matter, but failed to identify the snipers.

In February of 1947, on the night of the Butter Festival, the Regent Taktra suddenly canceled going to the Festival. It was customary

for the Regent and members of the government to pass in procession through the Festival area. The reason for his sudden decision was a suspicion that rebellious elements were lying in wait to ambush him and the heads of the government. Two weeks later, a mysterious parcel arrived through a favorite of the Regent, the Secretary-General Ngawang Namgyal. The parcel, which was addressed to the Regent from the Governor of Chamdo, was opened by a steward of the Secretary-General. A hand grenade inside the parcel exploded. However, it caused no injuries and little damage. The government laboriously conducted an investigation.

Almost a month later, the Kashag received from the Tibetan representatives in Nanking a wireless message, which said that ex-Regent Rating had written a letter to President Chiang Kai-shek, informing him of the unjust rule of Regent Taktra and of the sufferings of the Tibetan subjects. Rating had mentioned making preparations to overthrow the Regent and was asking for support from President Chiang. An emergency meeting took place between the Regent Taktra and the members of the Kashag. Two Kashag ministers were sent with government troops to the Rating monastery, with orders to bring the ex-Regent to Lhasa. On April 18, the day he was brought into Lhasa, monks of the Sera Che college prepared to descend upon the party and rescue the ex-Regent; but their plan failed, owing to the presence of the government troops.

Rating and his attendants were committed to house arrest in Lhasa. Rating had to surrender all his documents and correspondence for examination. Among the documents, the Tsongdu found ample evidence that the conspiracy was master-minded by the ex-Regent's attendants; chief among them was Nyungnas Lama. It was also found that the ex-Regent had made repeated attempts to avoid the use of violence; but he had been compelled into the conspiracy to overthrow the Regent and the government. The ex-Regent's attendants confessed finally to the ambush on Tsepon Lhalu, the case of the explosive parcel, the preparations to assault the Regent and the heads of the government on the night of the Butter Festival, and other attempts on the Regent Taktra's life.

In the process of the investigations and while under house arrest, ex-Regent Rating unexpectedly died on the eighteenth day of the third month of the Fire-Hog year (May 8, 1947). His sudden death caused some ill feeling and attempts at revolt among the monks of the Sera monastery and among the monks of Sera Che college in particular. The Tsongdu, along with representatives of the Rating estates, made a final examination of the body of the ex-Regent and reported that they did not find any injury on the body that might have caused his death. Meanwhile, government troops were able to quell the unrest among the monks. The ex-Regent's attendants who were found guilty of conspiracy were punished with sentences of life imprisonment or exile according to the degree of their involvement. Nyungnas Lama had already committed suicide.

Soon after this threat of a possible civil war was ended, the British government was scheduled to transfer its powers to the Indians. The Tibetan government began to worry whether Tibet would receive the same diplomatic support that it had received from Great Britain. In July 1947, the British Mission in Lhasa formally assured the government of Tibet that the governments of Great Britain and India would continue the relations that Tibet had enjoyed in its dealings with China. An understanding was reached that the government of India, as successor to the British government, would continue the same relations and adhere to the British obligations and rights of the treaties made with Tibet. It was also understood that Tibet would remain in contact with the British government through its High Commissioner in India, who could make visits to Tibet should his presence be required. On August 15, 1947 India became independent and the Tibetan government telegraphed its good wishes. In Tibet, the British trade agencies at Gyantse, Yatung, and Gartok, and the Mission in Lhasa, all became Indian offices.

On October 25th of the same year, the Tibetan government decided to send a Trade Delegation to India, the United Kingdom, the United States, and China. I was assigned to head the delegation and the other members were my younger brother, Khenchung Changkhyim, and Dapon Surkhang and Rimshi Pangdatshang. There were three reasons for dispatching the Trade Delegation:

1. Tibet's non-Asian exports, chiefly wool, followed by musk, furs, and yak-tails, were usually sold by way of India. All trade business was negotiated through India, which paid Tibet in rupees. The object of the Trade Delegation was to seek the relaxation of Indian control on Tibetan exports and to request payment in dollars or pounds sterling instead of rupees; otherwise, it would be necessary to seek direct trade relations with foreign countries. The Delegation was

also to look for import prospects and to find suitable machines for use in agriculture and in wool factories.

2. The Delegation was to purchase gold bullion for the backing of Tibetan currency.

3. As the world was not properly informed of Tibet's political status, and since what it did know was chiefly from Chinese sources, it was necessary for Tibet to open formal relations with other nations of the world. To demonstrate Tibet's independent and sovereign status, Tibetan passports were issued to the members of the Delegation for travel abroad. (These were the first official Tibetan passports ever issued for foreign travel.)

The Trade Delegation carried letters and presents from the Dalai Lama and the Tibetan government for the various heads of government they were to meet. In Delhi, the Delegation met with Viceroy Lord Mountbatten, Prime Minister Jawaharlal Nehru, and other Indian leaders, and discussed commercial matters. The leaders of India extended to the Delegation every assistance and expressed their goodwill towards Tibet. Later on, the Delegation met Mahatma Gandhi, who was then residing at the Birla House in Delhi. When I presented him with a ceremonial scarf (khatag), Mahatma Gandhi asked whether the scarf was made in Tibet. When I informed him that the materials for ceremonial scarves were imported, he was very surprised and stressed the importance of manufacturing in one's own country the goods one uses. This, and other profoundly straightforward advice by the Mahatma, deeply moved all the members of the Tibetan Trade Delegation.

Arriving in Nanking an January 31, 1948, the Delegation was informed of the sad news of the assassination of Mahatma Gandhi. Members of the Delegation deeply regretted the shocking news. In Lhasa, the government of Tibet conveyed its condolences by holding a national prayer in the Jokhang temple.

While in the Chinese capital, the Trade Delegation met with President Chiang Kai-shek and various leaders of the Chinese government and conducted discussions on the importation of tea and other goods to Tibet through two routes: one through Tachienlu, the other through India. The route through India would be for tea being imported from Yunnan.

At that time, the elections were in full swing and the Chinese government invited the Trade Delegation to attend the National Assembly, which was about to convene to adopt a constitution; but the Delegation members firmly refused to attend the Chinese National Assembly, stating that they were in China for the purpose of trade negotiations. Following the reelection of Chiang Kai-shek and with the instructions of the Tibetan government, the Delegation personally congratulated President Chiang Kai-shek and Vice-President Li Tsung-jen.

During their stay in China, the head of the so-called Commission or Mongolian and Tibetan Affairs, as well as Shen Tsung-lien, formerly Chinese liaison officer in Lhasa and now Secretary-General of the Shanghai Municipal Government, advised the Delegation members against visiting the United Kingdom and the United States. Should the Tibetans visit these Western countries, they were advised not to carry Tibetan passports. The Tibetan Delegation members refused to listen to these suggestions. Throughout their entire journey abroad, they carried Tibetan passports and travel documents, which were recognized and accepted by all the countries they visited; thus, they established another precedent supporting the independent status of Tibet.

The Delegation did not leave China without paying courtesy calls on the American Ambassador, John L. Stuart; the British Ambassador, Sir Ralph Skrine Stevenson; and the Indian Ambassador, Sardar K. M. Panikkar.

When the Delegation arrived in the United States, it was met by the Secretary of State, George Marshall. At that time, the Chinese Ambassador to the United States, Wellington Koo, expressed his desire to accompany the Tibetan Delegation in their meeting with the Secretary of State; but the Delegation refused the company of the Chinese Ambassador, despite his protest. The Delegation members informed the Chinese that the Delegation had been meeting various heads of governments and that the Chinese Ambassador had no right to accompany them at the State Department, or anywhere else. The State Department also found it unnecessary that the Chinese Ambassador should accompany the Tibetan Delegation.

In Washington, the Trade Delegation discussed matters concerning the export of wool and the purchase of gold bullion for backing Tibetan currency. During their stay in the United States, the Delegation members visited several agricultural, livestock, and industrial sites. They also purchased samples of agricultural implements to test in Tibet. Through their old friend, Colonel Ilia Tolstoy, the members met General Dwight D. Eisenhower, who was then President of Columbia University. The General expressed his appreciation and thanks to the Tibetan government for lending assistance to the American flyers who crash-landed in Tibet during the War.

In England, the Trade Delegation met with Prime Minister Attlee. Visits to the foreign and commerce ministries were made and discussions on trade possibilities were held.

When the Delegation arrived back in India, its members continued their trade discussions with the Indian government. They also expressed their desire of stationing a Tibetan representative in India. The Indian government agreed to the establishment of a Tibetan Trade Mission in India. This Trade Mission was intended as a step towards an eventual diplomatic mission in India.

The Indian government informed the Trade Delegation that as Tibet was trading indirectly with the United States and the United Kingdom, with the goods going via India, Tibetans not on government business could not be paid in dollars or pounds sterling; but if the export was by the government of Tibet, then the government of India would pay the Tibetan government in dollars or pounds sterling. The Indian government further stated that import items going directly to Tibet, via India, would be transshipped without Indian duty.

While I was in Delhi, Prime Minister Nehru personally informed me that Tibet could not remain isolated any longer and must change with the times. Back in Lhasa, I made a full, detailed report to the Kashag and the Tsongdu and strongly suggested the need and importance of diplomatic relations with India and other nations of the world.

About that time, the Communists were rising to power in China. Certain members of the Nationalist Chinese Mission in Lhasa and some Chinese traders put up a restaurant in the Tibetan capital. This restaurant, it was often reported to the Tibetan government, served as a channel for Communist propaganda. The Tibetan government did not wish to see any disturbances or foreign propaganda of any kind in Tibet. Knowing that the Chinese Mission was first established as a temporary means to settle pending disputes between Tibet and China and not as a permanent diplomatic mission, the government of Tibet, in July 1949, issued orders for the immediate departure of the Mission staff, as well as those Chinese traders concerned, through India to China. They were permitted to take their Tibetan wives, if they were willing to go, and to take all their properties along with them. Free transportation was provided to them up to the Indian border.

Shortly afterwards, the American Ambassador in India, Loy Henderson, wrote to me saying that the American radio commentator, Lowell Thomas, and his son, Lowell Thomas, Jr., wished to visit Lhasa. The Ambassador asked me to make it possible for the two adventurers to visit Lhasa. I informed the Foreign Bureau of this request and expressed the need for the world to know more about Tibet. The Foreign Bureau gave the necessary permits and within a few weeks, Lowell Thomas and his son were on their way to Lhasa. At Yatung, they met the Chinese, who were proceeding on their way back to China, via India. In Lhasa, they met with the Dalai Lama, the Regent, the Kashag, the Foreign Bureau, and many officials of the Tibetan government. After a little over one week in Lhasa, they journeyed back to their own country. Tibet received good publicity from their radio and television shows and from the book *Out of This World,* written by Lowell Thomas, Jr.

About that time, the United States Vice-Consul General, Douglas S. Mackiernam, accompanied by Frank Bessag and three White Russian friends, fled from Sinkiang towards Tibet, when the province fell into the hands of the Communists. After an arduous journey, they arrived in Tibet in May 1950 at a small district called Nagtsang. The United States government had, in the meantime, requested the Tibetan government, through the Indian government, to receive the Americans and to extend all necessary assistance. Accordingly, the Tibetan government sent instructions to the various check-posts, informing the guards of the expected arrival of the Americans, who were to be granted entry. Unfortunately, the Americans and their Russian friends had arrived at the Nagtsang check-post before the instructions from Lhasa. The guards, out of suspicion, recklessly fired on the Americans and their friends, killing the Vice-Consul General and two of the White Russians. The incident was most regrettable. The Lhasa authorities punished the guards for their recklessness in the presence of Frank Bessag, the surviving American, and his Russian friend.

18

The Communist Chinese Invasion

In October 1949, with the Communist regime in full control of main-land China, Radio Peking announced that Tibet was a part of China and that the People's Liberation Army would march into Tibet to lib-erate the Tibetans from foreign imperialists. The Tibetan government reacted strongly to the Peking announcement by stating that the rela-tionship between Tibet and China had been that of "priest and pa-tron" and that Tibet had never been a part of China. Moreover, there was no necessity for liberating Tibet from foreign imperialists as no foreign power controlled Tibet.

A year later, the Tibetan government appointed Tsecha Thubten Gyalpo and me as leaders of a special delegation to negotiate with China for the maintenance of Tibetan independence. The following is a summary in English translation of the contents of the credentials is-sued to the leaders of the delegation by the Tsongdu on the fifteenth day of the twelfth month of the Earth-Ox year (1950):

> Tibet, the Abode of Snow, ruled by the successive reincarna-tions of Chenresi (Avalokiteśvara) is an independent and peace loving country dedicated to religion. The country's peace is being disturbed and endangered by possible infiltration of defeated Chinese soldiers during the civil war in China, and though the Foreign Bureau of the government of Tibet has addressed a letter dated the twelfth day of the ninth month of the Earth-Ox year to Mao Tse-tung, Chairman of Communist China, to use his au-thority in checking Chinese troops from crossing into Tibetan territory, the Chinese have kept the request unanswered. Instead, radio announcements from Sining and Peking claimed Tibet as a part of China and instigated the people to the liberation of Tibet. The Delegation, with full authority to deal with matters con-

cerning Tibet, is to proceed for negotiations on the following
subjects:

    1. concerning the unanswered letter to Chairman Mao Tse-
tung from the Foreign Bureau of the Government of Tibet;

    2. concerning the atrocious radio announcements from Sining
and Peking;

    3. to secure an assurance that the territorial integrity of Tibet
will not be violated; and

    4. to inform the government of China that the people and
government of Tibet will not tolerate any interference in the
successive rule of the Dalai Lama, and they will maintain their
independence.

    The Delegation is instructed to negotiate on the above subjects
with a Chinese representative at a place close to China.

In India, while we sought the necessary visas to proceed to Hong
Kong, the Chinese informed us that their Ambassador was due to arrive in Delhi shortly and that we should open negotiations through
him. In Delhi, I met Prime Minister Nehru and informed him that
our mission was about to negotiate with China in regard to the maintenance of Tibetan independence. The Indian Prime Minister was also
informed that the treaty of 1904 and the Simla Convention of 1914
between the governments of Tibet and British India required the participation of the British government of India—an obligation now assumed by the government of India—in any negotiations that Tibet
made with a foreign country. I explained to the Prime Minister that if
he desired peace in Asia, Tibet should be recognized as an independent
buffer State. I told him that if two powerful nations bordered each
other, there would inevitably be friction between them. I strongly
urged the Prime Minister not to look to the immediate gain; but to
look into the future and consider the greater advantage to India's security if India supported the maintenance of Tibet's independence.
Meanwhile, the Chinese Ambassador, Yüan Chung-Hsien, arrived in
the Indian capital, and I held talks with him for several days; but
there was no satisfactory outcome. Finally, he asked me to accept the
following two points and to proceed to China in confirmation of the
agreement. The two points were that (1) China should handle matters concerning Tibetan national defense, and that (2) Tibet should
be recognized as part of China.

I informed the Chinese Ambassador that I would not agree to his proposals but that I would be glad to inform my government of them. Accordingly, I cabled my government in Lhasa and received an immediate reply instructing me not to accept the Chinese proposals. Before I could convey the message to the Chinese Ambassador, Chinese armed forces unexpectedly attacked eastern Tibet from eight different directions. The attack was on the twenty-third day of the seventh month of the Iron-Tiger year (October 7, 1950). I informed the Chinese Ambassador of the reports that I had received from my government and asked him to urge the government of China to withdraw its troops from Tibetan soil. The government of India was also informed of the Communist aggression in eastern Tibet.

On the eleventh day of the tenth month of the Iron-Tiger year (November 17, 1950) the Tsongdu offered the Dalai Lama full ruling power, even though he was only fifteen years old at the time, and Regent Taktra resigned from office. A few weeks later, the Dalai Lama, at the suggestion of the Tsongdu, left for Yatung. He appointed Lozang Tashi and Lukhangwa as joint Prime Ministers to managed the affairs of the country.

Before the Dalai Lama left Lhasa, the Chinese authorities in Ch'inghai province forced the Dalai Lama's eldest brother, Thubten J. Norbu, to proceed to Lhasa and persuade the Dalai Lama and the Tibetan government to accept Chinese rule over Tibet. They promised to reward him well for his services. Norbu, who had witnessed several months of Communist Chinese brutality and expansionist policies, grasped this opportunity to go to Lhasa and warn the Dalai Lama against the threatening dangers being imposed by the Chinese. Later, Norbu found it impossible to remain in Tibet and went to India, and from there to America.

The government of Tibet contended that Tibet was a sovereign and independent country at the time of the Chinese violation of its territorial integrity. Yet, on October 25, 1950, the People's Republic of China announced that "People's army units have been ordered to advance into Tibet to free three million Tibetans from the imperialist oppression and to consolidate national defenses on the western borders of China." [1] This announcement was made after the Chinese forces had already invaded Tibet on October 7. In the *Manifesto by Tibetan Leaders,* it is stated:

1. Chanakya Sen, *Tibet Disappears* (Bombay, 1960), p. 65.

To us Tibetans, the phrase "the liberation of Tibet," in its moral and spiritual implications, is a deadly mockery. The country of a free people was invaded and occupied under the pretext of liberation. Liberation from whom and what? Ours was a happy country with a solvent government and a contended people till the Chinese invasion of 1950.

On October 26, 1950, the government of India protested to the People's Republic of China against the use of force in Tibet and stated that the invasion was not in the interests of China or of peace. Two days later, a request reached the government of India from the government of Tibet, asking for India's help. On November 6 of the same year, the Foreign Under-Secretary to the British government, Ernest Davies, in a statement made to the House of Commons, said that Great Britain deplored the Chinese invasion and use of force in Tibet and "fully supported the stand taken by the Government of India." [2]

On November 7, in an appeal dated the twenty-seventh day of the ninth month of the Iron-Tiger year, which I cabled on November 11, 1950 to the United Nations Organization from Kalimpong, the Tibetan Kashag and Tsongdu protested against the Chinese invasion, which they called a flagrant act of aggression. The appeal to the United Nations stated in part:

> The armed invasion of Tibet for the incorporation of Tibet in communist China through sheer physical force is a clear case of aggression. As long as the people of Tibet are compelled by force to become a part of China against their will and consent, the present invasion of Tibet will be the grossest instance of the violation of the weak by the strong. We therefore appeal through you to the nations of the world to intercede on our behalf and restrain Chinese aggression. [3]

El Salvador formally raised the Tibetan question before the Secretary-General of the United Nations; but, following the Indian delegate's assertion that a peaceful solution, mutually advantageous to Tibet, China, and India, could be reached without a discussion in the United Nations, the steering committee of the General Assembly

2. *Tibet Disappears*, p. 66.
3. The complete text of the appeal to the United Nations is given in DALAI, pp. 249–53.

moved to postpone the Tibetan appeal. Although Great Britain had had good relations with Tibet and had concluded treaties with Tibet as a sovereign power—a clear mark of her recognition of Tibet's independence—the British delegate asserted that the legal position of Tibet was not very clear. This was a bitter disappointment to the Tibetans, because the British were well informed and clear about the Tibetan situation.

Three days after the British Foreign Under-Secretary's statement in the House of Commons, Indian Deputy Prime Minister and Minister of Home Affairs, Sardar Vallabhai Patel, said in New Delhi that "to use the sword against the traditionally peace-loving Tibetan people was unjustified. No other country in the world is as peace-loving as Tibet. The Chinese government did not follow India's advice to settle the Tibetan issue peacefully. They marched their armies into Tibet and explained this action by talking of foreign interests intriguing in Tibet against China. But this fear is unfounded." [4]

In an address to the Indian Parliament on November 14th, India's President, Rajendra Prasad, said:

> My Government have been consistently following a policy of friendship with our great neighbour country, China. It was a matter of deep regret to us, therefore, that the Chinese Government should have undertaken military operations in Tibet, when the way of peaceful negotiations was open to them. Tibet is not only a neighbour of India, but has had close cultural and other ties with us for ages past. India must, therefore, necessarily concern herself with what happens in Tibet and hope that the autonomy of this peaceful country will be preserved.[5]

When the Dalai Lama arrived at Yatung in November, 1950, the Kashag telegraphed me to come there immediately. On my arrival at Yatung, I reported the negotiations I had carried on in India. As the Indian government had not been of effective help and because the United Nations had postponed the Tibetan question, the Tibetan government appointed Dzasa Surkhang Surpa and a Secretary-General, Chosphel Thubten, to proceed to India to patch up the relations with the Communist Chinese government through its Ambassador in Delhi. The Chinese Ambassador welcomed this delegation and advised

4. *Tibet Disappears*, p. 66.
5. Ibid.

them to send a similar one to Peking. Subsequently, Dzasa Khemey and Secretary-General Thubten Tenthar were sent from Yatung to Peking. Khenchung Thubten Lekmon and Rimshi Sampo Sey were sent from Lhasa to Chamdo, where they joined the previously imprisoned Governor Ngabo, and then proceeded onto Peking.

Once in Chinese hands, the Tibetan Delegation had no alternative but to fall prey to Chinese pressure and to serve as an instrument for the construction of the so-called "Agreement on Measures for the Peaceful Liberation of Tibet," commonly referred to as the 17 Article Agreement of May 23, 1951.[6] It is to be noted that the Tibetan Delegation was not allowed to refer to the Dalai Lama or the Tibetan government for additional instructions. On top of this contempt and disregard for the generally accepted rules of international law and practices, "the Chinese forged duplicate Tibetan seals in Peking, and forced our delegation to seal the documents with them." [7]

Meanwhile at Yatung, the Dalai Lama arranged to have some relics of Lord Buddha and his disciples Śariputra and Maudgalyayana brought from the Indian Mahabodhi Society in Calcutta. The Dalai Lama held a grand reception and a religious ceremony, at which thousands of Buddhists from India, Bhutan, and Sikkim congregated to pay homage to the young Buddhist leader of Tibet.

In July 1951, General Chang Ching-wu, newly appointed Commissioner and Administrator of Civil and Military Affairs of Tibet, arrived at Yatung and requested the Dalai Lama to return to Lhasa. On the seventeenth day of the fifth month of the Iron-Hare year (July 24, 1951), the Dalai Lama departed from Yatung. I accompanied his party up to Phari and there received the permission of the Tibetan government to remain in India. The Dalai Lama reached Lhasa on the thirteenth day of the sixth month of the Iron-Hare year (August 17, 1951). On September 9th, several thousand Chinese Communist troops arrived in Lhasa under the command of Wang Chi-mei. These were followed soon after by some 20,000 Chinese troops under the command of Chang Kuo-hua and T'an Kuan-san.

With the arrival in Lhasa of the so-called Chinese Liberation forces, the oppression of the Tibetan people began. The Chinese forcibly demanded that the Tibetan government supply them with land for mili-

6. The complete text of this agreement is given in RICHARDSON, pp. 275–78, and in Ling Nai-min, *Tibetan Sourcebook* (Hong Kong, 1964), pp. 19–23.

7. DALAI, p. 88.

tary camps, in addition to enormous amounts of food for their soldiers. As a result, the stable Tibetan economy broke down. Tibetan resources ran low and prices rose many times. For the first time in history, the people of Lhasa were on the verge of famine. The people protested against the illegal measures adopted by the Chinese, but conditions continued to go from bad to worse.

The two Tibetan Prime Ministers, Lukhangwa and Lozang Tashi, strongly opposed the way in which the Chinese were handling Tibetan affairs and expressed their disapproval of Chinese policy. Lukhangwa asserted that the Chinese demand for enormous amounts of food could not be met, because Tibet's resources were just sufficient for her own needs. He stated that he saw no reason why such a massive Chinese force should be stationed in Lhasa. It was clear that the aim of the Chinese was political domination, which was to be effected after they had established complete physical domination of the Tibetan government and country. The unjust extortion of Tibetan resources and the armed suppression of Tibetans with grievances had brought the people to the verge of starvation. Lukhangwa, with courage and determination, asserted that the Chinese themselves had violated the so-called 17 Article Agreement, which they had forced on the Tibetans, and that it was therefore, absurd to refer to the terms of that agreement. He openly demanded the withdrawal of the Chinese forces, which had illegally occupied Tibet.

The grievances of the Tibetan people resulted in the forwarding of a six-point petition to the Tibetan government and to the Chinese General, Chang Ching-wu. The Chinese authorities accused the two Prime Ministers of conspiracy and of being imperialist agents backing the protest movement. They strongly demanded that the Dalai Lama remove Lukhangwa, who they claimed had obstructed their so-called welfare program. They warned that if the Dalai Lama would not remove him, troops would be called in to do so.

The Dalai Lama was placed in a difficult position, for, as he said, "I greatly admired Lukhangwa's courage in standing up to the Chinese, but now I had to decide whether to let him continue, or whether to bow yet again to a Chinese demand." He really had no choice but to meet the Chinese demands, for "to oppose and anger the Chinese authorities . . . could only lead us further along the vicious circle of repression and popular resentment." [8] Accordingly, the two Prime

8. Ibid., p. 97.

Ministers resigned on the second day of the third month of the Water-Dragon year (1952). Moreover, the Chinese authorities pressured the Tibetan government to imprison five of the Tibetan people's representatives, who had protested and were responsible for forwarding the six-point petition.

Let us turn now to the subject of the Panchen Lama. Three years after the death of the sixth Panchen Lama, the officials of Tashilhunpo, with the help of the Tibetan government and the other attendants of the Panchen Lama who had proceeded to Sining, began to look for the reincarnation of the Panchen Lama. In 1944 the officials of Tashilhunpo discovered two candidates, while the attendants at Sining discovered one. The government asked that all three candidates be brought to Tashilhunpo to undergo the traditional religious tests for the final selection of the true rebirth of the Panchen Lama. The attendants at Sining, however, requested the government to confirm their candidate as the Panchen Lama, promising to bring the candidate to Tibet if the government would accede to their request. Meanwhile, the Sining candidate was initiated into monkhood at the Kumbum monastery. The Tibetan government brought the other two candidates from Kham and initiated them into monkhood, one at the Drepung monastery, the other at Tashilhunpo.

A few years passed without the issue being resolved. The Nationalist government of China at first gave financial assistance, without making any commitments of recognition to the Sining candidate. However, when the Tibetan government asked the Chinese Mission in Lhasa to leave, the Nationalist government of China sent a representative to the Kumbum monastery, and on August 10, 1949, without resorting to any of the usual tests, officially recognized the Sining candidate as the reincarnation of the Panchen Lama. A few weeks later, Sining, the capital of Ch'ing-hai province, fell into the hands of the Communists. The Panchen Lama also fell into their hands. The Nationalist government had moved to Formosa, and the Governor of Ch'ing-hai, Ma Pu-fang, had deserted the province.

Soon after, the Panchen Lama, under the control of the Chinese Communists, felt compelled to support Mao Tse-tung and Chu Teh in their so-called liberation of Tibet. In 1951, during the signing of the so-called 17 Article Agreement, the Tibetan Delegation had no alternative but to recognize the Sining candidate as the seventh Panchen Lama. It is to be noted that while the Tibetan government regards the present Panchen Lama as the seventh in line, the attendants of the Panchen Lama claim him to be the tenth reincarnation. The difference stems from a disagreement concerning whether the first three rebirths are to be counted or not.

Following the compulsory resignation of the two Prime Ministers, the Panchen Lama, escorted by a large number of Communist Chinese troops, arrived in Lhasa by way of Sining on the fourth day of the third month of the Water-Dragon year (April 28, 1952). After calling on the Dalai Lama in the Potala, the Panchen Lama continued on to Tashilhunpo at Shigatse.

In the meantime, the Chinese began the construction of two roads between Lhasa and China, one from Szechuan via Kham, the other from Lanchow via Sining. An airfield was erected at Dam, some ninety miles north of Lhasa. Numerous political prisoners from China and thousands of laborers from Tibet were made to work on the roads. The Chinese publicly promised that the airfields and the highways would be used only for the benefit of the Tibetans; but, when work was completed, military supplies for their troops in Tibet began pouring in from China, marking yet another step in the consolidation of their dictatorial hold over Tibet.

The government of Tibet informed the Chinese that it would continue to introduce reforms in accordance with the local customs and prevailing conditions. There is a Tibetan saying that only when a house is built, can one live in it; only when the fruit is ripe, can one enjoy eating it. Accordingly, the Dalai Lama established a special committee, Legchos Lekhung, to deal with the reforms. This committee always found the Chinese obstructing them in their work, for the latter were bent on carrying out reforms in their own way.

In 1954 the Peking government invited the Dalai Lama and the Panchen Lama to attend the Chinese People's National Assembly in Peking. The Tibetan people were very much against the Dalai Lama proceeding to China for fear that he might be prevented from returning to Tibet. Amid scenes of great sorrow and the weeping of his people, the Dalai Lama had to leave for Peking on the eleventh day of the fifth month of the Wood-Horse year (July 11, 1954).

On his arrival in Peking, he attended the People's National Assembly and met several times with Chairman Mao Tse-tung, Vice-Chairman Chu Teh, and Prime Minister Chou En-lai. The Dalai Lama also met the Soviet leaders, Nikita Khrushchev and Nikolai Bulganin, at a reception on Chinese National Day. India's Prime Minister Nehru was also present and was met by the Dalai Lama. On all these occasions, the Dalai Lama was restricted from speaking freely. He was taken on a sightseeing tour of China, and to his birthplace near Kumbum.

Before his departure for Lhasa in March 1955, the Peking government proposed setting up a "Preparatory Committee for the Autonomous Region of Tibet." This move by the Chinese seemed ostensibly to promise participation in Chinese affairs by representatives from various regions of Tibet; but, in practice, such representatives were to be appointed only after approval by the Chinese government, which would naturally select its own favorites.

During his stay in China, the Dalai Lama and the Chinese government received thousands of letters from all over Tibet, requesting his immediate and safe return. On his way back to Lhasa, the Dalai Lama received invitations from all parts of the province of Kham, but he was able to visit only those towns and monasteries that lay on his route. To such places as Lithang, Chating, and Bah, he sent his junior tutor, Trijang Rimpoche, as his representative. Chung Rimpoche was sent to the district of Nyarong, and Karmapa Rimpoche to Derge and Nangchen, as his personal representatives.

Earlier, when the Dalai Lama had left Lhasa for China, his elder brother, Gyalo Thondup, Khenchung Lozang Gyaltsen, and I formed and headed a Committee for Tibetan Social Welfare (Bod-kyi Bde-don tshogs-pa). This Committee forwarded several letters to the Dalai Lama and Chairman Mao Tse-tung, emphasizing the fact that the absence of the Dalai Lama from Tibet was contrary to the wishes of the Tibetan people. The Committee requested his safe and immediate return to Lhasa. The Committee also forwarded a letter to Prime Minister Nehru, who was soon to proceed to Peking, requesting him to use his offices in making the Dalai Lama's immediate return possible.

On April 29, 1954, the government of India and the government of the People's Republic of China had signed an agreement, widely known as Panch Shila, or Five Principles of Peaceful Coexistence. In brief, that agreement called for the establishment of Chinese trade agencies in India, and Indian agencies in Tibet. It regulated the places where trade could be conducted in both countries, and also regulated the routes for traders, pilgrims, and officials.[9] Although the Panch Shila agreement dealt with the promotion of trade and cultural intercourse

9. The complete text of this agreement is given in RICHARDSON, pp. 278–85, and Ling, *Tibetan Sourcebook*, pp. 66–69.

between Tibet and India, the Tibetans were not a party to the agreement.

The Plenipotentiary of the government of India, Nedyam Raghavan, in his letter to Chang Han-fu, the Deputy Minister of Foreign Affairs of the government of the People's Republic of China, dated April 29, 1954, agreed on behalf of his government to withdraw the military escorts stationed at Yatung and Gyantse in Tibet, and to hand over to the Peking government, at a reasonable price, the postal, telegraph, and public telephone services, as well as the rest houses and land in Indian possession.

Following Article I of the Panch Shila agreement, India established trade agencies at Yatung, Gyantse, and Gartok, and China established hers at New Delhi, Calcutta, and Kalimpong. Because mutual noninterference in each other's internal affairs was one of the five principles agreed upon by China and India, the Chinese felt free to commit all kinds of atrocities in Tibet without regard to Indian feelings. India was now robbed of her 1904 and 1914 treaty rights, both as a mediating power on matters concerning Tibet and as a power with full rights to negotiate directly with the Tibetan government. The Panch Shila agreement was to be in force eight years. Because of current conditions, it was not renewed and accordingly expired on July 2, 1962, following which, the Indian trade agencies in Tibet and the Chinese trade agencies in India were closed.

In July 1954, a small lake, located at a place called Nyero on the Tibet–Bhutan border, broke open, and its rushing waters caused serious flooding of Gyantse, Panam, and Shigatse. The flood took the lives of hundreds of people, including the members of the Indian trade agency at Gyantse, along with their families and staff. Considerable land and property along the Nyangchu river were damaged.

In 1956 the Peking government sent Marshal Ch'en I, the Deputy Prime Minister, to preside at the inauguration of the Preparatory Committee for the Autonomous Region of Tibet. The Kashag ministers and all government officials had to go as far as Kidtsel Luding, one mile northwest of Norbulingka, to receive the Chinese representative. The Chinese authorities in Lhasa stressed that the Dalai Lama should also go to Kidtsel Luding. Strong criticisms were expressed by government officials and the Tibetan people; but the Dalai Lama agreed to go, for he felt that by doing so he could improve relations with the Chinese and gradually reduce their subversive activities.[10]

10. DALAI, p. 132.

Marshal Ch'en I arrived at Lhasa on the fifth day of the third month of the Fire-Ape year (April 17, 1956). A week later, the Preparatory Committee for the Autonomous Region of Tibet was officially inaugurated. The Dalai Lama was the Chairman; the Panchen Lama was first Vice-Chairman; Chang Kuo-hua, the second Vice-Chairman, and Ngawang Jigme Ngabo, Secretary General. The Committee had fifty-one members; but only fifteen of them, including the Dalai Lama, represented the Tibetan government. There were eleven members from among the leading monasteries, religious sects, civil committees, and prominent people. Ten more members represented the "Chamdo Liberation Committee," and a similar number represented the "Panchen Lama's Committee." The remaining five members were Chinese. The Committee was divided into thirteen departments, whose branches were established in every district of Tibet. The district offices were run jointly by a Chinese and a Tibetan officer, who functioned as commissioners. The Committee functioned only on matters that the Chinese authorities had already decided. Far from having a hand in the decision making, the Tibetan representatives could neither bring forward new proposals nor express any disagreement with Chinese decisions.

The Dalai Lama himself said:

Twenty of the members, although they were Tibetans, were representing the Chamdo Liberation Committee and the committee set up in the Panchen Lama's western district. These were both purely Chinese creations. Their representatives owed their positions mainly to Chinese support, and in return they had to support any Chinese proposition; though the Chamdo representatives did behave more reasonably than the Panchen Lama's. With this solid block of controlled votes, in addition to those of the five Chinese members, the Committee was powerless—a mere façade of Tibetan representation behind which all the effective power was exercised by the Chinese. In fact, all basic policy was decided by another body called the Committee of the Chinese Communist Party in Tibet, which had no Tibetan members. We were allowed to discuss the minor points, but we could never make any major changes. Although I was nominally chairman, there was nothing much I could do. Sometimes it was almost laughable to see how the proceedings were controlled and regulated, so that plans already completed in the other committee received a pointless and empty discussion and then were passed. But often I felt embarrassed at these meetings. I saw that the Chinese had only made me chairman in order to give an added appearance of Tibetan authority to their schemes.[11]

It was the year 1956 and India was preparing for the Buddha Jayanti, the two thousand five hundredth anniversary of the birth of the Lord Buddha. In the spring of the year, the Maharaj Kumar of Sikkim, who was President of the Mahabodhi Society of India, traveled to Lhasa with a letter from the Society, inviting the Dalai Lama to attend the Buddha Jayanti celebrations in India. The Dalai Lama gladly accepted the invitation. As the time for the Dalai Lama's departure for India drew near, the Chinese authorities in Lhasa insisted that his presence was necessary in the Tibetan capital. There was a lot of work for the Preparatory Committee, and there had been several uprisings in the provinces of Kham and Amdo. Subsequently, Trijang Rimpoche, the junior tutor of the Dalai Lama, was appointed as a representative of the Dalai Lama and he made preparations to go to India.

As this was an important Buddhist occasion, the lamas of the great monasteries of Lhasa and the suburbs, the people of Lhasa, and others strongly voiced their opinion that the Dalai Lama himself ought to attend the Buddha Jayanti. Moreover, Prime Minister Nehru had advised Peking that it would be beneficial if the Dalai Lama could come to India for the celebrations. The Chinese authorities finally agreed to let the Dalai Lama make the trip and arrangements were subsequently made for him to be accompanied by the Panchen Lama, the Dalai Lama's two tutors, and three council ministers. Before the departure of the party, the Chinese did not fail to instruct the Dalai Lama on what to do, and they gave him prepared speeches to read.

After riding on horseback only one day in order to cross the Nathu La pass, the Dalai Lama traveled by car from Lhasa to Siliguri, where he boarded a special plane at the Bagdogra airport, bound for Delhi. On November 25, 1956, the Dalai Lama arrived at the Palam airport in the Indian capital, where he was received by India's Vice-President, its Prime Minister, and many other leaders and foreign dignitaries. The Dalai Lama attended a UNESCO meeting and on one occasion

11. DALAI, p. 133.

made a speech in which he traced the path of Buddhism from India to Tibet and described its present position in his country.[12] Disregarding all Chinese instructions and prepared speeches, he went on to say that while all the world was preaching peace, there were instances where tiny independent nations were being devoured by strong and large nations. This, he emphasized, should not pass unnoticed.

From New Delhi, the Dalai Lama went on a pilgrimage to most of the sacred places of India. He visited many industrial sites as well. From Kalimpong, Gyalo Thondup, Khenchung Lozang Gyaltsen and I led some of the members of the Committee for Tibetan Social Welfare and we journeyed with the Dalai Lama's party. We met many times with the council ministers and informed them that we had heard that the Chinese were resorting to "forced reforms" in Kham and Amdo and that these reforms were being strongly resisted by the local people. We also had heard that the Chinese were violating the 17 Article Agreement and were killing monks and destroying religious institutions in those regions. We disclosed these and many other statements that we had heard, and then questioned members of the Dalai Lama's party as to their reliability and whether there was danger that such atrocities would be committed in Ü-Tsang as well.

For some time, the council ministers did not give us a clear reply, but then one day, during a period of leisure, they likened Tibet to an egg placed under the raised foot of an elephant. The elephant was China, and the life of the egg depended upon the elephant's action. We asked them whether they had any plans for extricating the country from such a deplorable situation; but the officials were wary of each other, and none, even if he did have any such plans, attempted to give us a clear picture of the Tibetan situation under Chinese rule.

For many days we pressed them to grasp this opportunity and make it possible for the Dalai Lama to remain in India, at least for the time being. During such a time, peaceful negotiations might be conducted with the Peking government through the Indian government. We could then hope that a favorable settlement would be reached for the future of the country. The council ministers said that they would refer these suggestions to Peking. We do not know whether they did or not, but it is clear that the Dalai Lama had spoken earlier to Prime Minister Nehru of his desire "to stay in India until we could win back our

12. See the Appendix.

freedom by peaceful means." [13] The Indian Prime Minister advised the Dalai Lama to return to Tibet and work peacefully with the Chinese, relying on the 17 Article Agreement. He promised to discuss the matter with the Chinese Prime Minister, Chou En-lai, who was coming to India. It was eventually decided that the Dalai Lama should return to Lhasa.

While the Dalai Lama was in Delhi, Mao Tse-tung made a public announcement on February 7, 1957, that Tibet was not ready for the introduction of new reforms. At the same time, the Communist Chinese authorities in Tibet announced that land reforms for Tibet would be postponed for six years. If after this period, the Tibetan people were still unwilling to accept reforms, then the introduction of the reforms would again be postponed for fifteen, or even fifty, years. The Chinese authorites in Lhasa also announced that the Preparatory Committee for the Autonomous Region of Tibet would be reduced in size.

Before the Dalai Lama left Delhi, he personally extended an invitation to Prime Minister Nehru to visit Tibet, an invitation that was gladly accepted by the Prime Minister. Later events in Tibet caused the invitation to be withdrawn by the Chinese.

On the eve of his departure from India, the Dalai Lama was invited to visit Kalimpong, a Tibetan trade center and a home for many Tibetan émigrés. The Chinese, however, objected to this visit on the pretext that there were imperialist and Kuomintang agents in Kalimpong who might harm the person of the Dalai Lama. Nevertheless, the Dalai Lama visited Kalimpong and remained a week at Bhutan House as the guest of Rani Chuni Dorji, mother of Jigme Dorji, the late Prime Minister of Bhutan.

In Kalimpong, the Dalai Lama attended religious functions and preached to the hundreds of people who flocked to hear him and to receive his blessing. Once more, as the guest of the late Maharaja of Sikkim, the Dalai Lama held similar functions in Gangtok. His departure to Lhasa was delayed temporarily by reports of heavy snowfall in Tibet. Finally, on the eleventh day of the twelfth month of the Fire-Ape year (1957), the Dalai Lama, accompanied by his retinue, departed for Lhasa, where he arrived on April 1, 1957. Some three weeks earlier, out of fear for the lives of the Panchen Lama and Ngawang Jigme Ngabo, the Chinese had them flown to Lhasa by aircraft.

13. DALAI, p. 148.

While in India, the Panchen Lama had invited the Dalai Lama to visit Tashilhunpo, when returning home to Lhasa. In the course of his journey, the Dalai Lama was met by a high-ranking representative of the Panchen Lama, who renewed the invitation to visit Tashilhunpo. When the Dalai Lama and his retinue reached Gyantse, he was met by leading officials of the Tibetan government, who requested him to visit Shigatse Dzong, before proceeding to the Tashilhunpo monastery. Shigatse Dzong was a place of historic importance, for it was there that the great fifth Dalai Lama was led in state and enthroned by Gushri Khan in 1642 as the supreme authority over all Tibet from Tachienlu in the east up to Ladakh's border in the west. The Dalai Lama then visited Shigatse Dzong for three days and afterwards spent two days at Tashilhunpo, before traveling on to Lhasa.

In Lhasa, the Chinese, in complete disregard of their earlier statements of slowing down reforms, now resorted to full-scale propaganda methods to influence the Tibetan mind toward accepting their reforms. The Tibetan government drew up a plan to introduce necessary reforms in accordance with the will of the people, the customs, and the prevailing conditions. The Tibetan government was fully aware of the need for change, but it wished to introduce changes in a peaceful and orderly manner, without compulsion or social disruption. Accordingly, the Tibetan government put proposals to the Chinese authorities for certain reforms; but, as these proposals did not fit in with the Chinese plans, they were completely ignored.

The Dalai Lama himself referred to reform in a statement issued at a press conference held in Mussoorie, India on June 20, 1959, saying:

> At this point I wish to emphasize that I and my government have never been opposed to the reforms which are necessary in the social, economic, and political systems prevailing in Tibet. We have no desire to disguise the fact that ours is an ancient society, and that we must introduce immediate changes in the interests of the people of Tibet. In fact, during the last nine years several reforms were proposed by me and my government, but every time these measures were strenuously opposed by the Chinese in spite of popular demand for them, with the result that nothing was done for the betterment of the social and economic conditions of the people. In particular, it was my earnest desire that the system of land tenure should be radically changed without

further delay and the large landed estates acquired by the State on payment of compensation for distribution among the tillers of the soil. But the Chinese authorities deliberately put every obstacle in the way of carrying out this just and reasonable reform.[14]

From 1957 on, the Communist Chinese engaged in intensive preparations in the building up of their military forces. This no doubt indicated that they were prepared to use force in carrying out reforms whether or not the Tibetans chose to go along with their plans.

14. The full body of the Dalai Lama's statement is given in *Dalai Lama and India* (New Delhi, 1959), pp. 158–62, edited by A. V. Rau.

19

The Revolt

By 1958 the Tibetan peoples of the Kham and Amdo regions were taking to the mountains as guerrilla fighters. The Chinese had used artillery to shell monasteries and towns without mercy. Cases of genocide were widespread. The resistance movement had grown considerably and gradually spread to other provinces of Tibet. The Chinese authorities actually informed the Dalai Lama that unless he went along with their policy, they would have to regard him as they did Gungthang Lama and Shar Kalden Gyatso, two well-known Amdo lamas. This was a warning to the Dalai Lama, because Shar Kalden Gyatso and Gunthang Lama had been imprisoned for repeatedly opposing the Chinese.

At the same time, local Tibetan newspapers, dated November 28, 1958, in Kantse, carried Chinese propaganda, which blasphemously denounced religion and accused the Lord Buddha of being a reactionary. The same denouncements were made in the local newspapers of Sining and Tachienlu. Day by day, conditions in Tibet became more tense. In Lhasa, the Chinese announced that all Khampas, Amdowas, and other people from eastern Tibet, residing in Lhasa, Shigatse, and surrounding areas, would have to return to their native regions. If these orders were not heeded, then the people from those regions would be arrested and forcibly returned to eastern Tibet.

The eastern Tibetan people, who were headed by Adruk Gompo Tashi, went quite openly to a district called Drigu in the south, where they formed a stronghold of several thousand men and made contact with leaders of various resistance movements all over Tibet. At Drigu, the revolutionary group formed an army, called the Danglang Tensung Makhar, or Voluntary National Defense Army. Resistance increased and attacks on Chinese convoys and military camps became frequent. Increasing numbers of people who had suffered under the Chinese now found their way to the revolutionary camps to join in the fight against their oppressors. It was at this time that the Committee for Tibetan Social Welfare in India, becoming concerned about the serious conditions in Tibet and fearing the destruction of that beautiful land, its religion, people, and monasteries, appealed to the freedom-loving nations of the world to intercede on behalf of Tibet and bring about peace in the country.

In southern Tibet, the local people suffered to some extent from the growing strength of the Voluntary National Defense Army; however, they bore the burden of giving support and supplies to the Army, because they knew it was fighting for Tibet's independence. There were many instances when Chinese troops, disguised as Tibetan Khampas, fell upon the local people inflicting much damage and suffering on them. This cruel Chinese policy was intended to disunite the fighters and the local people; fortunately, the local people were well aware of such things.

A change in Chinese policy took place. The Chinese armies had been trying to crush the revolts in eastern Tibet, but with little success. Instead, their attacks had created even more hatred and opposition. The Chinese therefore insisted that the Tibetan government should take action against the resistance forces by dispatching Tibetan troops to suppress the revolts. The Tibetan government pondered over this matter and concluded that if Tibetan troops were sent to fight the Voluntary National Defense Army, it would be a question of Tibetans killing Tibetans. This was the worst possible thing that could happen and was out of the question. Another possibility was that Tibetan troops sent to cope with the revolts might instead join the revolutionary forces, resulting in greater disturbances and more suffering for the Tibetan people. The Chinese had already threatened to use heavily armed Chinese troops to crush the revolt if the Tibetan government did not take action. The government was reluctant to do anything, but eventually a decision was made to send government representatives to various revolutionary posts and to try to persuade the guerrillas to lay down their arms peacefully. This plan was carried out, but the representatives failed to fulfill their missions.

In the same year, the Tibetan people were hoping for the promised visit of Prime Minister Jawaharlal Nehru. A visit from that world famous statesman would indeed have helped Tibet's cause, for the In-

dian Prime Minister would have seen for himself the actual conditions
in the country. His presence might even have led to a peaceful settlement of the conflict between the Tibetans and the Chinese. When the
Prime Minister expressed his desire to make the visit in that year, the
Chinese authorities informed him that conditions in the country were
bad and that they would not be able to guarantee his safety. The
Prime Minister was politely asked to postpone his visit indefinitely.

By the end of 1958, the Tibetan resistance movement had grown so
much in strength that it was in a position to control completely almost all the districts of southern Tibet and numerous areas in eastern
Tibet. The Tibetan government, while trying to settle peacefully all
conflicts in favor of Tibet, felt its chances dwindling as the Chinese
steadily strengthened their forces. News continued to reach Lhasa of
the victories of the Tibetan Army and intense feelings of patriotism
inspired the people in and around Lhasa, but over it all reigned a constant anxiety for the safety of the Dalai Lama's person.

Then, in February 1959, during the Monlam festival, when the
Dalai Lama took his final examinations as a Master of Metaphysics, the
Chinese authorities invited him to see a dramatic show. They informed
the commander of the Dalai Lama's bodyguard that the Dalai Lama
was to come to the Chinese military camp unescorted. This was highly
irregular. Customarily, wherever the Dalai Lama went, he was escorted by his bodyguards, and troops would line the route. The Chinese request was discussed by the government officials, who regarded
the invitation with suspicion. Word went around that the Dalai Lama
was to visit the Chinese military camp and the people of Lhasa feared
that he might be kidnapped by the Communists.

The Dalai Lama was to visit the Chinese camp on the tenth of
March. On that day, some 30,000 Tibetans from Lhasa surrounded
the Norbulingka in an attempt to protect the Dalai Lama from the
Chinese. The Tibetan people protested angrily and demonstrated
against the Chinese. At the same time, reports reached India of the
critical situation in Tibet, and the world's newspapers soon broke the
news of the Tibetan uprising. Hundreds of Tibetans living in Kalimpong sent repeated telegrams to Prime Minister Nehru, asking the
government of India to intervene in the interests of Tibet and humanity. Later, a deputation of Tibetans living in northern India, headed
by Prime Minister Lukhangwa, arrived in Delhi and met with Prime
Minister Nehru and leaders of India to seek their intervention and as-

sistance. During this time, there had been numerous instances of Tibetans, who, shocked and saddened by news of tragic events in Tibet, died or became mentally ill.

In Lhasa, several officials of the government of Tibet, together with leaders chosen by the populace, held an emergency meeting and declared that Tibet no longer recognized Chinese authority based on the 17 Article Agreement. This was followed by mass demonstrations against the Communist regime. The spirit of freedom inspired the people. Tibetan soldiers who had been made to wear Chinese uniforms discarded them and put on Tibetan uniforms. Meanwhile, the Dalai Lama made repeated attempts to reduce the mounting tension. He wrote letters to the Chinese General, T'an Kuan-san, that were no more than efforts to placate the Chinese and persuade them to desist from violence. They were letters written during hours of desperation, turmoil, and confusion.

The Dalai Lama himself said, "I replied to all his letters to gain time—time for anger to cool on both sides, and time for me to urge moderation of the Lhasan people . . . my most urgent moral duty at that moment was to prevent a totally disastrous clash between my unarmed people and the Chinese army." [1]

Wild confusion and uncertainty reigned everywhere in Lhasa, and the Voluntary National Defense Army and guerrilla fighters had cut all Chinese communications in southern Tibet. Uprisings followed in many other regions. Representatives of the Lhasa people approached the residence of the Indian Consul General asking for his intervention. Later on, thousands of women and children flocked to the Indian and Nepalese consulates to seek help.

The Tibetans assembled to protect the Dalai Lama. Gathering what arms they could find, they began to set up defensive posts all around the Norbulingka. On the night of March 17, 1959, the Dalai Lama, in disguise, escaped and fled towards India. The Chinese did not know of his escape, even though the Dalai Lama and his party passed close by a Chinese troop encampment.

After reaching the south bank of the Tsangpo River, the Dalai Lama was under the protection of the guerrilla fighters. On hearing that the Chinese had dissolved the Tibetan government, the Dalai Lama and his party immediately formed a new temporary government on March 29, 1959, at Yugyal Lhuntse, during their flight to

1. DALAI, p. 187.

India. When they reached Tsona, the Dalai Lama dispatched two emissaries to India. These reached the Indian border check-post at Kanzeymane, near Chuthangmu, and requested political asylum for the Dalai Lama and the Tibetan refugees. Soon after, Prime Minister Nehru officially announced in the Lok Sabha that the Government of India had granted asylum to the Dalai Lama.

When the Dalai Lama reached Tezpur on April 18, he announced:

> On March 17, two or three mortar shells were fired in the direction of the Norbulingka palace. Fortunately, the shells fell in a pond nearby. After this, the Advisers became alive to the danger to the person of the Dalai Lama and in those difficult circumstances, it became imperative for the Dalai Lama, the members of his family, and his high officials to leave Lhasa.[2]

On March 19, two days after the Dalai Lama's flight from Lhasa, the Chinese had shelled the Norbulingka, the Potala, and other strategic places in Lhasa. The shelling was followed by tank and infantry attacks. Some 12,000 people were mercilessly killed, and many were taken prisoners. Not until the third day did the Chinese learn of the Dalai Lama's escape; they immediately sent troops and aircraft in pursuit, but failed to spot the fleeing party. It was not long before thousands of Tibetan refugees, in pitiful conditions, began crossing into India and neighboring countries over all possible routes.

On his arrival in India, the Dalai Lama was given a warm welcome. Letters reached him from many world leaders, expressing sympathy at the tragic events and joy at his safe arrival in India. With his arduous flight to freedom over, the Dalai Lama, with his entourage, settled down in Mussoorie, a summer resort town in the hills of northern India. Newsmen from around the world crowded into Mussoorie to hear what the Dalai Lama had to say; but in the hope that peaceful negotiations might be effected with the Chinese government, the Dalai Lama refrained from making any press statements for a few months.

On April 24th, Prime Minister Nehru met with the Dalai Lama at Mussoorie. Then, on May 30th, Indian supporters of Tibet's independence held a convention in Calcutta, presided over by Jayaprakash Narayan, the Sarvodaya leader. The convention passed a resolution agreeing to set up an Afro-Asian committee to help promote a sympathetic climate of opinion on Tibet.

2. *Dalai Lama and India*, pp. 156–57.

On June 20th, the Dalai Lama held his first press conference and gave a clear picture of the political status that he desired for his country. He said, "I and my Government are . . . fully prepared to welcome a peaceful and amicable solution of the present tragic problem, provided that such a solution guarantees the preservation of the rights and powers which Tibet has enjoyed and exercised without any interference prior to 1950." [3]

In Mussoorie, officials of the Dalai Lama held a meeting at which it was decided to look to the major problems of relief and welfare of the Tibetan refugees, who had arrived by the thousands. I myself was appointed the official representative of the Dalai Lama in New Delhi to see to the growing need of refugee relief and resettlement. A Central Relief Committee was set up to coordinate the help received from various voluntary agencies and from governments of various foreign countries. The government of India gave much assistance and established village settlements in suitable districts.

A few months later, the Dalai Lama visited Delhi and met with the heads of the Indian government and various dignitaries of foreign countries. At this time, the possibility of bringing the Tibetan question into the United Nations was discussed. Accordingly, the Dalai Lama, in a speech delivered at Delhi on September 5, 1959, said, "It is in these circumstances that despite the advice which we have received from the Government of India, we have decided to appeal to the U.N. It is our cherished hope and our fervent faith that whatever be the result of this appeal, the cause of truth and humanity will ultimately triumph." [4]

Soon afterwards, the Federation of Malaya and the Republic of Ireland secured the inclusion of the Tibetan case on the agenda of the fourteenth session of the United Nations. The Dalai Lama assigned his elder brother, Gyalo Thondup, Rinchen Sadutshang, and me to represent Tibet and to seek support for the Tibetan case. On October 9, amid heated opposition from the Communist bloc, the General Committee of the United Nations debated whether the Tibetan question should be included for discussion in the General Assembly. By the middle of October, the General Assembly considered the General Committee's recommendation that the Tibetan issue be discussed. A

3. *Dalai Lama and India*, p. 162.

4. The text of the Dalai Lama's appeal to the United Nations, dated September 9, 1959, is given in DALAI, pp. 253–55.

resolution was finally passed by a vote of 45 to 9, with 26 abstentions. Costa Rica's vote was later recorded in favor of the resolution. The resolution, without making any reference to the Communist Chinese or their invasion and occupation of Tibet, stated, in part:

> Mindful also of the distinctive cultural and religious heritage of the people of Tibet and of the autonomy which they have traditionally enjoyed . . . [the General Assembly] 1. Affirms its belief that respect for the principles of the Charter and of the Universal Declaration of Human Rights is essential for the evolution of a peaceful world based on the rule of law, 2. Calls for respect for the fundamental human rights of the Tibetan people and for their distinctive cultural and religious life.[5]

5. The full text of the Resolution, with a list of the countries casting votes, is given in RICHARDSON, pp. 286–87.

Conclusion

Tibet's historical and political development clearly shows that it was a sovereign country, which enjoyed the right to negotiate treaties and to have direct relations with her neighbors. During World War I, Tibet offered to send her soldiers to fight on the side of the British. During World War II, she remained neutral in spite of the combined pressure brought to bear by the governments of Great Britain, China, and the United States for permission to transport war materials and supplies to China through Tibet. This alone is conclusive proof that Tibet controlled her own affairs, internally and externally. Tibet had her own national defense forces and even sent soldiers abroad for military training. She had her own postage and currency, and had direct trade relations with her neighbors. Tibetan representatives participated in the first Asian Conference in New Delhi, carrying their own national flag as a symbol of Tibetan independence. Most significant of all is the fact that Tibetan delegates traveled around the world on *Tibetan* passports, which were accepted as legal documents by the United States, the United Kingdom, and other countries. Finally, in the 1960 report to the International Commission of Jurists by the Legal Inquiry Committee on Tibet, the following is stated:

> The view of the Committee was that Tibet was at the very least a *de facto* independent State when the Agreement on Peaceful Measures in Tibet was signed in 1951, and the repudiation of this agreement by the Tibetan Government in 1959 was found to be fully justified. . . . Tibet demonstrated from 1913 to 1950 the conditions of statehood as generally accepted under international law.[1]

With all of these demonstrable sovereign rights, why was Tibet unable to defend herself from the Communist Chinese invasion and the violation of her independence?

Some of the major causes of Tibet's crisis may be summarized as follows:

1. *Tibet and the Chinese People's Republic* (Geneva, 1960), p. 5.

1. The world was not informed of the historical evidences of Tibet's independence.

2. The world was not clearly informed of the true nature of the "priest-patron" relationship between the Sakya lamas and the Mongol khans, and later on, between the Dalai Lamas and the Manchu emperors.

3. It was the policy of the British government of India and the Manchu Court of China to isolate Tibet from the rest of the world, which gave China the means by which to paint a false picture of Tibet's international position and to obstruct Tibet from revealing its political independence.

4. With the end of World War II, neighboring India became independent of the British, while China passed under a Communist regime. India, being deeply involved in her own development as an independent country, coupled with her continual conflict with Pakistan, lost sight of what was happening to Tibet. Pakistan leaned to the West for friendship and support and India, pursuing a policy of non-alignment, sought to make friends with Communist China. This resulted in India implementing a soft policy towards China in regard to Tibet, which finally paved the way for an easy invasion of Tibet by China in 1950, under the pretext of liberating Tibet from "foreign imperialists." As long as the Chinese Communists remain in Tibet, there will be no peace and security for the neighboring independent countries, a fact clearly demonstrated by the Chinese invasion of India in October 1962.

It is difficult to predict what the future holds for Tibet. Relying on the historical point of view and the belief that truth must triumph in the end, Tibet should eventually regain her independence. Tibetans have suffered greatly. The brutal suppression of a country and people so peace-loving as the Tibetans has shocked and awakened the free nations of the world. Tibetans in their own country remain in constant terror and even though they deeply desire freedom, that desire can not be effectively expressed under the overwhelming weight and brutality of Communist Chinese power.

It is those thousands of Tibetans who have taken refuge in India and other countries who must ensure the survival of their distinct creed and the preservation of their religion and culture, under the light of truth and the sound leadership of the Dalai Lama. The refugees in their plight must now wake to the need for unity among themselves and to the importance of education. Tibetan morale is higher than ever; but this alone is not the way to regain freedom. It is important that the world be continuously informed of the question of Tibet and that Tibet should seek increasing support and lasting friendship from the freedom-loving nations of the United Nations. Even former Soviet Premier, Nikita Khrushchev, called for the freedom of all colonial people, and the fact remains that Tibet is now in the position of a colonial country. Tibet looks hopefully, therefore, for support even from Russia.

The Chinese people as a whole are not to be blamed. The atrocities in Tibet are being committed by a few political leaders of Communist China. Power must be handled carefully, and the misuse of it is the curse of the present age. The Chinese are not Tibet's overlords, and there is a faint possibility that China will in time return Tibet to the Tibetans, just as many countries today are receiving their independence after being dominated by other nations. It is also possible that a time will come when the Chinese Communists, in accordance with their promise, will leave Tibet in the hands of the Tibetans after having developed the country. However, the realization of such possibilities seems remote and unlikely in view of current circumstances.

In this day and age, we have seen newly independent nations become involved in internal strife on account of either differing political ideologies or simply the love of political fame and power. We have also seen nations divide and become formidable foes of each other. The divisions of India and Pakistan, South Korea and North Korea, South Vietnam and North Vietnam, and the Congo are unforgettable instances of this. Tibetans must learn from these examples of political fragmentation.

Tibetans must not perpetuate provincialism or sectarianism. They should not be conscious of whether they come from Ü, Tsang, Kham, or Amdo; they must be conscious only of the fact that they are all Tibetans. They must be well organized and united to defend their rights; and they must strive to live and function under the leadership of the Dalai Lama in their struggle for a free, democratic state.

Appendix

1. LADAKHI LETTER OF AGREEMENT, 1842

The following is a translation of the original letter written in Tibetan:

Shri Khalsaji Apsarani Shri Maharajah; Lhasa representative Kalon Surkhang; investigator Dapon Peshi, commander cf forces; Balana, the representative of Gulam Kahandin; and the interpreter Amir Shah, have written this letter after sitting together. We have agreed that we have no ill-feelings because of the past war. The two kings will henceforth remain friends forever. The relationship between Maharajah Gulab Singh of Kashmir and the Lama Guru of Lhasa (Dalai Lama) is now established. The Maharajah Sahib, with God (Kunchok) as his witness, promises to recognize ancient boundaries, which should be looked after by each side without resorting to warfare. When the descendants of the early kings, who fled from Ladakh to Tibet, now return, they will be restored to their former stations. The annual envoy from Ladakh to Lhasa will not be stopped by Shri Maharajah. Trade between Ladakh and Tibet will continue as usual. Tibetan government traders coming into Ladakh will receive free transport and accommodations as before, and the Ladakhi envoy will, in turn, receive the same facilities in Lhasa. The Ladakhis take an oath before God (Kunchok) that they will not intrigue or create new troubles in Tibetan territory. We have agreed, with God as witness, that Shri Maharajah Sahib and the Lama Guru of Lhasa (Dalai Lama) will live together as members of the same household. We have written the above on the second of Assura, Sambhat 1899 (September 17, 1842).

Sealed by the Wazir, Dewan,
Balana, and Amir Shah.

2. TIBETAN LETTER OF AGREEMENT, 1842

The following is a translation of the original Tibetan letter:

This agreement is made in the interests of the friendship between the Lhasa authorities and Shri Maharajah Sahib and Maharajah Gulab Singh. On the thirteenth day of the eighth month of the Water-Tiger year (September 17, 1842), the Lhasa representative Kalon Surkang, investigator Dapon Peshi, Shri Raja Sahib Dewan Hari Chand and Wazir Ratun Sahib, the representative

327

of Shri Maharajah Sahib, sat together amicably with Kunchok (God) as
witness. This document has been drawn up to ensure the lasting friendship
of the Tibetans and the Ladakhis. We have agreed not to harm each other
in any way, and to look after the interests of our own territories. We agree
to continue trading in tea and cloth on the same terms as in the past, and
will not harm Ladakhi traders coming into Tibet. If any of our subjects stray
into your country, they should not be protected. We will forget past differences between the Lhasa authority and Shri Maharajah. The agreement
arrived at today will remain firmly established forever. Kunchok (God),
Mount Kailash, Lake Manasarowar, and Khochag Jowo have been called as
witnesses to this treaty.

Sealed by Kalon Surkhang
and Dapon Peshi.

3. Tibet-Ladakh Trade Agreement, 1853

The following is a translation of the Tibetan original:

During the last year, Kelzang Gyurme, a Tibetan government trader, has
not been able to bring a full quota of brick tea into Ladakh. Usually the
Ladakhis provide a certain number of horses to transport the tea, but this
year, they did not provide any, claiming that there was an insufficient quantity
of tea to be transported. Kelzang Gyurme, on the other hand, claims that
it is not a question of the quantity of tea brought in; but, of the number of
horses that are supposed to be supplied. As this has caused misunderstanding,
two Tibetan stewards of the Gartok Governor met with representatives
of Ladakh, Bisram Sahib and Kalon Rigzin, and a mediator, Yeshe Wangyal,
and concluded this agreement over future procedures.

It was agreed that the Ladakhis would supply horses to the Tibetan trade
agencies according to the limit previously agreed upon.

It was further agreed by the two governors of Gartok that they would
recommend to the Lhasa government that in the future more capable trade
agents should be sent to Ladakh; the Ladakhis agreed to send better envoys
to Tibet to pay the annual oath of allegiance.

Whenever Tibetan government trade agents arrive at Ladakh, they are to
be provided with kitchen boys and grooms for their horses, as in the past.
Tibetan traders bringing tea to Gartok and Ladakhi traders bringing cloth to
Gartok should trade only with each other, and not with any third party. The
boundary between Ladakh and Tibet will be maintained according to the
established custom.

Salt and wool carried from Rudok (a district in western Tibet) to
Ladakh should not be turned back. Similarly, *tsamba* (barley flour) and grain

taken from Ladakh to Rudok should not be restricted. The prices of commodities and custom duties must not be raised by traders on either side; they must be maintained at the previous level.

Tibetan traders carrying a permit from the Gartok Governor and Ladakhi traders carrying a similar permit from Thanedar are exempted from custom duties and need only make a token offering to the authorities. Traders without permits will have to pay a two per cent custom duty.

Both parties agree that the local inhabitants of the two countries will provide free transport and accommodations to special agents traveling in emergencies. These agents will carry letters of authority.

Tibetan and Ladakhi traders may freely graze their pack-animals at any place in both territories, on the condition that they do not bring domestic animals with them.

Local officials will cooperate with each other in implementing this agreement.

> Signed and sealed by Thanedar Bisram
> and Kalon Rigzin of Ladakh,
> and the two stewards of the
> Tibetan Governor at Gartok.
> Witnessed by Yeshe Wangyal.

4. Speech by His Holiness, the Dalai Lama, at the Symposium on Buddhism's Contribution to Art, Letters, and Philosophy on November 29, 1956, at New Delhi, India

Mr. Chairman, distinguished Prime Minister, fellow delegates, and friends.

His Holiness the Panchen Lama and I are highly honored by the opportunity to address this symposium before it concludes its deliberations this afternoon. We are indeed grateful to the Government of India and the Working Committee for the Buddha Jayanti celebrations in India for their very kind invitation to visit India during the 2,500th Anniversary of the Buddha's Parinirvana and for the excellent program of visits arranged for us.

As we are all interested in the development and spread of the Dharma, I am sure you will be interested to know something of the evolution and development of Buddhism in Tibet.

In the early seventh century, during the reign of the Tibetan King Srongtsan Gampo, Thonmi Sambhota and many other Tibetan students were deputed to India to learn the literature of the Dharma. Having learned Sanskrit grammar and literature thoroughly from Pandit Lha Rigba Sengge and other scholars of Kashmir, these students returned to Tibet. Thonmi

Sambhota invented the Tibetan script based on the Nagari and Sharda scripts of northern and central India respectively. They translated many books into Tibetan.

In the eighth century, during the reign of the Tibetan King Trisong Detsan, many great Indian scholars, such as Acharya Shantirakshita, Padma Sambhava, Bimala Mitra, and Kamala Shila, were invited to Tibet. Many Tibetan students, such as Ishes Wangbo and Berochana, studied Sanskrit and translated numerous books on Mahayana and Vajrayana into Tibetan. Seven Tibetan men became bhikshus. The cultural and spiritual relations of India and Tibet have gone on increasing ever since.

In the ninth century, the Tibetan King Tri-Ralpachen invited many scholars, such as Jina Mena, Surendra, Ratna Bodhi, and Bhodi Dhana Shila, who revived the old translations and rewrote them into a more standardized Tibetan language. During the reign of the cruel King Lang-darma, Buddhism declined to a low ebb, surviving only in remote Tibetan villages. But many great men, including notably Lachen Gonpa Rapsal, raised it again from its very foundations. Many Tibetan scholars, such as Rinchen Zangpo, Gyaltsen Sengge, and Tsultrim Gyalwa of Nagtso, came to India. Having completed their studies at Nalanda and Vikramashila viharas, they invited many un-rivaled Indian scholars, such as the great swami Dipamkarajnyana, Sakya Shri of Kashmir, and Mritijnyana to Tibet. In the course of time they translated all the teachings of the Buddha and the works of the Indian scholars into Tibetan. Thus the sun of the Dharma began to shine in the dark land of Tibet.

In those days it was not as easy to travel from Tibet to India as it is today. One had to measure the long, hazardous route from Tibet to India via Nepal on foot, step by step. One had to face the dangers of wild animals and oppressive summer heat to such an extent that out of a hundred students only three or four could survive and return to their homes. It is because of their gallant efforts and sacrifices that we received the teachings of the Blessed One in our country, and they even spread to the adjacent countries.

It is unfortunate that after A.D. 1200 Buddhism began to decline in India. Monasteries and viharas were destroyed and religous books were no longer disseminated; consequently the number of followers also decreased.

As a result of the incessant struggle of its people, India has achieved independence and has since made tremendous political, economic, and social progress. Being equally generous towards all faiths, India has shown great love and reverence for Buddhism and has even adopted the Dharma Chakra and Ashoka Pillar for its national emblem. This year, with a view to com-memorating the kindness shown by the Compassionate One, India is cele-brating the 2500th Anniversary of His Mahaparinirvana on a scale worthy of her great tradition. India has invited many distinguished guests from

Buddhist and non-Buddhist countries to these celebrations, and I consider myself extremely fortunate in being able to attend them. We are convinced that such great deeds of India will not only strengthen our faith in the Dharma in the East, but will also go a long way in the propagation of the eternal truths in the West.

In one of the Sutras the Lord Buddha had predicted that after 2500 years of His Parinirvana the Dharma would flourish in "the country of red-faced people." In the past, some of the Tibetan scholars had held that this prediction was meant for Tibet, but one scholar, Sakya Shri, has interpreted it otherwise. According to him, the prediction refers to Europe, where the Dharma may flourish hereafter, and some signs of this can be observed already. If the Dharma spreads all over the world, it will undoubtedly yield good fruits for our future life; but even in our present existence, hatred, exploitation of one by another, and the ways and deeds of violence will disappear, and the time will come when all will live in friendship and love in a prosperous and happy world. I am glad to have an opportunity of expressing my humble appreciation of the efforts which many peace-loving great countries are making day and night towards the freedom of small countries and the elimination of aggression and war. I feel that our lives would be entirely aimless if the Dharma which was brought to our land by great scholars at such immense cost were allowed to decay. For my part, I shall make every effort within my power to keep the Dharma alive, and I shall be grateful for your help and advice in the task of strengthening the Dharma in making it everlasting.

Friends, I thank you once again for the privilege of addressing this distinguished Assembly, and I shall devote my prayers for the fulfillment of the cause and success of the efforts of all who have gathered here for this Symposium on Buddhism, as well as for the prosperity and happiness of all beings throughout the entire universe.

Glossary of Tibetan Terms

Amban. Title of the imperial officials stationed in Lhasa from 1728 until 1912 as chief representatives of the Manchu Emperors. This position was filled only by high Manchu or Mongol officers.

Amdo (A-mdo). Tibetan name for the northeastern portion of ethnic Tibet, which became the Ch'ing-hai province of China in 1928.

Bande. Title of Buddhist monk-ministers during the early period.

Chang. A type of Tibetan beer made from fermented barley.

Chikyap Khenpo (Spyi-skyabs mkhan-po). Title of the chief minister of the monastic branch of the Tibetan government. Commonly called the Lord Chamberlain in English.

Chol-kha-sum. The three major regions of ethnic Tibet, including Ngari Korsum, Ü-Tsang, and Do-kham (*q.v.*).

Chosgyal (Chos-rgyal). "King of the Religion," a title of the early kings who patronized Buddhism.

Chu. River.

Dapon (Mda'-dpon). General of the army.

Do-kham (Mdo-khams). The eastern and northeastern portion of ethnic Tibet comprising Dotod (Khams) and Domed (A-mdo).

Dotsed (Rdo-tshad). A monetary unit equal to 50 *sang-gang*, valued in 1950 at 10 rupees.

Dri ('Bri). Female of the species *bos grunniens*, called yak in English, although only the male of the species is called *yak* (g. yag) in Tibetan.

Dzong (Rdzong). Name of the local-level administrative unit of the Tibetan government, as well as the fortress-like headquarters of the unit.

Dzongpon (Rdzong-dpon). Title of the administrator of a *dzong.*

Gelong (Dge-slong). Title of a fully ordained Buddhist monk.

Ge-lug-pa (Dge-lugs-pa). Name of the reformed, orthodox Yellow Hat sect of which the Dalai Lama is the head.

Getsul (Dge-tshul). A neophyte; one who has taken the first vows of Buddhist monkhood.

Gompa (Dgon-pa). A generic term for monasteries and nunneries.

Ka-gyu-pa (Bka'-rgyud-pa). A semi-reformed sect founded in Tibet by the translator Mar-pa (1012–97) and his disciples.

Kalon (Bka'-blon). Title of the ministers (also called *Shab-pe*) of the government council (*Kashag*).

Karma. Formerly, the smallest unit of weight of silver for coins.

Karma-pa. Name of a subsect of the *Ka-gyu-pa* established in the twelfth century at the monastery of Mtshur-phu.

Kashag (Bka'-shag). The administrative council of the Tibetan government composed of four ministers (*Kalon*).

Khal. A unit of measure equal to about thirty-two pounds.

Kham (Khams). Name of the eastern province of Tibet.

Khatag (Kha-btags). A ceremonial scarf of white silk or cotton.

La. A mountain pass.

Ngari Korsum (Mnga'-ris skor-gsum). Name of the western province of Tibet.

Nying-ma-pa. Name of the unreformed sect which follows the teachings of the 8th century Indian, Padma Sambhava.

Pön (Bon). Name of the prebuddhist, shamanistic religion of Tibet.

Ridro (Ri-khrod). A small monastery or hermitage.

Sa-kya-pa (Sa-skya-pa). A semi-reformed sect which takes its name from a monastic village in central Tibet. It was politically dominant in the time of the Mongol Emperors of China.

Sang. A banknote issued in denominations of 5, 10, 25, and 100. Valued in 1950 at 5 *sang* to one rupee.

Sang-gang. Formerly, a coin equal to 10 *sho-gang*.

Shab-pe (Zhabs-pad). Title of the ministers of the government council (*Kashag*).

Sho-gang. A coin equal to 10 karma.

Silon (Srid-blon). Title of the prime minister.

Tamka. A coin valued in 1950 as 4 *sang*.

Tishri (Chinese: Ti-shih). "Imperial Preceptor," title of the religious teacher of the Mongol Emperors.

Trikor (Khri-skor). An early administrative unit theoretically comprising ten thousand households; a myriarchy.

Trungyik Chemo (Drung-yig chen-mo). The council composed of four monk officials.

Tsang (Gtsang). The western province of the two central ones known together as Ü-Tsang. Its chief city is Shigatse.

Tsekhang (Rtsis-khang). The Finance Department.

Tsepon (Rtsis-dpon). Title of a Finance Minister.

Tsi-pa (Rtsis-pa). An astrologer; soothsayer.

Tso (Mtsho). Lake.

Tsongdu (Tshogs-'du). The National Assembly, composed of high officials both secular and monastic and representatives of the large monasteries.

Ü (Dbus). The eastern province of the two central provinces, together called *Ü-Tsang*, in which the capital Lhasa is located.

Bibliography

A. TIBETAN SOURCES

BCU-GNYIS Kun-dga' rgyal-mtshan, *Ngo-mtshar mdzad-pa bcu-gnyis* (A biography of the first Dalai Lama, Dge-'dun grub-pa).

BEE-DUR Sde-srid Sangs-rgyas rgya-mtsho, *Eee-durya ser-po* (An account of the Dge-lugs-pa sect).

BKA'-CHEMS *Bka'-chems ka-khol-ma* (The last testament of Srong-btsan sgam-po). A *gter-ma* (cached-treasure book) discovered by Jo-bo Rje Atisha.

BKA'-SHAG *Bka'-shag Documents* (A collection of treaties and agreements).

BKA'-THANG *Pad-ma bka'-thang* (An account of Padma Sambhava and the monastery of Bsam-yas).

BSE-RU Byang-chub rgyal-mtshan, *Rlangs pu-sti bse-ru* (An autobiography).

BSHAD-SGRA *Documents of Bshad-sgra* (preserved at the Gong-dkar gnas-gsar estate).

'BRAS-LJONGS *'Bras-ljongs rgyal-rabs* (Chronicles of Sikkim).

'BRUG-GI *'Brug-gi rgyal-rabs* (Chronicles of Bhutan).

BU-STON Bu-ston rin-chen grub, *Bsung-rab rin-po-che'i mdzod* (A history of Buddhism and its sects in Tibet).

CHENPO HORGYI 'Jam-dbyangs dge-pa'i bshes-gnyen, *Chen-po Hor-gyi bstan-bcos Gser-gyi deb-ther* (early Mongol history).

CHOS-KYI-SPRIN Man-dzu shri mi-tra, *Chos-kyi sprin-chen-po'i dbyangs* (A biography of 'Brug-pa Ngag-dbang rnam-rgyal).

CHU-RTA *Chu-rta Bka'-shag mgron-deb dangs-shel me-long* (The Kashag Diary of the Water-Horse year, 1822).

'DAB-BRGYA Pan-chen Blo-bzang ye-shes, *Dad-pa'i 'dab-brgya bzhad-par byed-pa'i nyi-ma* (A biography of Phur-lcog ngag-dbang byams-pa).

DANGS-SHEL Sgo-mang mtshan-zhabs ngag-dbang blo-bzang, *Dangs-shel me-long* (A biography of the twelfth Dalai Lama, 'Phrin-las rgya-mtsho).

DAR-HAN Dar-han mkhan-sprul Blo-bzang 'phrin-las rnam-rgyal,

Ngo-mtshar nor-bu'i 'phreng-ba (A biography of the tenth Dalai Lama, Tshul-Khrims rgya-mtsho).

DEB-DKAR   Dge-'dun chos-'phel, *Deb-ther dkar-po* (A short history of the reigns of Srong-btsan sgam-po and Khri-srong-lde-btsan).

DEB-DMAR   Tshal-pa Kun-dga' rdo-rje, *Deb-ther dmar-po* (A history of the early kings of Tibet).

DEB-SNGON   'Gos Lo-tsa-wa Gzhon-nu-dpal, *Deb-ther sngon-po* (A history of Buddhism in Tibet).

DGA'-STON   Dpa'-bo gtsug-lag 'phreng-ba, *Mkhas-pa'i dga'-ston* (A history of Buddhism in Tibet).

DMIGS-BU   Bka'-drung Nor-nang, *Deb-ther long-ba'i dmigs-bu* (An account of the Dalai Lamas and Regents and their Seals).

DOCUMENTS   *Miscellaneous Documents of the Government of Tibet.*

DPAG-BSAM   Sum-pa mkhan-po Ye-shes dpal-'byor, *Dpag-bsam ljon-bzang* (A religious history of Tibet).

GDUNG-RABS   Bsod-nams grags-pa rgyal-mtshan, *Sa-skya'i gdung-rabs rin-chen bang-mdzod* (A history of Sa-skya).

GLING-BU   Thub-bstan chos-'phel rgya-mtsho, *Ngo-mtshar gtam-gyi gling-bu* (An index to the 'Bum).

GOS-BZANG   *Du-ku-la'i gos-bzang* (Volumes 1–3, An autobiography by the fifth Dalai Lama, Ngag-dbang blo-bzang rgya-mtsho; Volumes 4–6, a biography of the fifth Dalai Lama by Sde-srid Sangs-rgyas rgya-mtsho).

GRUB-MTHA'   Thu-kwan chos-kyi nyi-ma, *Grub-mtha' shel-gyi me-long* (A comparative study of Buddhist sects in Tibet).

GSER-SDONG   Sde-srid Sangs-rgyas rgya-mtsho, *Gser-sdong 'dzam-gling rgyan-gcig dkar-chag* (A list of the contents of the fifth Dalai Lama's golden mausoleum).

'JAM-DBYANGS   Pan-chen Bsod-nams grags-pa, *'Jam-dbyangs chos-rje bkra-shis dpal-ldan-gyi rnam-thar* (A biography of 'Jam-dbyangs Chos-rje bkra-shis dpal-ldan).

'JUG-NGOGS   Mkhas-grub dge-legs dpal-bzang, *Dad-pa'i 'jug-ngogs* (A biography of Tsong-kha-pa).

KA-BSHAD   Ser-khang Nang-pa'i phyag-drung, *Ka-bshad* (A versified account of the Younghusband expedition to Lhasa in 1904).

KHANG-GSAR   *Notes of the Bka'-blon, Bkra-shis khang-gsar.*

LA-DAGS   *La-dags rgyal-rabs* (Chronicles of Ladakh).

LAM-YIG   Nag-mtsho Lo-tsa-ba, *Rnam-thar rgyas-pa,* also called *Lam-yig* (An account of Atisha's visit to Tibet).

LCANG-SKYA   Lcang-skya ho-thog-thu, *Dad-pa'i snye-ma* (A biography of the seventh Dalai Lama, Bskal-bzang rgya-mtsho).

LNGA-PA   Sde-srid Sangs-rgyas rgya-mtsho, *Lnga-pa drug-par 'phos-pa'i gtam* (An account relating to the sixth Dalai Lama, Tshangs-dbyangs rgya-mtsho).

LO-TSHIG   'Jam-dbyangs bshad-pa, *Lo-tshig gser-gyi nyi-ma* (A chronicle of famous lamas and monasteries).

MA-NI   *Ma-ni Bka'-'bum* (An account of the reign of Srong-btsan sgam-po). A *gter-ma* discovered by Grub-thob dngos-grub.

MDO-MKHAR   Mdo-mkhar zhabs-drung Tshe-ring dbang-rgyal, *Rtog-brjod* (An autobiography).

MDZES-RGYAN   Dge-slong sbyin-pa, *'Dzam-gling mdzes-rgyan* (A biography of the fourth Panchen Lama).

ME-LONG   Sa-skya Bsod-nams rgyal-mtshan, *Rgyal-rabs gsal-ba'i me-long* (A history of Tibet).

MI-DBANG   Mdo-mkhar zhabs-brung Tshe-ring- dbang-rgyal, *Mi-dbang rtog-brjod* (A biography of Mi-dbang Bsod-nams stobs-rgyas).

MTSHO-SNGON   Sum-pa mkhan-po Ye-shes dpal-'byor, *Mtsho-sngon lo-rgyus tshangs-glu gsar-snyan* (A history of the Kokonor region).

NOR-BU   Fifth Dalai Lama Ngag-dbang blo-bzang rgya-mtsho, *Nor-bu'i 'phreng-ba* (A biography of the fourth Dalai Lama, Yon-tan rgya-mtsho).

NYIN-'BYED   Kun-mkhyen pad-ma dkar-po, *Thub-bstan pad-ma rgyas-pa'i nyin-'byed* (A religious history of Tibet).

'OD-ZER   *Nyi-ma'i 'od-zer* (An anonymous biography of the third Panchen Lama Dpal-ldan ye-shes).

PAD-DKAR   Phur-lcog Ngag-dbang byams-pa, *Pad-dkar 'phreng-ba* (A history of the great monasteries of Tibet).

PAD-TSHA   Yongs-'dzin Lho-pa Blo-bzang bstan-'dzin, *Dad-pa'i pad-tshal bzhad-pa'i nyin-'byed* (A biography of the fifth Panchen Lama, Bstan-pa'i dbang-phyug).

PAN-CHEN   Pan-chen Blo-bzang ye-shes, *'Od-dkar can-gyi 'phreng-ba* (An autobiography).

'PHRENG-BA   Pan-chen Ye-shes rtse-mo, *Ngo-mtshar nor-bu'i 'phreng-ba* (A biography of the first Dalai Lama).

PHUR-LCOG   Phur-lcog yongs-'dzin Byams-pa tshul-khrims, *Rin-po-che'i 'phreng-ba* (A biography of the thirteenth Dalai Lama, Thub-bstan rgya-mtsho).

RAB-GSAL   Sde-srid Sangs-rgyas rgya-mtsho, *Rab-gsal gser-gyi snye-ma* (A biography of the sixth Dalai Lama, Tshangs-dbyangs rgya-mtsho).

RDO-RING   Bka'-blon Bstan-'dzin dpal-'byor rdo-ring (or) Dga'-bzhi, *Zol-med Gtam-gyi Rol-mo* (An autobiography).

RDZOGS-LDAN   Fifth Dalai Lama Ngag-dbang blo-bzang rgya-mtsho, *Rdzogs-ldan gzhon-nu'i dga'-ston* (A history of Tibet).

RNAM-THAR   Dka'-chen ye-shes rgyal-mtshan, *Lam-rim bla-ma rgyud-pa'i rnam-thar thub-bstan mdzes-rgyan* (A collection of short biographies of famous Lam-rim lamas).

ROL-MO   Dar-han mkhan-sprul Blo-bzang 'phrin-las rnam-rgyal, *Ngo-mtshar lha'i-rol-mo* (A biography of the eleventh Dalai Lama, Mkhas-grub rgya-mtsho).

SA-'BRUG   *Sa-'brug Bka'-shag mgron-deb* (The Kashag Diary of the Earth-Dragon year, 1808).

SBA-BZHED   Sba Gsal-snang, *Sba-bzhed* (A religious history of the reign of Khri-srong lde-btsan).

SHEL-BRAG   *Bka'-thang shel-brag* (An account of Padma Sambhava and the monastery of Bsam-yas).

SHING-'BRUG   *Shing-'brug Bka'-shag mgron-deb* (The Kashag Diary of the Wood-Dragon year, 1844).

SHING-RTA   Fifth Dalai Lama Ngag-dbang blo-bzang rgya-mtsho, *Dngos-grub shing-rta* (A biography of the third Dalai Lama, Bsod-nams rgya-mtsho).

SIMLA   *Tibetan Documents of the Simla Convention of 1914* (preserved by Bka'-blon Khri-smon).

SLE-LUNG   *Sle-lung rje-drung blo-bzang 'phrin-las* (An autobiography by Sle-lung rje-drung).

SPYOD-TSHUL   Pan-chen Blo-bzang chos-rgyan, *Rang-gi spyod-tshul gsal-ba ston-pa* (An autobiography by the first Panchen lama).

THANG-STONG   'Gyur-med bde-chen, *Nor-bu'i me-long* (A biography of the great saint, Thang-stong rgyal-po).

THUGS-RJE   Kun-mkhyen pad-ma dkar-po, *Thugs-rje chen-po'i zlos-gar* (An autobiography).

YANGS-RGYAN   Nag-shod bla-ma Bstan-'dzin shes-rab, *'Dzam-gling tha-gru yangs-pa'i rgyan* (A biography of the eighth Dalai Lama, 'Jam-dpal rgya-mtsho).

YID-'PHROG   Rgyud-smad dbu-mdzad 'Jam-dpal tshul-khrims and Bde-yangs rab-'byams Skal-bzang chos-'phel, *Dad-pa'i yid-'phrog* (A biography of the ninth Dalai Lama, Lung-rtog rgya-mtsho).

YIG-TSHANG   *Stag-sna'i yig-tshang mkhas-pa dga'-byed* (An anonymous
                 short history of Sa-skya).

ZLA-BA   Fifth Dalai Lama Ngag-dbang blo-bzang rgya-mtsho,
                 Zla-ba 'bum-phrag 'char-ba'i rdzing-bu (The teachings
                 and counsels of the fifth Dalai Lama).

B. WESTERN SOURCES

Ahmed, Zahiruddin, *China and Tibet, 1708–1959,* Oxford, 1960.

Aitchison, Sir Charles, *A Collection of Treaties, Engagements, and Sanads
    relating to India and Neighbouring Countries,* Vols. 12 and 14, Calcutta,
    1929–31.

Aoki, Bunkyo, *Study on Eearly Tibetan Chronicles,* Tokyo, 1955.

J. Bacot, F. W. Thomas, and Ch. Toussaint, *Documents de Touen-houang,
    relatifs à l'Histoire du Tibet,* Paris, 1946.

Barthold, W., *Encylopedia of Islam,* 4 (S–Z) Leiden, 1913–36.

Bell, Charles, *Portrait of the Dalai Lama,* London, 1946.

———, *Tibet: Past and Present,* Oxford, 1924.

Bretschneider, E., *On the Knowledge possessed by the Ancient Chinese of the
    Arabs,* London, 1871.

Bushell, S. W., "The Early History of Tibet from Chinese Sources," *JRAS,*
    New Series, 12 (1880), 435–541.

Cutting, Suydam, *The Fire Ox and Other Years,* New York, 1940.

Dalai Lama [14th], *My Land and My People,* New York, 1962.

Dalai Lama and India, A. V. Rau, ed., New Delhi, 1959.

Das, Sarat Chandra, "Contributions on the Religion, History, etc., of Tibet,"
    JASB, 51–1 (1882), 1–75.

———, *Journey to Lhasa and Central Tibet,* London, 1902.

———, "The Monasteries of Tibet," *JASB,* New Series, 1 (April 1905).

———, "A Short History of the House of Phagdu, which ruled over Tibet
    on the decline of Sakya till 1432 A.D.," *JASB,* New Series, 1 (August
    1905).

Dodwell, H. H., ed., *The Cambridge History of India,* 6, Cambridge, 1932.

Eliot, Charles, *Hinduism and Buddhism,* 3 vols., London, 1954.

Fillipo de Filippi, Editor, *An Account of Tibet: the Travels of Ippolito
    Desideri,* London, 1932.

Fisher, Margaret, Leo Rose, and Robert Huttenback, *Himalayan Battleground,*
    New York, 1963.

Francke, A. H., *Antiquities of Indian Tibet,* Tibetan Text, 2, Calcutta, 1926.

Frankfurter, Oscar, "Narratives of the Revolutions which took place in
    Siam in 1688," *Siam Society,* V–4 (Bangkok, 1908), 5–38.

Haarh, Erik, "The Identity of Tsu-chih-chien, the Tibetan 'King' who died in 804 AD," *Acta Orientalia, 25,* 1–2 (1963), 121–70.

Hitti, Philip K., *History of the Arabs,* London, 1956.

Hoffmann, Helmut, "Die Qarlug in der Tibetischen Literatur," *Oriens, 3* (Leiden, 1950), 190–208.

———, *The Religions of Tibet,* New York, 1961.

Holdich, Sir Thomas H., *Tibet, the Mysterious,* New York, 1906.

Howorth, Henry H., *History of the Mongols from the 9th to the 19th Century,* London, 1876.

International Commission of Jurists, *Tibet and the Chinese People's Republic,* Geneva, 1960.

Kawaguchi, Ekai, *Three Years in Tibet,* London, 1909.

Li Fang-kuei, "The Inscription of the Sino-Tibetan Treaty of 821–822," *T'oung Pao, 44,* 1–3 (1956), 1–99.

Li Tieh-tseng, *Tibet: Today and Yesterday,* New York, 1960.

Ling Nai-min, *Tibetan Sourcebook,* Hong Kong, 1964.

Ludwig, Ernest, *Visit of the Teshoo Lama to Peking* (Ch'ien Lung's Inscription), Peking, 1904.

Macdonald, David, *The Land of the Lama,* London, 1929.

———, *Twenty Years in Tibet,* London, 1932.

Markham, Clements R., *Narratives of the Mission of George Bogle to Tibet and of the Journey of Thomas Manning to Lhasa,* London, 1879.

Martin, Desmond, *The Rise of Chingis Khan and His Conquest of North China,* Baltimore, 1950.

Papers relating to Tibet (Presented to both Houses of Parliament by Command of His Majesty), London Cd. 1920 (1904), Cd. 2054 (1904), Cd. 2370 (1905).

Pelliot, Paul, *Histoire Ancienne du Tibet,* Paris, 1961.

Petech, Luciano, *China and Tibet in the Early 18th Century,* Leiden, 1950.

———, *A Study on the Chronicles of Ladakh,* Calcutta, 1939.

Report of the Officials of the Governments of India and the People's Republic of China on the Boundary Question, Ministry of External Affairs, Government of India (February 1961).

Richardson, Hugh E., "The Karma-pa Sect. A Historical Note," *JRAS* (October 1958), 139–64.

———, *A Short History of Tibet,* New York, 1962.

Rockhill, W. W., *The Dalai Lamas of Lhasa and Their Relations with the Manchu Emperors of China,* Leyden, 1910.

Roerich, George N., *The Blue Annals,* 2 vols., Calcutta, 1949, 1953.

———, *Trails to Inmost Asia,* New Haven, 1931.

Sandberg, Graham, *The Exploration of Tibet,* Calcutta, 1904.

Sen, Chanakya, *Tibet Disappears,* Bombay, 1960.

Shen, Tsung-lien and Liu, Shen-chi, *Tibet and the Tibetans*, Palo Alto, 1953.

Smith, Vincent A., *The Early History of India from 600 B.C. to the Muhammadan Conquest*, Oxford, 1904.

Stein, R. A., *Une Chronique Ancienne de bSam-yas: sBa-bžed*, Paris, 1961.

Teichman, Eric, *Travels of a Consular Officer in Eastern Tibet*, Cambridge, 1922.

Tucci, Giuseppe, "The Symbolism of the Temples of Bsam-yas," *East and West*, VI-4 (Rome, 1956), 279–81.

——, "The Tombs of the Tibetan Kings," *Serie Orientale Roma*, 1, Rome, 1950.

——, *Tibetan Painted Scrolls*, 3 vols., Rome, 1949.

Williams, E. T., *Tibet and Her Neighbors*, Berkeley, 1937.

Wood, W. A. R., *A History of Siam from the Earliest Times to the Year A.D. 1781*, London, 1926.

Wylie, Turrell, "A Standard System of Tibetan Transcription," *Harvard Journal of Asiatic Studies*, 22 (December 1959), 261–67.

Vira, Raghu, *Tibet: A Souvenir*, New Delhi, 1960.

Younghusband, Sir Francis, *India and Tibet*, London, 1910.

Yu Dawchyuan, "Love Songs of the Sixth Dalai Lama," *Academia Sinica Monograph*, Series A, No. 5, Peking, 1930.

Index